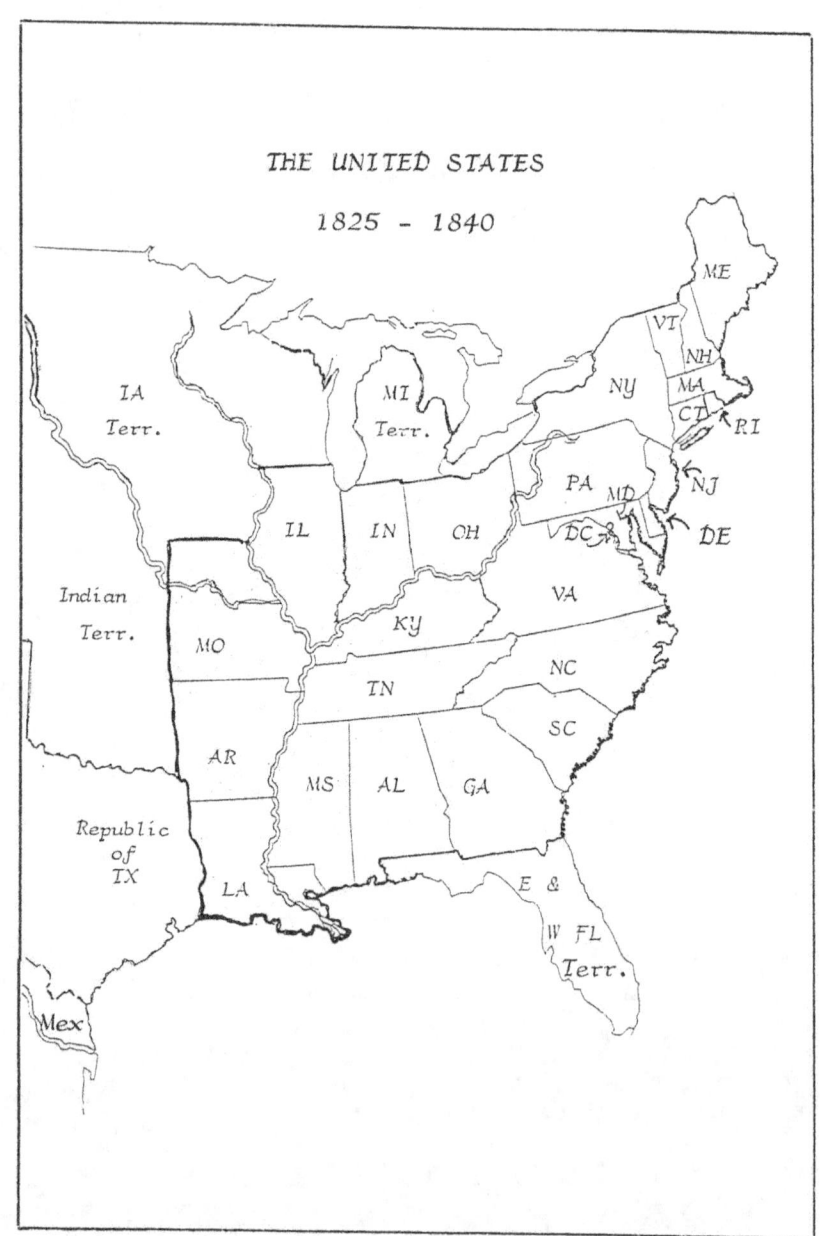

Genealogical Abstracts from Newspapers of the German Reformed Church

1830–1839

Barbara Manning

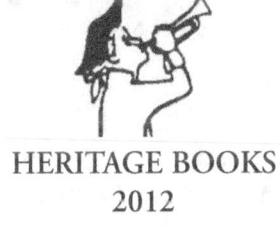

HERITAGE BOOKS
2012

HERITAGE BOOKS
AN IMPRINT OF HERITAGE BOOKS, INC.

Books, CDs, and more—Worldwide

For our listing of thousands of titles see our website at
www.HeritageBooks.com

Published 2012 by
HERITAGE BOOKS, INC.
Publishing Division
100 Railroad Ave. #104
Westminster, Maryland 21157

Copyright © 1992 Barbara Manning

Other Heritage Books by the author:
Genealogical Abstracts from Newspapers of the German Reformed Church, 1830–1839
Genealogical Abstracts from Newspapers of the German Reformed Church, 1840–1843

All rights reserved. No part of this book may be reproduced or transmitted in any form or by any means, electronic or mechanical, including photocopying, recording or by any information storage and retrieval system without written permission from the author, except for the inclusion of brief quotations in a review.

International Standard Book Numbers
Paperbound: 978-1-55613-626-9
Clothbound: 978-0-7884-9385-0

ACKNOWLEDGMENTS

I wish to thank the following people for the many hours of assistance they gave in the completion of this book. My husband, Dan; my son, Mark, who shared his computer expertise; James Goldwire and Mary F. Cox, for their suggestions and hours of proofreading. A special thank you to Kay Schellhase and Judy Witham, the staff of the Evangelical and Reformed Church Archives at Lancaster, Pa. Their many kindnesses, and the cheerful assistance they provided, were greatly appreciated. I believe the Archives, which has the most complete set of this newspaper of the German Reformed Church, has the only microfilm of the very early papers which I used to compile this book.

INTRODUCTION

It has been estimated that half of the German speaking people who settled in Pennsylvania prior to 1740 were affiliated with a Reformed Church. They migrated into Maryland, Virginia, and the Carolinas, taking their doctrines to new areas. An active mission service sent pastors to Indian Territory, Ohio, Indiana and Illinois. In November 1827, a monthly newspaper printed in English was published to help support their missionaries. Pastors sending in subscriptions began to include information about marriages and deaths in the communities they served, not just of members of their own church. The name of the newspaper was changed in 1832 to *The Messenger*. The office was moved from Carlisle, Pa. to York, Pa. in 1834, and soon began publishing a semi-monthly paper. In June of 1835, the office was moved to Chambersburg, Pa., and in September the paper was renamed *The Weekly Messenger of the German Reformed Church*.

The earliest issues were devoted to articles about doctrine and letters from ministers, and contain very little material of interest to genealogists. Prior to 1835 only issues of interest are cited. Issues after 1835 contain information from communities in <u>at least twenty two</u> of the states and territories, plus missions in China and Asia Minor. Names of victims of steamboat and train accidents, fire, floods, and lightning, as well as obituaries and wedding announcements, were printed.

Spelling, punctuation, abbreviations, and spacing varied widely from issue to issue, even within the same article. Substitutions in punctuation were common. Half of a pair of brackets often were omitted. The quality of education varied among the ministers who sent in material, the editors, and the copy boys who set the type. In addition, many people spoke heavily accented English, or had unusual names. Many ministers spoke and wrote German more fluently than English as did some members of their congregations. Whenever the dimensions of this book would allow, the same wording and spacing were used as appeared in the original newspaper, unless there were so few spaces between words as to be confusing. Words, particularly names, are spelled as originally written. The notation (sic) was not used for spacing or other minor errors found in the original paper, or almost every sentence would be interrupted. <u>Bold double slashes (//) are used to indicate the end of each article.</u> <u>A number was assigned to each date of the paper; that number, NOT the page number, was used to index this book.</u>

The editors acknowledged subscription payments, which were for past issues, current, and future issues, and for other publications, under the heading, **MONIES**. Sometimes, the same name appeared twice, and it is not always easy to determine whether there were two people with the same name, or one person paying twice. Under the heading, **FUNDS** or **SUBSCRIPTIONS**, were the names of those who pledged support for the activities of the church. The editors when mentioning another newspaper within an article, usually did not bother to italicize or underline the name of that paper. When the article was directly attributed to another newspaper, I placed the name in quotations at the end of the article.

In some articles a person has been referred to as "Mr. X." or "Mrs. Y." This device was used in the original paper, presumably because the person mentioned wished to remain anonymous.

All names were capitalized in this book to make them easier to locate on the page.

v

ABBREVIATIONS

Most of the abbreviations in this book are those found in the original papers. A variety of abbreviations were used for the states, which I have copied as written. When the state name was spelled out, I abbreviated, using modern postal zip code capital initials, viz.: IL, MD, PA.

There was no state of West Virginia during the period which this book covers. Some of the counties mentioned as being in Virginia are now a part of West Virginia.

"Ia." was most often used as an abbreviation for Iowa, but was also used for Indiana during the 1800's.

AM	America or American
ARC	Associate Reformed Church
DRC	Dutch Reformed Church
ENG	England or English
Evan. Luth.	Evangelical Lutheran
GER	Germany or German
GRC	German Reformed Church
inst.	instant (current month)
IRE	Ireland or Irish
MEX	Mexico or Mexican
Presby.	Presbyterian
RC	Roman Catholic
RDC	Reformed Dutch Church
ult.	ultimo (previous month)

THE MAGAZINE OF THE GERMAN REFORMED CHURCH

1. Jan. 1830/Extract from a letter from Malta, dated Sept. 12th reporting the marriage at Tinos of MR. KING, who is under the patronage of the NY Ladies Greek Committee, to MISS ANNA ASPASIA MENGOUS, by MR. RUFUS ANDERSON, Assistant Secretary of the American Board.//In the ship *Circassian* which sailed yesterday for Smyrna, the REV. JOSEPH BREWER and lady, accompanied by MISS MARY REYNOLDS, of New Haven and MASTER STEPHEN FIELD, of Stockbridge, Mass. a brother of Mrs. B., all destined for the island of Syra (Greece) where Mr. B. established a flourishing school, which has been under the care of DR. KORCK, of England --"NY Journal of Commerce."//DIED The REV. JOHN M. MASON, D. D. on Sunday morning, at the residence of his son in 4th st. For several years he has been unable to prosecute his public labor on account of his years and infirmities. Since the 1st of September, our city has been deprived of three of its most valuable ministers by death - BRUEN, GUNN, and MASON.--"NY Mercury."

2. May 1830/REV. C. BUCHER has become pastor of GRC at Middletown, Md., REV. D. ZACHARIAS has removed to Harrisburg, and the REV. J.F.DIEFFENBACHER has settled at Mercersburg, Pa.//DIED At the house of MR. J. HAMMON on the 24th ult. MR. JOSEPH H. HAMMON, aged 36 years, an elder in the GRC.--"Hagerstown Torch Light, March 18".

3. June 1830/DIED MRS. E. BUTLER, a native of CT, born Sept. 1798. She was married to DOCT. ELIZUR BUTLER in Oct 1820 and with him proceeded immediately to the Cherokee Nation to join the mission. They labored first at Brainerd, and for a season at Creekpath. The spring of 1826, they took charge of the station at Haweis, where the last three years and a half of life were spent. Her constitution was impaired by a cold taken on her way to her field of labor. She never after enjoyed good health; though she was generally able to manage the concerns of her family and

THE MAGAZINE OF THE GERMAN REFORMED CHURCH

teach a small school. In April last, DOCT. BUTLER having been called away more than 30 miles to attend MR. DAVID BROWN, who had been attacked with bleeding of the lungs, was summoned to return to his wife, who had experienced a similar attack. Severe spasms of the stomach followed. MESSRS.CHAMBERLIN and WORCESTER visited her. She was reduced to a feeble state, and on the morning of the 21st of Oct. her husband told her he hardly expected she would live through the day. MESSRS. WORCESTER and PROCTOR came that evening to offer comfort. About eleven o'clock, sunken eyes with a cadaverous countenance, indicated her speedy departure. The family were called together, and she gave each a farewell.

4. May 1831/Letter from ROBERT BAIRD, Agent of the American Sunday School Union, Augusta, Geo. to PROFESSOR MAYER, of York, Pa. giving account of the death of the REV. DANIEL YOUNG, assistant professor in the GRC Theological Seminary, York. MR. YOUNG arrived in Augusta about six or eight weeks since, in a declining state of health. He took up lodging at the house of MRS. KANE, where the REV. MR. TALMADGE boarded, and every thing (sic) was done by them, as well as by MR. MOORE, a brother of MRS. YOUNG residing here, and his physician, DR. FORD. Near 12 o'clock on March 6, a sudden violent hemorrhage of the lungs came on, and in a few minutes he expired from suffocation, or more properly strangulation. The next afternoon christian friends assembled to perform to the body the last offices. Suitable remarks were made by the REV.MR.CLINTON, and by the correspondent who had known the deceased at Princeton.//**DIED** On the 31st of March, at Chambersburg, Pa., MRS. ELIZABETH RAHAUSER, consort of the REV. FREDERICK RAHAUSER, and daughter of the REV. D. WAGNER, dec'd., late of York, Pa. in the 41st year of her age, of a protracted disease. She left a husband and four children, an aged mother, and brothers and sisters.

THE MAGAZINE OF THE GERMAN REFORMED CHURCH

5. Aug. 1831/**DIED** At his home in Shepherdstown Va. on the 15th of July, the REV. JACOB BEECHER. Obituary to follow in the next issue.

6. Sep. 1831/**DIED** The REV. JACOB BEECHER, late pastor in Shepherdstown, Martinsburg, and Smithfield, Va. at his home on Friday morning about 1 o'clock. He was born near Petersburg, Adams co, Pa. on the 2d day of May, A.D. 1799, and resided there until the spring of 1814, when his parents removed to Hagerstown, MD. In 1822 he entered the Academy at Hagerstown for a year, and then repaired to Jefferson College. In 1824 he completed his course, and immediately entered the Theological Seminary in Princeton, N. Jersey. After 18 months of study he was forced to leave due to declining health. He spent six months at Carlisle, Pa. in the study of the German language-and in the fall of 1826 he was ordained and labored as GRC pastor at the above three towns for about five years with frequent interruptions due to ill health. Only a few weeks have passed away since he returned from extensive usefulness abroad, to close his days in the midst of his flock whom he found destitute and scattered. He resumed his labors in this field. The success of the plan to raise a capital of $10000 for the Theological Seminary of our church in the winter of 1828 and 1829, which saved the institution, is due to him. He served a year on the Executive Committee to promote the establishment of Sunday Schools in the Valley of the Mississippi. The above from the obituary of the July 28 copy of the Martinsburg Gazette sent to our paper.

7. Oct. 1831/**DIED** The REV. JOHN H. RICE, D.D. President of the Union Theological Seminary in VA, Saturday evening, 3d inst. in the 54th year of his age.//Treasurer of the Education Society acknowledges $41 33 per GEO. BUCHER, Harrisburg, 9 06 Hagerstown, and 4 06 Salem Church, per REV. M. BRUNER, From H. S. CHAMBERSBURG, (sic) 5 00.

THE MESSENGER OF THE GERMAN REFORMED CHURCH

8. Jan. 1832/**NOTICE** After the 1st form of this number was set up, it was thought advisable by the Executive Commmittee, in view of the changes proposed, to substitute the title of "Messenger" for that of "Magazine", to preserve uniformity. The presentNo. (sic) will therefore be considerd the 1st of a new series of this publication- which was forgotten to be indicated.//**DIED** MRS. JANE ZACHARIAS, wife of the REV.DANIEL ZACHARIAS of Harrisburg, Pa. on the evening of the 26th of last November. She had been afflicted a long time with a disease, and has left a husband and infant daughter.//---on Tuesday the 13th ult. in Paradise township, York county, after a prolong- ed illness, REV. FRED. W. VANDERSLOOT, leaving a widow and a number of children.//**MONIES** for the Magazine. JOHN EBAUGH, $5.50, DAVID EBAUGH 5.50. MRS. JULY ANN HEDGES, $4.00. JOSEPH SMALL ofLAW RENCE (sic) 2.50, HENRY SCHLEIGH 2.50, REV. C. BECKER, 2.50. PETER SHAFFER, 1.50. JOHN LONG, 1.50, MRS. KOONS, 1.00, MRS. AUSTIN 1.00, MRS. CASSAT 1.00, M. DANNER 1.00, DR. SCHMUCKER 1.00, MARGARET SPANGLER 1,00, RICHARD RUSH 1.00, MRS. WENTZ 1.00, DR. FISK 1.00, JACOB LAMBERT, 1.00, J. B. BOOTHE, 1.00, H. ROSAMON 1.00, GEO. KIEHL 1.00, S. PROTZMAN 1.00 M. RIEKENBACH 1.00, JOHN SAILER 1.00, J. B. LATIMER 1.50.

9. Feb. 1832/**DIED** At his residence in York the 11th November, 1831, REV. GEORGE GEISTWEID, in the 70th year of his age. Remains committed to the GRC burying ground.//**LETTER** FR. W. HOOVER.

10. Apr. 1832/**DIED** On Monday the 13th Febr. in the 25th year of her age, MRS. JANE C. DIEFFEN- BACHER, wife of the REV. J. F. DIEFFENBACHER of Mercersburg, leaving a husband and babe.//**MONIES RECEIVED.** GEORGE BESORE, JACOB P. MILLER, REV. JOHN RUDY, MRS. B. M. SMITH, P. F. ROCKFELLER, each $1 00, WILLIAM WAGNER $2 50, GEORGE SMALL $1 00.// **LETTERS** GEO. BESORE, W. OVENBAGH, REV. B.S. SNECK, REV. S. K. DENIUS.

THE MESSENGER OF THE GERMAN REFORMED CHURCH

11. Nov. 1832/**DIED** JACOB WILLIAM DECHANT, late pastor in Berks County Pa. at the public house of MR. JOHN FORNEY, on the Reading road, about 9 miles from Lancaster, the night of October 5th. He was taken with premonitory symptoms of cholera previous to his departure from Frederick, on the morning of September 22. Anxious to return to his family, he imprudently set out the same day. After suffering much on the way he arrived on the evening of the 25th at the house of MR. FORNEY, a distance of nearly 100 miles where his further progress was prevented by an attack of cholera. The disease was checked, but he lingered in fever until the 5th of October when he expired. The REV. DANIEL HERTZ, who resides in the neighborhood, and was with him almost daily, says: "I sent for his wife and sons, who came in due time and saw their husband and father depart in peace. Today they have taken the corpse and are now on the way to his late residence. He has left a distressed widow and eight children to bewail their loss."//MR. HENRY WINROTH, late a student in the Theological Seminary at York, fallen victim to excessive application to study. He contracted a disease of the lungs and died on the 16th of October, about noon, at the house of his brother in law, MR. WILL, in Littlestown, Adams co. Pa. A motion of the Seminary students to appoint JOHN WM. HOFFMEIER, DANIEL G. BRAGONIER and GEORGE L. BROWN a committee to express a resolution, a Tribute of Affection and respect, offered for their fellow-student, of Petersburg, Pa. To be published in religious periodicals of the GRC, a resolution that we wear crape on our hats during this session as a testimony of respect. Signed by WM. C. BENNETT, Chairman and G. L. BROWN, Sec.//**LETTER** JEFFERSON WYNKOOP and J. F. SCHERMERHORN on measures to promote the best interests of the Reformed Churches in America-- (Christ. Int.).//**BENEFACTORS OF THE COMPLETED 50 DOLLAR SUBSCRIPTION LIST FOR THE SEMINARY** From York, Pa.: REV'D DR. CATHCART, MR. GEORGE SMALL,

THE MESSENGER OF THE GERMAN REFORMED CHURCH

From Easton, Pa.: REV'D THOMAS POMP, MR. PHILIP MEIXSEL, MESSRS SNYDER and BUTTS, MESSRS SEITZ and MEIXSEL, MESSRS LEIDY and LUTZ, and DR. WM. WESSEBHEFT, near Easton, From Littlestown, Pa.: MR. DAVID SHRIVER From Spring Mills, Centre co. Pa: REV'D P. S. FISHER From Milton, Pa.: REV'D H. WAGNER From Newville, Pa.: REV'D GEORGE LEIDY From Hagerstown, Md.: PETER SAILOR, D. MIDDLEKAUFF and RICKENBAUGH From Washington co. Md.: COL. D. SCHNEBLY From Frederick, Md.: REV'D J H. SMALTZ From Boonsborough, Md.: SAMUEL YONTZ, WILLIAM YONTZ, REV'D JOHN REBOUGH From Sharpsburg, Md.: JACOB MIDDLEKAUFF, SR., PHILIP GROVE, SENR. From Emmitsburg, Md.: HENRY RICKENBAUGH From Middletown valley, Md.: JACOB FLUCK, HENRY SHAEFFER, JACOB BISER, JOHN WILLIARD, PETER and JACOB BISER, PETER SHAFER, JOHN SHAFER, M. FLUCK & JOHN J. SMITH, JOHN COBLENTZ, HENRY LIGHDER, JOHN MICHAEL, PETER COBLENTZ, JACOB THOMAS (of JOHN) JNO. COBLENTZ and P. LIGHDER, J. REMSBURG & SONS, ISAAC BRANDENBURGER, JOHN BISER, GEORGE and D. MAHN, GEO. MAHN CHRISTOPHER MICHAEL, DANIEL and FRED'K. BISER, ABRAHAM and JOHN SUMMERS, DAVID BRANDENBERGER, J. SUMMERS and JOHN MAHN.// **BENEFACTORS FOR PROPOSED SECOND SUBSCRIPTION OF 50 DOLLARS** Middletown valley, Md.: HENRY COST, JOHN and JOSEPH STALEY, PHILIP KOBLENTZ, J. ADAM MAHN, JACOB and DANIEL BIEGLY, JOHN DERNER, JOHN FISTER, JACOB FISTER, GEORGE SHAFER, Widow MARY WILLIARD, JOSEPH SMITH and G. COST, PHILIP and JACOB FLOOK, From Boonsboro, Md.: HEN. THOMAS From Springmills, Centre co Pa.: REV'D B. S. SCHNECK Near Fred'k, Md.: HENRY ZIMMERMAN, JOHN ZIMMERMAN.//**MISC. PAID DONATIONS**. From Landisburg, Perry co. Pa.: MRS. BERNHEISEL, MR. J. WAGNER, MRS. M'CLURE, MRS. SHIVELY From Waynesburg, Pa.: LEWIS J. FORNEY, GEORGE BESORE From Franklin co. Pa.: PETER COOK, SAMUEL FREDERICK, Near Funkstown, Md.: JOHN KNODE Near Frederick, Md.: GEO. THOMAS No location: GEORGE COOK, J. COBLENTZ, FRED. STEMPLE From Middletown valley, Md.: J. FLUCK, D. RAUTZAHN, J. KOLLER, J. EVER-

THE MESSENGER OF THE GERMAN REFORMED CHURCH

HARD, CHRIS. SUMMERS, H. BURKITT, and MR. KELLER Unpaid from Middletown valley, Md.: FRED'K RUDY, WIDOW BOWLES, J. KEFAUVER, J. COBLENTZSMITH, T. GOLDEN, D. LEESER, SAMUEL DUTTEROH (near Fred'K) DAN'L COBLENTZ, MISS MARY KELLER, SAMUEL YASTE, D. KELLER, H. BRANDENBURGER Unpaid near Boonsborough, DAN'L THOMAS.//**FOR EDUCATION FUND.** By REV'D B. S. SCHNECK, from ZIEGLER'S and PETER'S, Cumberland co.//**MONIES** for Messenger for 1831 and 1832, $2 REV'D DIETRICH WILLERS, Fayette, Seneca co. N. Y., COL. DAVID SCHNEBLY $ 1.

12. Jan. 1833/**DIED** On the 23d of Dec. last, in Potter township, Centre county, Pa., REV. HENRY RASSMAN, in the 80th year of his age. This venerable brother had, long before his death, been compelled by the infirmities of age, to cease from his labors.//The 28th of Dec. 1832 at Bernville, Berks county, Pa., the REV. JOHN HAUTZ, in the 30th year of his age//At Gettysburg, Pa., sometime in Nov. 1832, the REV. WILLIAM RUNKEL, SEN. He was the oldest, we believe, except one, among his brethren, but we are not informed of his exact age//At Canton, OH, the REV. BENJAMIN FAUST, pastor of eight congregations.//**SUBSCRIPTIONS** From REV. J. B. ROBAUGH in Sharpsburg 2 50 From REV. ROBAUGH in Cross Roads 2 50, From REV. J. W. DECHANT 2 21, From MR. C. HICKEL, in part of his subscription to the Seminary 10 00 (The above sums were received through MR. REILY, in September, 1832, and were inadvertently omitted in our earlier number).//**EMBRAKATION** (sic) of MR. WM. C. SAMPSON, of Utica, N. York, and his wife, in the ship *Corvo*, CAPTAIN TOWNE, for Calcutta, on the 22d of Dec. He is to succeed MR. GARRET as printer to the Bombay mission. On the same ship, two missionaries of the American Baptist Board, the REV. MESSRS. WEBB and BROWN, their wives and an unmarried female, destined to the Burman mission.//**RECEIPTS** for the Messenger REV. GEO. SHOOK $2 00 REV. JOHN RUDY, PETER F. ROCKEFELLER, and JACOB P. MILLER, each 1 00.

THE MESSENGER OF THE GERMAN REFORMED CHURCH

13. Mar. 1833/**DIED** On the 10th of Feb. last at New Goshenhoppen, in Montgomery county, Pa. the REV. JOHN THEOBALD FABER in the 60th year of his age. He was preaching a funeral sermon a few days before his death, and near the close was stricken with palsy. It is remarkable that forty years before, REV. JOHN THEOBALD FABER, the father of the dec'd., while preaching a funeral sermon in the same pulpit, was attacked with the same disease, and died in a short time. REV. GEORGE WACK, who communicates these particulars, states that he lingered until the 10th day. His remains were interred, beside those of his father, under the alter of the church.//**A DONATION** to the Theological Library of two books by MRS. E. STEINER widow of the late JACOB STEINER, Esq. of Frederick, Md.//**EXAMINATION** will be held the first Wed. and Thurs. in April, of Classical and Theological students in York. DANIEL ZIEGLER.// **RECEIPTS** for the Messenger. From REV. THOMAS POMP, $5,50. COL. GEO. MAYER, $4,50. By REV. J. H. SMALTZ---from COL.HENRY KEMP, $6,50. From S. DICK, $1,00. From MRS. ELIZA REMSBURG and MRS. CATHARINE BRUNNER, each $1,00. From CHRISTIAN STEINER and ANDREW M'CLEARY, each $1,00. By REV. KROH--J. SHIRK, JOHN GLONINGER, JOHN GEORGE, WM. MOORE, JOHN WOLFSBERGER, WM. CHARLTON WEBB, JOHN B. MISH, each $1,00. By REV. J. REBOUGH - from JOHN B. WELTY, CHRISTIAN DEGENHARDT, JOSEPH BOWMAN, JOHN KRIDER, each $1,00. From J. ZELLERS, $1,00. JACOB COVER and ELIAS HEINER, each $1,00. From GEO. BESORE and PHILIP BEAMER, each $1 00. PETER SHELL, Esq. and J. H. HOFFIUS, each $2,50. From REV. WM. HENDEL, $2,00. From A. TAPPAN, $1,62 1/2.

14. May 1833/**DIED** At Shippensburg, on Friday morning, March 22d, very suddenly, REV. DIETRICH GRAVES, aged 58 years. He began his ministerial course near Uniontown and Taneytown, Md, and was called to Woodstock, Va. He removed last fall to Shippensburg.--"Messenger and Recorder".//**NEW**

THE MESSENGER OF THE GERMAN REFORMED CHURCH

SUBSCRIPTIONS to Seminary Fund: Huntingdon co. Pa. REV. JONATHAN ZELLER, Williamsburg, MR. JOHN LYON, Colerain Forges, MR. DANIEL BOGER, JACOB YOUNG, PETER SWOPE, DR. J. HOFFMAN, JOHN SWOPE, DR. WM. SWOPE, MR. HARBISSON, R. WILLIAMS. From Alexandria, Huntingdon Co.--MR. H. KNODE and C. BUCHER. Waterstreet (sic) & vicinity.--MICHAEL FETTERHOFF, SAMUEL HARNISH, JOHN KELLER, TOBIAS HARNISH, H. SPANG. Recd. by REV. B. S. SCHNECK, Trockenland, Northhampton Co. Pa. JACOB KERN, P. LICHTENWALDER, JOSEPH UNANGST, CHRISTIAN BROWN, JOHN ARNDT, JOHN RIDENOUR. LEWIS DEWART, Sunbury, DR. H. SCHNECK. Rec'd. from JACOB FISTER, A. MAHN 1 years interest on their subscriptions of 50,00. Rec'd. from JOHN LYON in part of his subscription, 10,00.//**A TEMPERANCE TRIUMPH,** at Plymouth, Mass. On 28th ult. DANIEL FROST, JUN. Esq. agent of the Temperance Society, requested the usual pledge of signatures at a public meeting, and to the astonishment of every body (sic) 200 names were returned. On the next evening an additional 225 names were obtained! On Sunday there was a third meeting and the number of new signatures was 310, making 735 names pledged to total absti-on (sic) three evenings, in one village which contains less than 5,000 inhabitants. --"N.Y. Observer."//**RECEIPTS** for the Messenger. By REV. B. S. SCHNECK--from P. SWOPE, DR. HOUTZ, MRS. SCHNECK (of Phila.), each 1,00. REV. GEO. GLESNER, and DANIEL ALBRIGHT (N. Carolina) 2,00.

15. July 1833/**DIED** MR. DANIEL HELFERICH, son of MR. DANIEL HELFERICH, SEN. of Lehigh county, Pa. a student of the Theological Seminary of the GRC, in York. He died on Wednesday morning the 19th of June, in this borough, after a short but painful illness, aged 20 years 6 months 2 days. Tribute of respect by D. BRAGONIER, chair and R. DOUGLAS, Secretary, at Student meeting, to wear crape on hats as testimony of respect for their fellow student, and this meeting to return their thanks to MR. and MRS. MORRIS for the attentions

THE MESSENGER OF THE GERMAN REFORMED CHURCH

given the dec'd. during his illness.//"The following obituary notice handed to the editor of the Messenger at the request of the mother and grandmother. She is the only child of MRS. HILL whose husband a few years ago attended our Synod at Harrisburg but has never returned. JOSEPHINE RACHEL ELENORA, only child of MARY HILL of Woodstock, Va. was born on the 6th of January, 1828; and departed this life May the 8th, 1833; aged 5 years 4 months and 2 days."//**RECEIPTS** for the Messenger. From MRS. ELIZ. KEPLINGER, $2; H. J. RAHAUSER, 1,00; GEO. L. BROWN, 1,00; AB. GARTMAN 50cts.; PETER TICE and M. HOKE, JACOB GARTMAN, each 1,00; REV. F. A. SHOLL, 4,00; NEHEMIAH DODGE, 1,50; MRS. BEECHER, 3,50; GEO. BOMBERGER (Northampton Co. Pa.)HENRY EYLENBERGER, MARGARET COOLBAUGH, DAVID EYLENBERGER and SARAH CHAMBERS, each 2,00; JACOB TROXEL of JNO., 4,50; D. & H. WELTY, JOHN COVER, PAUL HAUGH, each 1,00; JACOB COVER, PETER TROXEL, BARBARA SMITH, each 1,00; REV. JOHN CARES, 3,00; JOSHUA MOTTER, 2,00; ANN BARR, CATHARINE LIGHT, and MALVINA MILLER, each 1,00; JACOB LESHY DANIEL P. LANGE, each 1,00; REV. HENRY WAGNER, JOHN BODINE, WM. NICE, each 1,00; JAMES LEWARS, 2,00. By REV. JACOB DIFFENBACHER--from ABSOLOM RINKER, 3,00; CHR. HICKEL, JOSPEH BORDEN, MARY OTT, CHARLES JORDAN, JOSEPH ANDRECK, STEPHEN SCHAUMAN, GEORGE SANTZ, each 1,00; REV.JOHN BROWN 5,00; MICHAEL SEIBERT GEORGE WOLFF, Esq., each 2,00; DEWALT KIEFER 1,00; REV. H. BIBIGHAUS 2,00.

The paper moved to York, PA from Carlisle, PA.

16. Sep. 1833/**DIED** At Orwigsburg, Schuylkill Co. Pa. on the 27th of July, after a lingering illness, REV. JACOB LEYMEISTER, late pastor of six congregations in Lanc. county. His disease was contracted by close application to study and neglect of the requisite exercise, at the Seminary. This is the second instance of death from the same cause.//REV. D. WEISER of Selinsgrove

THE MESSENGER OF THE GERMAN REFORMED GHURCH

accepted a call from the congregation vacated by the death of REV. J. F. FABER. The REV. HENRY BASLER late of Union county has taken charge of the congregation vacated by the death of REV. J. W. DECHANT.//**STUDENTS** during the session of the Classical institution. Frederick city, MD: WILLIAM S. BANTZ, THEODORE S. BANTZ, JESSE STEINER. Hanover, Pa.: ABRAHAM KELLER Chambersburg, Pa.: JOHN G. WOLFF, EPHRAIM KIEFFER Lancaster city, Pa.: JONAS D. BACHMAN, HENRY D. MICHAEL, AMOS E. REIGART, JOHN H. A. BOMBERGER, and HENRY M. REIGART. Hanover, York county, Pa.: WILLIAM E. WIRT Millersburg, Dauphin county, Pa. EMANUEL V. GERHARD. Harrisburg, Pa.: EDWARD L. WOLF, JOHN A. STEHLEY. Somerset co. Pa.: WILLIAM CONRAD. Lancaster co. Pa.: JAMES H. LIGHTNER Philadelphia, Pa.: THOMAS M. BIBIGHAUS. Easton, Pa.: THOMAS H. R. POMP. Oxford, Adams county, Pa.: JEREMIAH HELLER. Quakerville, Bucks co. Pa.: ANDREW S. YOUNG. Berks co. Pa.: WILLIAM F. GERHARD. From Gettysburg, Pa.: JACOB BEAR. Richmond, Northampton county, Pa.: THEODORE C. W. HOFFEDITZ. Near York, Pa.: CHARLES J. BARNITZ, M'PHERSON BARNITZ From Saxony, Germany: FRANCIS M. RASCHIG. Salsbury, N. C.: JOSEPH LINGLE. Dauphin county, Pa.: CHRISTIAN W. FLANDERS. Cavetown, Md.: WILLIAM C. WEBB. Bakersville, Washington county, Md.: CHARLES F. M'CAULY. Leitersburg, Md.: SAMUEL B. LEITER. Baltimore, Md.: JAMES NUSSEAR. Washington co. Md.: WILLIAM F. COLLIFLOWER. Ellicot's Mills, Md.: F. UNCLES. Near Westminster, Frederick county Md.: WASHINGTON C. VAN BIBBER, ABRAHAM VAN BIBBER Burketsville, Md.: HENRY WILLIARD. Middletown, Md.: DANIEL FEETE. Martinsburg, Berkley co. Va.: CHRISTIAN W. DOLL, JOHN G. WOLFF. Shepherdstown, Va.: JOHN C. HENSEL. York, Pa.: HENRY BAUMGARDNER, GEO. A. HECKERT, CHARLES S. POOR, CHARLES A. HAY, GRANVILLE HARTMAN, ALEXANDER M. BARNITZ, DANIEL DECKER, ALEX. K. SPANGLER, DANIEL S. WAGNER, DAVID A. JONES, CHARLES RUTHRAUFF, WILLIAM G. VOGELSONG. Some of them are also members of Theological classes.

THE MESSENGER OF THE GERMAN REFORMED CHURCH

17. Oct. 1833/**DIED** DAVID LANG the 19th of June in Thorn Township, Perry county, OH, aged about thirty years. He studied Divinity with BROTHER WEIS in Lancaster, and in 1826 was ordained. DAVID WINTERS, Cor. Secretary. Dayton, July 9th, 1833.//**SUBSCRIPTIONS.** Obtained by D. BOSSLER, agent for the Seminary of the GRC, 1833. At Fredericktown--REV. CHARLES REIGHLEY, $100. GIDEON BANTZ, 150. Waynesboro' District--REV. G. M. GLESSNER, 50. DAVID BESHORE, 50. Hagerstown District--JACOB LECKRON, 50. Woodville, near Frederick--JOHN MILLER, 50. Glade District--GEORGE BARRICK, 50. LEWIS CRAMER, 50. MISS MARY CRAMER, 50. REV. JOHN W. HOFFMEIR, 50. Sharpsburg District--DANIEL FINFRUCK, 50. JOHN HOFFMAN, 50. Jefferson Middletown Valley--SEBASTIAN REMSBERG, 50. Loudon County, VA--JACOB SMITH, SAMUEL and PHILIP BAKER, 50. SMALLER SUBSCRIPTIONS Hagerstown District--ELI SMITH, 25, JOSEPH GROFF, 20, JOHN WOLFERSPERGER, 20, JAMES ZWISLER, JR., 10, JACOB MIDDLEKAUF, 10, JACOB RENNER, 5, ALEXANDER M'COMMON, 2. JACOB GRUBER, 2 MARTIN HAMMOND, 5. JACOB BRAGUNIER, 5. DANIEL SPIELMAN, 5. MISS ANN BEAR,5. SAMUEL PRETZMAN, 5. JOHN FUNK, 3. LEWIS FOUCK, 5. JOHN TICE, SEN. 5. JOHN TICE, JR. 5. GEORGE KIEHL, 2. DANIEL ULERY, 1. FREDERICK HUMRICKHOUSE, 2. RICHARD WISE, 5. GEORGE GOSSMAN, 50, cts. Glade District--JOHN OGLE, 25, GEORGE DEVELBISS, 10 DAVID CRAMER, 25 FREDERICK BAKER, 25, DAVID DEVELBISS, 10 HENRY CRAMER, 10 PHILIP H. CRAMER 10 Boonsboro' District--JOHN BLECHER, 20. JOSEPH LIGHDERT, 25. JACOB BRANTNER, 4. JOHN D. KEEDY, 20. GEORGE W. HARRIS, 4. MICHAEL HINDS 5. Frederick District--URIAH S. BANTZ, 25. GIDEON BANTZ, JR. 5. JOHN MARTIN, 5. JOHN MAHN, 5. JOHN KUNKEL, 10. FREDERICK RAMSBURG, 5. ABRAHAM KEMP, 10 HENRY SMITH, 1. JOHN ZIMMERMAN, 2. MISS ELIZABETH RAMSBURG, 5. JACOB ZIMMERMAN, 2. GEO. ZIMMERMAN, 2. MRS. ELIZABETH ZIMMERMAN, 1. M. E. BARTGIS, 2. DANIEL BENTZ, 2. ADAM STULL, 1. MRS. REBECCA RAMSBURG, 5. MICHAEL HOUCK, 10. MICHAEL THOMAS, 25. EZRA DOLL, 5. GEORGE GITTINGER, 25.

THE MESSENGER OF THE GERMAN REFORMED CHURCH

NICHOLAS WHITMOR, 50 cts. V. B. 6 1/4 cts. MRS. CHARLOTTE BUCKY, 50 cts. NICHOLAS HOLTZ, 25. DAVID KEMP, 20. CATHARINE & JONATHAN BRUNER, 20. MRS. ELIZABETH RAMSBURG, 5.

The July 1, 1834 issue describes the paper as a semi-monthly publication.

18. Sep. 15, 1834/**MARRIED** Tuesday morning the 2d inst. at Prospect Hill near Creagerstown, Md. by REV. E. HEINER, REV. J. W. HOFFMEIER to MISS LILLY ANN,daughter of the late GEORGE ZIMMERMAN, Esqr. of Frederick co. Md.//**LETTER** Canton, Nov. 1833, from REV. CHARLES GUTZLAFF, to the American Tract Society, seeking Tracts in Chinese as he has given out large numbers in Fuh-keen Province. MR. BRIDGMAN will acquaint you with our use of funds.//**MONIES.** By REV'D H. VANDYKE for DR. C. VANDYKE $4,25; for self 1,50; MISS SARAH HOYER $1,25; MR. DANIEL WEAVER 25 cts. MISS ANNETTE GOLDMAN $1,25. MR CHRISTOPHER HICKEL $1,25. By REV'D B.C WOLFF for MRS M BEIDELMAN, DR F. L. CRANE, MR JOSEPH LAUBACH, DANIEL W. BUTZ, each $1,50. By REV'D D. ZACHARIAS for MRS HARRIET WIESTLING and MRS SUSAN BUCHER, each $1,25. MR JOHN ZINN and GEO. SMALL, each $1,00. By REV'D B.S. SCHNECK for self $2,25, MR CHRISTIAN HOFFMAN $2,25, MRS MARY COOK $2,25, MR GEORGE BOMBERGER 25 cents, MR ROBERT M. HUEY $2,00, MRS SOPHIA P. YOUNG $1,25.//**SEMINARY FUND** MR. PETER HILLGERD, $25 00 ISAAC HILLGERD, 25 00 PHILIP HILLGERD 15 00. To 2nd Professorship; MR. CHRISTOPHER HICKEL $10 00. To Education Fund by REV. D. ZACHARIAS, from MRS SUSAN BUCHER, MR. C. F. MINICH, MRS CATHARINE Z. ZACHARIAS, each $5.00.

19. Nov. 1, 1834/**DIED** At Mansfield, OH on Friday July 25th in the 71 year of her age,MRS. ANN HOFFMAN. consort of REV. JAMES HOFFMAN. She was severely attacked with cholera on the preceding Thursday morning.//The 2d of August, 8 days after the preceding event, REV.JAMES HOFFMAN, hus-

MESSENGER OF THE GERMAN REFORMED CHURCH

band of the deceased, in the 75 year of his age, at the same place. //**MONEYS.** By REV. J. H. HOFFMEYER from MESSRS DANIEL ROUSER, JOHN YOUNG, SOLOMON CREAGER, each $ 1.50; By REV. G. GLESNER from MESSRS JOHN LECKRONE, WM. AUGHINBAUGH, JOHN GILBERT, JOHN HEAFNER, GEO. BESORE, each $ 1.50. By REV. E. HEINER from MESSRS JOHN TROXEL, JOHN SHEETS, WM. BOULDEN JACOB SHOVER, each $ 1.50, and PETER TROXEL $ 1.25; Rec'd from MR MICHAEL HENSELL AND COL. JACOB MYERS, each $2.25; from GEO. WOLFF Esqr. $ 1.25. By MR NEHEMIAH DODGE from MISS E. NAGLE $ 3.00. By REV. S. GUTELIUS from MR CONRAD UPPERMAN $5.25, REV. DAVID KAEMMERER $2.25, MR BENJAMIN FAHNESTOCK $5.75, REV. H. B. IBEKEN $ 2.25, MRS SUSAN SHEA $1.00, MR MARTIN RAHM, Esqr. $4.25, MR SAMUEL FAHNESTOCK $2.25 MESSRS. E. and F. FABER $2.25, REV. LUTHER HALSEY $5.75, MISS MARY EAKLE $1.00; MISS CATHARINE SHAFER _?_, MR ISAAC McCAULEY $2.00, GEO. SMITH, Esq $3.25, MR PHILIP GROVE $1.00. Paid to REV. H. MILLER, REV. L. BIBIGHOUSE $1. MRS BEECHER $2. REV. N. DODGE $1.50. ALEX. HENRY $3. BENJAMIN W. RICHARDS $3. J. V. KRUG $1. PHILIP APPLE $1 MR. ODENHEIMER $2 REV. W. T. SPROLE $3. //**BOARD FOR FOREIGN MISSIONS** elected at Utica, N. Y.: Hon. JOHN COTTON SMITH, LL.D. President. Hon. STEPHEN VAN RANSSELAER, LL. D. Vice President. His Honor SAMUEL ARMSTRONG, JOHN TAPPAN, Esq. Hon. SAMUEL HUBBARD, REV. WARREN FAY, D.D., REV. B. B. WISNER, D. D., CHARLES STODDARD, Esq. Prudential Committee. REV. CALVIN CHAPIN, D. D. Recording Secretary. REV. B. B. WISNER, D. D., REV. RUFUS ANDERSON, REV. DAVID GREENE, Cor. Secretaries. HENRY HILL, Esq. Treasurer. DANIEL NOYES, Esq. W. J. HUBBARD, Esq. Auditors. //**GERMAN BOOKS** at the REILY and VOGELSONG bookstore.

20. Apr. 1, 1835/**DIED** At Manchester, Md. March 12th. MRS. ANN CATHARINE GEIGER, wife of REV. JACOB GEIGER, after a short but severe illness, age 33 years, 9 months and 11 days. She left a husband and seven children.

THE MESSENGER OF THE GERMAN REFORMED CHURCH

21. May 15, 1835/**DIED** On the 1st of April last MRS. CATHARINE HEYSER, consort of JACOB HEYSER, Esq. of the borough of Chambersburg, in the 63d year of her age.//**DONATION** to the Seminary from MR. JOHN COBLENTZ, SEN. by REV. J. C. BUCHER, his pledge with interest $54 62 1/2 - to the Education Fund by MISSES SERENA SHEPHERD and HENRIETTA SHEPHERD, infant children of MR. JAMES SHEPHERD (Shepherdstown, Va.) $1.68 3/4.//**MONEYS RECEIVED** By REV'D STEPHEN STALEY from MESSRS. JONATHAN WENNER $4.25; DAVID WIRE $3.25; JACOB SMITH $3.25; JACOB SHUMAKER $2.25; DR H. S. WUNDER, MESSRS MICHAEL SOUDER, and JOHN YAKEY, each $1.50; MESSRS ANTHONY ROSENBERGER and THOMAS GRIGGS, each $2.75; MR SIMON YAKEY 33 1/3 cents; REV. S. STALEY $2.42. By MR J. B. AYRES from DR DANIEL HOUTZ $2.00; MR GEORGE H. BUCHER $1.50. By MR G. W. WILLIARD from MRS SARAH WILLIARD $3.75. By MR CHARLES McCAULY from JOHN SHAFER JUNR. $1.50. By REV. J. B. REBOUGH from MR PHILIP GROVE $1.00. By MISS SARAH EBERT $1.50. By MR. HENRY WILLIARD from ADAM TRUMBLE, WILLIAM KARN, and Vestry at Burketsville, each 75 cts.

No issues while paper moved to Chambersburg, PA.

22. July 18, 1835/**BEQUESTS**. HASTUR M. CHILDERS, of the Parish of Carroll, LA, died 18th December last. Extracts of his will, as reported in the "New Orleans Bulletin".--"Having entire control of the following negroes; namely,--PAT and family, and as many come to my share in the division of the personal property* between my wife MATILDA and myself, to be emancipated as soon as provision can be made by the Legislature of the State and conveyance to Liberia, my wish is that they shall be furnished from my estate, with tools, provisions, and good common clothing sufficient to last them one year, also the passage money. My body servant, LEWIS, and sore neck FANNY, I wish to have bought, if they should not fall to my lot, and be emancipated and five hun-

WEEKLY MESSENGER OF THE GERMAN REFORMED CHURCH

dred dollars be given to each. I appoint HORACE PRENTISS and JAMES H. HICKS, to make the necessary provision. I wish to have MARTHA SELLERS to have given her five thousand dollars provided she lives to maturity--to NARCISSA J. HEWLETT, one thousand dollars for her name that was given to my daughter who is now no more--to my mother DICEY HARRIS an annuity of 5 hundred dollars a year during her life-time. Her son HUSTON HARRIS a donation of four thousand dollars. It is my wish that HORACE PRENTISS, JAMES G. HICKS, and WILLIAM HENDERSON, of Warrenton be my executors. *about thirty negroes.//HENRY SMITH, bookseller of Chambersburg offers Psalms & Hymns.

No issues are available until Sep. 2, 1835, when the paper became a weekly edition.

23. Sep. 2, 1835/**DIED** At Frederick, MD, on the 10th ult. MRS. JULIA ANN HEDGES in the 61st year of her age.

24. Sep. 16, 1835/**SEMINARY FUND** collections by the REV. DAVID BOSSLER, Agent. HENRY WELTY $5 00 WM. HEITSHU 20 00 GIDEON BANTZ 100 00 ABRAHAM KIEFFER 13 60 JACOB SHOEMAKER 10 00 JOHN DARNER 3 00 JOSEPH SMITH 3 00 JOHN MICHAEL 3 00 JOHN P. COBLENTZ 6 00 HENRY WERTZ 10 00 DANIEL SMITH 0 87 COL. D. SCHNEBLY 50 00 RICHARD WISE 5 00 WM. WEBB 2 00 JOHN BLECHER 22 35 STEPHEN STALY 3 00 JOHN SCHLEY 5 25 WM. ROHRBACK 5 00 DANIEL CHRISTIAN 13 43 ISAAC BRANDENBERGER 3 00 SEV. E. REBOUGH (sic) 3 00 HENRY REMSBERG 17 53 JOHN WILLIARD 28 00 DANIEL & FRED'K. BISER 6 00 JOHN & STEPHEN STALY 6 00 JOHN MARTIN 5 00 JACOB BISER 26 50 JACOB BISER 26 50 (sic) DANIEL BRANDENBERGER 3 00 PETER SANDER 1 00 CHRISTIAN BOLLINGER $25 00 SAMUEL BECKER 35 00 ADAM MAHN 28 00 JOHN FISTER 28 00 GEORGE SCHAFFER 43 60 JACOBTHOMAS, of JNO. 25 00 (sic) PETER SCHAFFER 57 50 JOHN HERMAN 53 75 HENRY MIDDLEKAUFF 6 00 DANIEL SCHNEBLY 30 00 PETER SAILER 54 95 DAVID

WEEKLY MESSENGER OF THE GERMAN REFORMED CHURCH

MAHN 3 00 MISS ANN BEAR 5 00 JOHN HOFFMAN 3 00 STEPHEN MARTIN 16 66 CHRISTOPHER MICHAEL 22 00 JOHN TRAUP 4 00 JOHN MILLER 1 75 JOHN D. KEEDY 2 40 SAMUEL MOLER 5 00 HENRY MICHAEL 5 00 JOHN SCHAFFER 30 94 PETER BISER 26 50 LEWIS RODRICK 5 00 JOHN BISER 3 00 HENRY HERSPERGER 5 00 WM. LUCKEN 10 00 JACOB FLUCK 15 00 HENRY LEIGHDER 31 00 Div. HagerstownBank (sic) 34 50 W. WAGNER, Secr'y.//Contingent Fund REV. D. WILLERS $15 00. **//MONEYS** for Messenger. From GEORGE BESORE $2; JACOB BESORE 2; ANDREW P. FREESE 2; MRS. B. M. SMITH 2; DAVID BESORE 2; SAMUEL BESORE, Mansfield, OH, 2; HENRY SOHN, do. 2; MRS. S. SLOAN 2; HENRY SMITH, of DANIEL, 2; by JOHN C. HENSEL, from ELI CRAMPTON; (sic) from GEO. GROVE 2.// The REV. MESSRS. T. HOFFEDITZ and B. C. WOLFF, appointed to carry into effect a resolution for the "Society for the reief of widows and Clergymen of the GRC".

25. Sep. 23, 1835/**DIED** Sunday night, 23d August at Englishtown, Monmouth co. NJ, IRA CONDICT GULICK, a member of the Sophomore class in the College of NJ. Mr. G. was a younger brother of the REV. PETER J. GULICK, of the Sandwich mission.//Morning ofthe 6th inst. in Brooklyn, N. Y. RICHARD DURYEE, President of the Sabbath School Union of RDC.//The REV. DOCTOR WILLIAM NEVINS, pastor of the First Presbyterian Church in this city on Monday evening last, illness in the 38th year of his age. MRS. NEVINS died very suddenly about a year ago of cholera; their 2 or 3 small children are therefore left orphans.--"Lutheran Observer"//MISSES PINNEO Female School at Chambersburg, Pa. Boarding department will be under the control of MRS. SARAH FINDLAY. References: REV. J. M'KNIGHT, Hon. ALEX'R THOMSON, Hon. GEO. CHAMBERS, REV. HENRY L. RICE, T. HARTLEY CRAWFORD, Esq. BARNARD WOLF, Esq. WM. HEYSER, Esq. FRED'D (sic) SMITH, Esq. DR. P. FAHNESTOCK.

26. Sep. 30, 1835/**DIED** At Frederick Md., Thurs-

WEEKLY MESSENGER OF THE GERMAN REFORMED CHURCH

day the 24th instant, in the 19th year of her age, MISS MARTHA INGLES, an affectionate daughter and sister.//Thursday morning, the REV. WM. M. MURRAY,D. D, pastor of the RDC, in Market st. NY.//The second commencement of PA College, conferring the Degree of Bachelor of Arts on the following gentlemen, viz:

    M. G. DALE, of Lancaster, Pa.
    A. B. SHUMAN, of Cumberland County
    C. F. STOEVER, of Lebonon, Pa.
    W. R. RUTHRAUFF, of York, Pa.
    A. R. STEVENSON, of Gettysburg, Pa.
    EZRA KELLER, of Middletown, Md.
    D. F. BITTLE, of do.
    THEOPHILUS STORKE, Salisbury, N. C.,
Class Valedictorian.
The Honorary degree Doctor of Divinity:
    REV. JOHN BACHMAN, of Charleston, S. C.
    REV. GEO. A. LINTNER, of Schoharie, N. Y.//

MAIL ROBBERY MR. WILLIAM DUTCHER, Milford, Pike county, the proprietor of the stage house there was arrested last week on charge of having purloined letters from the mail containing money and has acknowledged that he was guilty. Agent MR. PLITT was sent by the Post Master General to ferret out the perpetrator of the thefts on the route from Oswego to Jersey City. He deposited a letter containing counterfeit bills and seven dollars in good money in the Post office at Carbondale. At the first Post Office in NJ, after leaving Milford, he examined the mail and found the package was missing. He returned to Milford with the Post Master, and requested him to go to MR. DUTCHER'S, call for something to drink, and give him in payment a 20 dollar bill. This he did, and obtained two of the counterfeit bills. DUTCHER was then arrested.--"Wayne Co. Herald"//

MONEYS for Messenger. By REV. MR. GOOD, from HENRY SHAEFFER, SR., $2; JACOB BARR 1 50; GEORGE FOUK 1 25; and JOS. GOOD, 2--by REV. JOHN CARES, from GEORGE WOLFF, Esq., 75 c; WM. BOOTHE, Esq., 2; JACOB WAGNER, Esq., 3; GEORGE KING, 2; DANIEL

WEEKLY MESSENGER OF THE GERMAN REFORMED CHURCH

SMALL, P. M. 1--by the REV. J. GEBHART, from JACOB SCHAFFNER, 75 c; PETER HOLTZMAN, 75 c; ISAAC GERHART 75c; VALENTINE ULRICH, 75c; TOBIAS BICKELL, 75c; JOHN BUFFINGTON, 75c; JACOB MEUNICH, 75c; JOSEPH MILLER, 75c; DANIEL A. MUENICH, 75c; by REV. MR. REBOUGH, from J. B. WELTY, 1 25.

27. Oct. 7, 1835/**MURDERER CONVICTED.** In Orange co., NY PETER G. CRINE, will be executed for the murder of his wife.

28. Oct. 14, 1835/**MARRIED** On the 7th inst., at Quincy, by the REV. H. L. RICE, MR. JOHN SNIDER, to MISS MARTHA L. daughter of GEORGE WERTZ, Esq. all of said place.//On Thursday the 8th inst. by the REV. H. L. RICE, MR. DAVID JOHNSON, to MISS CATHARINE VANDERAU, both of Guilford township, Franklin county, Pa.//**ROBBERY & SUICIDE** On the 29th ult. a MR. HOLSTEIN fell in with a person at a tavern in New Castle, Pa.--the next morning the stranger accompanied Mr. H. on his way home, but after riding a few miles demanded his money, at the same time presenting a pistol to enforce the demand. Mr. H. gave up his money, but was fired at--a second pistol was fired at MR. HOLSTEIN by the robber, who rode off. Alarm being given, pursuit was made and the robber overtaken. Told he was a prisoner, he drew a pistol, and threatened to shoot the first that attempted to take him; but being surrounded and having been called a murderer, he put his pistol to his temple and shot himself, under the impression he had killed HOLSTEIN. His clothes were marked J. CALDWELL.//**HONESTY** Yesterday afternoon MR. FARRINGTON, merchant, of Coffee House Slip, stepped into hack No. 39, driven by THOMAS BLAKE, with a package of $30,000 in his hand and rode to his residence in Fourth street. He left the package on the seat of the carriage, supposing it was in his pocket. Shortly after he missed his money, but as he had not taken notice of the hack number, he knew not where to look. While contem-

WEEKLY MESSENGER OF THE GERMAN REFORMED CHURCH

plating what step he had best take to recover his money, honest BLAKE drove up to his house, money in hand. MR. FARRINGTON generously tendered him $800 as a reward, but he refused. We understand that Mr. F. intends to present BLAKE an elegant carriage, horses, and harness--"N. Y. Times."//**MURDER.** It was noticed in this paper, last week, that PETER G. CRINE, was lately tried in Orange co., NY, for the murder of his wife, convicted and sentenced to be executed. From a report of the trial we make the following extract, which presents one of the most horrid scenes of the fiendish influence of Intemperance we have ever observed. MARIA CRINE, 12 years of age last April; examined by the court, and she was sworn; is the daughter of PETER G. CRINE, remembers the night her mother died; father came home about dusk; her mother and her brothers and sisters, five in number at home; her mother in bed; her father told her to get up and pull her frock off; deceased obeyed him; father pushed her back on the bed, sent DECATUR (her brother) our for a whip about four feet long; whipped the deceased on the bed; then pulled her out on the floor. Told the witness to go to the neighbors, and tell them her mother had fell down stairs; and that she fell in the fire and burnt herself; said they must never tell any one if they did he would be hung or go to jail for life; witness went to AMOS and NATHAN WILCOX'S, AARON HOWELL'S and MR. SMITH'S in company with THEODORE, her brother; mother was well and sound before father came home that evening.//GEORGE KING, Esq. York, Pa. is Treasurer of Board of Missions of GRC.// JOHN SMITH, Chambersburg, Pa. is appointed to receive money due for the 'Messenger of the GRC' and subscriptions for the "Weekly Messenger". WILLIAM HEYSER, Esq. of Chambersburg, is Treasurer of the Synod, to whom all collections and contributions will be paid.//**MONIES RECEIVED** By W. A. GOOD, from JOSHUA HOFFMAN 2--By REV. B. C. WOLFF, MISS EVE FABER 2; MRS. M. BE___MAN 2--By

WEEKLY MESSENGER OF THE GERMAN REFORMED CHURCH

REV. W. C. BENNET, from MAJ. JACOB BA RIER (sic) 2; COL. JOHN C. BARNHARDT 2; HENRY CLODFELTER 2; DAVID CORREE 2; W. BENNET 2--By C. F. HOFFMEYER, from ANDREW BAUSMAN 1; CHRISTIAN G?? 2, W. F. SHEFLER 2--By MARTIN RICKENBAUGH, from WILLIAM ??ER 2; JACOB WILLIAMS 1; SIMON SNYDER 2--By M?? KIEFFER, from MRS. ELIZABETH GREEN 2; HENRY BEAVER 2--By EPHRAM KIEFFER, from PETER MORITZ 2; D?? WILSON 2; MICHAEL GROSSMAN 1 25; JACOB MILLER 1; JOHN BOWLES 1 25; PETER SWIGERT 2; MISS MARY MINNICH 2.

29. Oct 21, 1835/**DIED** Near Taneytown, Md., at the residence of his father, MR. ABRAHAM HAWK in the nineteenth year of his age, on Wednesday the 7th October, 1835. He enjoyed good health till within ten or twelve days of his death. He left parents, brothers and sisterss. {Communicated}

30. Oct. 28, 1835/**MARRIED** The 22d inst. by the REV. JACOB MAYER, MR. ANDREW SNIVELY, to MISS MARY GARLIU, both of Franklin Co. Pa.//Many will recollect that the 4th of March, the brig *Rover*, CAPT. OUTERBRIDGE, sailed from this port with 71 emigrants for Liberia. Forty-one were from Claiborne county, twenty-seven from Adams county MS, and three from this city. We are happy to learn that they had a safe passage, but ARMISTED PRICE died a few days after landing, of the consumption he had when he left here--"New Orleans Observer"./**TRAGEDY** near Dillsburg, York county, a few days since. MR. MATTHIAS BLACK was bit about six weeks previous by a dog supposed to be mad. On Tuesday last, he felt unwell and at the sight of water was taken with spasms and died on the 22d inst., leaving a wife and several children.--"Gett'g Star."//**MONIES** From DAVID SCHREIVER $2--by REV. E. HEINER, from JAMES SLICK 2--- by DAVID SCHREIVER, from JACOB SCHREIVER 5- from G. CALLIFLOWER 2--by REV. M. DOUGLASS from D. M. CUSHWA 2, D.H. DOLL 2, MISS ROSANNA DOLL 2, MRS. LYDIA STEPHENS 2, MRS. McCLELLAND 1, MISS MARY

WEEKLY MESSENGER OF THE GERMAN REFORMED CHURCH

RILLEMORE 2, PETER REINER 2---by E. C. KEIFER, from P. HULL 1, MRS. LYDIA SPANGLER 2, JOSEPH HESSON 1 25--by J. PRITTS, from HENRY SNIVELY 2- by REV. D. ZACHARIAS, from D. SMITH 2, D. STOCKMAN 2, C. THOMAS 2, C. KEMP 2, P. THOMAS 2, J. ZIMMERMAN 2, MRS. M. BUCKEY 2, H. STOCKMAN 2, C. WIEDRICH 2, G. ZIMMERMAN 2. G. COLLIFLOWER $0 75.--By E. KIEFER, from R. CRAWFORD, $4.

No marriages or deaths in Nov. 4, 1835 issue.

31. Nov. 11, 1835/**DIED** MR. HENRY STITZEL, of Richmond township, in this county, occasioned by the sting of a bee, on the 25th ult. He was in the act of drinking cider, in which there was a bee unperceived, which stung him upon the tongue and caused his death in less than one hour.//The dwelling house of JOSEPH ELLIS was consumed on the morning of Wednesday last, in Brooks, (Me.) Five of his sons and a hired man perished in the flames!--"Belfast Journal".//**AN ACCIDENT** In Oxford, in this county, on Saturday week. A number of children were playing near a small shop where a loaded gun had been carelessly left in a corner. A small lad picked it up and threatened to shoot the girls. They all ran, with the exception of REBECCA CHRIST, daughter of MR. JONATHAN CHRIST, deceased; the lad snapped the gun; it went off, and the load lodged in the little girl. She lived until the next day. Her age was nearly eight years, and she was the only daughter of a widow.--"Adams Sent."//On Tuesday last, there was a Steam Boat launch at the shipyard in Fulton. The signal for starting was the firing of a cannon. The man with the match cried out for the crowd to clear the way, and touched off the cannon. The crowd did not move fast enough; one young man by the name of THORPE, who was within six feet of the cannon's muzzle was most horribly mangled.-"Cincinnati Repub."//**PERJURY.** At the late court for Portage county, OH, COL. W. R. WASHINGTON was convicted of perjury, and

WEEKLY MESSENGER OF THE GERMAN REFORMED CHURCH

sentenced to seven years. He was a man of property and standing, whose avarice prompted him.

32. Nov. 18, 1835/**MARRIED** On Wednesday morning last, by REV. B. S. SCHNECK, MR. JACOB WEIDNER to MRS. MARIA SLAYBAUGH, both of Adams county, Pa.//**DIED** On the evening of the 21st ult., at his residence in the city of Frederick, after a protracted illness, JOHN SCHLEY, Esq., aged 69 years, late Clerk of the Frederick County Court. {Communicated}.//**POISON.** The wife of JOHN EARLS of Lycoming county, Pa., died very suddenly, and suspicions excited of her having been poisoned, DR. EDWARD KITTOE proceeded to Philadelphia with the contents of her stomach, for an examination which resulted in the discovery of an extraordinary quantity of arsenic. On the Doctor's return her husband was immediately arrested on the charge of having administered the fatal drug to the deceased.//**REWARD.** $50,000 will be given on delivery to the Committee of Vigilance, for the Parish of East Feliciana, La., of the notorious abolitionist ARTHUR TAPPAN, of NY. Jackson, La. Oct 15, 1835.--"LA Journal."//**MONIES** for paper. By HENRY WILLARD, from JOHN G. SMITH 75, THOMAS ELMES 2 50, REV. A BARNES 2, REV. J. H. SMALTZ 75, PETER SHAFER 4, JOHN WILLARD 4. By SAMUEL R. FISHER, from MISS CATHARINE ENGERD, W. and C. C. RILE, JOHN BAUM, JOHN BENNER, SAMUEL R. FISHER, each $2--By HENRY WILLIARD, from REV. J. H. SMALTZ, REV. JJGEIGER, JOHN C. ALLBURGER, MARTIN GANT, CHARLOTTE MOSER, SUSAN B. MITCHELL, DR. J. D. GARROTT, C_ SCHAEFFER, GEO. KARN, JOHN KELLER JOSHUA BISER, JOHN NICHODEMUS, GEO. W. WILLIARD each 2, JOHN FINK and SAMUEL GARVER each 1 25, J. G. SMITH 4 25.--By DANIEL FEETE, from JACOB FLOOK OF JNO., JOSEPH WISE JOHN H. FLOOK, DAVID CRAMER, FRED'K. RUDY, ELIAS SCHOLL, DAN BANGHER, ELIZ. A. MOTTER, LEWIS CRAMER, HENRY CRAMER and GEO. DEVILBISS, each 2. By WILLIAM F. COLLIFLOWER, from ANDREW SNIVELY, JOHN McCLAIN, and JOHN WORLEY, each 2--By REV. B. S. SCHNECK, from GEO.

WEEKLY MESSENGER OF THE GERMAN REFORMED CHURCH

HECK 2--From JACOB THOMAS (of JOHN,) Middletown, Md. 2--By HENRY COST, Jefferson, Md. from JOHN COST, JOHN KEFAUVER, MICHAEL THOMAS, LEWIS RODERICK,each 2, HENRY COST ?. From GEORGE MARTIN and J. E. HOUSER, each 2--By REV. D. ZACHARIAS, Frederick, Md. from FREDERICK REMSBURG, HENRY ZIMMERMAN, MISS CATHARINE HEITSHU, JOHN HARGET, GEO. GOTTINGER, each 2. By J. PRITTS, from MRS. JOS. CULBERTSON 2. By REV. B. S. SO???, from A. E. E. DUNCAN 2. NOTICE: $2 00 acknowledged from WM. STO??R. Ought to have been WM. STONEBRAKER.

33. Dec. 2, 1835/**MARRIED** Thursday evening last, in Frederick City, by REV. MR. ZACHARIAS MR. JACOB ROHR to MRS. ELIZABETH REMSBURG.//**DIED** MRS. MARY SMITH Thursday last, relict of DANIEL SMITH late of this borough, in the 62nd year of her age. On Sabbath her remains were interred in the cemetery of the GRC. {Communicated}.//REV. J. F. LANNEAU has transferred to the Synod of SC and GA, fifty Shares in the Bank for a Scholarship. MR. LANNEAU contemplates leaving his native city as missionary to Syria and the Holy Land, and is founding the Scholarship to leave a memorial of his regard for the Churches of the South.--"Com. Adv."//**MONIES RECEIVED.** By REV. J. REBOUGH, from JOSEPH STONEBRAKER, PHILIP GROVE, Esq. MRS. CATHARINE MILLER, (of JAC.) MRS. MARY MILLER,(of JNO.) each $2, SAMUEL STONEBRAKER $5, MISS MARIA HOUSER, $1 00. By DAVID SHRIVER, Esq. from HENRY SHRIVER, GEORGE WILL, LUDWIG STUDY, G. & J. DATROW, SNYDER & KREPS, JOHN SPANGLER, J. & N. MARK JOHN WEIKERT, JR., JACOB STERNER, and ENOCH LEFEVER, each $2. By REV. D. ZACHARIAS from DAVID ZIMMERMAN, JOHN HILDEBRAND, ANDREW McCLEARY, and ABRAHAM GETZENDANNER, each $2. By REV. S. GUTELIUS, from MISS CLARISSA WAMPLER $1, and GEORGE WILL, Esq. 75 cts. By REV. E. HEINER, from MRS. HARRIET MOTTER, JACOB TROXEL, JOSEPH MORITZ, JACOB MYERS, and MRS. CATHARINE TROXEL, each $2. By REV. D. ZIEGLER, from A. HARRIS, Wrightsville, 2; ADAM PAULUS, York, 2; SAMUEL LEVER,

WEEKLY MESSENGER OF THE GERMAN REFORMED CHURCH

Windsor, York co., 2. REV. JOHN BROWN 1, REV. G. GLESSNER 1. By REV. S. GUTELIUS, from MISS CLARISSA WAMPLER, 1; GEORGE WILL, Esq. 75 cts.; KREPS & SNYDER 1; E. LEFEVER 75 cts, and HENRY WIRT 1. From DAVID SHRIVER 2, REV. JNO. BROWN 4. By REV. G. GIESSNER, for JOHN HARTELL 1.75; JACOB MANN 1.50; JOHN CLOPPER 1.75; GEORGE PENTZ 1 75; B. ZIMMERMAN 1.75; REV. G. GLESSNER 1.00; GEORGE LEIDY 1.75.//REV. J. N. MOFFATT, junior editor of the Western Methodist, has ended his relationship and expects to commence publication in Natchez. REV. MR. WAMNER to fill his place.

34. Dec. 9, 1835/**DIED** In Easton, (Miss.) Aug. 3d, MRS. RUTH POOL widow of the late Deacon SAMUEL POOL, aged ninety-seven years. At age 20, early in 1759, MRS. POOL, whose maiden name was FULLERTON, was married to MR. SAMUEL POOL, then of Bridgewater, with whom she lived near sevnty-one years. At the death of her husband in Dec. 1830, their descendants were 271, 251 were then living. At the time of her decease, her descendants were ten children, (nine living,) seventy-two grand-children, two hundred fortyfive great-grand children, and seventeen great-great-grand-children; of whom one hundred and thirty-eight are the offspring of her two 1st born children who were twin sisters.--"Christian Register."// MR. DANIEL GAMBER, employed in the Saw Mill of MR. H. HALDEMAN, near Columbia, on Saturday 21st ult. having been thrown on the log directly before the saw, which was in motion, was cut in so dreadful a manner he died in about two hours. The saw entered at the right shoulder taking off the arm, entering so far as to touch the spine, the muscles torn to shreds. The lungs were perfectly visible and were torn by the saw.-"Lanc. Union."//**MONEYS** received for Weekly Messenger. By MR. JOHN BESORE, (Waynesboro') from JEREMIAH HELLER and HENRY LEIDY, (Cavetown) each 2. By REV. JEHN (sic) RUDY (NY) from GEORGE FRALEIGH, PHILIP H. MOORE, HENRY CRAMER, HENRY WHITEMAN,

WEEKLY MESSENGER OF THE GERMAN REFORMED CHURCH

PETER P. MOORE, REV. JOHN RUDY, JACOB P. MILLER, REV. CHARLES KNAUSE, and P. F. ROCKEFELLER, each 2. By REV. H. L. RICE, from JOHN CELL 2; MRS. CALHOUN 2. By MR. DANIEL H. DOLL, (Martinsburg, Va.) from MISS SUSAN GROVE, BERNARD DOLL, C. D. WOLFF, JOSEPH PALISGROVE and JACOB SHOWERS, (Urbana, OH) each, 2. By REV. J. F. BERG, (Harrisburg) from GEO. H. BOCHER, FREDERICK BOAS, G. MISH, each 2, and N. CALENDER, 2.//**MONEYS** For the Messenger. By REV. JOHN Rudy, from P. F. ROCKEFELLER, JACOB P. MILLER, and REV. JOHN RUDY, each 1; N. CALLENDER 2.//**PANTHER** As three negroes belonging to the Hon. J. M. WHITE, were passing near Monticello, one was attacted (sic) by a large panther and hurled to the ground. His companions rescued him and they dispatched the monster.--Talahassee, (FL,) Nov. 14.//A panther measuring seven feet two inches, and weighing between 90 and 100 pounds, was killed in MR. WAKEMAN'S woods about three miles south of this village on Sunday last, by MR. DANIEL RAMSDALE. -"Saratoga Centinel, Dec 1".//**EXECUTION** JOHN W. COWAN, the cruel murderer of his wife and two children, was hung yesterday (in a field, near Mill Creek). He was swung from the scaffold at a quarter past one o'clock. An immense concourse of people, probably to twenty thousand, were congregated. The scene of yesterday, it seems to us, must have convinced every body who witnessed them, that executions should always be made privately.--"Cincinnati Whig." Facts of the Murder as related by the "Beaver Argus" to MR. HENRY of the Messenger - J. W. COWAN, the wretched being who butchered his wife and two children at Cincinnati, on the 10th of October last, married the daughter of MR. A. SINCLAIR, a tradesman of Wood street, Pittsburgh; and now in business at Jefferson, Ashtabula co., OH. MR. SINCLAIR'S daughter MARY became acquainted with him near six years ago and after several months they were married at her father's house in Pittsburgh. He took to intoxicating draught, and in little more

WEEKLY MESSENGER OF THE GERMAN REFORMED CHURCH

than a year from the time of his marriage, was confined for his abuse of his wife. Under the promise never to touch a drop his wife left the roof of her father where she had sought shelter, with him and her two babes for Cincinnati in May last. He reverted to his former abusive habits. Said at his trial that he recollects nothing of the deed till he saw the wound he had inflicted, and it occurred to him that he would have to die for it; then to save his children from disgrace, he thought he would kill them. He dispatched the little girl, the youngest, and then the boy, THOMAS. He then returned to MARY, his wife, to strike her more blows. He was burst in upon before he could take his own life. The funeral of Mrs. C. was attended to by an immense crowd on Sabbath afternoon, 15th inst. REV. MR. LINN delivered an appropriate address, and they were buried in the same coffin, a child on each arm.

35. Dec. 16, 1835/**MARRIED** In Mercersburg, the 8th inst. by the REV. THOMAS CREIGH, REV. GEORGE PORTER, of Williamsport, Washington county, Md., to MISS SUSANNA E. LITTLE, daughter of DR. P. LITTLE, of the former place.//**MONEYS** for Weekly Messenger & Messenger. By REV. H. L. RICE, from LEWIS DENIG, Esq. 75. By REV. J. C. BUCHER, from JOHN COBLENTZ, (of JOHN) for 1834 and 35 $2 00, JACOB WEAVER, for 1835, 75 cts., JOHN REMSBURG, JR., 75. By REV H. L. RICE, from LEWIS DENIG, Esq. 2, MICHAEL WHITMORE, $2 00. By REV. B. S. SCHNECK, from REV. F. RAHAUSER, $2. By REV. J. C. BUCHER, from JOHN COBLENTZ (of JOHN) $2, JACOB WEAVER, 1; JOHN MICHAEL, 2; JOHN REMSBURG, JR., 2; DAVID BRANDENBERG, 2; JOSEPH DANNER, 2; PHILIP FLOOK, 2; JOHN P. COBLENTZ, 2; PETER SOUDER, 2; JOHN FISTER, for 2 copies, 4; and J. C. BUCHER, 50 cts.

36. Dec. 30, 1835/**MARRIED** On the 22d inst, by the REV. HENRY L. RICE, MR. JAMES DUFFIELD to MISS MARY WALLACE, both of the vicinity of Cham-

WEEKLY MESSENGER OF THE GERMAN REFORMED CHURCH

bersburg.**//DIED** The 21st inst. in this borough, MRS. MARY ANNA GREENAWALT, in the 49th year of her age. In a feeble state of health for a number of years, unable to walk, she was confined to her chamber six years.**//**On the 14th inst., at the house of her aunt, MRS. SLOAN, relict of DR. SLOAN, MISS MARY BOYLIN, who had emigrated from IRE about 2 years ago.**//**On Sunday the 13th inst., in Westminster, Md., MRS. CATHARINE FORREY, consort of DR. FORREY, and daughter of DR. P. FAHNESTOCK of this place.**//**On the 11th of December near Middletown, Md, MRS. LYDIA LEAZER, consort of MR. DANIEL LEAZER, in the 40th year of her age, leaving a husband and six children. **//MONEYS** for Weekly Messenger. By DR. GROSSMAN (Centre county) from JA'S DUNCAN, Esq. $5; DAVID DUNCAN, Esq. 2; DOCTOR WILSON 2; JOHN STRUNK, 1. By REV. E. HEINER, from JOHN ZIMMERMAN, PETER TROXEL,JACOB SHOVER, H. WERTZ and JACOB SHRINER, each $2. From REV. J. B. KNIPE $5.

37. Jan. 6, 1836**/DIED** MRS. AVERY, wife of MR. JONAS B. AVERY, of New Milford, was so severely burned by her cloths taking fire while sitting near the fireside some days since, as to occasion her death--"Susquehannan Register."**//STEAMBOAT DISASTER.** The Steamboat *Oglethorpe*, CAPT. LEWIS, owned by MESSRS, HARPER and MR. WM. DUNCAN of this city and Augusta, burst her boilers on Tuesday evening last, at the wharf at Purysburg; the explosion caused the death of the Mate Captain, and two Engineers, all white men, and two of the hands colored. The rest 5 or 6, were injured.--Savannah, Geo. Dec. 17.**//ARREST** D. N. BABCOCK, the absconding cashier of the Clinton Branch of the New Orleans Bank was arrested near this city on Monday night. The arrest, we learn from the "Patriot", was made by two vigilant police officers,MESSRS. HAYS and JEFFERS. He was examined before JOSEPH SHANE, Esq. and committed to await the requisition of the authorities of LA.--"Baltimore American".**//LETTER** from MR. G.

WEEKLY MESSENGER OF THE GERMAN REFORMED CHURCH

W. McELROY, who went out with the Savannah expedition, to the editors of the "Commercial Advertiser", from Liberia, dated Oct. 15, states he has been there nearly two months, and he is very impressed by the health and crops of the colony. //**MONIES** for the "Magazine" and "Messengers". From PETER SNIDER, (Franklin co.) from 1829 to 1835, $8 00. By MR. J. H. BOMBERGER, from REV. DR. HENDEL, 1 75. JOHN HARPER 3 75. From JACOB SHARP $1 25; MR. HARTMAN, Greencastle, 2 00; by REV. J. F. BERG, from MR. GEO. ZINN, MRS. NAGLE, MRS. GOODMAN, MISS HOYER and D. BOAS each $2 00. By DANIEL SMALL, Esq. from LEONARD RATHFONG, (Wrightsville) $2 00; HENRY LEBER 2 00, and HENRY RUBY, 1 00. From REV. TH. L. HOFFEDITZ $2 00. By SIMON DRUM, Esq. (Greensburg) from JOHN GRAFF PLEASANT UNITY, $2. WILLLIAM SKELLY $2 00, and DANIEL KEAL 1 25. By C. F. HOFFMEIER, Esq. Lancaster, from A. WOLF $? ?, M. WESTHEAFER, $4 00. A. PETERS, A. WOLF, M. WESTHEAFER, C. McCLEARY, W. E. HAVERSTICK, G. WEILER and W. COOPER, each 25 cents.

38. Jan. 13, 1836/**MARRIED** On the 5th inst. by REV. D. DENNY, MR. L. W. GOSNALL, merchant, of Baltimore to MISS ADELINE KITE, of Chambersburg. //By REV. J. M'KNIGHT, the evening of the same day, MR. JAMES PATTON, to MISS MARGARET CAMPBEL, both of St. Thomas township, Franklin county.// On the 31st ult., MR. JACOB BARRIER, JR. to MISS AMELIA GRIMES, by the REV. W. C. BENNETT, all of Davidson county, N. C.//At Mackinac, REV. FRANCIS DENTON, Missionary to Indians of the North West, from the Canton of Switzerland, to MISS PORCIA SKINNER, teacher at the Mission School at Mackinac.//**DIED** In Chambersburg, on Saturday morning last, MISS SARAH B. CRAWFORD, eldest daughter of THOS. HARTLEY CRAWFORD, Esq.//**MONIES** for the papers. By M. RICKENBAUGH, from MICHAEL SEIBERT $5 00--By REV. R. DOUGLAS, (Shepherdstown,) from MRS. M. RINEHART, and MARTIN ROUCH, each $1 50.--By REV. E. HEINER, from WM.

WEEKLY MESSENGER OF THE GERMAN REFORMED CHURCH

FISHER, (Taneytown,) $2 00.--REV. D. WINTERS, (Dayton, O.) $2. -- By M. RICKENBAUGH, (Hagerstown,) from JOHN SHAFER, JR., PRETZMAN & FUNK, JOHN WOLFERSBERGER, JOHN TICE, JR. GEO. KIEHL, MICHAEL SEIBERT, SAMUEL J. DOWNEY, GEO. CHRISTIAN, HENRY FREANER, ANDREW KERSHNER, and JOSEPH NEWCOMER, each $2 00; SAMUEL GILBERT, $1 00.- By REV. JOHN CARES, from PETER SCHULTZ, DANIEL WEAVER, and JOHN CARES, each $2 00.--MR. HEISER, (Lebanon,) 1 00.-By REV. GEO. LEOPOLD (Va.) from JACOB JORDAN, P. PRINCE, F. HOFFMAN, JOHN PENNYWITT and C. HITCHEL, each 2 00. -- By REV. R. DOUGLAS, from MESSRS. JOHN MILLER, MICHAEL HENSEL, JOHN N. SHELL, A. SUMMERS, GEO. LEOMAN, H. STAUB, and MRS. ELIZABETH KEPLINGER, each 2 00, & H. WISENAIL 1 00.--By the REV. E. HEINER, from J. HERBAUGH, E. HERBAUGH, H. HERBAUGH, (Adams co.,) AND M. ZACHARIAS (Emmittsburg,) each 2 00. --From REV. D. WINTERS, (Dayton, O.,) 3 00.-- By the REV. W. C. BENNET, [N. C.] from GEORGE LONG, PETER LEONARD, PETER ADER, JOHN HEDRICK, PETER S. BOLDENHAMER, COL. GEO. BARNHART and PHILIP BARRIER, each 2 00 and ALEXANDER MICHAEL 1 00.// **DONATIONS** from NC & SC. Reported by WM. C. RANKIN, formerly a member of the Lutheran Church. From JONAS BART, J. CARPENTER, ADAM DELLINGER, each 1 00. C. BART, 50 P. WARLACK, 37 1/2 G. SUMMEY, 5 00 REV. WM. RANKIN and family 6 00 PETER SUMMEY, 3 00. SITCHEL SUBER, DAVID SUBER, MICHEAL SUBER, each 1 00. SAMUEL D. BANNAN, JOSEPH ALYMINE, DANIEL SUBER 50.

39. Jan. 20, 1836/**MARRIED & DIED** In this town, the 22d inst, by REV. D. LIMMERICK, MR. WM. B. SUTHERLAND to MISS SARAH MURRAY,daughter of MR. JOHN MURRAY, all of Wheeling. Died, at Steubenville, on the morning of the 24th inst. MRS. SARAH SUTHERLAND, wife of MR. WM. B. SUTHERLAND, only child of MR. JOHN MURRAY, of Wheeling. The happy couple left Wheeling on the 23d to spend the holidays with friends at Steubenville. The following morning, the lovely and accomplished

WEEKLY MESSENGER OF THE GERMAN REFORMED CHURCH

bride was a corpse ? (sic).-"Wheeling Times Dec. 26."//**LETTER** JAMES FARRELL, Tampico, December 13, to MESSRS. DUBOIS & GARRETSON, N. Orleans. "JONAS H. SEWARD, I, and 26 companions are to be shot, according to court martial of Mexican soldiers, tomorrow, for an attack on this city. I got a wound in the head and another in the hand. No money can save us; they want to defer others from the cause of Liberty."//The NY American announces the death of DR. DAVID HOSACK, esteemed for forty-five years as a medical practitioner.

40. Jan. 27, 1836/**ACCIDENT** -- REV. JOSEPH PRENTICE, late rector of the Episcopal Churches at Catskill & Athens. Mr. P. left his residence, near Catskill, on a visit to this city. At Coxsackie, the residence of his married daughter, he had taken his place on the seat of the stage, with the driver, when by sudden overturn, he was thrown upon the ground, the stage falling upon his head, crushed it. About dusk a horse rushed into the barnyard of MR. NASH who knew the horse to be that of MR. WAGER. Search was made; Mr. W. was found dead, his skull badly fractured.---"Hudson Gaz."//**TRIAL** of MRS. REBECCA PEAK for the alleged crime of murder by mingling arsenick in hash which she administered to three members of her family, the result of which was the death of one of them, MR. EPHRAIM PEAK, terminated on Saturday. She was found guilty and sentenced to be hung.--"Chelsea Vt. Dem."//**BATTLE** casualties at Withlacoochee as reported by W. J. MILLS, Lt. Col. by dispatch from Jacksonville, FL. On the 28th ult., ten men, dining at the house of ERASTUS ROGERS were fired upon. Dead: GEN. THOMPSON, Indian Agent, WILEY THOMPSON, LIEUT. CONSTANTINE SMITH, ERASTUS ROGERS, SUGS and HITZLER. All were scalped within 250 yards of Camp King. Day before yesterday, SOLANO'S house, seven miles from Picolata was burned and a man named YANOVER shot. CAPT. HEBBARD, of the steamer *Florida*, arrived to day, says that all communication be-

WEEKLY MESSENGER OF THE GERMAN REFORMED CHURCH

tween Picolata and St. Augustine is interdicted. Wounded in battle Dec. 31st, 1835 Militia, 4th Reg. COL. WARREN, MAJ, COOPER (sic), severely, LT. JOHN YOUMANS, privates JNO. HIGGINBOTHAM, JAMES TYSON--slightly. GEN. CLINCH had one ball through his cap, one through his jacket sleeve. Aggregate, 4 killed, 59 wounded, out of 227 men. //ISAAC M'GUIRE who was shot a few days since by GEDNEY, has since died, says the"Whig".

41. Feb. 3, 1836/**MARRIED** In Middletown, Md. on the 14th ult. by the REV. J. C. BUCHER, MR. DANIEL WOLFINGER of Leitersburg, Wash. co., Md., to MISS SUSANNAH, daughter of the late JACOB ALEXANDER, dec'd, of Middletown, Md.//Near Middletown, Frederick county, Md., on the 28th ult., by the REV.J.C. BUCHER, MR. PETER BRANDENBURG to MISS HANNAH M., daughter of the late MR. DAVID GAVER, all of Middletown Valley, Frederick co., Md.//**DIED** Near Burkettsville, Fred. co., Md., on the 3d ult., after a protracted illness, MR. DAVID GAVER, aged 55 years and 11 months.//In Harrisburg, on Tuesday week, JAMES TRIMBLE, Esq. late Deputy Secretary of the Commonwealth of PA, at an advanced age.//Near Jefferson, Fred. co., Md., on the 22d of January, at the house of her brother CAPT. WM. LAKIN, MISS ELEANORA, youngest daughter of the late ABR. LAKIN, aged 36 years,3 months, and 20 days.//In the borough of Lebanon, Pa., after a protracted illness, on the 22d ult. the HON. JOHN GLONINGER, in the 78th year of his age. He filled many public offices, civil and military, taking part in the battle of Staten Island, as also in that of Trenton. After the termination of the revolutionary war, he was appointed Justice of the Peace for Lancaster county. Sabbath last his remains were conveyed to the silent tomb. [Communicated.//At the residence of MRS. ELIZA GRIGGS, on Sunday morning, the 29th of December 1835, MR. G. DUVAL POLK, in the 23d year of his age--eldest son of the late ROBERT POLK, Esq., of Washington City, D.C. [NB A

WEEKLY MESSENGER OF THE GERMAN REFORMED CHURCH

memoir by DUVAL POLK copied from the Free Press states that the subject was deprived of his father at an early age, and that he engaged in the mercantile business in that city. He planned to study for the ministry. BAM]--"Charlestown Free Press."//**MASSACRE** reported from Indian Key, 14th Jan 1836. On the 6th inst., at New River, the Indians commenced hostilities upon the family of MR. WILLIAM COOLY, murdering his wife, 3 children, and MR. JOSEPH FLINTON, a Teacher in the family. Burnt his house, took all his Horses and two negro slaves, as is supposed, they not having been found among the slain. A Spaniard by the name of EMANNEL (sic) is also missing. Every man' woman and child was compelled to fly for their lives. Among the sufferers were MRS. RIGBY, her two daughters and one son. They ran 12 miles through woods to take refuge at Cape Florida light, Key Biscayne. Here it was proposed to make a stand with MR. DUBOSE the keeper of the light. A vessel hove in sight and took the sixty to this place.//**MONIES** for the papers. By REV. J. C. BUCHER, from HENRY GROSS, Jefferson, Md., $3.00; JOHN COBLENTZ, SR., 75 cents, PETER COBLENTZ, JR., $3.00. From P. ROFFENSBERGER, (Gettysburg) $1. By REV. J. C. BUCHER, from HENRY GROSS $2.00; JOHN COBLENTZ, SR., 2; PETER BISER, 2; R. & R. SHAFFER, 2; JOHN DERNER, 2; HENRY COCHRAN, 1; PETER COBLENTZ, JR. $3.00. By C. F. HOFFMEIER, from A. PETERS, $2; HENRY MARKLY, 1. By M. RICKENBAUGH, from REV. WM. A. GOOD, M. FUNK, MRS. M. E. SHAFER, (Funkstown) DANIEL ZELLER, SAMUEL WELTY AND JACOB SUMNER, each $2.

42. Feb. 10, 1836//**DIED** At Frederick, Md., on the 27th ult. REV. F. D. SCHAEFFER, D. D. many years pastor of GLC in Philadelphia, aged 76 years.//The 1st inst. in Harrisburg, LEWIS KRUMBHAUR, Esq., member of the House of Representatives, from Philadelphia city.//**SWINDLER** among the Shakers. "NATHAN SHARP, great head of the shaker establishment near Lebanon, has taken one

WEEKLY MESSENGER OF THE GERMAN REFORMED CHURCH

of thesisters to wife, and pocketing a large sum of money (some say $100,000,) has put out."---"Zanesville (OH) Gazette."//The first payment on the pledges for a THEOLOGICAL EDIFICE is payable to DANIEL SHAFER, Esq. or MR. JAMES O. CARSON, Mercersburg. JOHN SMITH, JAMES O. CARSON, GEO. BESORE, DANIEL SHAFER, Building Committee.//**EDUCATION FUND** J. CARES, Treasurer, acknowledges from MRS. H. H. ZELLERS, in REV. J. ZELLERS congregation, Huntingdon county, Pa., $5,00.

43. Feb. 17, 1836/**MARRIED** On Thursday evening last, by the REV. MR. WOLFF, at the parsonage of the GRC of Easton, MR. WILLIAM H. POMP, to MISS MARY ANN, daughter of P. YOUNG, Esq. all of that place.//By the same, at the same time and place, REV. JOSEPH L. BERG, Pastor of the Harrisburg, Pa. GRC to MISS ELEANORA, daughter of REV. THOMAS POMP, of Easton.//By the REV. GEO. BOYD, in St. John's Church, Philadelphia, the REV. BENJAMIN HUTCHINS late rector of St. John's Church, York, to MISS MARY H. SPANGLER, of the borough of York, PA, daughter of EMANUEL (dec'd) & JANE SPANGLER.//In Alleghenytown, on Tuesday evening, 19th ult. by the REV. JOSEPH PAINTER, the Hon. ROBERT ORR to MISS MARTHA GRIER.//Near Lincolnton, N. C., on Thursday evening, January 28th, 1836 by the REV. MR. FRITCHEY, MR. PETER FINGER, Merchant, of Rutherford county, N. C., to MISS CATHARINE WARACK, of Lincoln county.//**DIED** The 30th of December last in Lincoln county, N. C., CAPT. JOHN YODER, in the 73d year of his age.--- Eight weeks previous he was deprived by paralytic affection, of the use of speech, and of his right side.//In Lancaster, Pa. on Sunday morning last, the Honorable WALTER FRANKLIN, President Judge of the Courts of Common Pleas, in his 63d year.//**MONIES** for the newspapers. From M. GROSSMAN 75; by DANIEL H. DOLL, from DANIEL REEL Darksville, 2 25; ABS. F. GEPHART, Circleville, O. 2; and J. R. W. POLK, balance 75 cts; REITER & Co. Pittsburg, 2; from REV. R. DUENGER, Mar-

WEEKLY MESSENGER OF THE GERMAN REFORMED CHURCH

tinsburg, 2; from JOHN J. SMITH, Middletown, Md. 2; GEORGE COOK, Green Castle, 2; from REV. PAUL WEIDMAN 2; by REV. J. GULDIN, from JOHN ROBERTS, JOHN BROWNBACK, HENRY KEELY, and LEVI NYCE, 2. From REV. P. WEIDMAN 3.

44. Mar. 2, 1836/**MARRIED** On the 23d of January last, in Baltimore, by the REV. E. HEINER, MR. JOHN PARLEY, to MISS ELLEN MORRISON//On the 23d of February last, by the same, MR. JACOB YELT, to MISS ELIZABETH STANFORD.//**DIED** At Auburn, on the 12th ult., MATTHEW LA RUE PERRINE, D. D., Professor at the Theological Seminary, aged 59 years.//At Staunton, Augusta Co., Va., very suddenly, REV. DR. CONRAD SPEECE.//**MONIES** for the newspapers. From JOHN COOK, Esq., [Mercersburg,] 2, SIMON RUPLEY, [Green Castle] 2; by REV. ELIAS HEINER from JOHN RODENMAYER 2, BOYER and DIFFENDERFER 2, JOHN HEINER, JR. 1; from JOHN HERMAN 2. Correction---Monies received by MOSES KEEFER should have been credited to DAVID and JACOB STEVER, instead of STERER, as was stated. Names should be written plainly.//**SUICIDE** Friday last the steamboat *Mediterranean* from New Orleans, left the body of RICHARD D. HALSEY of NY at our town for burial, who committed suicide the 29th ult., by stabbing himself through the abdomen. The causes given for the deed are contradictory. It is said he left NY city a few months since and settled in Natchez with a view of practising the law; that he became enamored of a widow lady of beauty and wealth, neglected his pursuits, squandered his money, and in a fit of dispair, committed the deed. He was thought to be about 25 years old.(Date line: Randolph, Tenn. Feb. 2)

45. Mar. 9, 1836/**MARRIED** On Wednesday evening the 24th ult., in the city of NY, by the REV. CHARLES KNOUSE, MR. WILLIAM A. B. CLEMENT, of the firm of WORCESTER and CLEMENT, Albany, to MISS ELIZABETH, daughter of REV. JOHN RUDY, late of Germantown, Columbia county, N. Y.//At Ange-

lica, Allegheny county, on the evening of the 18th ult., by the REV. L. HULL, DR. MARCUS WHITMAN, of Rushville, to MISS NARCISSA PRENTISS, of the former place.--DR. WHITMAN and his wife are destined to the mission beyond the Rocky Mountains. The pastor was assisted by REV. WILLIAM BRIDGMAN of Friendship.--"N. Y Evan."//On the 2d ult., at Martinsburg, Bedford county, Pa. by the REV. MR. ZELLERS, MR. LEVI SLINGLUFF, merchant, to MISS ELIZA, daughter of CAPT. GEORGE FORE all of that place.//**AUCTION** of pews at the Presby. Church at the corner of Duane and Church streets took place. Among the purchasers were MESSRS. G. & G. HOWLAND, STEPHEN WHITNEY, ROBERT BULOID, N. GRAHAM, &c.--"N. Y. Herald".//**MONIES** for the papers. From HENRY COBLENTZ 25 cts., by REV. P. S. FISHER, from JOHN STRUCK, 87 1-2 cts., and HENRY SCHWARTZ, (Belle-fonte) $1 37 1-2. By REV. J. C. BUCHER from HENRY COBLENTZ 2. By REV. P. S. FISHER, Centre co., from H. SCHWARTZ, 1. VALENTINE MEYER, 2. WILLIAM KELLER 2. F. RUDD 2. By M. RICKENBAUGH from JOHN KNODE, MARTIN HAMMOND, SAMUEL NEWMAN, JACOB BRAGONIER, JR., each $2.// **EXAMINATION** of the Theological Seminary students on the first Wednesday in April, DANIEL ZIEGLER.

46. Mar. 16, 1836/**MARRIED** On Thursday the 10th inst. by REV. HENRY L. RICE, MR. DAVID WELLS, to MISS CHRISTINA FREYDINGER, both of this borough. //**DIED** In this borough, the 9th inst., in the 25th year of her age, MRS. ELIZABETH WHITMORE, daughter of CHRISTIAN WOLFF, Esq. consort of MR. JOHN WHITMORE. For more than three years MRS. WHITMORE endured much bodily and mental affliction.//In Philadelphia, on Wednesday, the 8th inst. MRS. MARTHA MADEIRA, wife of MR. GEORGE A. MADEIRA, of Chambersburg.//On the 1st inst., in Lewistown, Pa., CHRISTIAN HOFFMAN, in the 51st year of his age.//In Petersburg, OH, on the 15th January, MRS. MARGARET LEMMON, daughter of MATTHIAS SHIRK, dec'd. formerly of Newholland, Pa., after a severe illness of three weeks.//On Tues-

day the 8th inst. at her residence Chestnut Hill in the 73d year of her age, RACHAEL (sic) youngest daughter of the late REV. MICHAEL SCHLATTER, GRC Minister.--"Nat. Gaz."//**MONIES.** From MRS. SUSAN B. SHEA, 75 cts.//**LETTERS.** HENRY MICKLY, JACOB HALLER, DANIEL SMALL, ADAM YOUNG (Logansport, IN) M. ROUNSAVILLE, W. DUANE MORGAN.

47. Mar. 30, 1836/**MARRIED** In Guilford county, N. C.,the 10th inst.,by REV. J. H. CRAWFORD, MR. AMBROSE INGOLD to MISS REBECCA FOUST.//The 13th inst., by REV. WM. PAULI, MR. WILLIAM YOUNG, of Philadelphia, to MISS SARAH BISHOP, of Reading. //Near Utica, on the 24th, by REV. JOHN WM. HOFFMEIER, MR. DAVID COBLENTZ, near Middletown, to MISS MARY M., youngest daughter of COL. JACOB CRAMER.//On the 20th inst. by the REV. MR. GOOD, MR. SAMUEL MYERS, of Shepherdstown, Va., to MISS POLLY PRICE of MD.//**DIED** On the 14th ult in New Orleans, MR. WM. B. HENDEL, printer, a native of Carlisle, Cumberland county, Pa.--The deceased has a wife and child in Philadelphia.//In Orange county, N. C., on the 9th ult., MR. GEO. FOUST, SR.//**DONATION** by the Female Benevolent Society of $30 to the Board of Education. CATHARINE MORTON, Pres't. GERTRUDE V. D. RICE, Sec'y.//**FIRE.** Wednesday morning 16th inst., the stables of MR. J. MURPHY, 11th street, NY, were destroyed by fire.//**CURE** for hydrophobia offered by GUY RICHARDS of St. Andrews, L. C. as was used in Canada by six persons who were bit. "3 T. oyster shell lime, add egg to give consistency of soft dough, fry in olive oil or butter. Eat this cake, and abstain from food or drink, at least six hours. Repeat 3 mornings in succession." For information of the writer's character, refer to CHARLES H. CASTLE, Esq. Cashier of City Bank, Montreal.

48. Apr. 6, 1836/**MARRIED** The 11th ult. by REV. W. C. BENNET, MR. JOHN HEDRICK, to MISS PHOEBE BARRIER, all of Davidson county, N. Carolina.// **$50 PLEDGE.** ROBERT DOUGLAS, Missionary scheme.

WEEKLY MESSENGER OF THE GERMAN REFORMED CHURCH

//MONIES By GEO. BESORE from PHILIP AUGHENBAUGH 1 50. From PETER COOK, 75. By JOHN KOOKEN from JAMES HAYS, MRS. GREGG, JOHN PATTON, Esq. each $1 00. By REV. JOHN REBO, from MARY EAKLE 2, and ELIZABETH SMITH 1. By GEO. BESORE, from DAVID M. LIVERS and PHILIP AUGHENBAUGH each 2. By M. KIEFER, from JACOB HOSSLER, (Mercersburg) 2. PETER COOK, (Fayetteville,) 2, and HENRY RICKENBAUGH, (Emmittsburg,) 2.**//HEIRS.** The Albany Advertiser says, there is a search for heirs of HUGH, JOHN and DANIEL MOSHER, in this country, to whom an estate has descended in England.**//LETTERS.** JOSEPH LAUBACH, AQUILA B. MILLER, Esq.

49. Apr. 13, 1836**/MARRIED** On the 24th ult., by REV. E. HEINER, MR. CHARLES A. OBERTEUFFER, to MISS MARY L. PENNINGTON all of Baltimore//Thursday evening last, by the same, MR. JOHN R. PEDRICK of Philadelphia, to MISS SARAH ANN GRUBB of Baltimore.//The 28th ult. by REV. JACOB SCHOLL, the Hon. JOHN JUNKIN to MISS SUSANNA GUSS all of Perry co'ty.//The 31st ult. by REV. F. RAHAUSER, MR. ISAAC OSTAINGER, of Green, to MISS ELEANOR ECKERMAN, of Letterkenny township, Franklin county.//The same day, by the same, MR. WILLIAM RICHEY, to MISS SARAH SPECH, of Fayetteville.//
//DIED The 4th inst., MRS. SARAH JANE ESSIG, of this county, aged 34 years.//In Middle Paxton, Dauphin county,Pa. MISS RACHEL GROSS,daughter of ABRAHAM GROSS,dec'd,in the 20th year of her age.

50. Apr. 20, 1836**/MARRIED** In Middletown, Md., the 29th March, by REV. J. C. BUCHER, MR. DANIEL FLOOK, of JACOB, to MISS ANN ALEXANDER, all of Middletown Valley.//On the 7th of April, by the same, MR. NICHOLAS LUDY to MISS ELIZABETH LOGAN, all of the Valley.//On the 24th ult., by REV. D. ZACHARIAS, MR. JOHN H. ROHRER, to MISS REBECCA SAMSEL.//On the 29th, by the same, MR. GRAFTON J. RICE to MISS ANN M. R. BIRELY, all of Frederick City.//On the 31st, by the same, MR. HENRY KAUFMAN to MISS CATHRINE DOLL, both of Frederick

WEEKLY MESSENGER OF THE GERMAN REFORMED CHURCH

city.//On the 12th inst., by REV. MR. GLESSNER, MR. JAMES CHARITON of Chambersburg to MISS CATHARINE, daughter of MR. JACOB SNIVELY, of Antrim township, of this county.//On the 14th inst., by REV. HENRY L. RICE, MR. DAVID TATE, of Bloody Run, Bedford county, to MISS MARTHA L. BLACK, of the vicinty of Fayetteville.//Thursday the 31st ult., in the borough of Allegheny, by REV. E. P. SWIFT, REV. JOSEPH S. TRAVELLI, of Philadelphia, to MISS SUSAN, daughter of JOHN IRWIN, Esq., of Allegheny.--MR. TRAVELLI and wife expect to sail for Singapore, as missionaries.//**DIED** In Philadelphia, last week, WILLIAM RAWLE, a Lawyer.//On Friday afternoon last, at his residence in Bedford county, MR. CHRISTIAN ROEMER, innkeeper. He left a wife and large family.//March 27th, near Middletown, Md. CATHARINE, eldest daughter of MR. JONATHAN KELLER, in the 5th year of her age.//On the 6th of April, after a short painful illness, JOSEPHUS, only son of the same JONATHAN KELLER, in his 2d year.//Near Lovettsville, Loudon county, Va., the 1st of April, after a short illness MRS. BARBARA YAKY, consort of MR. SIMON YAKY, in the 64th year of her age, leaving a husband and sons.//Another soldier of the Revolution, at his residence in this borough, Friday morning last, in the 79th year of his age, ALEXANDER RUSSELL, Esq. He left Princeton College for the battle, was commissioned Ensign, and subsequently First Lieutenant in CAPT. ALEXANDER's company, PA Line regiment, commanded by COL. IRWIN, and served until 1779, having been at Brandywine, Monmouth, Whitehorse, Paoli, and Germantown. He was a good husband and father.-"Get. Star."//MRS. FOLLY was sentenced last week in Hackensack to three years at hard labor in the State Prison for the death of a little black girl belonging to her husband. The Newark Daily Advertiser described the scene. //**MONIES.** From J. GROVE (Hanover) 75 cts.; from GEORGE REINER (by REV. D. ZACHARIAS) $2 75. MRS. WAMPLER, JACOB HECK, and CHRISTIAN DOBLER, each $2.00. By REV. JONATHAN ZELLER, from B. ISENBERG

WEEKLY MESSENGER OF THE GERMAN REFORMED CHURCH

ENOCH ISENBERG, HENRY HUBLER, LEWIS KNODE, JACOB HUYETT,each $2.00. From JACOB GROVE, REV. SAMUEL GUTELIUS, HENRY WINEBRENNER, HENRY WIRT, each $2.00,GEORGE STOUFER $1.00. By REV. D.ZACHARIAS, from GEO. REINER, GIDEON BANTZ, SR., JOHN KUNKLE each $2.00. By REV. JOHN B. REBO, from J. KEEDY, ANDREW RENTCH, J.B. REBO, JACOB BUCK, E. MORRISON, each $2.00. By REV. J. C. GULDIN, from JOHN HEISTER, ROBERT UMSTEAD, JOHN SHIMER, MANASSEH HUGHES, DANIEL HOFFMAN, JR., each $2.00.//MR. J. B. PERRAULT appointed Cashier of the Citizens Bank, MR. MARTIN GORDON, JR., succeeded him as cashier of the Union Bank.--New Orleans paper.

51. Apr. 27, 1836/**MARRIED** Tuesday morning last in this place, by REV. B. S. SCHNECK, MR. DAVID M. MONTGOMERY of Chambersburg, to MISS JULIET C. BEATTY, formerly of the city of Philadelphia.// On the 14th inst., by REV. WM. A. GOOD, MR. MARTIN FUNK to MISS SUSAN SAILOR, all of Washington co., Md.//Saturday the 10th inst., by the same, MR. JACOB HELSINGER, to MISS ANN SLAER, all of Washington co, Md.//On the 19th inst., by REV. DANIEL ZACHARIAS, MR. JACOB LINN, to MISS EMILY ANN COLE, all of Fred. city.//The 21st inst. by the same, MR. GEORGE THOMAS, of HENRY, to MISS JULIANN HARGETT, all of Fred. co. Md.//The evening of the 7th inst., by REV. H. B. SHAFFNER, MR. J. J. LIBHART, to MISS HARRIET, daughter of MR. JOHN H. GOODMAN, all of Marietta, Pa.//**DIED** At Redhook, Duchess county, NY, on the 28th of March last, MR. JACOB C. MILLER, in the 73d year of his age. The last twelve years he was afflicted with an inenrable cancer, and the last six months has been obliged to sit day and night in a chair.//Suddenly, Sunday afternoon last, MAJ. ROBERT ALLISON, of this borough. He entered the army at the commencement of the Revolution, and served until its close. His remains were interred in the Presby. burying ground, with military honors yesterday.//**MONIES** By JACOB ALBERT, from DAVID LUPFER, JOHN FULWILER, HENRY SNYDER, HENRY

WEEKLY MESSENGER OF THE GERMAN REFORMED CHURCH

FETTER, WM. HUNTER, Esq., each $2 00. By REV. J. W. HOFFMIER, from JACOB FIROR JACOB BARRICK, each 2.

No marriages or deaths in the May 4, 1836 issue.

52. May 11, 1836/**MARRIED** In Clearspring, Md., on the 3d inst., by REV. M. BRAGUNIER, MR. JOHN GARVER, of Gettysburg Seminary, to MISS ELENORA KERSHNER, of Clearspring.//The 28th ult. by REV. F. RAHAUSER, MR. JACOB McFEREN, to MISS ELIZABETH DOSH, both of Guilford township.// **DIED** At Prattsville, the 26th of April, in the 29th year of his age, REV. HAMILTON VAN DYCK, pastor of the RDC in that place. He graduated from Hamilton College in his 20th year, and entered the GRC Seminary, at York. His health was impaired, and the charge he assumed was extensive. In his father's house he was restored so as to be able, in the Spring of 1833, to attend to some ministerial duty. The simultaneous onset of fistula, dyspepsia, phthesis brought him to his grave.--- "May 5, N. York Christian Intelligencer".

53. May 18, 1836/**MARRIED** By REV. B. S. SCHNECK on Tuesday last, MR. EMANUEL CROSSLAN, of Franklin co. to MISS REBECCA TAYLOR, of Michigan Territory.//At Patterson, N. J.. on the 10th inst. by REV. JOHN A. LIDDLE, REV. JOHN C. VAN DERVOOT of the first RDC at Patterson, to MISS GLORVINN ELIZABETH NOTTINGHAM, eldest daughter of the late DR. JOHN NOTTINGHAM, Marbletown, Ulster co. //**DIED** MISS SOPHIA WADDLE, Superintendant of the GR Sabbath School of Baltimore. She died on Thursday evening the 5th of May. (Communicated). //In Lincoln county, on the 21st ult, HUTCHINS G. BURTON, Esq. Ex-Governor of NC and Representative in Congress.//On the 26th ult., at his residence, near Somerville, N. J. JOHN P. VROOM, Esq., in the 52d year of his age.//Suddenly, on the 30th ult. in Philadelphia, the Hon. RICHARD J. MANNING, a Representative from SC.//**FUND** for

- 41 -

WEEKLY MESSENGER OF THE GERMAN REFORMED CHURCH

Missionary Society --letter from Rutherford Co., N. C./ D. MICHAEL $1 MRS. CHURCH 50 G. CORPENING 1 00 A. CORPENING 1 00 THOMAS JANES 3 00 J. H. FARNEY 3 00 TH. D. REED 2 00 WM. WALTON 1 00 JAMES YOUNG 1 00 S. LANTZ 25 A. SHULL 50 JACOB DELLINGER 1 00 J. METZ 37 1/2 J. RAMSOUR 1 50 R. H. BURTON 2 50 J. LANTZ 50 JACOB LANTZ 1 00 J. S. SHUFORD, Esq. 3 00 J. EDWARDS 50 J. FIPBER 50 J. C. BARNHARDT 2 00 M. BARRIER 50 GEORGE BARNHARDT 1 00 From S. C. Newberg District E. SUBER 1 00 From Lexington District REV. DR. E. HAZELIUS 2 00 S. HUFFMAN 1 00 JACOB FELEKLEY 50 From Richland District R. SA_LEY 5 00 North Carolina J. A. KENEDY 2 00 THOMAS FORNEY 1 00 R. HARMAN 1 00 E. SICELOFF 1 02 1/2 REV. W. C. RANKIN 3 00 N. BARTEE 1 00 REV. WM C. BENNET 2 00 C. HOULSHAUSER 1 00 R. HUIL 1 00 THOMAS WHITE 1 00 D. CORRELL 87 1/2 P. CORRELL 50 A. SHUPING 50 J. LITAKEDS 25 M. WARLACH 50 R. FINGER 50 A. HOUSER 50 JACOB RAMSOUR 4 00 L. F. HENDERSON 1 00 ISAAC ERWIN 1 00 COL. J. HOKE 5 00 D. RAMSOUR 3 00 A. RAMSOUR 2 00 ALD. RAMSOUR 50 ANDREW MOTZ 50 J. GRAHAM 50 A. H. LORETZ 1 00 J. T. ALEXANDER 50 F. A HOKE 1 00 W. H. MICHAEL 50 DR. S. SIMPSONS 50 THOMAS SHUFORD 50 A. R. BARTER 50 J. A. WALLACE 1 00 DANIEL HOKE 1 00 SOLOMON RAMSOUR 1 00 BENEDICT JETURS 50 E. S. SHUFORD 1 00 REV. C. A. CEROEL 50 G. R. SHUFORD 1 00 LAVINA WILFANG 1 00 JAMES J. SUMMEY 1 00 Widow SUMMEY 25 W. B. RUTHERFORD 2 00 JAMES M. SMITH 1 00 ABEL SHUFORD 1 00 COL. J. REINHARDT 2 00.

54. May 25, 1836/**MARRIED** At Wilmington, Del. Wednesday the 4th inst. by REV. E. W. GILBERT, REV. ARTHUR GRANGER, of Meriden, Conn. to MISS SARAH ALCORN, daughter of W. ROMAN of the former place.//Near Sharpsburg, Md. by REV. J. REBOUGH, MR. JOHN S. SHOWMAN, to MISS LAVINA HAMMOND.//On Tuesday the 22d March, at Boonsborough, by REV. J. REBOUGH. MR. HIRAM ARNSPERGER, to MISS MARY ANN, daughter of JOSEPH WEAST, Esq., of Boonsboro'.//On the 27th March, by REV. JOHN REBOUGH,

WEEKLY MESSENGER OF THE GERMAN REFORMED CHURCH

MR. EZEKIAL CHENEY to MISS JANE ROC.//The 11th of April, by REV. JOHN REBOUGH, MR. JOHN SPIELMAN to MISS SOPHIA WOLFF all of Washington county, Md.//On the 12th inst. at Friends' Meeting, Germantown, JOHN A. WARDNER, M. D., of Springfield, Clarke county, OH, to ELIZABETH BROWNE, daughter of the late REUBEN HAINES, Esq.//**DIED** In Harrisburg on the 10th inst. MRS. MARY WIESTLING, relict of the late DR. SAM'L WIESTLING, in the 72d year of her age.//**MOTHER'S PLEA** MARGARET SMITH, a widowed mother of Boonsborough, Wash'n co. Md., requests information on her son GEORGE, 11 years of age, stout built, sandy hair (which is disposed to curl, (large blue eyes, (sic) full face and open countenace. She is led to the belief that the man HUME has taken him to Western country, probably Louisville, KY. HUME is about 5 feet 11 inches high, of dark complexion, down look, light hair interspersed with grey:--he had with him two horses. He decamped this county leaving a number of bills unpaid.

55. June 1, 1836/**MARRIED** On Thursday evening the 19th ult. by REV. J. T. MARSHALL DAVIE, REV. JAMES MUNSON OLMSTEAD of Juniata county to MISS CLEMENTINE M. GUNDAKER, youngest daughter of the late MICHAEL GUNDAKER, of Lancaster city.//At York, Pa., Monday morning, the 23d ult., by REV. J. OSWALD, MR. EMANUEL K. ZIEGLER, of Baltimore, Md., to MISS CASSANDRA, daughter of MR. SAMUEL WEISER, SR., of the borough of York.//On Tuesday evening last by REV. D. ZACHARIAS, MR. GEORGE A. REIGHLY to MISS MARY ANN TURNER, all of Frederick city, Md.//The 25th ult. by the REV. MR. C. P. KRAUTH, President of PA College, MR. ISAAC BAKER, of Winchester, VA, to MISS RACHEL WELSH, of Gettysburg.//On the 26th ult. by REV. F. S. MINES, REV. AUSTIN DICKINSON editor of the "National Preacher", to MISS LAURA W. GAUMP, all of this city.//**DIED** At Pottsville, Pa., Tuesday 17th inst., suddenly, the Hon. E. G. BRADFORD, of York lately Associate Judge of the District

WEEKLY MESSENGER OF THE GERMAN REFORMED CHURCH

Court for Lancaster and York.//**A SUPPOSED MURDER** An aged female by the name of MARTHA POAG, residing in this county, disappeared the 25th April last. She was last seen going, accompanied by a pet dog to the house of a neighbor. The dog returned home alone--which has never been the case before--together with the fact she was reputed to be quite wealthy.--"Cecil (Md.) G =" (sic).// The extensive plantations of COL. CROWELL, GEN. M'DONELLS, GEN. ABERCROMBIE, and MR. JONATHAN HUDSON have been burnt by the Indians. The steamer *Hyperion*, in coming up the Chattahoochie was fired upon--and two pilots and one passenger killed. Saturday night, Agent of the Telegraph Line MR. ADAMS, and two drivers GREEN and HICKS, attempting to remove the horses from the stage road were killed. "Charleston Cour. May 19".// **MONIES** By REV. J. F. DIEFFENBACHER, from DANIEL HOTTEL 2, and LAWRENCE KELLER,50C.; from REV. J. ZUILCH 3, GEO. WEBER 4.//**LETTERS** DANIEL SHAFER, ABRAHAM CLAPP,Esq.,N. C. THOMAS SHAW, H.CRONISE, JOHN W. WATSON, H. F. W. SCHULTZE, JOHN WILFANG.

56. June 8, 1836/**MARRIED** On the 12th inst. by REV. DANIEL ZACHARIAS, MR. CHRISTIAN ZACHARIAS, to MISS SARAH PICKING, all of Frederick co.//On the 24th ult. by the same, MR. JOHN PHEBUS, to MISS ELIZABETH C. ELLIS all of Frederick county. //At Philadelphia, on Wednesday morning, by REV. STEPHEN H. TYNG, D. D., WILLIS G. CLARK, Editor of the Philadelphia Gazette, to ANNE POYNTELL, daughter of ROBERT A. CALDELEUGH, Esq.//At Washington, on Tuesday morning, the 31st ult. by the REV. MR. HIGHBEE, DANIEL WESLEY MIDDLETON, to MISS HENRIETTA VAN DYKE, both of that city.//At Hanover, York county, on Sunday morning, by REV. MR. GUTELIUS, MR. HENRY BEITZEL, of York, to MISS ANNA MARY, eldest daughter of ADAM EISHELBERGER, sheriff of York county.//On Tuesday the 24th ult., by the REV. JOHN COLLINS, MR. MICHAEL LUPFER, Esq., of Bloomfield, to MISS ELIZA EMERICH, of Millerstown, Perry county.//On Thursday

WEEKLY MESSENGER OF THE GERMAN REFORMED CHURCH

the 26th ult., by the REV. W. T. SPROLE, FRANCIS DEAL, Esq., to MISS SUSANNAH H. HOFFMAN, both of Philadelphia county.//On Tuesday last, by the REV. JACOB MEYERS, of Mercersburg, MR. CHRISTIAN HOOVER to MISS FRANCES RHODE, both of this county.//On the same day by REV. GEORGE ??, MR. OWEN ASTON, of Pittsburg, to MRS. ESTHER ASTON, of Chambersburg.//On the 26th ult., by the REV. MR. RUTHRAUFF, MR. SAMUEL WINROTT of Adams county to MISS SARAH ANN WINEBRENNER, of York county.//On the 29th ult. by REV. F. L. HERMAN, JR. of Union Co. Pa., MR. JOHN SMITH, editor of the "New Berlin Advocate and Northwestern Eagle" to MISS LUCINDA SEABOLD, both of New Berlin, Union Co.// **DIED** In Baltimore, on Thursday last, MR. SAMUEL HIMES, of Hanover, York co. Pa., in the 53d of his age//Particulars on the death of the following individuals which were reported two weeks ago. At Baltimore, Thursday the 5th inst., MISS SOPHIA WADDLE, aged about 30 years. It is supposed death was hastened by exposure of herself, and unwearied exertions to promote the interests of the institutions of the GRC.-Thursday morning last, in the 54th year of his age, of and affection of the liver, MR. JACOB GROVE, an indulgent parent. //On the 21st ult., MARGARETTA CHAMBERS, infant daughter of JOHN S. KERR, of Green township.//**MONEYS** for Messenger. By REV. J. CARES, from REV. J.CRAWFORD, 1 37 1/2 by MR. REILY, from COL. DAVID SCHNEBLY, 1 50, and MISS AMELIA RAHAUSER, 1 50. From P. ZIMMERMAN, Berlin, Pa., 2. by REV. J. RUDY, from JOHN DRUM, [Poughkeepsie, N. Y.] 2; by REV. J. PENCE 3; by CHARLES F. HOFFMEIER, Esq. from E. M. HASTINGS 2, and GERHART METZGER 1; by REV. H. B. SHAFFNER, from DAVID SHOFF, ELIJAH KEEN, MAGD. KAPP, JOSHUA KEEN, THOMAS RODEMAN, MICHAEL KRAMER, GEORGE KELLER, JACOB HURSH, JACOB KEEN, HENRY KEEN JOHN ECKMAN, JOHN HOLLINGER, each 2; D. HELM and WIKERT 1;

57. June 15, 1836/**MARRIED** On Tuesday week in this borough, by the REV. JOHN N. HOFFMAN, MR.

WEEKLY MESSENGER OF THE GERMAN REFORMED CHURCH

JONATHAN DECHERT of TN, to MISS REBECCA HOFFMAN, of this place.//**DIED** The 11th inst., MARY LOUTZENHEISER, only child of MR. JOHN SMITH this borough, near the close of her fourth year. To her parents her decease must be deeply afflictive as she was their fourth flower that fell before the frost of death. She sweetly fell asleep after twelve days severe suffering.//Sunday morning, the 5th inst., at the residence of her father, MR. H. W. BAKER, in Winchester, Va., MRS. MARY CATHARINE KURTZ, in the 31st year of her age, wife of REV. B. KURTZ, Editor of the Lutheran Observer.//On Friday evening, 7th inst., HORATIO McPHERSON, Esq. Cashier of the Washington County Bank, after an illness of two months in the 35th year of his age.//**MONEYS** From HENRY NYMAN, SR. $1. From MISS ELIZA GREENAWALT $2, JACOB HOAK 2.//It is known to most readers that the German Missionary, GUTZLAFF, has long labored among the vast population of China. He will be joined ere long, we hope, by MR. ROBERTS, MR. and MRS. TRAVELLI.//**LETTERS** MRS. L. ALLEMAN, AARON MULL

58. June 22, 1836/**MARRIED** On the 4th inst. by REV. ALEXANDER SHARP, MR. JAMES WILSON, Esq. to MRS. JUNE DEVOR both of Concord, Franklin county Pa.//**DIED** In Shippensburg on the 9th inst. MAJ. JOSEPH McKINNEY in the 72nd year of his age.//In Frederick City, Md., the 8th inst. MRS. HANNAH MARGARET GETZENDANNER, in the 58th year of her age.//**MONIES RECEIVED** B. REIFF, Esq. 2 25; by M. RICKENBAUGH [agent] from DANIEL ZELLERS, 75, DAVID ZELLERS 1 50, GEO. KEAL 50, REV. W. A. GOOD 75. By JOSEPH LEITER, from JOHN CLOPER 2, JOSEPH LEITER 2 JOHN BEAR 1; from B. REIFF, Esq. 2 75. By M. RICKENBAUGH, from SAMUEL MERCHANT 1, MISS SOPHIA FORCE V. PENTZER, each 2; by REV. J. W. HOFFMEIER, from WILLIAM DEAN [Clarksburg] 2 JOHN CRAMER [Walkerville] 2, and MICHAEL ZIMMERMAN [Creagerstown] 1 75; from MRS. M'CLELLAN [Strasburg,] 1.//**PLEDGES FOR THE MISSIONARY FUND** from REV. J. C. BUCHER, $20 paid, $50 00 pledged.

WEEKLY MESSENGER OF THE GERMAN REFORMED CHURCH

59. June 29, 1836/**MARRIED** On Tuesday the 21st inst. by REV. HENRY AURAND, MR. JACOB SEITS to MISS BARBARA NICKEY, both of Cumberland co, Pa. //Thursday the 9th inst., by REV. H. AURAND, MR. WILLIAM H. SMITH, of Spring Forge, to MISS MARY ANN WILSON, of Perry co., Pa.//Thursday the 16th inst., by REV. D. ZACHARIAS, MR. JOHN MICHAEL KOLB to MISS CHRISTIANA C. HANE, all of Frederick, Md.//In Cavetown, Md. on the 5th inst., by REV. MR. CLINE, MR. ARTHUR B. WEBB to MISS MARY A. YOUNG.//On the 17th inst. by REV. WM A. GOOD, MR. THEOPHILUS BROST to MISS ELIZABETH KEILER, all of Hagerstown, Md.//On the 8th inst., by the REV. MR. BERG, MR. GEORGE LAUMAN to MISS LOUISA CRABB, all of Harrisburg, Pa.//On Tuesday evening the 21st inst., by REV. D. DENNY, MR. JOHN GREENAWALT to MISS MARY, daughter of CAPT. JOHN McCLINTIC both of Chambersburg.//**DIED** In Philadelphia Sunday morning the 19th inst., FREDERICK WOLBERT, Alderman, in the 68th year of his age.

60. July 6, 1836//**MARRIED** On Thursday evening last by REV. D. DENNY, REV. BENJAMIN S. SCHNECK, editor of the Weekly Messenger, to MISS REBECCA, only daughter of the Hon. JAMES RIDDLE, all of Chambersburg, Pa.//In St. Thomas, on the 21st ult, by REV. MR. ROTHROCK, MR. JOHN RENSCH, to MISS MARGARETTA MILLER.//**DIED** JAMES MADISON, Ex-President of the US, in the 85th year of his age at his residence in Orange co. VA.//At his residence, near Mercersburg, on the 12th inst. REV. THOMAS B. CLARKSON of the ARC.//At her residence in Mercersburg, Wednesday, 8th inst., MRS, (sic) ELIZABETH MARTIN, widow of DR. MARTIN, aged sixty years.//On Tuesday morning, 23d inst., this borough, MRS. MARY HART, wife of MR. C. HART, in her 23d year.//**MONEYS RECEIVED** By JOSHUA MOTTER, Esq., from ABRAHAM KRISE 75C.; FREDERICK RECKER 2 50. DAVID ESSOM and JACOB GARVER, each 2; By JAMES POTTER, Esq. from MRS. A. GREGG and WM. HUGHES, Esq. each 2.//**LYNCHING** REV. A. W. KITCHELL of Morris county, N. J. was taken by citi-

zens of Hillsborough, Ga., tarred, feathered and rode through town on a rail, being *suspected* to be an agent of the Abolition Society.

61. July 13, 1836/**MARRIED** Thursday the 15th of May,at Boonsborough, Md.,by REV. J. REBOUGH, MR. GEORGE LOUGHRIDGE, to MISS ELIZABETH FUNK.//By the same, on Sunday, the 29th of May, in Sharpsburg, Md, MR. GEORGE MOSE, to MISS MARY M'COY.// By the same on the 2d of June, MR. GEORGE MACE, to MISS MARGARET PARKS.//By the same on the 28th ult., MR. HIRAM WIEST, to MISS SUSAN HORINE, fourth daughter of JNO. HORINE, Esq., of Washington Co. Md.//At Albany, N. Y., the 28th ult., by the REV. C. GATES, PETER M'NAUGHTEN M D., of Scottsville, Monroe Co., to MISS JANE, daughter of the late SAMUEL M'ELROY, Esq., of the former place.//By the same at Red-hook, N. Y. MR. NICHOLAS SIMMONS to MISS HELEN RIGHTER.//Tuesday the 5th inst. in St. Thomas by the REV. MR. ROTHROCK MR. WILLIAM SMITH, to MISS MARY MORGAN, all of Franklin Co, Pa.//**DIED** In April last, MRS. SUSANNA NYMAN, consort of HENRY NYMAN, SR., in the 49th year of her age, leaving a large family of children.//**MONIES RECEIVED.** From JOHN BEAVER, (Loudon,) and HENRY SNIVELY (Greencastle,) each 2; By REV. JACOB GEIGER, (Manchester, Md.) from JOHN S. MARTIN, LEVI MAXFIELD, JOHN KRANTZ, WESLEY W. GARNER, and JACOB GEIGER each 2.

62. July 20, 1836/**MARRIED** Near Middletown, Md. on the 21st of June, 1836, by REV. J. C. BUCHER, MR. ABRAHAM BOWLES, [of JOHN,] to MISS REBECCA HYATT, daughter of MR. WM. HYATT, all of Middletown valley, Frederick co., Md.//**DIED** Substance of the following notices was furnished by the surviving partner of the deceased: MRS. CATHARINE RANKIN was born in the county of Tyrone, IRE, July 16, 1785. Her parents emigrated to this country when she was about six years old, and settled in Blount county, E. TN, where she resided until her marriage to WM. C. RANKIN, in

WEEKLY MESSENGER OF THE GERMAN REFORMED CHURCH

1815. Her health failed previous to her marriage, and was never restored. Before day, on the morning of the 5th of June, A. D. 1828, her immortal spirit took flight. **ALSO** Departed this life, on the 21st of June, 1836, MRS. ELIZABETH B. RANKIN, second wife of REV. WM. C. RANKIN of NC, in her 33d year. After an illness of three months she was called to leave her husband and children.//Near Middletown, Frederick county, Md. the eve of the 24th June, 1836, after a long distressing illness, MRS. MARY ICOFF, widowed consort of MR. ADOLPH ICOFF, deceased, aged 75 years, 8 months and 24 days.//In Philadelphia on the 17th inst., the Right REV. WM WHITE, D. D., senior Bishop in the Protestant Episcopal Church in the 89th year of his age.//The Rev. Professor GREGG, of the W. R. College, who died at Hudson. He had just returned from N. E. where he had recently married to a niece of the Hon. DAN'L WEBSTER.//**MONIES.** By REV. J. C. BUCHER, from HENRY FEETE and V. W. WELSH, (Burketsville) each $2, JOHN STEHLY 2 75. ADAM VONDERAU, Esq. $2, by GEO. BESORE, from JAMAS McCOY, JR. (Quincy,) 2. By REV. ISAAC GERHART, from W. SCHNEIDER 2, J. MILLER, J. BUFFINGTON and J. MUENCH, each 1. By REV. D. GRING, from SOLOMON E__ (sic) and DANIEL LANTZ, each 2, D. GRING, 2 75.//**SUICIDE.** Papers Monday recorded the sad death of a young German Student LEWIS C. HENNINGER, who shot himself on the Battery on Saturday evening, between 9 and 10 o'clock. Through MR. S. F. B. MORSE, Prof.in the N. Y. University, we have it in our power to give details. His real name was LEWIS HENNINGER CLAUSING; HENNINGER being his mother's name; by this he chose to be known in this country, the better to avoid, as he believed, the persecution of his enemies. CLAUSING was a student at the University of Heidelberg. About the time of the assasination of KOTZEBUE at Manheim by SANDS, a student of the same university, CLAUSING was under arrest. It would seem that the Jesuits, after many years discontinuance, had ventured to

WEEKLY MESSENGER OF THE GERMAN REFORMED CHURCH

innovate those odius public processions of the host, at the passing of which in the streets all are required to be uncovered, and to fall upon their knees. CLAUSING was among the spectators, but ignorant of the custom, he neither moved his cap from his head nor his German pipe from his mouth. A fierce ecclesiastic from the procession struck off his cap. CLAUSING seized it and put it on his head when several others forced him to remove his cap. He marked the man who insulted him determined on revenge. He procured pistols, proceeded to the man's house, shot and wounded him severely in the face. He delivered himself to the Police of the University, and was imprisoned. He had been imprisoned 11 months, awaiting his sentence. The SAND's case roused the Government to punish political offenses with rigor. Besides his crime, it was learned that he belonged to a secret Republican Association. He learned that death would be his doom. By aid of his associates, he effected an escape to this country.--"N. Y. Journal of Commerce.".

63. July 27, 1836/**MARRIED** On the 7th inst., at Mount Carbon by the REV. MR. BRUNER, HENRY VETHAKE, Esq., President of Washington College, Lexington, VA to MISS ELIZA SEELY, of Carlisle, Pa. //**DIED** In Baltimore the 19th inst., MARTHA VIRGINIA, daughter of REV. E. HEINER, aged 5 months 2 weeks and 6 days.//Two days since, we recorded the marriage of REV. JARVIS GREGG, Professor of Sacred Rhetoric in Western Reserve College, to a lady of NH, niece of the Hon, DANIEL WEBSTER; and now we are called upon to note his death. He arrived at Hudson last week, - on Sunday morning had a sudden and severe attack of billious fever and Tuesday night sunk into the sleep of death. "Cleveland (OH) Gazette.".// **FIRE** At 4 o'clock this morning, the large brick building occupied as the printing establishment of DANIEL FANSHAW for the American Bible Society was completely riddled inside.--"N. Y. Jour. Com. July 20."

WEEKLY MESSENGER OF THE GERMAN REFORMED CHURCH

64. Aug. 3, 1836/**MARRIED** Thursday 20th June by REV. HENRY AURAND, MR. JAMES ARMSTRONG, to MISS REBECCA GILMORE, both of Carlisle.//On Thursday, by the same, MR. JACOB RICKENBAUGH to MISS ELIZA BUTCHER, both of Lisburn, Cumberland county.// **DIED** ANDREW CAROTHERS, Esq., of this borough. He died yesterday at his residence, after a protracted illness in the 59th year of his age. His death is a public calamity, particularly for those upon whom his liberality was bestowed.---"Car. Ex."//**A REWARD** of two hundred dollars for the apprehension of JOSEPH CRAMER, charged with murder. He is about 28, 5 foot 7 1/2 inches high, slender form, fair complexion, light hair. He has a sore on his face, and a fresh cut on his cheek, his ears are borred, he speaks broken English. A reward of two hundred dollars is likewise offered for the apprehension of two men who murdered JOHN CLARK, an Englishman, on the 29th ult. in Philadelphia county. One of the perpetrators is about 5 feet 11 inches in height with dark hair and whiskers. The other is described to be 5 ft. 5 or six inches high, broad shouldered, stoutly made, somewhat marked with smallpox, with sandy hair, and whiskers.//MR. JESSEY RAY, of Jefferson County, in this State, just returned from KY, informs us that within a quarter of a mile of Paris, in Edgar county, IL, he saw twelve Indians who had been slain in camp by about sixty intoxicated inhabitants of the town, and the surviving two were pursued through the woods. St. Louis, July 5.---"Republican."// **MONIES.** Z. SPANGLER, J. B. WENTZ, P. A. SMALL, WILLIAM JOHNSON, GEO. SMALL, each 75cts. GEORGE WILLIARD $4. M. DANNER, MARTIN AUSTIN, SAMUEL WAGNER, H. WILLIARD, DR. H. McCLELLEN, WILLIAM BEITZEL, JACOB STEHLEY, each $2. By REV. JONATHAN ZELLER, from GEORGE BIEGLE, SAMUEL KELLER, and WILLIAM LOVE, each $2. GEORGE WILLIARD $1.// **LETTERS** WILLIAM and C. C. RILE, THOMAS HEMPHILL.

No marriages or deaths Aug. 10th or 17th issues.

WEEKLY MESSENGER OF THE GERMAN REFORMED CHURCH

65. Aug. 24, 1836/**MARRIED** On Thursday the 11th of August, by the REV. MR. WYNCOOP, MR. WILLIAM D. M'KINSTRY, to MISS MARGARET SCHNEBLY, daughter of DANIEL SCHNEBLY, Esq. of Hagers-town.// **DIED** Sunday morning, in Cambellstown, Franklin co, MRS. MARY ROTHROCK, wife of REV. MR. ROTHROCK, aged about 23 years.//In NJ on the 29th of July, REV. WILLIAM BURROUGHS, in the 36th year of his age, late pastor of the Central Presby. Church of the Northern Liberties. His disease was consumption.//At Huntingdon, Pa. on the 14th inst., after a few days illness, REV. JOHN W. JAMES, Rector of Christ Church, Philadelphia.// Suddenly, at Harrisonburg, Va., on his way to the Springs, MICHAEL T. SIMPSON, Esq., formerly of PA, but the last few years a resident of this District. On the 7th, his remains were taken to the Methodist burying ground, where the services were performed by the Presbyterian minister.--- "Georgetown Metropolitan."//On Wednesday evening last, a boy about 14 years of age, a son of MR. WM. CLINE, of Adamsburgh, was riding upon a wagon, loaded with stone, and in going down a small declivity, attempted to draw the rubber of the locking machine, in leaning over the side of the wagon to do so, lost his balance and fell, the wheel passed over his head and crushed it. Greensburg paper.//**SUICIDE**. On Thursday the 4th inst., CAPT. MOSES LA??A, of Mountpleasant township this county, by hanging himself to the limb of a tree. We are informed that he had for some time been subject to occasional fits of mental alienation. He was about 50 years of age, sustained an excellent character for morality. He left a widowed mother and two sisters, with whom he resided.-Ib.//MR. W. REYNOLDS, on advise from DRS. F. B. BARCLAY and W. WATSON, of this place, went to Philadelphia for the purpose of having a stone removed from his bladder by DR. RANDOLPH, the first surgeon to perform this in that city.

66. Aug. 31, 1836/**MARRIED** On Tuesday morning,

WEEKLY MESSENGER OF THE GERMAN REFORMED CHURCH

23d inst., by REV. B. S. SCHNECK, MR. JOHN HINE, to MISS MARTHA BURKHOLDER all of Franklin County //**MONEYS** By REV. J.C. GULDIN, from DAVID GRUBB, JR.$2 50; Hon. GEO. CHAMBERS $2,MRS. T. H. CRAWFORD $2; by REV. JOHN WM. HOFFMEIER, from DR. ROBERT CUMMING, DAN'L SNOOK, FREDERICK BARRICK, SOLOMON CREAGER, HENRY SAILOR, each $2.//**A FATAL ACCIDENT** reported Aug. 20. DAVID HARP a well-digger by trade, placed himself at the mouth of an alley in Frederick, MD on Tuesday last, while a man was driving a steer of a most vicious disposition down the street. The steer inflicted so terrible a wound about the thigh and down the leg, that he died in a few hours. This should be a warning to drivers and to citizens.//**ORGANIST WANTED** Of good moral character, for the GRC at York, Pa. It is necessary to understand both languages. DANIEL WEAVER, Pres't of the Vestry.

67. Sep. 14, 1836/**MARRIED** At the residence of MAXWELL WILSON, Esq., in Lincoln county NC, on Thursday evening, the 18th ult., by REV. J. G. FRITCHEY, WILLIAM T. BENNETT, Esq. to MISS NANCY C., eldest daughter of MOSES ALEXANDER, Esq., all of Iredell co. N. C.//In Philadelphia on the 2d ult., by REV. MR. BERKEY, MR. GEORGE HOSKINS, of Cincinnati, OH, to MISS MARION EDWARDINIA STEINMETZ.//In Orwigsburg, Schuylkill co., Pa., by the REV. MR. HARPEL, REV. GEORGE JENNINGS to MISS MARIA, daughter of GEORGE ROUSH, Esq.//**DIED** Near Hagerstown, n Saturday the 10th inst., MRS. PHILIPINA HAIGIS, in the 38th year of her age// Near Hagerstown, the 9th inst., HEZEKIAH, son of DAVID MIDDLEKAUFF, in the 14th year of his age. //On Saturday evening, the 10th inst, WILLIAM HEYSER, SEN., of Hagerstown.//On the 1st inst., in Upper Bern, Berks co., Pa., in the 45th year of his age, VALENTINE WAGNER, Esq.

68. Sep. 21, 1836/**MARRIED** In Baltimore, by the REV. E. HEINER, MR. THOMAS BENTLY to MISS CATHARINE DYKES.//In Reading on the 9th inst., by the

WEEKLY MESSENGER OF THE GERMAN REFORMED CHURCH

REV. WILLIAM PAULI, MR. JOHN TROUP, of Mercersburg, to MISS. MARY KIRCHOFF, of Carlisle.//At Washington, on Wednesday evening, by REV. J. C. SMITH of Georgetown, REV. MASON NOBLE, pastor of the Fourth Presbyterian Church, to ANN CATHARINE only daughter of B. F. PLEASANTS, Esq. all of that city.//On the 8th inst. by REV. DR. CUYLER, JEREMIAH ROSEBERRY, M. D., of Freemansburg, Pa., to MISS. CAROLINE MERRIL, of Philadelphia.//**DIED** Sunday morning, the 4th September, at her residence, in York, MRS. ELLENORA GARDNER, relict of the late JACOB GARDNER, in the 82d year of her age.//On the 15th inst., REV. CYRUS H. JACOBS, Rector of the Episcopal Church in Martinsburg, Va.//On the 5th inst.at Frederick City, MD, COL. FREDERICK EICHELBERGER, formerly of York county, in the 54th year of his age.//On Friday morning last at the residence of his mother, in the city of Lancaster, THOS. BYRD COLEMAN, Esq., in the 43d year of his age.//On Friday evening last, in Hanover, MRS. _____ (sic) WELSH, consort of MR. BENJAMIN WELSH of that place.//On the 13th inst. at Staten Island, N.Y. COL. AARON BURR, formerly Vice President of the US in the 81st year of his age.//**LETTERS** W. J. MAXWELL, SAMUEL PAGUE.

69. Sep. 28, 1836/**MARRIED** On Tuesday, the 20th inst., by REV. MR. WYNKOOP, REV. ROBERT DOUGLAS, pastor of the GRC of Shepherdstown and Martinsburg, Va., to MISS MARY, daughter MR. (sic) JOHN ROBERTSON of Hagerstown, Md.//On the 23d ult. at Easton, Pa., by the REV. THOMAS POMP, the REV. JACOB GEIGER, pastor of the GRC of Manchester, Md. to MISS ESTHER GOBRECHT daughter of the late REV. J. GOBRECHT, of Allentown, Pa.//On Thursday the 15th inst, by the REV. MR. GEIGER, GEO. W. SLINGLUFF, Esq.,of Dover, OH, to MISS ANN daughter of JACOB SHRIVER, Esq.of Frederick county, Md.//**DIED** In Pittsburg, on Sabbath, the 11th inst., MRS. ELIZA consort of SAMUEL FAHNESTOCK, and daughter of JACOB HEYSER, Esq. of Chambersburg, leaving a husband and four children//In

WEEKLY MESSENGER OF THE GERMAN REFORMED CHURCH

Hagerstown, Md. MRS. ANN HEYSER, relict of CAPT. WILLIAM HEYSER, long since deceased, in the 94th year of her age. Mrs. H. was a native of Switzerland, and emigrated to this country with her parents at an early age.//We were shown a beautiful Bonnet made at Goshen by MISS W. CATHCART, in imitation of the Tuscan straw. The Silk and red top grass were raised on her father's farm. "Northampton Courier."//**STRAMONIUM DEATH.** HENRY F. TABER, aged 5 years, son of WILLIAM TABER, of No. 16, Avenue A, NY, died Friday evening from the poisonous effects of some stramonium balls which he ate the previous Sunday.//**MONEYS** for Messenger. DANIEL CROUSE, Waynesborough, 1 50. By REV. D. G. BRAGONIER, from GEORGE YOUNGHEN (Hancock) 2, MRS. ELIZABETH LOOSE (Clearspring) 3. By REV. W. A. GOOD, from ELIJAH DECHERT, Esq.,G.&P.M. BUSHAR, HENRY ERMENTROUT, WM. LOTZ, REV. WM. PAULI, ESTHER HIGH, JACOB LONG, JACOB SOUDER, DR. ISAAC HEISTER, JACOB H. MILLER, LOUISA BOYER, NICHOLAS COLEMAN, HANNAH CROUSER, JACOB HAAK, JOSEPH GOOD, each 2, all of Reading, Pa. By REV. JOHN REBOUGH, from SAMUEL YONTZ, SAMUEL PRY, JOHN CRIDER (Boonsborough,) DANIEL GRIM, (Sharpsb'g.) each 2. By JOHN KOOKEN, from WM. METCALFE, JOHN SHAFER, and DR. P. W. LITTLE, each 2. From PHILIP HERTZEL, (Abbottstown,) 2. NICHOLAS KEEFER 2 50. By DAVID CORRELL, from D. CORRELL, HENRY SECHLER, DAVID BRADSHAW, each 2.

70. Oct. 12, 1836/**MARRIED** On Tuesday, the 20th ult., by REV. JOHN WALLACE, REV. JOHN W. SCOTT, of Steubenville, OH to MISS PHEBE, daughter of ROBERT JENKINS, Esq., of Lancaster Co. Pa.//The 2d inst.in Baltimore, by the REV. E. HEINER, MR. GEORGE S. PUMPHREY, to MISS MARY ANN DYKES, all of that city.//Thursday the 6th inst., by REV. JOHN CLEARY, MR. JOHN PATTERSON, of Juniata co. Pa., to MIS ELLEN, (sic) daughter of MR. WM. VAN DYKE of Mercersburg, Pa.//The Green Bay Democrat states MR. D. WHITNEY sold 1300 ac. for $20,000, on the Fox river.//**PLEDGES DUE.** REV. MR. BERG,

WEEKLY MESSENGER OF THE GERMAN REFORMED CHURCH

REV. P. S. FISHER, J. C. BECKER, J. CARES, T. L. HEFFEDITZ.//**MONEYS** For Messenger. By REV. J. C. BUCHER, from JOHN NEIGHBOURS 25c., JOHN KELLER 75c. By REV. R. DOUGLAS, from JOHN BORNFF 2 25, STEPHEN STALEY, JR. 3 50, JEPTHA HENSEL 6. By REV. W. C. BENNET, from JOHN HEINER 75c, PAUL HAUGH 2 75. By REV. DIEFFENBACHER, from ABSALOM RINKER 50c. ELIZABETH RINKER 75c. BY REV. J. C. BUCHER, from JOHN KELLER, JR. 2, MISS M. KELLER (Jefferson) 2, JOSEPH LONG (alias A. KOOGLE) 2. By REV. W. C. BENNET, from JACOB KOONTZ, JOSEPH KOONTZ, JOHN HEINER 25c., ISRAEL HEITSHU 3 50, JACOB FEASER 2. By REV. SAMUEL R. FISHER, from PHILIP HARTMAN, M. ZACHARIAS, ABIAH MARTIN, MRS. H. MOTTER, JOSEPH MORRITZ and WM. HAUGH, each 2. From MRS. JAMES ARMSTRONG (Balt.) 1. By REV. R. DOUGLAS, from REV. J. BLACK, MRS. AMELIA SHEPHERD, MISS ROSANNA DOLL, A. SUMMERS, JOHN SMURR, D. HAWN, JOHN BORUFF, HENRY STAUB, and ELIZABETH KEPLINGER, each 2. By REV. J. C. BECKER, from JOSEPH LABAUGH, 2. REV. J. H. SMALTZ, 2, MRS. R. ELY 2, JOHN GRANT 2. By REV. J. F. BERG, from GEORGE SMALL (Harrisburg), REV. J. F. BERG 2. By REV. S. HELFENSTEIN, JR., from FREDERICK HUBER, PHILIP HUBER, JOHN RILE, each 2; REV. S. HELFENSTEIN, JR.3. By REV. J. DIEFFENBACHER, from ELIZABETH RINKER 2 50, ISAAC HOTTEL 2, ELIZA EMSCHWILLER 2,ABSALOM RINKER 1 25. REV. F. RAHAUSER2.

71. Oct. 19, 1836/**MARRIED** On the 6th inst., at Freehold, N. J., by the REV. D. V. McCLEAN, REV. ISAAC V. BROWN, of Lawrenceville, to MRS. JANE AUGUSTA BRUEN, widow of MR. JOHN BRUEN, daughter of the late JOHN WATERS, ESQ., Planter Savannah, GA.//At German Valley, N. J. the 20th September, by REV. JAMES SCOTT, MR. FOREMAN, of the firm TITUS & FOREMAN, merchants, Easton, Pa., to MISS ANGELINE, daughter of LAWRENCE HOGAN, Esq., of the former place.//Thursday morning last, by the REV. MR. GUTELIUS, MR. HENRY WINEBRENNER, son of P. WINEBRENNER to MISS SARAH FORNEY, daughter of ADAM FORNEY, deceased, all of Hanover, Pa.//On

WEEKLY MESSENGER OF THE GERMAN REFORMED CHURCH

Tuesday the 27th September, by REV. J. G. ANSPACH, REV. DANIEL GRING, pastor of the GRC in Milton, Pa., to MISS CATHARINE MORRISON of the same place.//**ACCIDENT** Our fellow citizen, MR. JAMES M'GUIRE of this neighborhood, died at the tavern of JACOB NUBECK, below Gettysburg, on Tuesday 28 inst. of a hurt he received the previous Friday. He was driving a wagon and stopped for the night at Mr. N's---there being no hosler present, he went on top of a stack to get some hay. At descending from which he ???? on the end of a rake handle which entered his body near a foot and a half! He lingered in great pain until Friday. (sic) MR. M'GUIRE left a wife and two children. --"Oct. 14 Chambersburg Repos."//**MONEYS**. From JOSEPH McCAULEY and JACOB COUTER, each 2, from HENRY BOOZER (Old Fort, Centre co.) 2. By REV. J. C. GULDIN from LEVI SMITH, JESSE DAVIS, PETER BROWNBACH, JNO. KIMES, CHARLES LAW, JR., ALBERT TRAINER, each 2 50, and ALBERT TRAINER, (sic) CHARLES H. LEINBACH, WILLIAM BROWNBACH, each 2. EPHRAIM KIEFFER 2.//**LETTERS** A. S. E. DUNCAN, F. LEAS, SAMUEL RITTER, JAMES ALLEN, JOHN MOYER, SR.

72. Oct. 26, 1836/**MARRIED** In Cambridge, by REV. MR. WINSLOW, REV. LYMAN BEECHER, D. D. President of Lane Seminary, OH, to MRS. LYDIA JACKSON, of Boston.//On Thursday 6th inst. by the REV. J. B. KNIPE, MR. MADISON HECK, to MISS SARAH QUAY, all of Chester County, Pa.//On the 11th inst., by REV. HENRY L. RICE, MR. THOMAS QUANTRILI to MISS CAROLINE CLARK, both of Chambersburg.//The 20th inst., by REV. HENRY L. RICE, MR. JACOB SIDES to MISS MARY KEEFER, both of Franklin county.// In Rowan Co. N. C., on Thursday the 26th of May last, by REV. GEO. BOGER MR. DANIAL KERCHER, to MISS CYNTHIA SECHLER.//In Cabarrus Co., N. C., on Thursday the 8th of Sept., by the same, MR. JOHN FISHER to MISS SOPHIA FOIL.//The 28th Sept. in Spartanburg District, S. C., by the REV. HUGH HENDERSON, the REV. WM. C. RANKIN, of the GRC, Rutherford Co. N.C., to MISS JOANNA KELSO daugh-

WEEKLY MESSENGER OF THE GERMAN REFORMED CHURCH

ter of WM. KELSO, Esq., Spartanburg District, S. Carolina.//**DISTRESSING** A little girl 7 years old, named FRANCES JULIA ANDERSON, daughter of MR. ANDERSON, a teacher in this city, caught her clothes on fire attempting to toast bread while her mother was out. She died the next day at 12 o'clock. This was in Alleghany--her parents had recently moved from Philadelphia.//**MONEY** for Messenger. By REV. MR. KNIPE, from SAMUEL ACKER (Chester Springs) 2. By AMOS E. KREMER, from JOSEPH URBAN (C?) 4, DAVID BIXLER 2 50, WM. STREBIG (Mar?ville) 2, and MRS. LYDIA SPANGLER (York) 2. By REV. J. REBOUGH, from JOHN B. WELTY (Boonsborough, Md) 2, from MRS. MARY MILLER (of JOHN) and JOSEPH HIGHBARGER, each 2. From REV. J.S.EBAUGH 2.//**LETTER** SAMUEL HAHN.

73. Nov. 2, 1836/**MARRIED** The 13th ult., by the REV. MR. HACKE, MR. TIMOTHY JENNINGS to MISS. DOROTHY BLYHOLDER, both of Greensburg.//The 16th ult., by the same, MR. JACOB SHYBLER to MISS. VERONIKA, daughter of MR. JACOB KEPPEL both of Hempfield township.//On the 18th ult., by the same, MR. ISAAC SYLVIES to MISS MARGARET PORTER, both of Hempfield township.//On Thursday, September the 1st, at Delphi, IN, by the REV. JOHN STOCKER, R. C. GREEN, Esq. editor of the Delphi Oracle formerly of Lewistown, Mifflin co., to MISS. ZERUA AMELIA eldest daughter of DR. PHELPS of NY.//On Tuesday evening, September the 20th, in Bellefonte, Pa., by the REV. JAMES LINN, MR. S. T. SUGERT, senior editor of Centre Democrat, to MISS DEBORAH DUNLOP, all of the above mentioned place.//In York, Pa. on the 13th ult., by REV. A. H. LOCHMAN, the REV. SAMUEL SPRECHER pastor of the Ev. Luth. Church in Harrisburg, Pa. to MISS. CATHARINE, daughter of REV. DR. J. G. SCHMUCKER.//In the English Lutheran Church in Baltimore city, on Tuesday evening last, by the REV. J. G. MORRIS, the REV. P. RRIZER (sic) of IN, to MISS MARGARET P. ROGERS of that city.// The 11th ult. by REV. MR. GUTELIUS, MR. HENRY

WEEKLY MESSENGER OF THE GERMAN REFORMED CHURCH

CRAMER, of Frederick county Md. to MISS ANNA SAVERBIER, of Adams Co. Pa.//At Lancaster, Pa., Tuesday evening the 18th ult., by the REV. MARTIN BRUNER, MR. SAMUEL DORWART, to MISS HARRIET HEITSHU, daughter of MR. PHILIP HEITSHU, all of the city of Lancaster.//**DIED** On the 19th inst. at the residence of her father, near Hagerstown, MISS ELIZABETH, second daughter of MR. MICHAEL HAMMOND. On the day preceding her death she was so much improved as to warrant a discontinuance of the prescribed medicines.//On Sunday morning last, at the residence of DR. JOHN CREIGH, Carlisle, Pa. MRS. ANN H. CREIGH, wife of the REV. THOMAS CREIGH of Mercersburg, Franklin county, Pa. aged 27.//Suddenly on the 10th ult., at the residence of THOMAS JEFFERSON RANDOLPH, MRS. MARTHA RANDOLPH, widow of the late THOMAS MANN RANDOLPH, and daughter of THOMAS JEFFERSON.//In York, on the 17th ult. MR. FERDINAND L. SPANGLER, in the 31st year of his age.//The REV. ASA MESSER, D. D. LL. D. departed this life on the night of Tuesday last, in the 68th year of his age, the President of Brown University from 1802 until 1826.--"Prov. Cour."//On Tuesday morning, the 18th ult., after a short illness, MARGARET, daughter of the REV. HENRY HABLISTON in the 9th year of her age.//In Pittsburgh, on the morning of the 17th ult., JOHN BRECHBILL, about 27 years of age. He was a native of Cumberland county, in this state, residing in South Middleton township, five miles from Carlisle. He left home for the west in the latter part of September, in good health, but had been attacked by billious fever, and was received into the house of H. W. KAUFMAN, a friend of his youth. On the morning of the 18th ult. his remains were decently laid in the Cemetery of the GRC of this city - Pittsburg paper.//**MONEYS** for the Mission fund. DANIEL WEISER, $30//**MONEYS** for the Messenger. By C. F. HOFFMEIER, from GERHART METZGAR 1, JOHN LENHERR 1, and CHRISTIAN GAST 2.//**GAME** The Portland Argus states that at a recent shooting match in

WEEKLY MESSENGER OF THE GERMAN REFORMED CHURCH

Fryeburg (Mud c'ty) CAPT. HENRY BATCHELDER and five others brought in 1735 squirrels of all kinds, about 140 woodpeckers, blue jays, hawks, and owls. Another party, of CAPT. CHARLES and four others, brought in 1265 squirrels, over 100 woodpeckers and many other birds, amounting to nearly 3,850.//**DISTRESSING ACCIDENT.** As workmen on the new church erected for the Baptist society were completing the stone work on Saturday evening last, the main part of the gable end fell with a tremendous crash, carrying with it two men who were at work upon the staging. One was a German by the name of JOHN HAMLUN, and the other had but a few days previous arrived from MO, whose name was GWYNN. "Telegraph." Alton, IL Oct. 12//**LETTERS** ELI CRAMPTON, JAMES PEACOCK.

74. Nov. 9, 1836/**MARRIED** The 25th ult. by the REV. MR. GUTELIUS, MR. WILLIAM ROBERT, to MISS CHRISTIANA WISE, all of Adams county.//In Boonsboro, Md.,Sept.22d,by the REV. J. REBOUGH, MR. WILLIAM HOFFMAN, Merchant of Attica, IN, to MISS CAROLINE B., eldest daughter of the late LEONARD SHAFER, of Washington Co., Md.//Wednesday evening, 19th ult., by the same, MR. FRANKLIN BLACKFORD, to MISS ELIZABETH R. MILLER, all of Washington Co. Md.//**DIED** In Hanover, on the 25th ult., EMELINE MARGARETTA, daughter of MR. HENRY WIRT,aged 1 year, 1 month, and 20 days.//On Friday morning last, MISS MARY, eldest daughter of ARCHIBALD I. FINDLAY, Esq. of Chambersburg, aged about 6 years.//___, (sic) on the 3d inst. MR. MATHEW GIBBONS, an old resident of this Borough. //**MONEYS** for Messenger. From VALENTINE UHRICH, (Halifax) 1. By REV. JONATHAN ZELLERS, from SAMUEL HARNISH, SR. 2, JNO. AURANDT 2, and REV. J. ZELLERS 1. By C. F. HOFFMEIER, from WM. HEITSHU, 2. By REV. ROBERT DOUGLAS, from MISS SUSAN GROVE, MRS. MARY MILLER, GEORGE WOLFF, Esq., and SOLOMON ROPP, each 2. From J. H. A. BOMBERGER 2. By JACOB WELSH from ALBRIGHT & ALBAUGH (Hanover) 2. By REV. S. R. FISHER, from BENJAMIN KOONS

WEEKLY MESSENGER OF THE GERMAN REFORMED CHURCH

(Bruceville) HENRY WORTZ, each 2, and REV. S. R. FISHER 1. From GEORGE COOK, JR., 2. By REV. J. ZELLERS, from ABRAHAM DIVELY 2, HENRY KNODE 2, and REV. J. ZELLERS 1. By REV. J. HENSEL, from DAVID SHULTZ 3, JOHN HAWPE 2. From JOHN HIESTER (Mercersburg 2. (sic).

75. Nov. 16, 1836/**MARRIED** In Philadelphia, on the 8th inst., by the REV. G. DUFFIELD, the REV. JAMES O. STEDMAN, of NC, to MISS MARGARETTA HARBERT, of the former place.//In Huntingdon, Pa., on the 3d inst., by the REV. J. PEEBLES, THOMAS JACKSON, Esq., of Williamsburg, to MRS. ANN PATTON, daughter of DAVID McMURTRIE, of the former place//The 27th ult. by the REV. HENRY L. RICE, MR. JAMES WILSON, to MISS BARBARA WORLEY, both of the vicinity of Greencastle.//On the 3d inst. by the same, MR. GEORGE SNIDER of Guilford township, to MISS ANN CHRISTMAN, of St. Thomas township.//**MONEYS** for Messenger By JOHN KOOKEN, JR., from JAMES HAYS 1. By A. H. KREMER, from JACOB NEWMAN 1, MELCHOIR BRENDEL (St. Thomas) 1. By REV. D. ZACHARIAS, from CHARLES HALLER, MICHAEL ZIMMERMAN, CHRISTIAN KEMP, JOHN A. STEINER, and MRS. MARY BUCKEY, each 2, and JNO. BRUNER, LEWIS BRUNER, each 4. From REV. JOHN ALBERT and HENRY BITTINGER, [York Springs,] each 2. By AMOS H. KREMER, from CHARLES PENSIL, ELIAS GUMP, SOLOMON DIEHL, JOHN G. MARTIN, Esq., PETER SCHELL, Esq., and JOHN NYCUM, Esq., each 2. By REV. W. C. BENNET, from REV. W. C. RANKIN, and HENRY BARRIER, each 2. From A. BUSH 2.

76. Nov. 23, 1836/**MARRIED** At Easton, Pa., on Thursday evening, the 10th inst., by the REV. B. C. WOLFF, MR. WILLIAM HELLER, to MISS ANN ELIZA MIXSELL, daughter of C. MIXSELL, Esq.//On Thursday evening, the 10th inst., by the REV. JOHN S. REESE, MR. JOSHUA YINGLING, of New-market district to MISS MARGARET daughter of ISAAC SHRIVER, Esq., of Westminster, Md.//On the 5th inst., by the REV. MR. GUTELIUS, MR. GEORGE MILLER to MISS

WEEKLY MESSENGER OF THE GERMAN REFORMED CHURCH

MARY THEIBER, all of York county.//On the same day, by the same, MR. JOHN HANDESHELL to MISS JULIA ANN SCHOENEBRUCH, all of Adams county.//On the same day, by the same, MR. ADAM STRASBACH to MISS REBECCA THRONE, all of York county.//On the same day, by the same, MR. DANIEL SNYDER to MISS REBECCA FIESER all of Adams county.//**DIED** Mount Joy Tp. Lanc.co.Pa.,on the 9th inst., MR. TOBIAS BICKEL, of Gratztown, Dauphin co., in the 55th year of his age.//Middletown Valley, Md., October 28th, MR. V. W. WELSCH, in the 47th year of his age, member of the GRC at Burkettsville. He left five children to mourn the loss of an only parent.//At his residence in Hagerstown, Monday evening last, in the 60th year of his age, MR. DAVID MIDDLEKAUF, SEN.//At his residence near Hancock, on the 4th inst. CAPT. ABRAHAM NICODEMUS, leaving a wife and several small children. //**MONEYS** for Messenger. By M. RICKENBAUGH, from DAVID ZELLERS, (of JNO. $1. From WM. VONDERAU 3. By REV. J. C. BUCHER, from JOSEPH WISE 2, JACOB WEAVER 2 75. By REV. J. F. DIEFFENBACHER, from WM. HOTTEL 4, CHARLES JORDAN 1. By M. RICKENBAUGH, from JACOB KERSHNER, DAVID MIDDLEKAUF, JR. DANIEL MIDDLEKAUF, WILLIAM STONEBRAKER, and M. RICKENBAUGH, each $2. By REV. J. REBOUGH, from A. NEFF, JOHN GRICE, JOHN MILLER, of JNO., each $2, and ELIZ. and MARIA HOUSER $1. From MRS.McCLELLAND [Strasburg] 2. By REV. B. C. WOLFF, from WM. REWALT, MRS. MARY SHICK, each 2. From FREDERICK RUDD 2. By Hon, GEORGE CHAMBERS, from Hon. WM.HIESTER and HENRY SHIRK, [New Holland,] each 2. From DAVID WILSON 2. By J. O. WALKER, Esq., from JOHN F. LIPPARD 2, and REV. GEORGE BOGER [Concord, N. C.] 4, JOHN MOORE, JOHN C. BARNHART, [Mt. Comfort, N. C.] each 2. From ROBERT KING [Mercersburg] 2.//**MISTAKE** We acknowledged receipt of one dollar, each, from JACOB NEWMAN and MELCHOIR BRENDEL, for the Messenger.--The payments were not intended for this paper, but for the German 'Christliche Herold.' //**GREAT BEAR** We are informed that CAPTAIN JOHN

WEEKLY MESSENGER OF THE GERMAN REFORMED CHURCH

NOYES, of Greenwood, shot a bear the quarters of which weighed 401 pounds, when dressed. He sold one half of it for nine cents per pound, which was carried to Boston and disposed of at a handsome profit.//**A BODY!** From the Circleville, OH Telescope, we learn that a man, named JOHN BEAR, JR., was found on the tow-path of the canal, near that place. He formerly lived near Gettysburg, Pa., where his parents still reside.

77. Nov. 30, 1836/**MARRIED** On Thursday evening last, by REV. DAVID DENNY, MR. J. G. HEIST, of Winchester, VA, to MISS GEORGIANA, daughter of GEO. K. HARPER, of Chambersburg, Pa.//In Easton, Pa., evening of 22nd inst., by REV. B. C. WOLFF, MR. PETER YOUNG, to MISS MARY SHICK, all of that place//On the 17th inst., by REV. MR. HACKE, MR. JONATHAN STUMP, to MISS ELIZABETH SMITH, all of Westmoreland Co., Pa.//On the 8th inst., by REV. W. MILLER, MR. JOHN BAKER, Editor of the Lebanon Democrat, to MISS HARRIET MARKLEY, daughter of DANIEL MARKLEY, Cumberland Co. Pa.//On Thursday evening, 24th inst., by REV. MR. DE WITT, G. F. WEEBER, Esq. late Editor of the "Centre Berrichter," to MISS ELIZABETH DICKEY, both of this place.//The 10th inst., by REV. MR. ALLAN, MR. JOHN W. STURGES, of Fayette county, to MRS. EMMA HECBROTH of the borough of Greensburg.//Thursday the 10th inst., by the REV. MR. MEDHART, REV. CHARLES BARNITZ, of Philadelphia, to MISS CATHERINE FRANKS, of the same place.//On Tuesday the 15th inst., by the same, REV. H. MILLER, pastor of the Evan. Lutheran church in Williamsport, Md., to MISS CORNELIA S. second daughter of JOHN C. MOORE, of Philadelphia.//On the 10th inst. by REV. N. P. HACKE, MR. WILLIAM FISHER, of Mount Pleasant township to MISS ELIZABETH, daughter of MR. JOHN LEASURE, of Unity township, Westmoreland co.//On Tuesday, 15th inst. by the REV. MR. REIKA, MR. HENRY MYERS of Circleville, OH, to MISS ELVINIA A. FETTER of Lancaster, Pa.//At New Haven, Conn., on the 27th ult., by the REV. LEO-

WEEKLY MESSENGER OF THE GERMAN REFORMED CHURCH

NARD BACON, the REV. THOMAS BRAINARD, editor of the "Cincinnati Journal," to MRS. MARY WHITING, editor of the "Microcosm," New Haven.//**DIED** On Wednesday night, the 16th inst., JAMES C. GILLELAND, Esq. late editor of the Pittsburg Times.// Thursday last, at his residence in Green township. the Hon. WM. McKESSON, aged 56 years, an Associate Judge of the county.//Near Hagerstown on the 16th inst, MRS. SUSAN REINHART, in the 44th year of her age, leaving a husband and nine children.//**CASUALTY** We learn, says the Raleigh (N. C.) Register, by a letter from the REV. DR. WITHERSPOON, of Camdon, S. C., that WILLIAM P. FERRANT, Esq. of Onslow county, was killed by the overturning of the stage sixteen miles south of Cheraw on the 7th inst. His remains were interred on the farm of a MR. M'MILLAN.//As MRS. WEED, wife of MR. HENRY WEED of 39 Howard street NY, was attempting to swallow beefsteak on Saturday morning, it stuck in her throat and caused her death. She had for some time previous complained of quinsy and sore throat.//On Saturday the 5th inst. the Powder Mill of MR. JACOB JOHNSON, erected on the Swamp Creek, exploded, killing MR. JOHN WEYANT and WM. KOCH, both men of families, the former of Philadelphia.--"Norristown Register."//H. W. EVANS, Esq., proprieter of the Lanvale Factory in MD, abolished intoxicants on his premises.//**MISSIONARY DONATION** from NC: A. BECHLER $1, G. SUMMEY, Esq. 2 50, P. A. SUMMEY & J. S. E. SUMMEY 5, SOLOMON RAMSOUR 1, MICHAEL FINGER 50c., H. F. FOSTER 50c., JOSEPH FINGER 50c., J. NAUGLE 25c., PETER FAUST 3, J.H. FORNEY 1, RICHARD HARRIS, Esq. 1, HENRY FAUST 1, JACOB RAMSOUR 50c., DAVID RAMSOUR 50c., SOLOMON WARLICH 1, JOHN HAUS 25c. D. F. RAMSOUR 1, J. RAMSOUR 50c., PETER WARLICH 50c., PETER FINGER 1 REV. W. C. RANKIN 14, LOGAN CONRAD 50C., J. RAMSOUR, JR. 25c., JONAS BART, Esq. 50c.,

78. Dec. 7, 1836/**MARRIED** In Perry County, OH by the REV. MR. WINTERS, MR. DAVID BESORE, to MISS

WEEKLY MESSENGER OF THE GERMAN REFORMED CHURCH

MARY KLINGLER all of that county.//In Adams Co., Pa. on the 22nd ult. by the REV. MR. KELLER, MR. THOMAS J COOPER, Merchant of Gettysburg, to MRS. ELIZABETH FLOHR, of Franklin Township.//On the 24th, by the same, MR. GEO. KANN, to MISS SUSANNAH DEARDORF, both of Adams County.//On Tuesday, the 8th ult., at Vaucluse, the seat of WM. S. JONES, Esq., Frederick county, Va., MR. WM. H. KEIM, of Reading, Pa. to MISS LUCY JANE, daughter of GEN. THOMAS RANDOLPH.//Tuesday the 15th ult. by REV. WM. A. MUHLENBERG, D. D. of Flushing, in St. Johns Church, Brooklyn, the REV. JACOB W. DILLER, Assistant Minister of the same, to MISS ANGELINA, daughter of LOZEE VAN NOSTRAND Esq. of that city.//On Wednesday evening Nov. 23, in the Fifth Presbyterian Church, by REV. ROBERT KENNEDY, of Mercersburg, JAMES M. KENNEDY, merchant of Philadelphia, to MISS SIBILLA STONE, daughter of the late EVAN MORRIS, Chester county //Tuesday the 18th ult. by the REV. MR. WHITE, DR. JAMES DAVIDSON to MISS MARTHA ROBINSON, all of Antrim township, Franklin county, (Pa) - "Hagerstown Torchlight, Dec. 4."//**DIED** In the city of NY on Sunday the 20th of November, 1836, MRS. MARIANNE F. McELROY, wife of REV. J. McELROY, D. D. of NY, in the forty-first year of her age. She was the eldest daughter of the late JUDGE WALKER and was born on the 2d of November, 1795. Her education was substantial and she possessed a talent for writing. At the age of sixteen she was united in marriage to a gentleman of opulence. In a few brief years she was called to meet the sorrows of widowhood. In May, 1824, she became the wife of the pastor. She died of a protracted and painful disease.//At his residence, in Centre county, on the ___ (sic) inst. WILLIAM PATTON, Esq. in the 80th year of his age.//On the 29th of October last, MRS. SARAH JACK, wife of MAJ. JOSEPH JACK, of Westmoreland county and daughter of the late SAMUEL SLOAN, Esq. of Gettysburg.//**MONEYS** for Messenger By REV. SAMUEL R. FISHER, from JOHN COVER (Bruceville) 4, MARY

SMITH and ELI SMITH (Emmitsburg) each 2, RICHARD GILL (Millcreek, Va.) 2. From CHRISTIAN WOLFF, Esq.2. By DAVID SHRIVER, Esq. (Littlestown) from EGBERT ECKERT and MARTIN STEFFEY, each 2. By M. ROUNSAVILLE, Esq. (Lexington, N. C.) from HENRY BARRIER, JACOB BARRIER, ALEZANDER MICHAEL, JACOB LEONARD, and PETER LEONARD, each 2. From MRS. CULBERTSON 2, JOHN ZIEGLER 2, JACOB ZIEGLER 2, REV. F. A. SHOLL 2. By H. COST 2, from CAPT. WM. LAKIN 2, MRS. SUSAN LAKIN 1, MISS CATHARINE COST 2, HENRY COST 2, SEBASTIAN REMSBERG, JR., 3, and LOUIS RODERICK 2.//**WRECK** of the *Bristol,* which had sailed from Liverpool for N .York(where she belongs) (sic) 15th October. About two o'clock, last Monday morning, she went ashore in a gale on East Rockaway. Her mainmast and boats gone, 15 or 16 persons were hanging in the rigging. CAPT. SCHENCK left here with his schooner, to be assisted by ten men in a surf boat. At about 11 o'clock, P. M. the sea abated and the boats succeeded in taking off the captain, a portion of the crew, and some of the passengers. The cook and steward with a MR. DONNELLY, two MESSRS. CARLTON'S, cabin passengers, and about sixty steerage passengers perished.//**ORDINATION** Held in Christ Church, Richmond, Va. on the 6th ult., by the RIGHT REV. RICHARD CHANNING MOORE, D. D., REV. WILLIAM SCULL lately minister of a Lutheran congregation in Augusta county, VA, was admitted to the order of deacon.--"Southern Churchmen."

79. Dec. 21, 1836/**MARRIED** In Middletown, Md., December 15, 1836, by the REV. J. C. BUCHER, MR. ELIAS STEIN, to MISS ELIZABETH ANN REBECCA HESSONG all of Middletown Valley.//ISAAC MOTTER, of Williamsport, formerly of Emmittsburg, and son of LEWIS MOTTER, to MARY A., daughter of JOSEPH SNIVELY, of Franklin county, Pa.//In Hagerstown, Thursday the 24th Nov. by REV. C. F. SCHAEFFER, MR. JACOB ARNDT, to MISS ANN MARIA KERSHNER both of Washington county, Md.//In Sharpsburg, on the evening of 19th October by REV. MR. REBOUGH, MR.

WEEKLY MESSENGER OF THE GERMAN REFORMED CHURCH

FRANKLIN BLACKFORD to MISS ELIZABETH MILLER eldest daughter of MR. JACOB MILLER, Esq., all of Washington co., Md.//**DIED** Near Middletown Frederick county, Md., on the 12th day of December, 1836, after a protracted illness, MRS. HANNAH MANSON, a pious widow in her 63d year. She left two sons, one whose family she lived with.//The 15th of November in Pleasant Valley, Washington county, Md., after a protracted illness, MRS. CATHARINE, wife of MR. BENJAMIN GRIM, aged 31 years, 15 (sic) months and 5 days leaving a husband and 3 small children.//Near Burkettsville, Md., on the 24th of November at the house of MR. ERASMUS GARROT, MR. JONATHAN MOSS, eldest son of MR. CHARLES MOSS, near Buckeystown, Md., in his 25th year.//Near Middletown, Md., the 5th of December of croup, CHARLES WASHINGTON, second son of MR. JOHN COBLENTZ, (of JOHN PHILIP,) aged 2 years, 1 month 29 days.//Near Middletown, Md, on the 12th day of December, after a short illness, MARY CATHARINE, eldest daughter of DANIEL and SARAH KEFAUVER, in the third year of her age.// In NY, December 14, REV. JOHN R. McDOWULL, (sic) aged 35 years, formerly editor of "McDowell's (Moral Reform) Journal." Owing to difficulties between himself and the Female BenevolentSociety of NY, charges were preferred and he was suspended. He appealed to the General Assembly of 1837 (sic)--but death summoned him.//On the 15th inst, at the house of her son, DR. SHEFFER, in Petersburg, Adams co., Pa, MRS. MARY SHEFFER, formerly of York, at an advanced age.// On the 7th inst., MAJOR HENRY MYERS, of Adams co., Pa., aged about 42 years.//**AM. COLONIZATION SOCIETY'S** twentieth annual meeting, held Tuesday evening, 13th inst. Interesting addresses were delivered by DR. PROUDFIT and DR. REESE, of NY; MR. Z. C. LEE, of Baltimore, MR. GRENNELL, of MA; the REV. DR. HILL and REV. CHARLES W. ANDREWS, of VA; MR. G. W. P.CURTIS, of DC; and the REV. DR. LAURIE. The Annual Report was read by REV. MR. GURLEY, Secretary.--Washington paper.//**MISSIONARIES** The

WEEKLY MESSENGER OF THE GERMAN REFORMED CHURCH

The following gentlemen, several of whom will be accompanied by their wives, will embark early next week in the *Mary Frazier*, as Missionaries for the Sandwich Islands: REV. ISAAC BLISS, REV. DANIEL T.CONDE, REV. MARK LIVES, REV. THOMAS MASON, M.D, DR. SETH L. ANDREWS, MESSRS. AMOS S. COOKE, EDWARD BAILEY, WM. S. VAN DUZEE, CHARLES M'DONALD, ABNER WILCOX, HORTON O. KNAPP, RETHIEL MANN, EDWIN LOCKE, EDWARD JOHNSTON, SAMUEL N. CASTLE. MISS MARCIA M. SMITH, and MISS LUCIA G. SMITH.//**DEATH** The last issue of the Missionary Herald contains a narrative of the shipwreck of REV. ELI SMITH who was conveying his wife from Beyrout to Smyrna in the hope of benefitting her health. They reached Smyrna the 13th July, and we have before us a Smyrna paper of the 30th of September, with the following announcement:---- Died this morning at the village of Boujah, MRS. SARAH L SMITH, wife of REV. ELI SMITH, of Beyrout. While on passage to Smyrna, a few weeks since, this excellent lady was, by the wreck of the vessel, left for four days if (sic) a state of exposure on an inhospitable shore.//**MONEYS** for Messengers. From REV. GEORGE WEIS, $1. From MRS. WAMPLER 2. By REV. ELIAS HEINER, from MRS. ARMSTRONG 1, VALENTINE UHRIG 2, REV. E. HEINER 1, REV. H. HABLISTON 1. From REV. GEORGE WEIS (Lancaster, O.) 4. By REV. C. GATES, from GEORGE FRALEIGH, REV. C. GATES, each 2. By REV. H. AURAND, from SOLOMON SENTMAN 2, GEORGE KELLER 2, JOSEPH SHROM 1. An error in credit to V. SHOFF for 2 50 intended for 'Der Christliche Herold" from REV. W. CONRAD and V.SHOFF, each 1 25.//DR. SHOWMAN of NC, resolved to emancipate 17, viz: 9 females and 8 males, to be sent to Liberia, furnishing them with clothes, tools, and $1000.

80. Dec. 28, 1836/**MARRIED** On the 15th inst., by the REV. H. L. RICE, MR. HENRY SNIDER to MISS CATHARINE BOON both of this county.//On the same day, by the same, MR. JOSEPH CHRISTMAN, to MISS SUSANNA PICKING both of this county.//On the 22d

WEEKLY MESSENGER OF THE GERMAN REFORMED CHURCH

inst. by the same, MR. LEWIS WAMPLER to MISS JULIAN SHIVELY both of this borough.//On the same day, by the same, MR. FRANCIS B. FRENCH, of Newark, N. J., to MISS CATHARINE ANN BROWN, of this borough.//Tuesday, the 13th inst. by the REV. P. S. FISHER, MR. GEORGE LIVINGSTON, to MISS ELIZA ANN FORD, all of Penn's Valley, Centre co., Pa. //On Tuesday morning last, by the REV. R. BOND, MR. JACOB GILBERT, to MISS ELIZABETH SWIGART, both of Gettysburg.//On the 6th, by the REV. MR. SLAUGHTER, MR. LEWIS WELSH, of the Post Office Department, (formerly of this place,) to MISS SARAH ANN C. READ, daughter of the late JOHN M. READ, of Cumberland, Md.//**DIED** In the city of Lancaster, Pa., the 8th inst., DR. SAMUEL FAHNESTOCK, in the 73d year of his age.//On the 14th inst., in the city of Lancaster, COL. HENRY CARPENTER, in the 57th year of his age.//In Letterkenny township, Franklin county, Pa., on the ___ inst., (sic) MR. DEWALT KEEFER, (of ABRAHAM,) in the ___ (sic) year of his age. He has left an aged father to mourn his early departure. His remains were deposited in the burying ground of the GRC [Keefer's] of which he was a member.//On Tuesday the 20th inst., after a short painful indisposition, in the 38th year of her age, MRS. MARGARET SHCNEBLY, consort of DANIEL SCHNEBLY, Esq., of Hagerstown.//On Saturday, 12th ult. at his residence near Hagerstown, MR. JOHN DUSING, an old respected inhabitant of this county.// On Friday, 19th ult. MR. JOHN GRIMES, a respectable farmer of Washington Co., Md.//At his residence in Pleasant Valley, on the 4th November, in the 76th year of his age, MR. CONRAD THOMAS, a farmer of Washington county, Md.//In Washington township, Franklin County on the 17th inst., MR. PHILIP REED, in the 73d year of his age.// The Account of SUSANNA WAY, Adm'x of FREDERICK WAY, dec'd, late of Franklin County, will be presented to the Orphans' Court, for confirmation, on the Sixteenth day of January, 1837. JOS. PRITTS, Reg'r.//NORMAN CALLENDER, Druggist,

WEEKLY MESSENGER OF THE GERMAN REFORMED CHURCH

No. 22, Wood St., informs the public he is opening a new stock of Drugs, Medicines, Dye-Stuffs, Paints, Perfumery, Surgical Instruments &c &c. All orders will be promptly and carefully put up. Pittsburg, Dec. 1836.//**FOR SALE**. A pocket volume "Church Harmony," containing Psalm and Hymn Tunes, JOHN SMITH, Chambersburg, Pa.

81. Jan. 4, 1837/**MARRIED** On the 26th ult., by REV. D. G. BRAGONIER, MR. P. N. KRATZ, to MISS BARBARA FECHEN, all of Washington co., Md.//On the 13th ult., by REV. LEWIS C. B. HERMAN, MR. DAVID BECHTEL, of Colebrookdale, to MISS MATILDA LUDWIG of Amity, Berks Co., Pa.//On the 15th, by the same, MR. ELIAS HUNTSBERGER, to MISS SARAH HURTZ, both of Limerick, Montgomery Co., Pa.//In Philadelphia, on the 22nd ult., by the REV. MR. SPROLE, MR. RICHARD VANNEMAN to MISS MARY REEVES //On the 15th ult.,by the REV. MR. BRAGONIER, MR JACOB KERSHNER, to MISS SUSAN SPIEGLER, all of Washington Co., Md.//The 15th ult. by the REV, (sic) N. P. HACKE, MR. MATTHEW GORDON, to MISS DOROTHY, daughter of MR. CHRISTOPHER WALTHAUR, dec'd., both of North Huntingdon township, Westmoreland Co.//On the 20th ult. by the same, MR. JOHN SIECFRIED to MISS VERONICA, daughter of MR. JOHN BRINDLE, both of Unity township, Westmoreland co., Pa.//On Wednesday the 21st ult. by the REV. J.S. WOODS, MR. JAMES POTTER, JR. of Centre county, to MISS ISABELLA, daughter of JAS. CRISWELL, Esq. of Mifflin county.//Thursday the 22d ult. by the REV. J. RHODES, MR. JOHN GLENN, of OH, to MISS HANNAH JONES, of Patton township, Centre co.//On Tuesday the 27th ult. by the REV. J. STEWART MR. ROBERT L. WILLIAMS, to MISS JULIA DE HAVEN ATLEE, all of Centre co.//**DIED** Near Bakersville, Washington county, Md., the morning of the 27th ult., MR. ISAAC H. McCAULEY, aged 24 years 7 months; he had taken leave of the Classical Institution of our church, preparatory to the practice of Medicine.//In Canton, OH, MISS MATILDA DUNBAR, formerly of Mifflinburg, Union

WEEKLY MESSENGER OF THE GERMAN REFORMED CHURCH

Co., in the 26th year of her age.//The 22d ult., in Adams Co., Pa., MR. JOHN SHRIVER, in the 60th year of his age.//**A FIRE** destroyed the house of CHRISTIAN SULTNER, an honest industrious farmer of York, on the night of the 21st ult., together with nearly the whole of his furniture, clothing and $7 or $800 in money! (sic).//The Baltimore Gazette of Tuesday afternoon announces the death of DR. EDWARD ALCOCK, of that city and gives the following particulars: "His death was caused by a wound in his thigh of a pistol ball, the night of the 20th inst. MR. GEORGE STEUART was charged with having fired the pistol. The circumstances which led to the above result, originated, weeks ago, in a dispute of a political character..."

82. Jan. 11. 1837/**MARRIED** On the 5th inst. by REV. HENRY L. RICE, MR. HENRY BETZ to MISS JULIAN READ both of the vicinity of this Borough. //On the same day, by the same, MR. JOHN EBERLY to MISS ELIZA LEIDIG, both of the vicinity of this borough.//On the 3d inst. by the REV. MR. BRUNER, MR. DANIEL WERNER to MISS ESTHER BRENNER, of Reading, Berks Co.//On the 15th by the same, MR. JOHN KINSEY of Buffalo, N. Y. to MISS ANN MUSSELMAN, of Rapho tonship, Lancaster, co., Pa.//Same day by the same, MR. GEORGE BAKER, to MISS ELIZABETH SHERTZ, of Middletown, Dauphin County//On Thursday evening the 29th December, by the REV. MR. WYNCOOP, MR. WILLIAM ROBERTSON, to MISS SARAH ANN CLARK, both of Hagerstown, Md. //On the 24th Nov. last in Vicksburg, Miss. by the REV. MR. COX, MR. EDWARD SHANNON, Merchant of Vicksburg, to MISS A. C. KEALHOFFER, daughter of MR. JOHN KEALHOFFER, of Hagerstown, Md.//The 22d of Nov. by REV. MR. GEO. RIMER, MR. JOSEPH S. GRIM to MISS SARAH HUFFERD, both of Pleasant Valley.//**DIED** At her residence near Hagerstown, on Wednesday last, MRS. EVE OYSTER, an aged and respectable lady.//At his residence in Wooster, OH, on Thursday morning the 15th ult., after a short but painful illness of pleurisy, COL. JOHN

WEEKLY MESSENGER OF THE GERMAN REFORMED CHURCH

BARR, formerly of Washington county, Md., aged sixty-five years and four months.

83. Jan. 18, 1837/**MARRIED** On Tuesday morning, 10th inst. by the REV. DR. HENSHAW, MR. ISAAC H. LONG to MISS ELIZABETH C., daughter of the late WM. BALTZELL, Esq. all of Baltimore.//At Carlisle, Thursday the 5th inst. by REV. J. R. GOODMAN Chaplain of the U. S. Senate, W. MILNOR ROBERTS, Civil Engineer, to ANNIE, second daughter of Chief Justice GIBSON.//By REV. ISAAC GERHART, on the 5th inst. MR. DAVID NEIDIG, to CHRISTINA FLEISHER, all of Armstrong Valley, Dauphin co.// On Tuesday the 22d ult., by the REV. J. H. CRAWFORD, MR. JAMES BURNSIDES to MISS EMILY, daughter of DR. WILLIAM B. PRICE, of Guilford County, NC.//The 5th inst, by the same, MR. JOEL INGOLD, of Guilford County, to MISS SALLY M. WILSON, of New Salem, Randolph co., N. C.//On the 10th, by the REV. SAMUEL R. FISHER, MR. JOSEPH MORITZ, Merchant, to MISS MARY M. SMITH, all of Emmitsburg, Md.//**DIED** On the morning of the 27th ult. at his residence, near Frederick, JACOB BRENGLE, in the 63d year of his age.//At his residence, in the neighborhood of Buckeystown, on Wednesday last, after a short illness, MR. GEORGE KESLER, an aged citizen of this county.//On Friday Dec. 30th ult. MRS. MARIA SMALL, consort of CAPT. WM. SMALL of Frederick town, in the 30th year of her age.//On the 11th inst. in the 29th year of his age, after an illness of ten days, the REV. JOHN H. HOSKYNS, Vice President of St. Mary's College Baltimore.//On the 30th of December of a bilious pleurisy, MRS. MARY E. DASHIELL, in Baltimore, aged 69 years.//In the Borough of Easton, Pa., on the morning of the 5th inst. JESSE M. HOWELL, in the 48th year of his age.//In Indiana co., Pa. on the 31st ult. REV. N. SHARRETS, a respectable minister of the Lutheran Church, in the 35th year of his age.//On the 7th inst, in the Franklin County Almshouse JACOB WITZEL (from Germany) formerly Teacher of Music, in the 37th

WEEKLY MESSENGER OF THE GERMAN REFORMED CHURCH

year of his age.//**A SETTLEMENT** These passengers who were injured by the collision of the Denham train, received a total of eleven thousand three hundred and fifty dollars: JAMES THOMPSON, JOHN A. RUSS, JOSHUA HOWELL, THOMAS MURDOCH, CHARLES W. WH TE (sic) JOHN B. CUMMINS, BENJAMIN RANSON. Six other suits pend on the trial.

84. Jan. 25, 1837/**MARRIED** In Bellefont, Centre Co. Pa., on the 10th inst., by REV. JAMES LINN, MR. SAMUEL HUMES, of Lycoming co, to MISS RACHEL daughter of HAMILTON HUMES, Esq. of Bellefonte. //On the 15th, by REV. ISAAC GERHART, MR. HENRY WEBER, to MISS ANN HECKERT, daughter of PETER HECKERT Esq., all of Mahantongo Valley Northumberland co. Pa.//On Monday the 16th inst., in West Chester, Pa. by the REV. GEO. I. MILES, W. GUYER Esq., Editor of "Harrisburg Chronicle," to MISS ELIZA M'CORD, both of Harrisburg.//**DIED** On the 15th inst., SARAH HOMMAN, daughter of MR. J. HOMMAN, near this place.//In Philadelphia on the 18th inst., WM. W. WOODWARD, Theological Bookseller, aged 67 years.//**A CATASTROPHE** In Greenville, S. C. about the 3d December. A daughter of JOHN CROW, was returning home from a neighbors when she met her brother returning from a military muster. He jokingly said to his sister, I have a good mind to shoot you for being away so long, raised his rifle to his shoulder and snapped it, when it went off and the ball lodged in her body.---He ran home and returned with his father, when they found the girl in the agonies of death-"NY Evening Star".//J. D. PAXTON, Esq., of Adams county, has retired from the PA Board of Canal Commissioners, and PETER LEVERGOOD, of Cambria county, has been appointed.//**MONEYS** We have been instructed to transfer the credit of MR. SOLOMON CREAGER for $2 to MR. DANIEL FIROR. By J. J. SHUFORD, Esq. from ISAAC DOUGLASS 2. By JACOB HADE, from ANDREW SNIVELY, Esq. 2. From JOHN DENIG 1. By REV. JOHN W. HOFFMEIER, from JACOB DUDRO, JACOB CRAMER, GEO. BARRICK, (Walk-

WEEKLY MESSENGER OF THE GERMAN REFORMED CHURCH

ersville,) DANIEL HILDEBRAND, (Utica,) MICHAEL ZIMMERMAN, (Creagerstown,) each 2. By SAMUEL GROSSMAN, from GROSSMAN & STICKEL, 1. By REV. H. BASSLER, from DR. W. B. HAHN, 1, AARON MULL 1, ANDREW REED 1, H. BASSLER 2. By SIMON DRUM, Esq., from H. BUCMAN, WILLIAM SKILLY, and JACOB KOHRT, each 2. From REV. J. S. DUBBS, 5.

85. Feb. 1, 1837**/MARRIED** On Wednesday morning the 18th inst., in Shippensburg, Pa., by REV. N. J. STROH, MR. PETER S. ARTZ, merchant of that place, to MISS B. ANN, only daughter of ANTHONY CLIPPINGER, Esq. dec'd. of the same place.**//DIED** On Friday week, MRS. ELIZABETH SCHAEFFER, daughter of G. KREBS, Esq. late of Philadephia, and consort of REV. DR. SHAEFFER (sic) of Fredericktown. She has left a husband and six children. //In Walker township, Centre co., Pa. on the 8th ult., MRS. ELIZABETH NEIL, at an advanced age.// In Lamar Township, Centre co., on the 8th.,COL. WM McKIBBIN, an aged and respected citizen.//In Gibbonsville, NY, in the 48th year of his age, REV. ROBERT BRONK, minister in the RDC.//In the city of NY, on the 20th ult., ISAAC L. KIP, Esq. in the 70th year of his age, of the RDC.//Saddle River, N. Y., on the 16th ult., the REV. SAMUEL GOETSCHIUS, of the RDC, in the 85th year of his age.//In NY on the 20th ult., JOSIAH QGDEN (sic) HOFFMAN, Superior court Judge, in the 71st year of his age.//At his residence in Perry county on Saturday the 7th ult., COL. JOHN URIE, in the 77th year of his age. He has left a widow and daughter.//In Guilford Township, Franklin county on Saturday last, MRS. CATHERINE FRY, consort of ANDREW FRY, in the 76th year of her age.

86. Feb. 8, 1837**/MARRIED** Tuesday morning the 31st ult., by the REV. THO'S CREIGH, the REV. N. W. WHITE, Pastor of the Presby. Church in M'Connellsburg, Bedford county, Pa., to MISS SUSAN MAYERS, youngest daughter of MR. A. MAYERS, dec'd. late of the same place.//On Wednesday the

WEEKLY MESSENGER OF THE GERMAN REFORMED CHURCH

1st inst., by the REV. THOMAS CREIGH, MR. JOHN BARD, to MISS MARY P. EVANS both of Mercersburg.//On the same day, by the same, MR. SAMUEL VAN TREIS,of Hanover Iron Works Bedford co., to MISS SUSANNAH M. POE, near Greencastle, Franklin co.//On the 19th ult., by REV. A. L. HERMAN, MR. SAMUEL BENNET, to MISS MARY HIGH, all of Berks county, Pa.//On the 25th, by REV. ISAAC GERHART, MR. JACOB AUMILLER, to MISS ANN PIPER, both of Georgetown, Northumberland county, Pa.//On the 26th by the same, MR. SOLOMON MERTZ to ELIZABETH MAYER, both of Lyken's Valley, Dauphin county, Pa.//On the 19th ult.,by REV. H.E.F. VOIGHT, MR. CUNNINGHAM ANDERSON, to MRS. CHRISTIANA HUGUS, all of Mt. Pleasant, Westm'd co'ty, Pa.//On the 18th ult., by the REV. D. ZACHARIAS, MR. HENRY HOUCK to MISS MARY C. BRENGLE, all of Frederick, Md.//In Middletown, Md., on the 5th ult., by the REV. J. C. BUCHER, MR. JOSEPH WISE to MISS ELIZABETH, daughter of the late JACOB ALEXANDER, all of Middletown, Md.//By the same, in Middletown, Md., on the 11th ult. MR. RICHARD JOHNSON, of Harper's Ferry, Va., to MISS ELIZABETH, daughter of MR. GEO. KNODE, of Pleasant Valley, Wash'n c'y Md.//By the same, on the 15th ult., at Burketsville, Md. MR. DAVID BROWN to MISS MARIA, daughter of MR. GEORGE KNODE, all of Pleasant Valley Washington county.//**DIED** On the evening of the 13th of Jatuary, (sic) in Westmoreland County JANE KIRKPATRICK, widow of BENJAMIN KIRKPATRICK, formerly J. M'KEAN, of the Borough of Chambersburg, aged ninety-two years.//In Lurgan Township, Franklin County, on the evening of the 19th of January, JAMES M'KEE, Esq. in the sixty-eight (sic) year of his age.//**FIRE** On Wednesday last, the barn of MR. SAMUEL SMITH, of Antrim towship (sic) this county, took fire, and burned down. The dwelling of MR. SMITH took fire several times from sparks but was saved by the exertions of the few persons present--"Chambersburg Telegraph."//**MONIES** For Missionary Fund from Classis of NC, viz: DAVID J. RAMSOUR 22 1/2c.,

WEEKLY MESSENGER OF THE GERMAN REFORMED CHURCH

DAVID CONRAD 50c., THOMAS JANES $5, ELI RAMSOUR 25c., A. RANKIN, Esq. 50c., ISAAC ERWIN, Esq.$1, REV. W.C. RANKIN$13//**MONEYS** By REV.J.C. GULDIN, from DAVID STENDLER, GEORGE SLOYER, ABR. QUIG, JOHN DIEFENDERFER, DAVID BOYER (NewStore) WM. BUSH, each 2. From D. ALBRIGHT, Esq. 2. By JOHN COULTER, Esq.,from J. & D.RAMSOUR, JOHN RAMSOUR, (Tanner)SAM'L LANTZ, JOHN COULTER, JACOB RAMSOUR (Merchant) SOLOMON RAMSOUR, DR.A. RAMSOUR, DAVID RAMSOUR,(Tanner) COL. JOHN HOKE, each 2. By REV. J. C. BUCHER, from D. S. BISER, Esq. 4, JOSHUA BISER 2, O. F. HARLEY 1 25, PETER BISER, SR., 2.

87. Feb. 15, 1837/**MARRIED** Thursday, 24th ult., by REV. JOHN H. CRAWFORD, MR. IRA FIELDS to MISS ELIZA JOB, all of Guilford county, N. C.//On the 2d inst., by REV N. P. HACKE, MR. JACOB KEMMERER to MISS MAGDALENA, daughter of MR. DAVID BEAR, both of Westmoreland co.//On the 20th ult., by the REV. MR. BRAGONIER, MR. JOSHUA NEWCOMER, to MISS MARY A. ANKONY, all of Washington co., Md. //At Washington, D. C. on the 2d ult., by REV. DR. LAWRIE,RICHARD SOMERS SMITH,of Philadelphia, to ELLEN MARION, daughter of MATHEW ST. CLAIR CLARKE, of Washington city.//**DIED** On Wednesday last, in Green township, Franklin County, MRS. COVER, wife of MR. ANDREW COVER, at an advanced age.//Thursday last, after a lingering illness, MR. RUDOLPH OYERLY,an aged farmer of Green township.//In Beaver co., Pa., Dec. 11, DR. JOHN Y. BEAR, in the 24th year of his age, formerly of Millersburg, Dauphin co., Pa.//In Philadelphia, Feb. 7th, JOEL, aged 14 months; and on the evening of the same day ELIZABETH, aged 3 years and 5 months, the only children of MR. JOEL JONES, Esq., of that place.//In Hagerstown, on Thursday morning last, MRS. CATHARINE KERSHNER, consort of JONATHAN KERSHNER, aged 41 years.//**MURDERED.** REV. ISAIAH HARRIS, a minister of the Methodist Episcopal church, was waylaid and murdered on the 23d ult. in Surry co. near Cabin Pt., Va. When in about three or four hundred yards from

WEEKLY MESSENGER OF THE GERMAN REFORMED CHURCH

his house, he was shot through the head by some one behind the gig. The perpetrator had not been discovered.--"Rel. Telegraph."//MR. WILLIAM MORTON, of Lexington, bequeathed one-ninth of his estate, for the support of a school in that city for the education of poor children.--"Maysville Eagle."//MR. HUBBS, steward, will open a boarding house for the students of the Milledgeville, Geo. academy which burned on Jan. 19.//Blacking Manufacturer MR. CHARLES DAY left a 100,000 fund the interest for the use of poor blind.//**MONEYS.** By REV. JACOB SHOLL, from JACOB SMITH, (Newport) JACOB LONG, GEORGE ZINN, JOHN JUNKIN, Esq. JOHN KLINE, SAM'L LEIBY, & REV. J. SCHOLL, each $2. By REV. D. WEISER, from JA'S TAGGART, 2, CHA'S DUBBS 1, SOLOMON STELTZ 1, and D. WEISER.

88. Feb. 22, 1837/**MARRIED** The 26th of January last, by REV. JOHN RHOADE, MR. ISAAC PENNINGTON, to MISS SARAH KELLER, both of Penns Valley, Centre Co. Pa.//Near Middletown, Frederick county, Md. on the 2d inst., by REV. J. C. BUCHER, MR. JACOB FOGER, to MISS LYDIA DARNER, all of said county.//Near Mideltown, (sic) Md. by the same, on the 9th inst., MR. PERRY F. FLOOK son of JACOB of JOHN, to MISS DELENAH, youngest daughter of MR. BENJAMIN RAUTZAHN,dec'd.//Pleasant Valley Washington county, Md. on the 14th inst., by the same, MR. GEORGE W. BROWN, to MISS MARY ANN, youngest daughter of MR. JOHN BROWN, SR., all of said place.//On the 14th inst., by REV. N. P. HACKE, MR. WILLIAM FISHER, SEN. of Mountpleasant township, to MRS. CHRISTIANA BARNHARDT, Unity townsihp (sic) Westmoreland co. Pa.//In Mifflinburg, on the 5th inst. by the REV. J. H. FRIES, MR. DANIEL NEIHART to MRS. MARY HOLLOWBUSH, both of Millhall, Centre County.//**DIED** In Middletown Md., on the 4th inst., in the 80th year of her age, MRS. MARY M. ALEXANDER, consort of the late JACOB ALEXANDER.//Near Middletown, Mr., on Saturday the 4th inst. MR. SOLOMON RENNER, after a short illness, in the 47th year of his age.//On

WEEKLY MESSENGER OF THE GERMAN REFORMED CHURCH

the 13th inst. in Hagerstown, Md. PETER HUMRICK-HOUSE, respectable citizen, and a Soldier of the Revolution, in the 84th year of his age.//On the 19th inst ,in (sic) Guilford township, Franklin co. MRS. HANNAH WAKER.//At his residence near Ridgville, OH, on Saturday MR. FERGUS M'LEAN, father of JUDGE M'LEAN, at the advanced age of 90 years. He was one of the pioneers to this country, having emigrated from NJ and settled in 1796 on the spot where he died. He was for more than half century a member of the Presby. church --"Lebanon Ohio Star."//At Stoke Newington, ENG, on the 20th of December, MRS. MARY CLARK, relict of the late REV. ADAM CLARKE, L. L. D. (sic) in her 70th year.//At London, on the 24th of December, the REV. DR. RIPPON, aged 86, pastor of the Baptist Church in Carter-lane, Tooly street. DR. RIPPON succeeded the venerable and learned DR. JOHN GILL; by which that pastoral office of the church was filled by these individuals for 117 years.//**AN ACCIDENT** GEORGE BACKESTOW, JR. near Hummelstown, Dauphin county whilst out on a gaming excursion, week before last, on meeting with another person on the same business, proposed to trade fowling pieces, and while examining the other persons gun, having his own leaning on the brush near the fence it slipped down and the gun discharged its load into his body.//COL. ANDREWS U. S. Army, arrived at St. Augustine on the 11th inst., informs that JUMPER and ALLIGATOR came in under a flag of truce to surrender themselves to GEN. JESUP and that POWELL is on a island in the Wythlacoochee, with about one hundred and fifty followers and suppose he would come to terms.

89. Mar. 1, 1837/**MARRIED** On the 15th ult., in Hanover. Pa., by REV. MR. GUTELIUS, MR. ANDREW K. SHRIVER, of Carroll co. Md., to MISS CATHARINE, daughter of HENRY WIRT, Esq. of the former place.//On Thursday last, by REV. B. S. SCHNECK, MR. WILLIAM M'CLEERY, to MISS MARY, daughter of COL. JOHN SNIDER, all of Franklin co., Pa.//**DIED**

WEEKLY MESSENGER OF THE GERMAN REFORMED CHURCH

At Harpers-Ferry, Va., on the 6th inst. MRS. SARAH PATTON MIDDLETON, relict of MR. ROBERT F. MIDDLETON, aged about 70 years.//At Dayton, OH, on the 30th December,of Consumption, in the 35th year of her age, MRS. SARAH, wife of HENRY BARR, daughter of ANDREW HAYS, dec'd, formerly of Conestego township, Lancaster county.//In NY, on Monday 20th Feb., MRS. SARAH H. KREBS, wife of REV. JOHN M. KREBS, of that city, aged 30 years. **//A FIRE.** 24 buildings were destroyed at Bath, ME on the night of the 17th ult. when fire originated in a building occupied by PARSON SMITH and SAMUEL FOOTE.//WM. B. PAYNE, aged 33 years, a husband and father, expired in dreadful agony, in Baltimore. He was scratched by a dog in August last but thought nothing of it until Wednesday last, when hydrophobia symptoms developed.

90. March 8, 1837/**MARRIED** On the 21st ult., by REV. H. L. RICE, MR. JOHN MILLER, to MISS CATHARINE HAWK both of St Thomas township.//On Monday week, in Shippensburg, by L. DAVIS, Esq., MR. WILLIAM WELTY, of Emmitsburg, Md. to MISS ELIZA DUNLAP, of the former place.//On Tuesday the 7th inst. by REV. W. C. BENNET, MR. HENRY HUFFER, to MISS JULIA ANN BOYER.//Near Greencastle, Pa., on Tuesday last, by the same, MR. JOHN GRIMES, to MISS SABINA LANCASTER.//On Thursday last by REV. B. S. SCHNECK, MR. JOHN MILLER, to MISS FRANCES PAINTER, both of Franklin co., Pa.//In Harrisburg, on the 28th ult., by the REV. D. BOSSLER, MR. WILLIAM NOBLE, to MISS JULIAN FAUGHT, both of Carlisle.//**DIED** On Wednesday morning in this Borough of a pulmonary disease, MR. SAMUEL LOCHBAUM, aged about 26 years.//On Sunday afternoon last MRS. ELEANOR EYSTER, wife of MR. GEORGE EYSTER of this borough.//At Emmitsburg, Md. on the 1st inst. MRS.SUSANNAH, wife of MR. FREDERICK DREYER, in the 33d year of her age.//At the same place, on the 2d inst., after a protracted illness, MR. LEWIS MOTTER, SN., in the 63d year of his age.//**MONEYS** for paper. From DAVID LENHART

WEEKLY MESSENGER OF THE GERMAN REFORMED CHURCH

[Quincy] 2. By HENRY ECKERT, from MRS. CLARISSA LEAMAN 2, JAMES P. McILVAINE 2, GEORGE L. ECKERT 1. By REV. D. G. BRAGONIER, from JAMES DORRANCE 4 and REV. D. G. BRAGONIER 1. From JACOB HECK 2. By JOHN C. BUCHER, Esq., from FREDERICK KELLER, Esq. 2 and MISS SABINA KELKER 4. By DAVID WEIDNER from REV. MR. BIBIGHAUSE, MRS. SARAH ZIMMERMAN, and WM. H. WALLACE, each 2. By JACOB HADE, Esq., from JACOB SMITH 4, and JOSEPH FUSS 2.

91. March 15, 1837/**MARRIED** In York, Pa.,on the 2d inst., by the REV. L. MAYER, D. D., REV. EPHRAIM KEEFER,of the GRC, Bellefonte, to MISS ELEANOR SPANGLER, of the former place.//On the 2d inst., in Nittany Valley, Centre co., MR. MOSES FELMLEE, merchant, to MISS LOUISA, daughter of JOHN OYER, all of that place.//On Monday the 5th inst, by the REV. MR. ZACHARIAS, MR. HARRISON LOUGERBEAM to MISS FRANCES JENKINS, of Frederick, Md.//On Thursday last, by the same, MR. JAMES BOOTH to MISS MARY FRY.//In Chambersburg, Pa on the 13 inst by REV. W. C. BENNET, MR. WILLIAM REEVES, to MRS. SARAH THOMPSON, both of Franklin co., Pa.//On Thursday last, by the REV. MR. FOERSCH, MR. GEORGE KESSELRING, to MISS ELIZABETH GABEL, both of this place.//**DIED** At his residence in Lamar township, Centre co., on Friday the 10th ult., DAVID LAMB, in the 84th year of his age. The deceased was a soldier in the revolutionary struggles for American Freedom and Liberty.--He came to this country when it was a howling wilderness.//**MONEYS** By REV. J.B. KNIPE, from SAMUEL RICKSTINE 2 and J. B. KNIPE, 3. By REV. J. H. SMALTZ (thro' W. HEYSER, Esq.) from MRS. R. ELY, 2. By REV. H. MILLER, from PETER TICE (McConnellsb,g.) J. EVERHART, Esq. (Berks co.) each 2.//**TEMPERANCE DELEGATES** assembled in the Presby. church at Harrisburg, Tuesday 14th of February, and appointed the following officers: President, MATTHEW NEWKIRK of Philaphia; Vice Presidents, REV. WM. M. HALL, of Mifflin Co.; RICHARD WILSON, of Columbia Co.; FINDLAY

WEEKLY MESSENGER OF THE GERMAN REFORMED CHURCH

McGOWAN, of Perry Co., and JAMES BEATTY, of Crawford Co. Secretaries, DR. WILLIAM J. SLOAN, of Dauphin Co.; and GEO. M. PHILLIPS, of Cumberland Co. REV. T. P. HUNT, the celebrated lecturer, addressed the Convention.

92. Mar. 22, 1837/**MARRIED** Tuesday morning last by REV. R. DOUGLASS, MR. JOSEPH HOUSTON merchant of Clear Spring, Md. to MISS ELLEN MARY GREGORY, daughter of MR. ROBERT GREGORY, of Martinsburg, Va.//On the 9th inst., by REV. MR. CARES, MR. WILLIAM MECANDLESS to MISS SARAH ANN MOORE, both of York, Pa.//On Thursday morning last, by REV. MR. KERFOOT, REV. WALTER E. FRANKLIN, Rector of St. John's Church, to MISS CATHARINE H. DAYS, of York, Pa.//On Thursday, 9th inst. by the REV. H. AURAND, MR. JOHN WILEY to MISS BARBARA, daughter of JOSEPH SHROM, SR., all of Carlisle.//On the 12th inst., by REV. J. C. BUCHER, MR. JOSEPH LONG to MISS ANN MARIA BUZZARD, all of Middletown Valley, Md.//At the same time, by the same, MR. HENRY MICHAEL, to MISS SOPHIA, daughter of MR. PETER BISER, all of Middletown Valley, Md.//**DIED** In this place, on the 18th inst, CHRISTIAN L SUESSEROTT, in the 52d year of his age. Funeral Sermon will be preached on Friday evening next, in the Lutheran Church.//At her residence in Clear Spring, Md. on Monday last, the 13th inst. MRS. SARAH JACQUES, at an advanced age, consort of DR. LANCELOT JACQUES.//On Tuesday last after a short illness, at the house of MR. FREDERICK BRYAN, in Hagerstown, MISS SARAH NEWCOMER, youngest daughter of MR. CHRISTIAN NEWCOMER, former Sheriff of Washington county Md.//Same day, after a lingering illness, MR. HENRY MIDDLECAUFF, an old and respectable inhabitant of Hagerstown.//On Monday 13th inst. at his residence near this borough, in the 52d year of his age, MR. PETER LEHMAN.//REV. DR. PALMER, o (sic) Charleston, (S.C.) stated in the course of a sermon, Sabbath before last that there were five hundred colored members of his own church in good standing.//Through the vigi-

WEEKLY MESSENGER OF THE GERMAN REFORMED CHURCH

lance of Sheriff WM. WARD, JAMES PURSEL, who is charged with the murder of THOMAS CASEY, was taken in Hollidaysburg, Huntingdon county, and is confined, to await his trial at the April court. CONSTABLE HALL was in company with the Sheriff. --"Centre Dem."//JOHN W. SANFORD, of GA, to be agent for the Creek Indians. MONTFORT STOKES, of NC, agent for the Cherokee.//The Editor of "Der Christliche Zeitschrift," please send paper to J. ADAM MAIN, Middletown, Md., and acknowledge the following receipts for "Der Herold," -- viz: PETER SNYDER (Jacksonhall (sic) 1. GEO. A. MAHN (Middletown, Md.) 1, REV. J.C.BUCHER, balance, 25cts. MRS. KLINE (Landisburg) 1. Discontinued. JACOB SNIVELY, Landisburg 1.

93. Mar. 29, 1837//**MARRIED** On the 21st inst , by REV. J. N. HOFFMAN, JAMES NILL, Esq. Attorney at Law, to MISS ELIZABETH MYERS, both of this place//In Mansfield, OH, by REV. SOLOMON RITZ, REV. GEORGE LEITER, to MISS LEANNA MAIN, both of that place.//In Mercersburg, Pa., by the REV. PROFESSOR BERG, on Tuesday 21st inst., MR. JOHN HAVEN, to MISS MARY ANN HAMMEL, all of Franklin Co.//On Wednesday, 9th inst., by the same, MR. LAZARUS KENNEDY, to MISS SUSAN A. BREWER, all of Franklin County.//On the 16th ult., by the REV. J. REBOUGH, MR. JEREMIAH DRENNER, to MISS SUSAN FLOOK//Tuesday evening, 20th inst., by the same, MR. JOHN SHINDLE to MISS MARGARET, eldest daughter of GEORGE NEWKIRK, Esq., all of Washington Co., MD.//On the 16th, near Utica, by REV. J. W. HOFFMEIR, MR. JOHN WACHTER, son of JACOB WACHTER to MISS SNSAN, (sic) second daughter of JOHN CLEM, both of Frederick Co., Md.//Near Creagerstown, on the 23d, by the same, MR. ELIAS HAHN, to MISS CATHERINE ALBACK.//On the 16th inst., by the REV. SAMUEL R. FISHER, MR. DIETRICK ZECK, to MISS MARY ANN ROWE, all of Emmitsburg, Md.//On the 21st inst, by the same, MR. DANIEL SHEETZ, to MISS BARBARA ANN MEYERS both of Liberty Township, Adams Co., Pa.//On the 9th inst. by SAMUEL

WEEKLY MESSENGER OF THE GERMAN REFORMED CHURCH

MILLER, Esq., JOHN MORRIS, of Berks county, to LYDIA CADWALLADER, of Uwchlan, Chester county, Pa.//At Ashton Hall, on Thursday evening the 22d ult, by the REV. RICHARD WYNKOOP, MR. JOSEPH RENTCH, to MISS ELIZABETH SCHNEBLY, of Washington county, Md.//On the 12th inst., by the REV. CHALES F. SHAEFFER, MR. DAVID MIDDLECAUFF, to MRS. MARY ANN SWOPE, both of Washington Co., Md. //On Wednesday evening, the 22d inst., by the REV. MR. HEINER, MR. JAMES GRIFFITHS, to MISS SARAH ANN FAILS, both of Baltimore.//MR. JACOB KNABB, son of PETER KNABB, JR., of Oley, Berks Co., Pa., while returning home from this place (Reading) met with a melancholy accident.

94. Apr. 5, 1837/**MARRIED** On Thursday evening last, by the REV. MR. KENNEDY, MR. DAVID CUSHWA, son of CAPTAIN CUSHWA, to MISS SUSAN ZUCK of Welsh Run, Franklin co. Pa.//On February 15th, by REV. JOHN P. CLINE, MR. DANIEL BEARD to MISS ELIZABETH, eldest daughter of MR. GEO. COLLIFLOWER of Mercersburg, Pa.//On Tuesday evening the 21st inst. by the REV. A H. LOCHMAN, ALEXANDER H. BARNITZ, M. D. to MISS REBECCA, daughter of the Hon. GEORGE BARNITZ, all of York, Pa.//On the 16th inst., by the REV. D. ZACHARIAS MR. EDWARD TURBUT of Frederick city to MISS ELIZABETH S SPANGLER, daughter of the late COL. MICHAEL SPANGLER of York Pa.//_____, (sic) on the same day, by the same, MR. J. FABLER to MISS HARRIET SMITH, all of Frederick county, Md.//**DIED** At Harrisburg, Pa., Wednesday morning 22nd of March 1837, MRS. ANNA MARY, consort of MR. HENRY FREY, aged 52 years and 4 days. MRS. FREY suffered a very protracted and painful illness for nearly 4 months.//Near Frederick city ,on (sic) Monday 27th ult., CAPT. HENRY SMITH, in the 65th year of his age. On Tuesday following, his remains were taken to the cemetery of the GRC of Frederick city followed by his wife and children.//In Rowan co., N. C., on the 2d of Jan., at the residence of his brother-in-law, MR. FISHER, MR.

WEEKLY MESSENGER OF THE GERMAN REFORMED CHURCH

JOSEPH LINGLE, formerly a student at the "Theological Seminary" York, Pa., in the 34th year of his age. His health was so impaired by consumption he was compelled to return to his parents after three years of study.//**DROWNING ACCIDENT.** We learn from the Gazette, of yesterday, that "on Saturday the 18th inst. 5 men started to cross the Susquehanna, at M'CALL'S Ferry in a skiff, which struck a rock, filled and sunk. The names of the dec'd were JAMES WILSON, SAMUEL PAYNE, of Lower Chanceford, and __ MOSIER, (sic) a Frenchman who had been at work on the canal near the Ferry. The bodies are not yet found."
//**DROWNED** MISS DORCAS MARSHALL, daughter of MR. GEORGE MARSHALL, SEN. of this county, aged about 16 years was drowned in the Bull Pasture river, in Bath county, week before last. Miss M. was on a visit to her uncle, and in attempting to cross on a foot log, was precipitated into the considerably swollen river.--"Staunton, Va. Spect."//
ROBBERY On Wednesday last,GEN. EDWARDS, cashier of a Branch Bank of the Valley in Leesburg, in VA, came up in the Rail Road cars, and proceeded to TALBOTT'S Hotel, and, on the ringing of the bell for dinner took his saddlebags in which the money was deposited, and placed them in the desk of the bar room, requesting that they be taken care of. The desk was not locked, nor the key in it. On return from dinner, he inquired for the saddlebags, but they were gone. On inquiry, one of the servants stated that he had seen a man come out of the bar room with the saddlebags and get into the stage. The Cashier pursued the stage. In the meantime the search was continued at the Hotel. The bags were found in the cellar and the twenty five thousand dollars was gone.//
MONEYS for Messengers. From JACOB KROH 2.25. The agent paid over the money long ago, without specifying the names we now acknowledge. This creates much difficulty, and leads to mistakes. By J. KROH, from FREDERICK CRAMER, JOHN LEIDY, THOMAS DUR, CHRISTIAN RANSBERK, JACOB KROH, JOHN

WEEKLY MESSENGER OF THE GERMAN REFORMED CHURCH

WALKER, JOHN DITTO, each $1. For 1833 H. CRAMER, C. RANSBERG, T. DUR, J. LEIDY, J. KROH, each $1. From J. HOUCK, Trough Creek) 2.50.--From ABRAHAM LIGHTNER 2.--From MAJ. HENRY SNIVELY Green Castle) 2.--BY REV. JON. ZELLER, from JNO. KYLE,--- SAMUEL HARNISH, JR.,---JOHN KELLER of JNO. JOHN SWOPE and LEWIS KNODE--each 2. By H. R. RIDDLE, from CHRIST'N DIETRICH (Green Castle) 2. From J. ROTH (Chambersburg) 2. By REV. J. C. BUCHER, from SAM. ZACHARIAS Harrisburg 2. By REV. HENRY BASSLER, from WM. REIFF (Skippack 1,HENRY HERRING 1, ABRAHAM STEINER (Schwenk's) 2, and SAMUEL GRUBB (Limerick) 1.--From MRS. McCLEERY (Quincy) 2. From JACOB KROH 3.25---by same, from DANIEL MILLER 2.25 and REV. J. L. SANDERS 2.25. From J. O. CARSON 3.25.

95. Apr. 12, 1837/**MARRIED** On Tuesday the 9th inst., by the REV. HENRY L. RICE, GEORGE K. HARPER, Esq., Editor of the Franklin Repository, to MISS JANE McCLINTIC all of Chambersburg.//On the same day, by the REV. DAVID DENNY, DR. WILLIAM CULBERTSON to MISS NANCY, eldest daughter of TH. G. McCULLOH, Esq., of Chambersburg.//On the 10th November, 1836, by WM. HUNTER, Esq., MR. HENRY MILLER of Juniata county, to MISS MARY ANN ROUSH of Millerstown, Perry county, Pa.//On Tuesday the 4th inst., by REV. D. ZACHARIAS, MR. WILLIAM MILLER, to MISS MARY ANN H. SMELSER both of Carroll county, Md.//Thursday the 6th inst., by the same, MR. SAMUEL HARGETT, to MISS ELANOR WATERS, both of Frederick county, Md.//On the 16th ult., by REV. JOHN G. WOLFF, MR. JACOB GROFF, to MISS MARY SHILICH, all of Chester County, Pa.//Tuesday, 14th ult., by REV. R. C. DEMME, MR. DAVID BUCHWALTER of Trap, Montgomery co., Pa., to MISS HANNAH L. EWALD, of Philadelphia.//On Wednesday, the 1st ult., by the REV. MR. KARN, MR. N. E. SLAYMAKER, to MARY, only daughter of ROBERT M'ILVAIN, dec'd.,of Strawsburg township, Lancaster Co.//On Thursday, the 2d ult., by the REV. MR. WALLACE, MR. N. E. KENZER, to LYDIA MARTHA,

daughter of JNO. WALLACE, Esq., of Earl, Lancaster Co.//On Tuesday, the 4th inst., by the REV. DANIEL ZACHARIAS, MR. CHARLES SHRIVER second son of the Hon. ABRAHAM SHRIVER, to MISS ANN ELIZA, only daughter of SAMUEL THOMAS late of Frederick county, Md.//In York, Pa., by the REV. DR. MAYER the REV. SAMUEL R. FISHER, pastor of the GRC, Emmitsburg, Md., to MISS ELLEN C. eldest daughter of DANIEL MAY, Esq., of the former place.// On the 23d ult., by REV. N. P. HACKE, MR. PETER WAUGHEMANN, to MISS MARY ANN, daughter of MR. HENRY LAUFFER, both of Westmoreland co.//On the 30th ult., by the same, MR. HENRY BUCHMANN, of Hempfield township, to MISS MARY, daughter of MR. PETER WHITEHEAD, of Westmoreland county.//On Thursday, the 30th ult., by the REV. MR. VOIGT, MR. PETER SMITH, of Buffalo township, Armstrong county to MISS ELIZABETH LONG, of Franklin township, Westmoreland county.//On Tuesday the 4th inst., by REV. LEANDER KERR, MR. OLIVER HILL of Licking Creek, to MISS NANCY KERNEY, of M'Connellsburg, Bedford county.//**DIED** In Hagerstown, on Thursday last in the 63d year of her age MRS. ROSAMOND H. KENNEDY, consort of the late THOMAS KENNEDY, Esq.//In Lancaster, Pa., Saturday the 1st inst., after a few days confinement to his bed, GEORGE LOUIS MAYER, Esq., of that city, in the 47th year of his age.//In Lancaster, on the morning of the 27th ult. the REV. JOHN S. BRENNEMAN, in the 24th year of his age.//In York, Pa., on Tuesday, 28th ult., MRS. ANNA BARBARA MAYER, mother of the REV. DR. MAYER, in the 79th year of her age.//At York Springs, Adams co., Pa., on the 28th ult., MRS. JUHA ANN BITTINGER, consort of MR. HENRY BITTINGER, and daughter of DOCTOR SHAFFER, in the ____ (sic) year of her age.//In Reading, Pa., CAPT. DANIEL D. B. KEIN, in the 65th year of his age.//Friday morning last, MR. JOHN WICKHAM, an old respectable inhabitant of Chambersburg.//**A DEBATE** At Marshall College between Goethean and Diagnothean Societies on the evening of the 26th inst., at Mercersburg, Pa.

WEEKLY MESSENGER OF THE GERMAN REFORMED CHURCH

G. PEARSON, P. GOSSLER, J. KOOKEN, JUN, G. W. WELKER, P. LITTLE, H. I. BROWN, Committee of Arrangement.//**EARTHQUAKE** From a letter from MR. CHANEBAND, British Consul, dated Beyroot, Jan. 25, 1837, addressed to JUDAH BENOLIET, Esq. of Gibralter. " Dear Sir:--I have a most painful task to perform, that of announcing the deaths of MR. and MRS. JOSHUA LEVY, of Staffet, and the greater part of their family. I address myself to you so that you may convey the melancholy tidings to MR. JOSHUA LEVY'S brother and other relatives he may have at your place after you have prepared them.//**THE TEMPERANCE SOCIETY** Officers elected Apr. 7 in the Methodist Episcopal Church Chambersburg. President-JAMES MORROW. Vice President-JOHN SMITH. Recording Sec.-WILSON REILLY. Corresponding Sec.-REV. RICHARD BOND. Treasurer-THOMAS J. WRIGHT. Managers--REV. HENRY L. RICE, JOSEPH MINNICK, GEORGE FLACK, JOHN DENIG, W. O. HICKOK, ROBERT M. BARD, JOSEPH PRITTS, WM. P. THOMSON. Committee of Solicitors--MRS. SARAH FINDLAY, MRS. COLHOUN, MRS. RICE, MRS. MARSHALL, MISS E. J. FINDLAY, MISS JANE DAVIS. ARCHIBALD BARD, ADAM HEIGHT, ROBERT VIRL, ALONZO FRY, A. H. FRENCH.//**FEMALE SEMINARY** Chambersburg run by the MISSES PINNEO is endorsed by the following: FRED'K. SMITH, WM. HEYSER, BARANARD WOLFF, A. I. FINDLAY, R. WASHINGTON, P. BERLIN, A. COLHOUN, A. THOMSON, P. FAHNESTOCK, JAMES CAMPBELL, GEO. K. HARPER//**MONEYS RECEIVED** By REV. D. ZACHARIAS, from JOHN SCHLEY 2 50, JONATHAN GERTZENDANNER 2 50, CASPAR MANTZ 4. By REV. RICHARD A. FISHER, from JACOB GASS 2, DANIEL DRUCKENMILLER 2, R. A. FISHER 1. By REV. D. WEISER, from DANIEL PENNYPACKER 2 GEORGE GERHART 1, HENRY TRUMBAUER 1, D. WEISER 1. By REV. JACOB MAYER, from DAVID EXLINE, PHILIP J. SHOEMAKER, each 2, HENRY DEAL and H. P. SHOEMAKER, each 2 50, REV. GEO. LEIDY and JAMES SPROBT, each 2. From GEORGE COLLIFLOWER 2 From HENRY SMITH (St. Thomas) 2. By JOHN C. BUCHER, from MRS. HARRIET WIESTLING 4. By MARTIN RICKENBAUGH, from SAMUEL WEAVER, MISS

WEEKLY MESSENGER OF THE GERMAN REFORMED CHURCH

SARAH KELLER, WM. KINKLE (Alexandria) VALENTINE PENTZER, GEO. WOLFERSPERGER, DAVID TROUB, JOSEPH POWLES, JACOB POWLES, DAVID ZELLER, each 2, and ADAM TROUB 3. PHILIP STOEHR (St. Thomas) 2. COL. CURTIS MILEY (St. Thomas)4. Transfer credit from MRS. R. ELY to MR. JOHN DAVISON, Trenton, N. J.

96. Apr. 19, 1837/**MARRIED** In Chambersburg, on the 14th ult., by REV B.S.SCHNECK, JAMES S. DURBORAW, printer to MISS NANCY SMITH.//By the REV. D. G. BRAGONIER on the 6th inst. MR. FREDERICK REFFLEY to MISS MARY BOYD.//On the evening of the same day by the same, MR. OLIVER ZELLERS, to MISS MARTHA, daughter of HENRY ANKENY, ESQ., all of Wash. Co. Md.//On the 6th inst.,at the residence of MR. ISAAC B. BURROWS in Lancaster county, by the REV. MR. EDWARD Y. BUCHANAN, THOMAS H. BURROWES, Esq. Secretary of the Commonwealth, to MISS SALOME, daughter of the late DR. JOHN S. CARPENTER.//**DIED** On the 22d March, after lingering pulmonary consumption, at his residence in Funkstown, Md., MR. GEORGE M. ELLIOTT, leaving a large young family. The funeral, on the 24th ult. was attended by a large concourse of citizens.//In Fayetteville, Franklin Co. on the 13th inst., PETER COOK HUSSEY, infant son of the REV. GEORGE ST. CLAIR HUSSEY.//In NY city on Thursday morning last, REV. LEWIS SMITH, JR., pastor of GRC in Forsyth street, in the 24th year of his ago (sic).-"N. Y. Evang."//In Gratztown, Dauphin Co., Pa., on the 10th inst., BARNARD RIEDY, in the 61st year of his ago (sic).//At the Saline reservation on Salt river, now owned by DR. ELY and one or two other gentlemen, an Artesian well has been sunk to 300 feet.--"Gen. Farmer".

97. Apr. 26, 1837/**MARRIED** On the 15th inst., by the REV. ISAAC GERHART, MR. CONRAD BACHMAN to MRS. ELIZABETH LENKER, all of Dauphin co., Pa.// On Thursday last by REV. D. ZACHARIAS, MR. ELIAS BAST to MISS MARY LAMBERT, all of Frederick co., Md.//On the same day, by the same, MR. DANIEL

WEEKLY MESSENGER OF THE GERMAN REFORMED CHURCH

C_LLER to MISS ANN MARIA HARGATE, both of Frederick county.//On the evening of the same day by the same, MR. JOHN A. STEINER of this city, to MISS ANN SOPHIA MYERS, of the vicinity of Frederick, Md.//At Antietam Hall Thursday the 30th of March, by the REV. MR. GLESSNER, MR. SAML. MIDDLECAUFF to MISS CATHARINE C. third daughter of MR. JOHN BARR all of Wash. co., Md.//In Green Castle, Pa., on Thursday the 30th ult., by the REV. MR. BUCHANAN, MR. JOHN F. EICHHOLTZ formerly of Williamsport, to MISS SUSAN, eldest daughter of MR. JOHN CURREY of Hagerstown.//Thursday the 6th inst., by REV. A. HELFENSTEIN, JR. MR. CHARLES ULRICH, to MISS CATHARINE FREYDINGER, of Wash. co., Md.//On the same day by the same, MR. DANIEL ZELLERS to MISS RACHEL PHEASANT, of Wash. co. Md.//On the 13th inst. by REV. HENRY AURAND, MR. JOHN REED, to MISS HANNAH DAVIS, both of Perry county.//On Thursday last by the same, MR. HENRY SPERA, of Monroe township, to MISS MARY ECHELBERGER, of Cumberland co.//Monday the 10th inst., by the same, MR. PETER ARTHUR, to MISS AMELIA ROBERTS both of Carlisle.//**DIED** In Mechanicsburg, Cumberland co., Pa., the 11th inst., REV. EMANUEL KELLER,in the 37th year of his age. //In Huntingdon, Pa.,on the 5th inst.,MRS. ELIZA WARTON, wife of SAMUEL WARTON, Esq., and daughter of PETER SWOPE,of that place, aged 29 years. //MRS. RACHEL BROMBACK,of East Vincent township, Chest__, has been robbed of two thousand dollars and murdered. She was 70 years old. "Phila. Sat. Cour."//Newington Academy, near Gloucester Court House, Va., property of JACOB TABB, Esq. of Norfolk was entirely destroyed by fire on the 6th inst.//ABNER JONES, Esq. of this city has made a donation of 25,000 dollars to the NY Theological Seminary. --"N. Y. Observer."//We learn from the Lexington (Ky) Observer, that the Faculty of the Transylvania Medical School has been dissolved. Investigation was made upon charges made by PROFESSOR DUDLEY against PROFESSOR CALDWELL and the latter dismissed.//The late Pastor of the Spruce

WEEKLY MESSENGER OF THE GERMAN REFORMED CHURCH

street Baptist Church, Philadelphia, REV. G. B. PERRY, has been elected President of Canton College, IL.//MICANOPY and PHILIP have surrendered.

98. May 3, 1837/**MARRIED** On Thursday last, by REV. S. SPRECHER, MR. DAVID M. ALTER, of Westmoreland co., to MISS MARGARET, daughter of GOVERNOR RITNER.//On the 20th ult, by REV. ISAAC GERHART, ISAAC UHLER, to MISS HANNAH HOFFMAN all of Lykens Valley, Dauphin co.//On the 25th, by the same, MR. JOSEPH LEBO to MISS SARAH SHEPLEY, of Armstrong's Valley, Dauphin co., Pa.//**DIED** In Lancaster co. Pa., on the 24th ult., MR. NATHANIEL ELLMAKER, father of AMOS ELLMAKER, Esq., at an advanced age.//In Beaver co. Pa., on the 12th ult., ABNER LEACOCK, Esq., aged 66 years.//**HOME MISSION FUNDS** received from Lincoln co., N. C. LEWIS DELLINGER, 25c.; DAVID DELLINGER, $1; MRS. ELVIRA SHUFORD, 50c.; REV. J. G.FRITCHEY, $2; A. RAMSOUR, 25c.; JACOB HILEMAN, 25c.; DAVID RAMSOUR, $1; JACOB RAMSOUR, $2; JACOB A. RAMSOUR, 50c.; PAUL KISLER, 50c.; LYMAN WOODFORD, $1; JACOB SHUFORD, $1; SOL. RUDISEL, 25c.; MISS SUSAN SHUFORD, 50C.; A. WARD, Esq., 50c.; F. TURNER, $2; JOHN LANG,50c.; A. ROMSOUR, 50c.; REV. W. C. RANKIN, $3; CALEB MILLER, 50c.; PETER SUMMEY, $1; MRS. SIMPSON, 25c.; B. JETTUN, 50c.; ELKANAH COULTER, 50c.; W. R. COULTER, 25c.; A. H. LARETZ 50c.; DAVID DICKEY, $1; THOMAS R. SHUFORD, 25c,; GEORGE SHUFORD, Esq., $1, DANIEL LARETZ,50C,;// **POISONED** Died on Saturday afternoon, April 8th, DR. R. P. HAYES, aged 50 years, after a confinement of nearly 11 months, with great suffering, in consequence of poison administered, without cause, by a negro girl, employed as cook, on the 12th of May last.--"Cincinnati Gaz."//**AN INQUEST** over the body of JOHN FREEZLIN, found dead near Concord, N. C. on the morning of the 18th inst. Verdict--the dec'd. came to his death by Intoxication!---"West. Car."//The 19th inst., PETER A. BROWNE, Esq., was appointed Professor of Geology and Mineralogy at Lafayette College, Easton, PA.

WEEKLY MESSENGER OF THE GERMAN REFORMED CHURCH

99. May 10, 1837//**MARRIED** In Shippensburg, on the first of May, by the REV. WM. C. BENNET, MR. PETER DEWALT, of Dover, OH, to MISS BARBARA ANN PAYNE, of Shippensburg, Cumberland co., Penn'a. //Near Shippensburg, on the second of May by the same, MR. GEORGE TRITT, to MISS MARIA NOECKER, all of Cumberland county, Pa.//In Hagerstown, Md., on the 19th ult., by the REV. MR. HELFENSTEIN, MR. HUGH L. GULLUHER, one of the editors of the VA Free Press, to MISS ELIZABETH C. BOWEN of Shepherdstown, Va.//In York by REV. J. CARES, MR. JOSEPH WATTS to MISS CATHARINE MYERS, all of that place.//By the same on the 16th ult., MR. JACOB HESS, to MISS SARAH EHRMAN.//In Burke co., N. C., by REV. W. C. RANKIN, MR. JOHN NULL, to MISS NANCY daughter of THOMAS WARD Esq.//Tuesday evening 2d inst., by REV. RICHARD BOND, MR. REXTON CHENOWITH, to MISS REBECCA GROVE, all of this place.//In Cabarnr (sic) N. C., on the 20th ult., by the REV. GEO. BOGER, MR. LEVI MOOSE, to MISS LAVINIA TROUTMAN.//March 23d by REV. J. F. BERG, MR. JOHN THOMPSON to MISS MARY ANN PEARSON both of Franklin co.//On the 18th ult., by the same, MR. JOHN DOYLE to MISS MARY COSLEY both of Franklin co.//On the 19th ult., by the same, MR. HIRAM SINSNEY to MISS MARIA HUBER both of Franklin co.//By REV. I. GERHART, on the 4th inst., MR. LEOPOLD DREYFUSS, merchant of Harrisburg, to MISS ELIZA, daughter of PHILIP HIRSH, of Lykens Valley, Dauphin co., Pa.//**DIED** In this borough, on Thursday last, MRS. CATHARINE BERLIN, relict of ADAM BERLIN, dec'd., at the advanced age of 92 years. She was a native of Alsace, in GER, and emigrated to this country between fifty and sixty years ago.//Thursday last in this borough, MRS. CATHARINE HECK consort of LUDWIG HECK Esq., in the 67th year of her age. Her remains were deposited in the burying ground of the Lutheran Church.//In this borough, on Thursday last, MR. WILLIAM S. DAVIS, aged about 47 years.//A short time since, at Canton, OH, MR. JACOB ECKART, formerly of this place.//At Pittsburg, MR. ADAM

WEEKLY MESSENGER OF THE GERMAN REFORMED CHURCH

COOK formerly a resident of this place.//In York on the 28th ult, JOHN WELSH, SEN., a Soldier of the revolution, aged 99 years.//At Cadiz, OH, on Monday the 17th ult., REV. JOHNSON WELCH, President of the College at New Athens.//In Frederick city, Md. on the 5th ult., REV. D. G. SCHAEFFER, formerly pastor of the Luth. cong. of that place in the 51st year of his age.//At Shepherdstown, Jefferson county, Va. on the 30th of March, MRS. CATHERINE SMITH, consort of MR. JOSEPH SMITH, in the 42d year of her age.//Wednesday, 3d inst., REV. HENRY L. RICE, in the 42nd year of his age. **//FISHING** At the Indian Head Landing of the Potomac with a seine GEO. H. SMOOT, Esq., took upwards of seven hundred thousand Herring besides a large number of Sturgeon, Shad, Rock Perch and every description of fish.//CLAYTON, the celebrated western aeronaut, who was to go up from Cincinnati on May 1, takes one or two passengers at $100 each.//**CONVENTION** of the friends of the integrity of the Union, assembled in the Court House at Harrisburgh, on Monday last, 1st inst., MR. McGRIFFIN, of Washington, (sic) occupying the chair pro tem. JUDGE BAIRD, of Washington County, was chosen President, and MORTON McMICHAEL, of Philadelphia, S. D. PATTERSON, of Dauphin, S. W. RANDALL, of Erie, JOSEPH WILLIAMS, of Delaware, were appointed Secretaries. Hon. T. B. DALLAS, Allegheny, THOMAS BELL, of Chester, COL. WALTER S. FRANKLIN, of York, GEORGE FISHER, of Dauphin, Hon. GEORGE CHAMBERS, of Franklin, SAMUEL H. LLOYD, of Lycoming, NATHANIEL EWING, of Fayette, JAMES M. PAULING of Montgomery, Hon. JOHN BREDIN, of Butler, GEN. THOMAS C. MILLER, of Adams, MARTIN STAMBAUGH, of Perry and MICHAEL HOLCOMB, of Cumberland, Vice-Presidents. Tuesday morning, MR. THADDEUS STEVENS of Adams, and other delegates took their seats. MR. KANE reported a preable (sic) and resolutions, which were adopted.-"U. S. Gaz."//We learn from JAMES KINZIE, Esq. of this city, on Saturday, the 18th inst., at about 5 miles from the mouth of the IL

WEEKLY MESSENGER OF THE GERMAN REFORMED CHURCH

River, through the obstinacy of two captains, a boat was sunk. MR. and MRS. GARRET, and MR. and MRS. POMEROY, of this city, saved.-"Chicago Commercial Advertiser."//**MONEYS** By REV. J. REBOUGH from HENRY THOMAS 3, PHILIP GROVE 2. DR. TOBIAS SELLERS, (Upper Hanover,) 2, A. MOSTELLER 2, JOSIAH HILLEGAS 1. ELIZA & MARIA HOUSER 1, SAMUEL FOUTZ 4, JACOB BUCK 2, HENRY THOMAS 4, J. CHRISTIAN & ERNSPERGER 2 25, By REV. PETER S. FISHER, from GEORGE YOUNGMAN 2. By PROF. BERG, from JOSEPH RENINGER (Greencastle) 2. GEO. STRICKLAND, JR.(Seltzer's Store)2. By JACOB HADE, Esq., from PETER STEIN, 4, CONRAD HERR 2. GEORGE PEARSON, HENRY SMITH of D., each 2. GEORGE COLLIFLOWER 2. By M. ROUNSAVILLE, from G. LENGS, 1 50, THOMAS JANES 2, A. MICHAEL,1 25. By GEORGE BESORE, from GEORGE MOWEN, 2. By REV. G. WACK, from JOHN BOILEAU (Norristown, transferred from F.W. HOOVER)2 //**LETTERS** JOHN GRICE, J. R. FILSON, HENRY KLINE.

100. May 17, 1837//**MARRIED** On Tuesday morning last, by REV. JOHN PEEBLES, DR. JOHN HARRIS, of Bellefonte, to MISS ELEANOR, daughter of WILLIAM ORBISON, Esq., of Huntingdon, Pa.//On the 20th ult. by the REV. MR. ZIEGLER, WILLIAM HILDEBRAND Esq. to MISS ELIZABETH GIEB both of East Berlin, Adam Co. (sic).//**DIED** In Frederick, on Thursday morning the 5th inst., MRS. ANN J. GRAHAM, the Relict of MAJ. JNO. GRAHAM and eldest daughter of the late GOV. THOS. JOHNSON, in the 69th year of her age.--"Fred. Times."//At his residence in Williamsport, Md. on the 7th inst., DR. WILLIAM VAN LEAR.//At the house of her father,JOHN RANKIN, Esq., of Bellefonte, on the morning of the 2d inst., MARY, wife of MR. ALFRIED ARMSTRONG of Harrisburg, in the 33d year of her age.//In Gettysburg on the 9th inst. SARAH AMELIA, youngest child of MR. SAMUEL S. FORNEY.//Near St. Thomas, Tuesday morning last, MR. ADAM RUDISILL, an old inhabitant of this county.//Salisbury, N. C. May 6.--COL. JOHN BRANDON, of this county, was accidentally killed on Wednesday last, by a tree his

hands were felling sliding back some ten or fifteen feet to where he was standing, and crushing him to death. The accident happened about 4 o'clock in the evening and he died about 11 the same evening.//A Coroner's Jury in the death of MR. FLEMING, gave the verdict "died of apoplexy, produced by mental excitement." N. Y. paper, May 10.//On Saturday afternoon the building on the corner of Liberty and William streets, fell to the ground with a tremendous crash burying two boys playing in the cellar. MICHAEL HAGAN, aged 8 years, of 43 Elm street, was killed instantaneously.//DR. WM. D. JENKS, planted this spring, 20,000 white Mulberry trees, for the purpose of feeding Silk Worms and proposes planting the same number next year.--"Frederick (Md.) Examiner."//**LIGHTNING**. Tuesday evening last, a barn belonging to MR. BARNITZ, in the south east part of the borough, was entirely consumed. Rain and the exertions of fire companies and citizens prevented fire from communicating to the adjacent buildings.---"Carlisle Volunteer."//**MONEYS**. From MISS SOPHIA WADDEL, $1.

101. May 24, 1837/**MARRIED** At Troy, N. Y., by the REV. DR. TUCKER, on the 18th ult., MR. JAMES W. JONES, a licentiate of the GRC, to MISS JANE ELIZA WALDORF of Redhook Duchess co., N. York.// At Alexandria, on Tuesday, the 9th inst., by the REV. MR. HILL, MR. JOHN WOOLVERTON, of the state of IN, to MISS ANN MARIA STEWART, of Alexandria, Pa.//On Thursday evening, 9th inst. by the REV. MATHEW SORIN, C. H. BIBIGHAUS, M. D. of the Northern Liberties, to MISS MARY ANN, daughter of MR. WILLIAM LAIRD, of Philadelphia.//**DIED** Sabbath, May 14th, at Redhook, N. Y., REV. GEORGE A. SHOOK, in the 35th year of his age. The deceased was born the 3d of May, 1803. At the age of 21, he graduated from Union College, Schenectady. A lingering, deep-rooted consumption had been preying on his body.//On Saturday last, in the 16th year of her age, MISS CATHARINE NOEL,

daughter of MR. JOHN NOEL of Chambersburg.//**TESTIMONY OF RESPECT** The Trustees of Marshall College take this method of expressing their deep sorrow, occasioned by the death of their estimable President and colleague, the REV. HENRY L. RICE. In testimony of regard for the dec'd., they will wear crape on their left arm for thirty days. P. W. LITTLE, Sec'y.//In Pursuance of a resolution of the Trustees of Marshall College twenty-five Beneficiaries will be admitted free of tuition; and twenty young men who design to prepare themselves for teaching school, into the English Department. Applications must be made to the Faculty, or to the following Committee: P. W. LITTLE. DANL. SHAFFER, WM. McKINSTRY.//The U. S. ship *S. Louis,* CAPT. PAINE, and *Concord,* CAPT. MIX arrived at Pensacola from Havana on 28th of April.//**MISSIONARY MASSACRE** We copy the following from a Boston paper of the 1st of May. Weekly Mess.--Boston May 1.--MR. WILLIAM M BARNARD, formerly second officer of the ship *Selma,* of New Bedford arrived in this port in the *Parachute* a few days since with a detailed account of the murder of 80 South Sea Island Missionary natives in the month of August, 1835, at Walls' Island. The English Missionaries at Keepland conceived the plan of attempting to introduce Christianity at Wallis' Island by sending native teachers and missionaries. Soon after landing, the whole number were murdered.//**AMERICAN LYCEUM** met in session in Philadelphia. WM. A. DUER of NY, President; SAMUEL L. SOUTHARD of N. J., G. W. RIDGELY of Pa., EDWARD EVERETT of Mass., P. W. RADCLIFF of Brooklyn, N. J., and JOHN GRISCOM of Philadelphia, Vice Presidents; ROBERT G. RANKIN of N. Y., Recording Sec'y.; WM. FORREST of N. Y., Treasurer; THEODORE DWIGHT, JR., of N.Y.; J. L. COMSTOCK, of Hartford, Ct., J. P. ESPY of Philadelphia, W. A. CLAYTON of Athens, Ga., J. M. STURTEVANT of IL, WM. C. WOODBRIDGE of Boston, B. C. PEERS of Lexington, Ky., ALVA WOOD of AL, W. B. CALHOUN of Springfield, Mass., N. SARGENT

WEEKLY MESSENGER OF THE GERMAN REFORMED CHURCH

of Phila., JAMES M. GARNETT of Va., CHARLES GODDARD of Zunesville (sic) OH, JAMES M. ALEXANDER of Princeton, N. J. Corresponding Secretaries; DENISON OLMSTEAD of New Haven, Ct., S. H. PENNINGTON of Newark, N. J., J. S. ROGERS, A. P HOLSEY, L. H. GALE, J. VAN RENSELLAER, ROBERT G. RANKIN, G. W. DISOWAY of NY, F. A. PACKARD of Phila., J. HEDGES of Newark, N. J., additional members of the Executive Committee. They urged Congress for provisions for systematic research and observation of Meteorology, setting forth the importance to farmer, mechanic and mariner. //On the 8th inst. fire broke out on the Steamboat *Ben Sherrod,* about 30 miles below Natchez, on her way to Louisville, with over 160 passengers. The account in the New Orleans Commercial Herald. "The captain saved his wife, but saw his two children perish. MR. SMITH saved his wife and one child. The nurse rushed madly through the flames with his daughter, and both perished. MR. GAMBLE'S wife, we understand, was burnt to death; he escaped although very badly burnt."

102. May 31, 1837/**MARRIED** In Rowan County, N. C., on Thursday evening, May 11th, by REV. J. G. FRITCHEY, MR. JACOB SLOOP, to MISS CATHERINE, eldest daughter of MR. JOHN CORRELL, of Rowan County, N. C.//In Frederick, on the 11th inst. by the REV. MR. HARKEY, REV. CHARLES MARTIN, Pastor of the Lutheran Church Martinsburgh, Va., to MISS ELIZA JANETTE CARLTON, daughter of the late THOMAS CARLTON, Esq., of Frederick.// **DIED** In this place, on Tuesday 21st inst., SARAH FINLEY, daughter of DR. FINLEY, aged 19 years.// **HAVANA LETTER** to the editor of the Presbyterian from REV. S. G. WINCHESTER dated April 4th, 1837 "Protestant worship is not allowed in any form on the Island. The British Consul requested of the Governor, in behalf of British subjects, permission to read the church service in private houses, which was refused. I visited the public burial ground. Ditches are dug into which the

bodies are thrown. They are taken to the ground in coffins, but the bodies are taken out and the coffins taken home to serve for other occasions" **//MONEYS RECEIVED.** By D. COULTER, from G. BOMBERGER, [Experiment Mills,] 2, HENRY SMITH [do,] $2, MISS CATHARINE COLEMAN 3, J. HOFFMAN, Esq. [Reading] 4, REV. W. PAULI 2. By REV. W. PAULI, from MISS HANNAH KROUSER 2. From JAMES McCOY [Quincy] 2. By D. COULTER, from MISS C. COLEMAN 2, REV. A. L. HERMAN, WM. WILSON, [Bath] and ABRAHAM GEORGE, each 2, HENRY SMITH 2, ISAAC SMITH [Up. Mt. Bethel] 1 25, GEORGE BOMBERGER [Exp't. Mills] 4. From REV. L. E. DIEFFENBACHER, from JOHN RINKER 2.//Whereas Brother HENRY HABLISTON is devoting his time and talents to objects foreign to his office; and inasmuch as he himself requests to withdraw from the Classis and Synod of the GRC---therefore, Resolved, That we no longer consider him a member of this Classis. The committee appointed to inquire into the matters relating to BROTHER HABLISTON are MESSRS. CARES, SHOLL, and WIRT.

103. June 7, 1837/**MARRIED** Middletown, Md., on the 23d of May, by REV. J. C. BUCHER, MR. DANIEL LEASER, to MISS MARY GRAVER, all of Middletown , (sic) Frederick county, Md.//Near Middletown, on the 25th of May by REV. J. C. BUCHER, DR. GEORGE W. MARIS to MISS ELIZABETH ANN, only daughter of the late MR. GEORGE MOTTER, all of Middletown Valley, Md.//On Thursday 25th ult., by REV. HENRY AURAND, MR. JOHN L. N. HALL to MISS ELIZABETH CAROTHERS, all of Carlisle, Pa.//On the same day by the same, MR. FRANCIS MICKEY, to MISS ELIZA STAUFFER all of Perry co., Pa.//On Tuesday morning, 23d ult., in Carlisle, Pa., by REV. JAMES WILLIAMSON, DR. WILLIAM HEPBURN, of Centre co., Pa., to MISS ELIZABETH IRVINE, only daughter of the late JOHN IRVINE, dec'd.,of Cumberland county, Pa.//At Lewistown, on the 18th ult, by REV. REV. JNO. S. EASTON, REV. ALEXANDER T. McGILL of Carlisle, to MISS ELLEN A. McCULLOCH, of Lewis-

ton, Mifflin county, Pa.//On the 1st inst., near Woodsboro, Md., by the REV. J. W. HOFFMEIER, MR. MICHAEL GRINDER, to MISS MARGARET ANN, second daughter of SAMUEL WILHIDE Esq., both of Frederick co.//On the 1st ult. by REV. J. GERHART, MR. GEORGE HOFFMAN, to MISS SUSAN, daughter of MR. JOHN MILLER, both of Armstrong's Valley, Dauphin co., Pa.//The 16th ult., by the same, MR. DAVID ZERBE of Northumberland co., to MISS MARGARETTA, daughter of JACOB MORITZ, of Dauphin co.//On the 21st u lt., (sic) by the same, MR. JACOB RATHFON to MISS MARY, daughter of MR. JOHN SHORA, both of Millersburg, Dauphin co., Pa.//**DIED** On the 17th of May near Taneytown, Carroll County, Md., MRS. MARY, consort of MR. JOHN HEINER, in the 44th year of her age, leaving a husband and several children.//On Friday the 26th ult., MRS. REBECCA HENDEL, consort of MR. BERNARD HENDEL, of Carlisle, Pa.//On Wednesday the 24th ult, at the residence of DR. J. C. HAYS, in Sharpsburg, Md., after a short illness, MISS JANE CHAPLINE, in the 80th year of her age.//**A MELANCHOLY ACCIDENT** On Tuesday last, WILLIAM, eldest son of MR. GEORGE BOWMAN, of this town, aged about thirteen years, was killed by the accidental discharge of a gun. The dec'd., his father and MR. J. K. HARRY, were out gunning about eight miles from Town. While stopped at a spring Mr. H. took up one of the guns and whilst examining it, it discharged, and the contents entered the cheek of the dec'd. between the eye and the mouth.--"Hagerstown T. Light, 1st inst."//The Grand Jury of Frederick county, Md., refused to find a bill against E. B. McPHERSON, for the robbery committed on the Teller of the Leesburg Bank.//Faculty of Marshall College resolved to wear crape on the left arm until July 12th in respect for the memory of REV. HENRY L. RICE, who died since adjournment. //**MONEYS** By H. J. BROWN, from ELIZABETH WATSON (Philadelphia) 1 25. By C. F. HOFFMEIER, from JOHN PEPPER (Strasbury) 2. AMOS H. KREMER, from JOHN PHILIPPE (Gephart's) 1 25, CHRISTIAN CRAMER

WEEKLY MESSENGER OF THE GERMAN REFORMED CHURCH

2, PETER PUTMAN 2, LUDWIG WELLER (Somerset) 2, JOHN SNYDER (Rastraver) 1 25, HENRY SNYDER 2, & FREDERICK SHEARER (Cookstown) 2. By H. F. W. SHULTZE, from VALENTINE MEYER 3, and JOHN NEIL, JR. 2. By REV. ISAAC GERHART, from JOHN NAGEL 4. By REV. JOHN PENCE, from REV. J. DESCOMBES 2, and JOHN PENCE 3. By JOHN C. BARNHART, from HENRY MOOSE (Salisbury) CASPAR HOLSHAUSER, DANIEL CARKER (Mt. Comfort) PAUL KLUTTS, and JOHN C. BARNHART, each 2. Editor "Der Christl. Zeitschrift" add MR. FREDERICK BROWNELLER, Perryopolis, Fayette co., Pa., to his list of subscribers. JOHN MAYER of Berrysburg, Dauphin co., Pa., paid $1, for which he will give credit, and charge us.

104. June 14, 1837/**DIED** On Monday last, MARY G. daughter of DR. N. B. LANE, of this borough, aged 18 months.//Monday the 5th inst., MRS. BARBARA TANNER of this county, at an advanced age. //On Saturday the 3rd inst. at the residence of her brother near Mercersburg, MISS JANE HAMILTON formerly of Dauphin Co., Pa.//**MONEY** By R. GOOD, from JOSEPH GOOD (Reading) 2.--By DAVID WEIDNER, (Phil'a.) from MRS. MARIA THOMAS, and MISS SARAH GIBSON, each2.--By REV. S. HELFENSTEIN, JR. from JOHN RILE, Esq. 2 50 HENRY RILE 2 50, A. YOST 2.

105. June 21, 1837/**MARRIED** On Tuesday morning, 13th inst., by REV. D. ZACHARIAS, MR. DAVID HARGATE to MISS REBECCA DUDRO, all of Frederick Co. Md.//**DIED** In Lancaster city, on the 30th ult., MRS. GERTRUDE HOFFMEIER, consort of REV. J. H. HOFFMEIER, in the 73rd year of her age. She endured much bodily suffering for 30 years. She was confined to her chamber since last autumn. She expressed a desire to see her son, who is in the ministry at some distance. Her sermon was delivered by REV. MR. BRUNER, aided in the other services by REV.MR. BECKER and REV.MR. REINECKE. //Saturday last, at the house of her son-in law, WILLIAM REYNOLDS, Esq., in Bedford, MRS. SARAH HOLLIDAY, relict of ADAM HOLLIDAY, Esq. formerly

WEEKLY MESSENGER OF THE GERMAN REFORMED CHURCH

of Hollidaysburg, Huntingdon co., in the 83rd year of her age.//MR. SCOTT of the New Jerusalem Church of London, will migrate with a colony to WI.//E. C. DELDVAN, Esq. of Albany, who was sued by brewers of Albany and Troy for libel in publishing a statement they mixed poisonous drugs with their beer has non-suited them.//A lad aged about nine years, son of MR. SAILOR, tobacconist, in Sixth, between Market and Arch street, on Tuesday ascended to the roof of his house, which is three stories high, to fly his kite. He slipped, and rolling over the eaves, fell to the ground. Marvellous to relate, he suffered little or no injury!--"Phil. Gazette."//The greatest calamity with which Baltimore has ever been visited was experienced Wednesday night. Heavy rains tore up the mill dams and wooden bridges on the waters of Jones's Falls which left its accustomed bed, coming down over the wall at Centre street where it takes a somewhat abrupt turn. Soap and Candle Factories of MESSRS. FRANCIS HYDE & Son, SAMUEL HYDE, and T. N. SMITH & Co., suffered extensive damage. The Coach factory of MR. ELISHA LEE sustained injury. The floor of the dwelling (sic) of MR. W. BROMWELL at Saratoga and Calvert, was under water. The house of JOHN MeKIM, JR. Esq (sic) near Orange Ally (sic) on Holliday street had water in the basement and parlours. The Sexton of the Presby. Church at the corner of Holliday & Saratoga, named JOHN WIEST, lived in a house adjoining it. The whole family, Wiest, his wife and three children drowned in their sleep. LEWIS SPIESE, a mechanic of this city, snatched a boy of 12 or 14 from the current at the Pratt street bridge. The Tannery of MR. GEO. APPOLD was inundated, also the Mail Coach Factory of MESSRS. STOCKTON & STOKES. Greatest losses were suffered by MESSRS. JOHN WILSON & Son, MESSRS. J. M. LAROUQUE & Co. druggists, MR. C. DIFFENDERFFER, MR. S. JACOB, MESSRS. J.& A. ROSS, grocers, MESSRS. J. & A. HERON, dry goods vendors. We are indebted to J. I. GROSS, Esq. Coronoer, for a list of inquests: CHRISTOPHER WIEST, wife and three children, Saratoga street. ____ (sic) DOUGHERTY, Concord and Water streets. CATHARINE DONNELLEY, Pratt street. JAMES DOYLE, Long wharf JACOB OCKLEY, Falls road. The following bodies are yet uncovered: JAMES KELLEY, HENRY LINEHAN, MR. DONNELLY, five on Falls road, names unknown. From "Patriot", and "American, June 17."//Died at Singapore, Asia, about the 15th December last, REV. EDWIN STEVENS, AM Missionary to China, age about 34. He was taken with fever after leaving Canton on his third tour. He went to Canton, in 1832, as Chaplain to AM seamen.//**MONEYS** By JOHN ZEIGLER from JOHN ZIMMERMAN, 1 25. By REV J. G. GULDIN from FRED'K KOONS and SAMUEL EISENBERGER, each 2. By HENRY KELLER, from JOHN HUNTER, Pinegrove, Centre co.) 4. GEORGE HECK 2. By DR. HOFIUS, (Bedford from DANIEL CROUSE, JAMES WEISEL, PETER MANN, HENRY REIMUND PHILIP MANN, each 2.

No marriages or deaths in July 5, 1837 issue.

106. July 12, 1837/**MARRIED** In Bedford, Pa. the 4th inst., by REV. MR. LEIDY, MR. PETER MANN, to MRS. MARY SCOVIL, all of Bedford county.//Thursday last, in Chambersburg, by REV. J.A. FOERSCH, MR. FREDERICK ECKERT, of St. Louis, Mo., to MISS CHRISTIANA KESSELRING, of the former place.// **DIED** On the 4th inst., GEORGE MATTHEW, only son of DANIEL M. SMYSER, Esq., of Gettysburg, age 1 year, 3 months, and 13 days.//In Orange county, NC, on the 7th ult., MRS. FOUST, relict of the late GEORGE FOUST at an advanced age. Like her husband, who entered into rest about twelve months ago she was a respectable member of the GRC. //MR. LUKE WHITMORE of Montville, Medina county, OH, and five of his children were taken ill on the 12th ult. Three of the children have since dec'd., and of the lives of the father and another child, scarce a hope remains. Physicians pronounce all three cases of poisoning. A post mortem of two bodies disclose evidence of vege-

WEEKLY MESSENGER OF THE GERMAN REFORMED CHURCH

table poison, but no circumstance can be traced showing when or what substance had been taken.--"Cleveland (OH) Gazette."//A small boy, MATTHEW DUFFY, found a roll of bank bills in Beekman street. He applied to DAVID GRAHAM, Esq., whose office was near, who told him to leave the money at the Police. The property was claimed by MR. J. C. LAWRENCE who gave him a $5 bill for his trouble.--"N. Y.Express".//Latter (sic) received from the REV. DR. RICHARDS, of Auburn, published in the Newark Advertiser, states that four students of the Theological Seminary were drowned in the Owasco lake, on Saturday, 25th ult. They were in a sail boat, when a sudden flaw (sic) overtook and ingulphed them. Their names were H. SMITH, of Johnson; WM. P. TUTTLE, of Newark, N. J.; WM. WOODBRIDGE, of Stockbridge, Mass.; and SIMEON S. JOHNSON, of Sweden, Monroe county. They were accompanied by a lad named WITHERELL, who saved himself, clinging to an oar. The body of TUTTLE has been found.//The British steamer, *Traveller*, arrived in Rochester yesterday, from Hamilton, Upper Canada, bringing news which will be received in Utica with satisfaction. A fellow named HARVEY has been charged with the robbery of the Oneida Bank.//**MONEYS** By E. THOMAS, Esq., from MRS. SUSAN DARE 2.--By JAMES POTTER, Esq., from JOHN KELLY, SR. 2 50, WILLIAM BARR 3, DAVID WISE 2, ALEXANDER McCOY 2, MRS. ROBERT PENNINGTON 4, WM. HUGHES 2, JAMES POTTER 2.--By REV. J. HELFENSTEIN, from MISS E. TOOL (Emmaus)2.--By H. J. BROWN from JOHN PAUL (Chester Co. 2.--By REV. RICHARD A. FISHER, from JACOB ALBRIGHT (Northumberland) 5. By WILLIAM HUNTER, Esq., from MISS WENRICH Thompsontown) 4.//**LETTER** W. H. KINKLE.

107. July 19, 1837/**MARRIED** On Thursday the 22d inst. by REV. WM. R. De WITT, MR. MARKS STOUFFER to MISS MARY ANN HARRIS, both of Middletown, Pa. //The 6th of July at Middleburg, Pa., by GEO. W. HEWITT, Esq., MR. WILLIAM HALL, to MRS. SARAH DILLON both of Hagerstown, Md.//**DIED** Near Green

WEEKLY MESSENGER OF THE GERMAN REFORMED CHURCH

castle, Pa., in the 73d year of his age, MR. DANIEL STALL.//In Yorksville, S. C., MR. J. W. CLARK, lately from PA, engaged to take charge of the Academy in Clemmonsville, Davison county, N. C. He was called away,(as was supposed, by a fit of apoplexy, less than an hour after eating a hearty breakfast. His age was supposed to be between 25 and 30; member of the Presby. Church. "Western Carolinian."//Lately, in Lincoln County N.C., REV. ROBERT TUCKER, in the 98th year of his age. He took a swallow of poison (Arsenic) through mistake for some tea he was using for a cough. He survived seven hours, suffering intensely.//On the 6th inst., after a lingering illness, MRS. WILHELMINA GOODMANSON, wife of MR. PETER GOODMANSON, of Frederick, Md., in the 23d year of her age.//Fire consumed the house of MR. H. GAY, in New Lebanon, Columbia county on the 3d ult. The aged mother of MR. GAY, who was infirm and sick, and his little daughter perished. Feathers taken from a bed on which MRS. G. had lain, who had died a few days previous, were washed and put in a room to dry. A little son remarked they were hot. //The Marlborough Hotel, has reopened, distilled and fermented liquors being excluded. A dinner was prepared for the opening of the house on the 4th inst., at which two hundred gentlemen partook. REV. MR. PIERPONT DR. BROWN of Medway, DR. W. CHAANNING, REV. DR. PIERCE of Brookline, REV. MR. TAYLOR, HARRISON GRAY, Esq., RICHARD FLETCHER, Esq., L. M. SARGENT, Esq., were present.//MR. P. H. KEMPER, of Cottage Farm, near Cincinnati, received a letter dated South Hanover, IN, from his son, MR. JAMES S. KEMPER, describing a tornado which struck the town the 5th inst., about 6 o'clock. MR. YOUNG's store, MR. BISHOP's house, DR. MATTHEW's house, MR. CHEEVER's house, COL. MORROW's house, MR. BUTLER's house, and PROFESSOR NILES' house were severely damaged.//MR. LAMB, MR. CHRISTIAN KEENER, MR. D. POLLARD, and MR. BALTZER SCHAEFFER, upwards of 80 years old, addressed a 4th of July

WEEKLY MESSENGER OF THE GERMAN REFORMED CHURCH

Baltimore Temperance meeting. MR.J. AIKEN of PA could not attend.--"Temperance Herald."//**MONEYS**. REV. C. F. HOFFMEIER, from COL. G.MAYER 4, GERHART METZGER 1, DAVID LONGNECKER 1, C. F. HOFFMEIER 1, SAMUEL DORWART 50c.-By REV. J. REBOUGH, fromJOHN D KEEDY 2.-By JOHN HOSLER,(Westmoreland co.) from J. REED and SAMUEL BROWNELLER, each 2. From W. J. HOSLER 2.--By GEO. WEBER, Esq., from CHRISTIAN BERGER and CAPT. PETER AUNEWALT, each 2, and G. WEBER 1.--From MRS. LYDIA VAN DYKE 2. From JACOB ZIEGLER (Harrisburg,) 2.--By H.ERMENTROUT, from ELIJAH DECHERT, Esq.,G. & P. BUSHAR, H. ERMENTROUT, MISS CATHARINE ERMENTROUT, MISS ESTHER HIGH, each 2.--By REV. S. R. FISHER, from GEO. W. GRIMES, (Taneytown,) WM. HAUGH, ABRAHAM KRISE,SR., (Emmitsburg) each 2, REV. S.R. FISHER 1. REV. JOHN H. SMALTZ 2 50--send your account to WM. HEYSER,Esq.//Philadelphia Courier of last Saturday notes dedication of the Second Presby. Church by the REV. DR. CUYLER. DR. GREEN will preach his half-century sermon, and DR. JANEWAY officiate. An inscription reads: "In memory of the REVEREND GILBERT TENNENT, the first pastor of this church, whose Evangelical labours, in concert with those of the REV. GEORGE WHITFIELD, were divinely blessed..A. D. MDCCXLIII. He died MDCCLXIV, in the 43d year of his age." A splendid organ constructed, direction of MR. KNAUFF.

108. July 26, 1837/**MARRIED** In Cabarrus County, NC, the 4th inst., by REV. GRAEBER, REV. GEORGE BOGER to MISS ELIZABETH FILE.//The 22th (sic) April, at the Missionary Station, Creek Path, Cherokee Nation, by WILLIAM POTTER, MR. ELIAS BOUDINOT,a native Cherokee, to MISS DELIGHT SARGENT, of Pawlet,VT.//Near Jefferson, Md.,by REV. J.C. BUCHER, MR. JOSEPH MYERS,of Washington Co., Md., to MISS HARRIET ANN REBECCA LAKIN, of the former place.//**DIED** The 6th inst. at Shippensburg, DR. R. K. PEEBLES, formerly of Vandalia, IL.//In Lancaster,the 10th inst.,at the residence of the REV. MR. BRUNER, MRS. ELIZABETH HUNT,

WEEKLY MESSENGER OF THE GERMAN REFORMED CHURCH

of Carlisle,in the 74th year of her ago. (sic)// Near Middletown, Md., on the 15th inst., GRANDISON LIVINGSTON, infant son of MR. SAMUEL BOWLUS. //The 17th inst., MR. JAMES BOWDEN, aged citizen of Emmittsburg.//At Jefferson,Frederick Co., Md.,on the 2d inst. MRS. BARBARA, consort of MR. HENRY CRUM, in the 59th year of her age.// When WOOD, who committed suicide a few weeks since in jail at Keene, murdered BAKER, both were intoxicated.--"Providence Courier."

109. August 2, 1837//**MARRIED** In Greencastle by REV. J. REBOUGH,on the 17th ult., MR. LEWIS FETTERER, to MISS CATHARINE STOLTZ,of Wash. co.,Md. //By the same on the 20th inst., MR. JOHN STEELE to MISS ANN MARIA TALHELM, all of Franklin co., Pa.//In this place, on Tuesday the 25th inst. by the REV. MR. DENNY, DR. G. W. HART, of Syracuse N. Y., to MISS MARIA LOUISA, daughter of the late DR. J. BOWIE.//**DIED** Thursday evening last, in this Borough, MRS. SARAH CHAMBERS, relict of the late CAPT. BENJAMIN CHAMBERS, in the 78th year of her age.//In Philadelphia, on the 28th ult. WM. S. COXE, M. D. in the 48th year of his age.//**CONFESSED** "Many of our readers will recollect the name of JOHN R. BUZZEL, indicted and tried some two years and a half ago for the Convent Riot. He was acquitted upon his trial. We learn, that BUZZEL is since dead, and that upon his death bead he confessed himself to have been one who set fire to the Convent"-"Boston Atlas". //**FIRE** A violent storm passed over Hanover, Pa. about 5 o'clock Wednesday evening. During the storm, the barn of MR. HENRY BOYER, near Pigeon Hills, was struck by lightening and consumed, with nearly all its contents.//**ARRESTED** An individual named JOHN MILLER, formerly a resident of Pa., after giving payment for a pair of shoes a $10 note on the Bank of Baltimore, and being informed it was counterfeit, gave good money in its place, starting soon after for Wellsburg, lest suspicion might be excited. Inquiries were

WEEKLY MESSENGER OF THE GERMAN REFORMED CHURCH

made on the subject, leading to immediate pursuit and arrest.//**MONEYS RECEIVED** for the funds of the H. M. Society of the N. C. Classis, from the 12th of May to the present date, viz: REV. W. C. RANKIN, (life member,) $10; J. COULTER,$1; JACOB RAMSOUR, JR., 50c.; MICHAEL FINGER, 50c.; PETER FINGER, 50c.; SOLOMON RAMSOUR, 50c.; DANIEL FINGER, 50c.; J. CARPENTER, 50c.; A. H. SHUFORD, Esq.,$1; JACOB SHUFORD, JR., 50c.; DANIEL WHITENER, 50c.; MR. MOORE, 25c.; A. CORPENING, 50c.; MRS. ALEXANDER, 25C; A. ALEXANDER, 50c.; THOMAS JANES,$5; PETER WARLICH, 50c. From Wythe County, VA:--HENRY HOTTLE, 50c.; DR. J. STANGER, 50c.;//**DISTRESSING**. Early in the morning, ISAAC HOLLINGSHEAD a lad in the employment of MR. BARTON FOULKE, on his return home was attacked by a large dog belonging to JESSE HOGE, seized by the leg and drawn from his horse. His head and face were torn and mangled to such a degree he died almost instantly. He was about twelve years of age. An individual passing aloag (sic) some hours after, was also attacked by the same dog, which he kept from pouncing by means of a large club. The savage animal was shot during the day.--"St. Clairsville (OH) Gazette."

110. Aug. 9, 1837/**MARRIED** On Tuesday evening, 1st inst., by the REV. MR. DENNY, MR. JAMES S. BLACK, merchant, to MISS MARY, daughter of G. K. HARPER, Esq. all of this borough.//In this place on the 3d inst., by REV. B. S. SCHNECK, MR. JACOB MILLER, to MISS PHEBE ANN SHYER, both of Franklin county, Pa.//On Tuesday evening, 25th ult., by REV. J. SECHLER, MR. FREDERICK ELDER METZGER to MISS ELIZA ANN EMBICH, both of Hanover, Pa.//On Tuesday evening, 27th ult., by the same, DR. JOHNSON, of Littlestown, Adams county, to MISS LOUISA, daughter of MR. HENRY WIRT, of Hanover, Pa.//**DIED** Suddenly at his residence in Natchez, on the 14th ult., DOCTOR JAMES DENNY, son of the REV. DAVID DENNY of this place.//Near Hagerstown at his residence on Thursday the 20th

WEEKLY MESSENGER OF THE GERMAN REFORMED CHURCH

of July last, MR. HENRY M'LAUGHLIN, in the 62d year of his age.//MR. BADGER, late editor of the Christian Advocate, Weekly Messenger, and other newspapers, having been subject of late to partial derangements, has found asylum in the Hartford Retreat for the Insane. It is but a few months since Mr. B. lost his wife; he continues his occupation "for the benefit of his orphan children".//**LONGEVITY.** RICHARD TAYLOR, the oldest pensioner in Chelsea Hospital England, died on the 10th of June, aged 104. He was a drummer boy at the battle of Culloden in 1745; his last action was that at Alexandria in Egypt where SIR RALPH ABERCROMBIE fell.//**AN INCINDIARY.** Sixteen houses were destroyed by fire on Wednesday night in New-Haven. The fire commenced in the store of GARDNER MORSE, Chapel street, and extended into Orange street, and was stopped at the house of DYER WHITE. It broke out at three different places at the same time--"NY Express."//**MONEYS.** From ISRAEL HEITSHU (Taney-town) 2. From REV. DIETRICH WILLERS 2 50. From GEO. COOK, Esq., (Grencastle) 2. By J. WENNER, Esq.(Lovettsville) from PETER COST 5, WILLIAM WIRE 2, SAMUEL BECKER 2 JON. WENNER 1.--By REV. C. ZWISLER, from JOHN HARE, MICHAEL TROUTMAN, and JOSEPH KEISER, each 2, and REV. C. ZWISLER 4. - From SOLOMON MILLER 2. By JOHN KOOKEN from JAS. T. BLAIR 1 25. By GEO. BESORE from JACOB BESORE 2. By DANIEL SHAFFER, Esq., from GEO. H. MARTIN 2 50, THOMAS REYNOLDS 4 50. From GEO. S. EYSTER 4. and WILLIAM CISNA 3, SAMUEL PECKMAN 2.//GEORGE COOK, Esq., appointed Postmaster of the new Upton Post office between Mercersburg and Greencastle.

111. Aug. 16, 1837/**MARRIED** On the 8th inst. by REV. G. GLESSNER,at the residence of MARTIN NEWCOMER, Esq., MR. MELCHIOR SNIVELY, to MISS ELIZA NEWCOMER, all of Franklin co., Pa.//At Lebanon Pa. on the 13th inst., by REV. HENRY WAGNER MR. LEONARD NEGLY, to MISS PRISCILLA HAUER, all of that place.//On the 13th ult., at Marion, AL, by

WEEKLY MESSENGER OF THE GERMAN REFORMED CHURCH

the REV. MR. BAKER, DR. JOHN OSWALD, late of Baltimore, Md., to MISS JANETTA A. McROBERTS, of Prince Edward county, Va.//**DIED** Near Kutztown, Berks co., Pa. 23d July,of typhus fever, CHARLES FREDERICK, son of the REV. C. G. HERMAN, in the 14th year of his age.//Near Lebanon, on the 4th inst., MRS. HOFFER, relict of the late GEORGE HOFFER, in the 74th year of her age.//At Monongahela Washington co., Pa. July 28, JOHN H. RAIGUEL, son of ABRAHAM RAIGUEL of Lebanon county, Pa., in the 37th year of his age.//**LOST** REBECCA PLOTZ, aged about 73, who calls herself REBECCA LANDER, who was in a deranged state of mind, and who will be recognized by her white locks being shorn close, made her escape a few weeks since, from her husband, MR. PHILIP PLOTZ, at Marksborough, Warren county, NJ. She is supposed to be in the neighborhood of Easton, Penn.//Considerable excitement has prevailed since Wednesday morning last, in consequence of a robbery committed on Tuesday night at the dwelling of MR. A. W. STERLING, merchant,of this place, of about $18,000.--"York Pa. Gazette of the 1st inst."// **MONEYS RECEIVED** By REV. HENRY MILLER, from sundry persons $12 50. From REV. C. G. HERMAN 5. By DR. BENJ. WIESTLING, from MRS. LOUISA LOWMAN 5, JOHN HICKS 2 50, and B. WIESTLING 2 50. From REV. HENRY MILLER 4. From G. WEISER, Esq. 2. By GEORGE BESORE, from CHRISTIAN WELKER 4 and J. R. WELSH 2. By REV. J. W. HOFFMEIER, from DANIEL SNOOK and D. HILDEBRAND, each 2, and J. W. HOFFMEIER 1. From JAMES CHARITON 4. By H. ERMENTROUT from MISS C. COLEMAN 2, JACOB SEUDER 2, JOHN ECKERT 1. From MRS. SUSAN SLOAN 2. From DAVID CROUSE 2. From JOHN GILBERT [Waynesborough] 2, HENRY MILLER [Cook's Store] 2,

112. Aug. 23, 1837/**MARRIED** On Thursday, the 3d inst. by REV. J. SHOLL, MR. DAVID SNYDER to MRS. SUSANNAH CHARTERS, both of Landisburg, Pa.//**DIED** On Tuesday night, 15th inst., ALEXANDER COLHOUN, Esq., Cashier of the Chambersburg Bank, aged 53

WEEKLY MESSENGER OF THE GERMAN REFORMED CHURCH

years.//In York, Pa., the 25th ult., in the 71st year of her age, MRS. MAGDALENE GEISTWEIT, relict of the late REV. GEO. GEISTWEIT, minister of the GRC. She was afflicted with a wen of unusual size, attached to the left side of her face from which she suffered greatly toward the last, and which terminated her existance.//On the morning of the 10th inst, suddenly, at her residence in the same place in the 78th year of her age, ANNA MARIA WAGNER, relict of REV. D. WAGNER, for many years minister of the GRC in York, Pa.//**A LETTER** from REV. MR. GUTZLAFF dated Macao, Feb. 9, 1837 to the Sun. School Journal. There was trouble with the school. Chinese girls entrusted to MRS. GUTZLAFF went away as fast as they came. Afterwards, dreadful rumors of a barbarian daring to teach celestials subsided. There are now twenty-five children learning English, reading Christian books, and the Chinese New Testament. //Second annual meeting of the Society for the Diffusion of Useful Knowledge in China was held at No. 2, American Hong, Canton, on March1 10th. REV. MR. BRIDGEMAN and DR. PARKER, AM missionaries, took part. MR. JARDINE is President. The celebrated GUTZLAFF is one of the Secretaries. Also MR. BRIDGEMAN, and MR. MORRISON, son of the late REV. DR. MORRISON.--"Christian Intel."

113. Aug. 30, 1837/**MARRIED** At Welsh Run, on Tuesday, 8th inst., by the REV. MR. KENNEDY, DR. JOHN DUFFIELD to MISS MARTHA BLAIR all of Franklin county, Pa.//On the 23d inst., by the REV. MR. DUBBS, MR. WM. H. BLUMER, one of the editors of the "Friedensbote," of Allentown, to MISS MARY BIERY, (daughter of JOSEPH BIERY) of South-Whitehall, Lehigh county.//On the 22d inst. by the same, MR. JACOB HOEGH to MISS MATILDA CANDY, both of Millerstown.//On the same day, by the same, MR. GEORGE HAAF, of Lowell, to MISS ANNA STAFFERT of South-Whitehall.//**DIED** At the Glade the 18th of August, ANN ELIZABETH COCKY, infant daughter of REV. J. W. HOFFMEIER, aged 6 months.

WEEKLY MESSENGER OF THE GERMAN REFORMED CHURCH

//___, near Creagerstown, on the 16th of August, ELIZABETH JANE, second daughter of MR. MARTIN EICHELBERGER, aged 5 years.//___, at the residence of his brother, EDWARD COLEMAN, Esq. in the city of Philadelphia, on Friday, the 18th inst. WILLIAM COLEMAN, Esq. of Lancaster in the 62d year of his age.//GEN. JOHN FLOYD, many years a distinguished member of Congress, and Governor of VA, died lately at the Sweet Springs, in that state.//In Boalsburg, Centre county, Pa., August 11, DOCTOR THOMAS Z. COVERLY, in the 32d year of his age.//**A LETTER** from ERNST. WILHELM MUELLER, Sec'y. of the Rhinish Miss. Soc., regarding the sending of a misssionary to America.//**CHOLERA!** REV. MR. BREWER, American Missionary in Smyrna, writes, under date of May 24, The pestilence is sweeping the city and vicinity.

114. Sep. 6, 1837/**MARRIED** On the 23d ult. by REV. R. S. GRIER, MR. ANDREW REA, (merchant,) of Emmitsburg to MISS SARAH JANE MALONY of the same place//On the 29th ult. by REV. D. ZACHARIAS, MR. GEORGE W. LOCK to MISS REBECCA ANN GORDON, both of Jefferson, Va.//On the 22d ult., by REV. ISAAC GERHART, MR. JOHN MUMMERT, to MISS MARY GRIMES, all of Lykens Valley, Dauphin Co.//On the 29th, by the same, MR.JACOB DREVITZ, to MISS ANN MAYER, of Armstrong's Valley.//On the same day by same, MR. JOHN HECKERT, to MISS MARGARET TSIHOPP, (sic) all of Mahantongs Valley.//On the evening of the 26th inst.,by REV. E. HEINER, MR. WM. S. WONDERLY, of Philadelphia,to MISS ELEANOR P. daughter of the late E. CUMMINGS, Esq. this city.//On the 13th ult. near Middletown, Frederick county, Md., by REV. J. C.BUCHER, MR. GEORGE W. KOONTZ,to MISS REBECCA LONG all of Middletown Valley, Md.//**DIED** On the 7th ult., near Jefferson, Frederick county, Md., LEWIS HAMILTON, infant son of MR. JACOB FLOOK, in the 2d year of his age.//On the 21st ult., near Jefferson, Md., ELIZABETH ELEANOR daughter of MR. HENRY FEASTER, in the 2d year of her age.//Near Jefferson, Md.

after a painful illness, LLOYD W. L., youngest son of the late LLOYD LUCKETT, in the 13th year of his age.//On the 7th ult., in the 32d year of her age, MRS. MINERVA NEAL.//On the 26th inst., FRANCIS EPHRAIM, son PETER THOMAS, (sic) aged 5 years, 2 months and 22 days.//On the 25th ult., MR. JAMES KIRKER, of North Huntingdon township, put an end to his existance, by shooting himself through the head with a rifle. He was alone in the house, his wife and child being at her fathers, in the neighborhood; and it appears he sat upon the bed, placed the muzzle of the gun under his chin, and set it off with his toes. The deceased was a man in the prime of life, of rather intemperate habits, and doubtless committed the act in a fit of insanity.--"PA Argus."//**ACCIDENT** The Hon. CHARLES J. KILGOUR, Judge of the Montgomery County Court, lost his life a few days since. He was on his return home to Rockville, Md., from one of his farms near Leesburg, Va., riding in a barouche, when, it is supposed, his horse took fright and ran off, and he was thrown out, his skull fractured. The accident occurred near Poole's Ville.//**ACCIDENT** On Thursday, the 9th ult., MR. SAMUEL RUMBAUGH, son of MR. WILLIAM RUMBAUGH, aged 21 years went over the Kiskiminetas river, to bring home the horses and took his gun along to shoot fish in the river. After having shot several times, he set his gun among some old salt barrels which were lying on the shore and went for the horses. On his return he caught the gun which discharged fatally.//**A FIRE BY LIGHTNING** On the 30th ult. the Swiss Barn of JACOB GILBERT, Esq., near Millersburg, Dauphin county was struck by lightning, and burnt to the ground.//Readers will remember, that some weeks ago, we published an account of a robbery at the house of MR. A. W. STERLING, merchant. We have seen in various papers a paragraph, originating, we believe, in the Miner's Journal at Pottsville stating that MR. STERLING had been arrested at Reading. We deem it due to correct this report,

WEEKLY MESSENGER OF THE GERMAN REFORMED CHURCH

which is altogether untrue and unfounded, and to state that he is now doing business at his old stand.--"Gazette. York, Pa., August 29".

115. Sep. 13, 1837//**MARRIED** In Carlisle, Pa., on Tuesday morning, 29th ult., by the REV. W. T. SPROLE, REV. WILLIAM FULLER, pastor of the Presbyterian church, Conneaut, OH, to MISS MARGARETTA KNOX, daughter of the late JOSEPH KNOX, Esq., of the former place.//In Franklin county, Pa. on the 27th ult., by the REV. D. G. BRAGONIER, MR. ISAAC SUFFICOOL to MISS MARY, daughter of JOSEPH PHENICA, Esq.//On the 5th inst., by the REV. MR. WATSON, MR. ANDREW MEHAFFEY of Lancaster city to MISS ELIZABETH, daughter of JOHN B. McPHERSON, Esq., of Gettysburg.//In NY, 29th ult., by the REV. DR. MILNOR, the REV. ALFRED LOUDERBACK, of Sunbury, P.,to MISS SUSAN OPHELIA HORTON, of NY. //By REV. GEO. A. LEOPOLD, August 17, MR. GEORGE DANNER to MISS SARAH JORDAN, both of Augusta county, Va.//On the 22d August, by the same, MR. HENRY WYNANT to MISS LYDIA, daughter of the REV. JNO. BROWN, of Rockingham co.,Va.//On Thursday last, by REV. D. ZACHARIAS, MR. FREDERICK KEEFER to MISS ELIZABETH HIMBURY both of Frederick, Md. //**DIED** Suddenly on the evening of the 6th inst. at his residence, near York, Pa., MR. WILLIAM JOHNSTON, in the 64th year of his age. (Communicated.)//CHRISTIAN D. WOLFF, Esq. departed this life on the morning of the second inst, at his residence in Martinsburg, Va. His afflictions were painful and protracted. His death was the more distressing because he was in the prime of life, being about 38 years of age. He has left an aged father and mother, an affectionate wife, and six helpless children. On Sabbath afternoon his remains were followed to the grave by a large concourse.//On the 31st ult., CHARLES EDWARD, infant son of EZRA DOLL, aged three years, six months, and twenty-seven days.//**MELANCHOLY DEATH** MR. EDWARD WEBSTER, a respectable young man living in the vicinity of Richmond (IN) and on the

eve of being married, was found dead about four miles from that place, supposed to have fallen from his horse.//**MONEYS RECEIVED.** By EMANUEL THOMAS, from ANN CATH. THOMAS, 2. From SOLOMON HAMER, 2 25. By JAMES WISEMAN, Esq. from DAVID SMITH, 2 50, and DANIEL TUSSEY, 2 50. From COL. JACOB MYERS, (Martinsburg, Va.) 10 00. By C. F. HOFFMEIER, from JOHN ECKMAN, 2. By REV. G. A. LEOPOLD, from PETER PRINCE, FREDERICK HOFFMAN, CHRISTIAN HICKLE, JOHN PENNYWITT, JACOB JORDAN, JACOB BURNER and B. HAMMOND, each 2, and G. A. LEOPOLD, 5. By J. C. BUCHER, from GEO. RUPP, 4. By R. ROEMER, from ADAM KNEPPER, 2. Received for "Der Herold," one dollar from FRED. MECHTLY, Nittany Valley.//The REV. JACOB HELFFENSTEIN, of Allentown, has accepted a call to the first Free Presby. church, NY city.//Papers of the present week have announced the death of REV. H. G. O. DWIGHT Missionary at Symrna. He embarked for his work in (sic) January 7th, 1830, and devoted himself, in the first instance, to an exploring tour through Armenia and adjacent countries with MR. SMITH. Since the above was set in type the following has been received:---A letter has been received from REV. H. G. O. DWIGHT, Missionary of the A. B. C. F. M. at Constantinople, stating that his wife and one of his children died of the plague, in the early part of July - the child on the sixth - the mother two days after. The latest date in the letter is July 12th. MR. DWIGHT was then in quarantine, and well. The date of the account from the English paper not being given, there may be a mistake.--"Christian Intel."//We learn on good authority that MARCUS C. HOKE merchant of Lincolnton, N. C. was killed in an affray by MR. LOGAN HENDERSON on Saturday last--the death wound was given with a " Bowie Knife." We are also informed that MR. HENDERSON acted in self-defense.--"Western Carolinian."

116. Sep. 20, 1837/**MARRIED** On the 31st ult. by the REV. MR. ALBERT, MR. DAVID SHULL, of New

WEEKLY MESSENGER OF THE GERMAN REFORMED CHURCH

Chester, (Pine-town,) to MISS SARAH EHRHART, of Hamilton township, Adams Co.//The 31st of Aug. by the REV. A. L. HERMAN, MR. CHARLES W. PORTER, to MRS. ELLEN J. DEISCHER, both of Maidencreek, Berks Co.//On Saturday last, by the REV. GERMAN, MR. SAMUEL REICHENBAUCH, to MISS ANNA DANY, and MR. CHARLES DAUBERT, to MISS ELIZABETH REINBOLD, all of Upper Milford, Lehigh county.//On the 5th inst., by the REV. MR. DUBBS, MR. CHARLES WEIDE, to MISS SARAH KERSCHNER both of South Whitehall, Lehigh Co.//On the 3d inst., by the same, MR. CHARLES GUTH, of South Whitehall, to MISS MARIA MILLER of Macungie.//Sunday evening the 27 ult., by REV. AUGUSTUS PAULI, MR. LEWIS BECKHART, to MRS. SUSAN BICKEL, both of Reading.//On the 22d ult., in Lincoln Co., N. C., by the REV. J. G. FRITCHY, MR. MAXWELL WARLICK, to MISS CATHARINE M., only daughter of JOHN COULTER, Esq.//On the 7th inst. in Baltimore by REV. J. G. MORRIS, MR. JOSEPH GARRETSON, of York, to MISS ELLEN, daughter of JOHN M. EBERMAN, Esq., of Harrisburg.//On the 7th inst., by REV. S. R. FISHER, MR. SAMUEL STRICKLAND, to MISS MARGARET STEM, all of Frederick county, Md.//**DIED** The morning of the 27th ult. at his residence in Hereford, Baltimore county, REVD. ANDREW HEMPHILL, for many years an eminent itinerant minister of the M. E. Church, aged 60//On the 17th inst. in this borough, JOHN FRIDINGER, at an advanced age.//**ACCIDENT** About nine o'clock on Friday morning, the 8th inst, a scaffold nearly forty feet high in the new Catholic Church, at the corner of Court and Dean, Brooklyn, gave way with thirteen carpenters, who were working on it. JOHN FISHER, a man advanced in life, and having a large family, was killed on the spot, his head being literally smashed to pieces. Another man, named DUFF, had both his thighs broken, and FINN, GOOLEY and COOKE, each had a leg broken. CRAWFORD had his face frightfully cut. COMERFORD, BROWN and CORIGAN, escaped with little or no injury; but the other five were so badly injured as to leave little hopes for their recovery. Last winter, when the walls were nearly ready to put the roof on, the whole building fell to the ground.--'Jour. of Com."// **MONEYS RECEIVED.** From DAVID GROSSMAN 2, JACOB HECK (Gettysburg) 4. By REV. A. P. FREEZE, from D. BULGER 2, and JOHN HARNISH (Hollidaysburg) 2. **//DELEGATES** to Synod: Ministers. Primarii: M. BRUNER, H. B. SCHAFFNER, T. H. LEINBACH. Alternates: P. MOYER, D. HERTZ, A. L. HERMAN. Elders. Primarii: DR. H. SCHNECK, JACOB SWOPE, G. MATZ. Alternates: R. GOSHEN, J. WEIDNER, H. FEASTER. Brother BOSSLER having presented his credentials from the Classis of MD was received as a member. BROTHER BERKY obtained an honorable dismission.

117. Sep. 27, 1837/**MARRIED** On the 31st ult. at Winchester, Va. by REV. D. H. RIDDLE, of Pittsburg, Pa., REV. HENRY R. WILSON of Shippensburg, Penn., to MISS SARAH ELIZABETH, third daughter of MR. JAMES LITTLE, dec'd., of Winchester. //In Franklin co., Pa., on the 27th ult., by REV. D. G. BRAGONIER, MR. ISAAC SUFFICOOL, to MISS MARY, daughter of JOSEPH PHENICO, Esq.//The death of REV. H.G.O. DWIGHT of Constantinople, is contradicted by letter from the Missionary Rooms at Boston; but the same letter announces the death of his wife and one child by the plague.//**FUNDS** from the Home Missionary Society of the NC Classis of the GRC, viz: JACOB BARRIER, DANIEL LEONARD, MR. LOCKE, ANDREW SHUFORD, E. P. COULTER, JOHN REINHAARDT, MICHAEL HOKE, Esq., JOHN WILFANG, Esq., JOHN MOTZ, PETER HARMAN, MRS. L. WILFANG, GEORGE IKERD, GEORGE M. MOTZ, each 50. JOHN C. BARNHARDT, DAVID CORREL, DR. A. RAMSOUR, JOHN RAMSOUR, (T.), each 1 00. COL. JOHN HOKE, REV. JOHN G. FRITCHEY, DAVID RAMSOUR, (M.), each 2 00. JACOB RAMSOUR, (M.) 3 00.//**MONEYS RECEIVED** By JOHN BROWN, from DANIEL WHITMORE, JOHN BROWN, each $2; by MARTIN RECKENBAUGH, Esq. from JOSHUA HOFFMAN, WM. STONEBRAKER, JACOB SUMMERS, S. J. DOWNEY, HENRY SHAFER, DAN'L SCHNEBLY, Esq. each $2, and ANDREW KERSHNER, Esq., JOHN ADAMS, each

$4; by HUGH SHAW, Esq. from PETER OGLE, $1; by JOHN B. WELTY, Esq. (Boonsboro) from JACOB MYERS $1, and JOHN NICHODEMUS, JACOB NICHODEMUS, and J. B. WELTY, each $2. from JOHN HEINER, JR. 2, JOSEPH BURG 2.//**LETTERS** GEO. KLUTS, R. K. WRIGHT

118. Oct. 11, 1837/**MARRIED** On the 10th ult. in Adams County, Pa. by REV. JACOB BEAR, MR. JOSEPH BLACK, of MD, to MISS ELIZABETH MOOSE, of Adams County.//On the 24th ult. by the same, MR. PETER FEHL, to MISS ELIZABETH SILICK, of Adams County. //Near Green Castle, on Thursday the 7th of September, by REV. JOHN REBAUGH, MR. JOHN MUTERSBAUGH, to MISS SARAH BRACHE of Franklin county. //In Green Castle, on Thursday, the 21st, by the same, MR. WILLIAM BOYERS to MISS ANN MARIA PHEASANT, of Washington Co., Md.//In Green Castle, on Sunday, the 24th, by the same, MR. JONATHAN GOWAN to MISS ELIZA HATHFIELD of Hagerstown, Md. //On Wednesday evening last, by the REV. RICHARD BOND, MR. MATTHEW SMITH, to MISS ELEANOR FINDLAY, youngest daughter of COL. JOHN FINDLAY, Post Master, all of this place.//**DIED** Menallen township, Adams Co., on the 29th ult., ANNA MARY HUSTON, in the 39th year of her age.//On the 27th ult., at the Glade, MRS. ELIZABETH, widow of the late GEORGE ZIMMERMAN, and mother-in-law of the REV'D. J. W. HOFFMEIER, in the 55th year of her age.//At the Orange county, NY, Circuit, JAMES DECKER was tried on an indictment for enticing from her parents without their consent, and marrying a girl under fourteen years of age, named MARGARET RELYEA. This offence is punishable by imprisonment in the State Prison for a term not exceeding three years or confinement in county jail for a term not exceeding one year, or a fine of one thousand dollars, or by both of the latter. The prisoner is a young man about nineteen years of age, and probably not aware of the nature of the offence. He wept freely while the jury were out; the parties reside in the village of Warwick and from the testimony it ap-

peared that the bride was a willing victim. On the morning of her elopement she proceeded on foot with her intended and his sister, from Warwick to Edenville, with the view of having the marriage solemnized before ESQUIRE HOUSTON. That gentleman being absent from home, the bride suggested going on to Amity. The jury returned a verdict of guilty.//**MONEYS RECEIVED** By REV. J. SECHLER, from CHRISTIAN WIRT 2. By D. H. DOLL, from JOSEPH PALSGROVE 62 1/2, D. REEL 2.25, C. D. WOLFF 2, JONATHAN CUSHWA 1, and D. M. CUSHWA 1.50. From GEO. WOLFF, Esq. 2. By REV. HENRY WILLIARD, from JOHN WILLIARD, JUN. 2.

119. Oct. 18, 1837/**MARRIED** In Green Castle, on the 5th inst. by REV. J. REBAUGH, MR. JOHN RAUM, to MISS NANCY STEPHENS, of Sharpsburg, Washington county, Md.//On Thursday last, by the same, MR. HENRY LAWVER, to MISS NANCY HEATH, of Washington county, Md.//On the same day by the same, MR. JOHN HERSHBERGER to MISS MARY SMITH.//On the same day, by the same, MR. JOSEPH CUNNINGHAM, to MISS ELIZABETH SPICKLER, all of Washington county, Md.//**DIED** In Green Castle, on the 30th ult. MR. JACOB STINER, in the 70th year of his age, for 40 years a respectable inhabitant of this county. He was a son of REV. CONRAD STINER, one of the earliest ministers of the Reformed Church in America.//SAMUEL JAUDON, Esq., late Cashier of the Bank of the US, has been appointed agent of that institution, to reside at London, and JOS. COWPERWAITE, Esq., been elected Cashier to supply the vacancy.//**SHIPWRECK.** The Ship *Amelia Thompson,* from NY, reports that on the 23d ult., in lat. 32 23, long. 73, fell in with a vessel bottom up, on which there were two men in a very exhausted state; it was the *Pennsylvania,* of Saybrook, Williams; (sic) she sailed from NY on the 10th ult. with twenty-one passengers, and a crew of six; she capsized the night of the 16th. Captain and crew on deck, supposed to be immediately lost, as well as seven passengers drowned

below: the remainder survived in the hold with the cargo until the succeeding Monday, when WILSON and DAUGHERTY, by great exertion, effected their escape. In the hope of finding some of the rest alive, CAPTAIN T. sent the boat to scuttle the vessel; they found one man alive, but quite senseless; the others floating around, all dead. This man was taken on board the *Amelia,* where he expired on the second day. WILSON and DAUGHERTY are on board the *Amelia* quite recovered.//On account of travel distance, due to the removal of the Seminary from York to Mercersburg, the following were elected at the meeting in Sunbury.

LEWIS DENIG, Esq. in the room of JACOB SPANGLER, Esq.
J. E. BRADY, Esq. vice W. D. GOBRECHT.
JACOB HOSSLER -   - M. DANNER.
DR. J. H. HOFIUS - JNO. HARTMAN.
D.CROUSE,Waynesboro', W. WAGNER.
STEPHEN KEEFER -   - GEORGE KING. (sic)
Remainder of the old Board continue in office.

120. Oct. 25, 1837/**MARRIED** By REV. DAVID DENNY on the 17th inst., W. MILEY AMMONS of OH,to MISS MARGARET C. GABBY of this vicinity.//At the residence of REVD. CHARLES G. HERMAN near Cootstown Pa., on the 12th inst. by REVD. AUGUSTUS L. HERMAN, MR. WILLOUGHBY FOGLE, of Lehigh Co. to MISS MARIA F., daughter of REVD. CHARLES G. HERMAN.// On the 12th inst., by REV. MR. SECHLER, MR. SAMUEL P. YOUNG, to MISS MARGARET E. WILL, both of Adams county.//**AN ACCIDENT** on Section 11 of the Gettysburg Rail Road on Monday last, resulted in the death of WM J. SEABROOLS, a sub-contractor, and an Irish laborer. Whilst the hands were at work in a pit, a large quanity of dirt unexpectedly fell in on the dec'd; killing the laborer instantaneously. Mr. S. survived about 3 hours. "Gettysburg Star."//**MONEYS RECEIVED.** By REV. S. B. LEITER, from DANIEL BESORE 2, MESSRS. LEPPO, WISE, and D. LEITER, (Mansfield) 5. By REV. J. SECHLER, from CHARLES WINEBRENNER, JACOB FORNEY,

WEEKLY MESSENGER OF THE GERMAN REFORMED CHURCH

JOHN FLICKINGER, JACOB WIRT, each 2. From HENRY SHRIVER 2. From DANIEL H. SCHNEBLY (Bakersville) 2. By D. WEIDNER, from MRS. ADELINE SCHNECK 2. //**PRESIDENT'S APPOINTMENTS, as Consuls** HENRY E. COLEMAN, for Tobasco in MEX. WM. P. GILLIA___, for Monterey, MEX. JOSE MARIA CANTANOS, for San Blas in MEX. FERDINAND GARDNER, for Cape Verde Islands. EDWARD F. RIVINUS, for Dresden, Saxony. JOHN M. MARTSON, for Palermo, Sicily. JOSEPH F. SANCHEZ, Marshall of Eastern FL.//**LETTERS** DANIEL LANTZ, JUN., HENRY C. NEINSTEDT, JOHN WILFONG.

121. Nov. 1, 1837/**MARRIED** On Wednesday morning 25th ult., by REV. DAVID DENNY, REV. BENJAMIN KURTZ, editor of Lutheran Observer, to MISS MARY COLHOUN, daughter of the late ALEXANDER COLHOUN, Esq., of this place.//Near Shippensburg, on the 26th ult.by REV. W. C. BENNET, MR. BENJAMIN RAMP to MISS SARAH MAPPS, all of Cumberland, co. Pa. (sic).//On the 17th ult., by REV. MR. SMITH, MR. SAMUEL SADLER, of Adams co.to MISS NANCY AMANDA, daughter of FRANCIS LEAS, Esq. of Littlestown.// On the 19th inst.by REV. MR. FOERSCH MR. JOHN P. STALLINGS,of Washington City, to MISS C. WILHELMINA SEYFFERLY of Emmittsburg, Md. //On the 15th inst. by REV. MR. ZACHARIAS, MR. OTHO REAL, of Frederick County, to MISS CATHARINE MARY, daughter of MR. JOHN HANE, of Frederick City, Md.//On the 15th of October, at Point of Rocks, Frederick county, Md., by REV. DANIEL FEETE, MR. JOHN RUSSEL to MISS CATHARINE R. SMITH, all of Loudon county, Va.//**DIED** Recently at Mobile of Bilious (sic) Fever, REV. WHEELOCK S. STONE, in the 30th year of his age, formerly of Northumberland, Pa. //At Burkettsville Frederick county, Md., on the 20th of October, MR. JACOB RAVERTZ, in the 74th year of his age.//Near Burkettsville the 19th of October, MARGARET ANN E., daughter of MR. JOHN SMITH, in the 3d year of her age.//Near Middletown, Md. the 29th of September, 1837, JOHN, 3d son of MR. JOHN MICHAEL, aged 6 years, 8 months and 4 days.//At his residence in Antrim township

WEEKLY MESSENGER OF THE GERMAN REFORMED CHURCH

on Thursday morning last, MR. JACOB SNIVELY.//We learn that MR. H. B. CROOM, who with his entire family perished by the wreck of the *Home*, was a member of the Lyceum of Natural History in this city. He was a resident of Charleston, but being in feeble health spent his summers at the North. MR. KENNEDY, a member of the Sophomore Class in Yale, was on his way to his home in Charleston. REV. GEORGE COWLES, who also perished was pastor of a Congregational Church in Danvers, Mass. His lady was a sister of REV. MR. ADAMS of the Broom street church in this city, and daughter of the Preceptor of Phillips Academy, Andover. CAPTAIN ALFRED HILL,of Portsmouth, secured his wife to a plank, which overturned in the breakers, and she was lost.-"N. Y. Journal of Commerce."//The Ship *Susquehanna,* from Philadelphia for Liverpool, captured by Pirates, off the Capes of the Delaware.--**Passengers:** M. HUMPHREY, lady, two children and servant; ANN RAWLE, MARY W. RAWLE, HENRY MARTIN, RACHEL SHARPE, HENRY C. CORBITT, EDWARD PLEASANT of Philadelphia; ESTHER HOPPIN, of Providence, R. I MARY ANN and ANNA REILLY, Cincinnati; JAMES SAUL, New Orleans; WM. H. GRAY, of Norfolk, Va.; WM. B. McCRONE, of New Castle, Del; HENRY FOX, of Bristol, Eng: 40 in steerage. A man named MITCHELL is the leader; he is 6 feet 2 inches high stoutly made, has lost one eye and has a large scar on his throat. For two years previous to March last, he was an inmate of the Penitentiary in this city. The other named BRENNER has also been in the Penitentiary; he has a family, we understand, at Kensington. COMMODORE RIDGELY despatched *Porpoise* Brig of War in pursuit, and the Cutter *Galiatin* of this port, with the following officers. Lieutenants, J. M. DALE, Commander, ARTHUR LEWIS, EDMUND BYRNE; Sailing Master, WILLIAM TATUM; Passed Midshipman, CARTER B. POINDEXTER, S. DECATUR HURST, D. ROSS CRAWFORD,(of Chambersb'g); WILLIAM WATERS,Boatswain; Midshipman, ST. GEORGE CALLENDER NOLAND; ALEXANDER RUSSEL, Gunner.--"Philadelphia Inquirer."

WEEKLY MESSENGER OF THE GERMAN REFORMED CHURCH

CAPT. DRINKER of the ship *Girard*, from Liverpool did not see or hear anything of the piracy until he was informed that the pilot boat *Mary Ann* had brought a report. **Crew and passengers.** THOMAS B. CROPPER, Captain; THOMAS WAYNE, Philadelphia, First Mate; JOHN WILLIAMS, NY, Second Mate; THEOPHILUS H. SWAIN, Philadelphia, Carpenter; THEODORE C. MYRIC, Philadelphia, Sail Maker; SAMUEL KEEN, Pa., First Steward; LEHMAN FITZGERALD, Philad., Second Steward; JOSEPH HOLLAND, Philad. First Cook; JAMES DUNN, Philadephia, Second Cook. Seamen--WILLIAM SMITH, NY; ROBERT LEWIS, Philad; GEORGE FOXWELL, Md.; JAS. WILLIAMS, NY; MERRIT SHECKELS, Baltimore; WM. R. FLOYD, Mass.; CHARLES SQUIRE, NY; FRED'K. CLUBB, Va.; WM. MASSY, Philad. JOSEPH D. NASON, ME; JAMES HALL, Philad.; THOMAS HEWITT, N. Y.; FRANCIS WILLIAMS, NY; JOHN BROWN, New Orleans; SAMUEL BARTLETT, ME. Boys-GEORGE C. GRAHAM, Easton, Md.; JOHN ROBERTS, WILLIAM SEYMOUR, HENRY COPES. Steerage. HENRY JACKSON, JACOB ROBB, ANDREW KAIGN, JAS. KEANEDY, wife and two children, JAMES MURRAY, ELIZABETH M'GILLAN, MICHAEL SMITH, MARY MONTGOMERY, JOHN IRWIN, MARY CASSADY, ROBT. SWAN, ANDREW LONG, DAVID LAIRD, wife and two children, RICHARD DOLLAND, ISABELLA RICHARDSON, ROBT. CAMPBELL, MARGARET ROACH, JOHN M'PHELLAMY, WILLIAM MARSHALL, JOHN SEWELL, JOHN CHAMBERS, FLEMING WILSON, MICHAEL CARNEY, wife and infant, W. S. DALGREW, STEWART ELLISON, JAS. M'FALL, ROBT. PIGGFORD, PETER DONAGHUE, CHARLES HENRY, WM. NIMMO, wife and child, JAMES LYNN, WM. CLAIR, 2 unknown.--"Philadelphia Ledger of yesterday." Lewis, Del., H. F. RODNEY writes to MR. J. COFFEE that pilots, MR. JAMES M. WEST and MR. EDWARD MAUL, report the ship captured.//**MONIES.** From REV. J. W. HAMM $2.50, by REV. S. GUTELIUS, from MRS. WM. McCLELLAN $4; by GEO. BESORE, from JOHN LECRONE $2, and JACOB R. WELSH $2; by REV. B. C. WOLFF, from PETER SNIDER (Easton) $2 in advance; by H. ERMENTROUT, from SAMUEL BOYER, of Boyerstown $2; from WM. BERRY $2; by M. KEEFER; from DR. W. HENDEL $5, MISS HANNAH KRAUSER $2.

WEEKLY MESSENGER OF THE GERMAN REFORMED CHURCH

122. Nov. 8, 1837/**MARRIED** On Thursday the 19th ult., by REV. DAVID M'KINNEY, MR. JOHN IRVIN, JR. of Nelson county, KY to MISS ANN H., daughter of REV. JAMES LINN of Bellefonte, Pa.//In York, Pa., 2d week in October, by REV. JONATHAN OSWALD, REV. SOLOMON OSWALD of Boonsboro', Md., to MISS SUSAN SMYSER, only daughter of HENRY SMYSER, Esq., of the former place.//By REV. J. BEAR, on the 21st ult., MR. JOSIAH FICKES, to MISS ELIZABETH ANN DORNARICE, all of Adams county Pa.//By the same, on the 2d inst., MR. JOHN FOTE, JR., to MISS SUSAN STALLSMITH, all of Adams county, Pa.//**DIED** On the 13th inst., CATHARINE, youngest daughter of WALTER KEMP, Fred'k Co., Md., aged 12 years, 6 months and 14 days. For 8 months of her life, she labored under the influence of a complicated disorder which baffled human skill, and for the last 5 months she was entirely confined to her bed. The groans and shrieks of the sufferer, occasioned by intense bodily pains are impressed upon those who visited her in her sickness.//On Saturday afternoon week, a daughter of MR. SAMUEL DIEHL, aged about six years, who was playing about a press, where they were busied in making cider, put her hand in to take an apple when the nut caught it, and drew in her arm. Before the horse could be checked, it was horribly mangled till above the elbow.--Gangrene having taken place, the arm was amputated on Thursday last, by DR. BERLUCHY, of this place, assisted by DR. STEWARD, of Petersburg. Strong hopes are entertained of her recovery.--"Gettysburg Sentinel."

123. Nov. 15, 1837/**MARRIED** Thursday evening 2d inst., by REV. MR. HEINER, MR. GEORGE C. RODENMEYER to MISS MARTHA ANN, second daughter of MR. JOHN F. COOK, all of Baltimore.//In this place, on Thursday evening last, by REV. B. S. SCHNECK, MR. DANIEL RHOADS, of Adams county, Pa. to MISS MARY SHOOP, of Washington county, Md.//At the same time, by the same, MR. ABRAHAM LEHMAN, to MISS MARY COUTER, all of Chambersburg.//Thursday

WEEKLY MESSENGER OF THE GERMAN REFORMED CHURCH

the 26th October, by REV. MR. HELFENSTEIN, MR. GEORGE ALBERT, to MISS LOUISA ANN, daughter of MR. JACOB POWLES all of Hagerstown.//In Cavetown on the 5th ult.by REV. JOHN P. KLINE, MR. GEORGE FOCKLERto MISS MARGARET MORGAN, all of Cavetown. **//DIED** On Friday the 3d inst., at his residence in the city of Frederick, after an illness of a few days, MR. VALENTINE J. BRUNNER, in the 41st year of his age.**//ARSON** commenced in the stable of MR. REDGRAVE, which with six valuable horses, were burned. The fire communicated with buildings on Spring court which were destroyed. The dwelling of MR. L. TAYLOR, with nearly its whole contents, were consumed. An attempt was made on Monday morning to set fire to the Chronicle office, but it was discovered in time to prevent serious damage.//KEOKUCK, BLACK HAWK, and the principal Indian chiefs, with their squaws and papooses, will visit the National Theatre this evening.--"Courier and Enquirer."

124. Nov. 22, 1837/**MARRIED** On the 5th inst. by REV. MR. ALBERT, MR. JACOB BASHOAR, to MISS EVE STONESIFER--both of the neighborhood of Littlestown.//The 13th inst. by REV. C.P. KRAUTH, D.D., REV. D. F. BITTLE of Augusta County, Va. to MISS LOUISA C. KRAUTH of Gettysburg.//On the 2d inst. by REV. MR. KELLER, MR. DAVID CAMP to MISS SARAH BUCHER--both of Cashtown, Adams county.// On the 9th inst. by the same, MR. JACOB MARK, of Cashtown, to MISS LYDIA FISSLE, of Cumberland township, Adams Co.//On the 10th inst. by same, MR. ADAM EPPLY, Merchant, to MISS JANE, daughter of REV. MR. GRIER, all of Adams Co., Pa.//In Rowan county, N. C. the 14th of September last by REV. PHILIP A. STROBEL, REV. SAMUEL ROTHROCK, Pastor of the Lutheran church Salisbury, N. C., to MISS AMELIA AREY, daughter of PETER AREY, Esq.//The seventh inst., by the REV. P. SAHM, St. Thomas, Franklin county, MR. JOHN KEMMERER, to MISS ANN MAUCK, both of McConnellsburg, Bedford county.// Near Sharpsburg, on the 8th inst. MR. EZRA J.

WEEKLY MESSENGER OF THE GERMAN REFORMED CHURCH

SNYDER, to MISS SARAH ANN STAUBS, both of Washington county, Md.//At Lancaster, (Pa.) on the 1st inst. WILLIAM B. FORDNEY, Esq., to ELLEN, daughter of WM. JENKINS, Esq. both of that city. //On the 7th inst. THOMAS E. FRANKLIN, Esq. to SERENA ANGELICA, daughter of GEO. MAYER, Esq., both of Lancaster.//At Harrisburg, Pa., on the 2nd inst. REV. JOHN WINNEBRENNER, to MISS MARY MITCHELL, both of that place.//On the 5th inst. by REV. MR. GEO. WACK, MR. LAWRENCE NUSS to MISS VERONICA RUTH of Montgomery County.//On the same day by the same, MR. WILLIAM BEYER to MISS ELIZABETH CASSEL all of Worcester,Montgomery county. //On Thursday the 9th, by the same, MR. SAMUEL BOAZ, to MISS SARAH KNIPE, all of Gwynedd, Montgomery county.//On the 12th inst.by REV. H. GERHARD, MR. JACOB SHULL of Upper Salford township, Montgomery county, to MRS. CATHARINE HEISLER, of Milford township, Bucks county.//**DIED** Danville, Ky, on November 2d, in the 26th year of her age, MRS. FRANCES B. YOUNG, consort of REV. JOHN C. YOUNG, President of Centre College, and eldest daughter of the late JOSEPH CABELL BRECKENRIDGE. //**FROM NOV. MISSIONARY HERALD** In Greece--MESSRS. HOUSTON and LEYBURN have removed from Scio, to Mane, or Sparta. Odessa--As the result of the labours of MR. SCHAUFFLER, a powerful work of grace is advancing here. From Constantinople---August 1. The health of MR. DWIGHT and his three surviving children is good.

125. Nov. 29, 1837/**MARRIED** On Thursday the 9th inst., by REV. MR. GREENLEAF, EDWARD B. GRUBB, Esq. of Mount Hope, Lancaster county, to MISS EUPHEMIA B. second daughter of ISAAC B. PARKER, Esq. of Carlisle.//On Thursday last, in Harrisburg, MR. GEO. AUGHINBAUGH, of Carlisle, to MISS ANN MYTINGER, of Harrisburg.//On Monday evening last, by REV. MR. LIPSCOMB, DR. ANDREW HETICH, of Bucyrus, OH, (lately of Chambersburg) to MISS AMELIA FLANAGAN, daughter of JNO. FLANAGAN, Esq. of Waynesborough.//On Wednesday morning last, by

WEEKLY MESSENGER OF THE GERMAN REFORMED CHURCH

the REV. MR. BUCHANAN, MR. F. COOPER,merchant of Pittsburg to MISS LUCRETIA B. FLANAGAN, daughter of JNO. FLANAGAN, Esq. of Waynesborough.//Thursday last, by Rev. J. N. HOFFMAN, MR. JEREMIAH KEEFER, to MISS HANNAH KEEFER.//On Tuesday last, by the same, MR. JAMES DOUGHERTY to MISS SUSANNA ZIEGLER, all of this county.//On the 14th inst. by REV. MR. KELLER, MR. WM. BARNHEISEL to MISS CATHARINE, youngest daughter of REV. J. W. HEIM, both of Perry County.//On the 16th inst. by REV. MR. HARKEY, REV. THEOPHILUS J. STORKE, of Winchester, Va., to MISS MARY JANE LYNCH, of Frederick county, Md.//**DIED** In Philadelphia on Friday, Nov. 17, REV. JAMES PATTERSON, in the 57th year of his age, 23 years pastor of the Presby. church in the Northern Liberties.//At his residence, near Jefferson, Frederick county, Md. on Saturday evening last, JOHN COST, Esq. at an advanced age.//The high constable arrested six for the blood spilt in Lower Canada between the government and the party of MR. PAPINEAU. MESSRS. ANDRE OUIMET, president of "fils de la liberte," J. DUBEC, FRANS TRAVENIER, GEO. De BOUCHERVILLE, advocate,DR. SIMARD, and a student at law, named LEBLANC. Not served: DR. O'CALLAGHAN, THOMAS S. BROWN, RODOLPHE DESRIVIERES and OVIDE PERRAULT.

126. Dec. 6, 1837/**MARRIED** On the 28th inst. by REV. H. R. WILSON, MR. JOHN B. DUNCAN, of Southampton Township, to MISS MARGARETTA CRISWELL, second daughter of MR. JOHN CRISWELL.//Thursday the 23d ult.,by REV.D.DENNY, MR. GEORGE LINHEART to MISS MARY SIMMS, both of Green Castle.//Wednesday the 29th ult., by the REV. N. G. WHITE of McConnelsburg, REV. THOMAS CREIGH, pastor of the Presby. Church, Mercersburg, to MISS JANE M. GRUBB, of the same place, daughter of MR. JOSEPH GRUBB.//On Tuesday the 28th by REV.D. DENNY, DR. H. A. BUTLER, to MISS SOPHIA, daughter of MR. GODFREY GREENAWALT of this place.//By REV. J. HELLER, on the 23d of November, JESSE COWGAR, to MISS MARY ANN D. KEISTER, both of Pendleton Co.

WEEKLY MESSENGER OF THE GERMAN REFORMED CHURCH

VA.//On the same day, in Woodstock, Va. by REV. J.F. DIEFFENBACHER, MR. JOSEPH SOUTH formerly of Huntingdon Co. Pa. to MISS JANE McAFFEE, of the former place.//On the 16th ult. by REV. CHARLES F. SCHAEFFER, MR.JOHN M. ERNST to MISS CATHARINE ENTLER, both of Shepherdstown, Va.//The 23d ult. by the same, MR. WARREN R. WILLIAMSON, to MISS ANN MARIA SUTTER, both of Middletown,Md.//On the 23d ult. near Bakersville, by REV. JOHN W. HOFFMEIER, MR. HARVEY STONEBREAKER, to MISS ANGELICA RENCH, eldest daughter of DANIEL RENCH dec'd.// **DIED** On the 9th ult. in St. Louis, MO, MR. WILLIAM COWAN of Mercersburg, Pa., aged 28 years, 1 month 20 days.//On the 21st inst. MRS. MARY JANE BRACKENRIDGE, wife of MR. JOHNBRACKENRIDGE, of Shippensburg, in the 23d year of her age.//On Wednesday last,in York, aged precisely 76 years, MRS. BARBARA MORRIS, widow of the late DR. JOHN MORRIS.//MRS. MICHAEL C. DUNN and her daughter, whilst riding in a carriage near Nashville TN, jumped out for fear of being upset, resulting in the death of Mrs. D. and serious injury to her daughter.//MR. JOHN REINECKE was ordained as the pastor of the Shrewsbury Charge, York county, on Wednesday Nov. 15.//We learn by letter from REV. CHARLES G. HERMAN that missionary JOSEPH WOLFF, visited Cootstown, Berks County, Pa.//In JOHN EVANS vs. Westchester Rail Road the jury awarded the plaintiff $3,500 for injuries he sustained through the carelessness of the driver.--"Phila. Gazette."//**GERMAN MISSIONARIES.** We learn from the Lutheran Observer,clergymen from the Rhenish Missionary Institute at Barmen, Prussia, arrived in this country. They are REV. LEWIS NOLLAU, to join REV. MR. NIEZ, who arrived here a year ago to labor among Indians, REV. MAXIMILIAN OERTEL, among the emigrants in NY city. MR. JOHN MUELHAEUSER, to operate among the emigrant children.

127. Dec. 13, 1837/**MARRIED** On Thursday last in this place, by the REV. B. S. SCHNECK, MR. JOHN SHRADER, to MISS ROSANNA PENTZINGER, both of the

WEEKLY MESSENGER OF THE GERMAN REFORMED CHURCH

vicinity of Green-castle.//At Middletown, Frederick Co., Md., Thursday evening last, by REV. J. C. BUCHER, MR. JACOB YOUNG to MRS. ANN L. PERRY, all of Middletown, Md.//On the 5th inst. near New Chester,by REV. JACOB BEAR, MR. HENRY THOMAS to MISS ELIZABETH,third daughter of MR. NICHOLAS TAUGHINBAUGH, all of Adams Co., Pa.//On the 5th inst. by REV. JOHN MOODY, MR. JESSE KILGORE, of Newton township, to MISS MARY QUIGLY, eldest daughter of MR. JOSEPH QUIGLY, of Hopewell township, Cumberland county.//On the 8th of Nov.near Sharpsburg, by REV. JOHN W. HOFFMEIER, MR. EZRA J. SNYDER to MISS SARAH ANN STAUBS both of Washington county, Md.//On the 30th by the same, MR. BENJAMIN SWINGLEY to MISS CATHARINE HERSHEY.//On Tuesday evening week, by REV. J. SECHLER, MR. FREDERICK KROFT of Baltimore, to MISS ELIZABETH, daughter of MR. JOHN BLAIR, SEN.,of Hanover.//On the 28th ult. by the REV. MR. GEIGER, MR. JACOB SHARRETZ, of Manheim township, York county, to MISS SARAH ANN, daughter of MR. JOHN KERLINGER, of Carroll co., Md.//**DIED** On the 28th of Nov. near Sharpsburg,ELIZABETH SARAH, daughter of MR. SAMUEL GROVE, aged 6 years 3 months & 2 days.// **MONEYS** By WM. GLESSNER, from JOHN BENTZ $4, JOHN BRUNNER (of JB.) 2, ADAM WOLFE 2. By D. H. DOLL, from JACOB SHOWERS (OH) 4, MARY KILMER, MICHAEL SEIBERT, LYDIA STEPHENS, MARY MILLER, D. H. DOLL each 2, and GEO. M. WILSON 1. By REV. J. BEAR, from J. G. HARTZEL 2.

128. Dec. 20, 1837/**MARRIED** Tuesday, 5th inst., by REV. MR. GEIGER, MR. JOHN T. DIETUS, of Baltimore, to MISS JULIA, daughter of MR. PETER K. GETTIER, of Manchester district, Baltimore co.// On the same day, by the same, MR. JESSE SENTZ to MISS ELIZABETH LUCKENBAUGH, both of Manchester, Baltimore co., Md.//**DIED** In Philadelphia, Friday morning last, the celebrated DR. PHILIP SYNG PHYSIC in the 70th year of his age.//On the 10th inst. at her residence in Tiffin, MRS. ELIZA HEDGES, aged about 40 years, consort of JOSIAH

WEEKLY MESSENGER OF THE GERMAN REFORMED CHURCH

HEDGES, Esq. of that place.//Near Burkettsville, Sunday the 26th of November last, GIDEON BISER, in the 26th year of his age, after an illness of eight weeks.//On the 2nd inst. in Waynesboro', after a lingering illness, MARY ELIZABETH SMITH, daughter of MR.JOHN SMITH,in her sixteenth year. **//POWDER MILL EXPLODED** On Monday the 4th inst., the property of MR. DANIEL JACOBY, of Sumnytown, situate (sic) in Marlborough township,Montgomery county, Pa., was completely destroyed.**//ARREST** We last week noticed the murder of MR. SOLOMON CHAMBERS, of Adams county, since which we learn that THOMAS SNOWDEN, Son-in-Law of the dec'd. has been arrested.--"Tel."**//A TRAIN WRECK** Among those injured when the Engine was thrown from the track by a raised rail, were MRS. ROCHELLE, MISS BLOW, MISS KING, MISS SIMMONS, of Southampton, MR. NOE of Norfolk, MR. CROCKER of Jackson N. C.; MR. MILLS LAWRENCE, COL. ROCHELLE, NELSON HODGES, MR. BLOCKER, MR. OWENS, MR. HALL and MR. BLOW the train agent. Two servants of COL. PRESTON and the servant of COL. DOWNING of FL were wounded. As soon as they could be extricated, they were conveyed to ROCHELLE's where every attention was rendered. Those unhurt besides COL. PRESTON of the U. S. Senate and lady, were COL. DOWNING, MRS. STEWART, MR. DUNHAM of FL, MRS. and MISS PEAL, and MR. BANKS, of Augusta, Geo., who was riding on the engine, and jumped off at the moment of concussion. P. S. The cars have come in and announce the death of MRS. ROCHELLE and MISS BLOW. Only MISS SIMMONS and MR. CROCKER are in danger.**//MONEY.** From REV. GEO. LEIDY 2, and SAMUEL STATLER 2. By REV. E. HEINER, from MICHAEL HOFFMAN 4, BOYER & DIEFFENDERFER 2, J. J. MYERS 2 and GEO. RICHSTEIN 2. By REV. I. GERHART, from EDWARD BICKEL 2, DR. BESHLER 2, REV. I. GERHART 1. From MRS. MARGARET SPANGLER 2. By REV. D. ZIEGLER from W. CALDWELL, Esq. [Dover]2. HENRY BETZ 2. By DAVID WEIDNER (Philadelphia,) from J.G. SMITH and REV. J.F. BERG, each 4, GEO. TROUTMAN, SEN., C. LEIDY, SAML. MEARS, SARAH ANN

WEEKLY MESSENGER OF THE GERMAN REFORMED CHURCH

GIBSON, JOHN ALBURGER, DANL. WELKER(Mercersburg) each 2. For "Christliche Zeitschrift," by REV. G. LEIDY, from FRED. BRECHBILL, LEONARD WENDEL, MR. RADEBAUGH, JONATHAN HEIGELROTH, H. OTTO,each 1 dollar.//**FOR SALE** Sacred Music, by D. WEIDNER, Race street and HOGAN & THOMPSON, Market street, Philadelphia; DAVID CUSHING (successor to JOSEPH JEWETT) Baltimore; PATTERSON & INGRAM, Pittsburg JOHN FISHER & Son, Wheeling; JOHN RITTER, Reading; JOHN R. WILSON, Martinsburg, Va; JOHN BEAR, Lancaster; G.S. PETERS, Harrisburg; S.H. BUCHLER Gettysburg; REILY & VOGELSONG, York; JAMES LANDON, Carlisle; and HENRY SMITH Chambersburg, Pa.

129. Dec. 27, 1837/**MARRIED** On the 7th inst. by the REV. J. HELLER, MR. WILLIAM WALDSON, to MISS NANCY SMITH both of Pendleton county, VA.//On the 14th inst., by REV. A. P. FREEZE, MR. DANIEL EILER, to MISS SOPHIA GORSHON, both of Frederick county, Md.//On the 19th, by the same, MR. MICHAEL ZIMMERMAN to MISS HANNAH WOOD, both of Frederick county, Md.//On the 19th inst., by REV. D. HERTZ, MR. AMOS FASSNACHT, to MISS LUCY KILLIAN, all of Lancaster county.//On the 14th, by the same, MR. JESSE KILLIAN, to MISS ELIZABETH HOWERTER also of Lancaster county.//On the same day at the house of CHARLES WILSON, by REV. ROBERT KENNEDY, MR. JOSIAH KEEFER late of Chambersburg, to MISS REBECCA ANN MACKEY, of Welsh Run, Pa.// **DIED** In Greencastle, on the 15th inst. REV. J. RUTHRAUFF, SEN. in the 74th year of his age.//In Carlisle, on the 16th inst., ARTHUR W. CHAMBERS, eldest son of DR. WM CHAMBERS, in the 21st year of his age.//In Shippensburg, on the 19th, WILLIAM B. FULWILER, in the 24th year of his age.// At Utica Mills, Frederick county, Md. MR. HENRY HILL, in the 50th year of his age.//On Tuesday night 19th, REBECCA M. daughter ofMR. JOHN RADEBAUGH, of this place, aged about 12 years. This is the third death in the family of Mr. R. within in the last 4 months.//**KILLED** On Thursday evening 14th inst., a black man named GEORGE JACKSON

WEEKLY MESSENGER OF THE GERMAN REFORMED CHURCH

was killed in a scuffle with THOMAS JOHNSTON, a coloured man, at the residence of the latter, adjoining this borough. It appeared in evidence before the inquest held over the body of the dec'd. that JACKSON went to the room of JOHNSTON for the purpose of fighting him. JACKSON sprang on JOHNSTON who then struck him with a brick bat fracturing his skull, from the effects of which he died.--"Chambersburg Teleg."//**MONEYS RECEIVED** By REV. S. LEITER, from P. YEATZ $2.00.

130. Jan. 3, 1838/**MARRIED** On the 12th ult. by the REV. MR. GLESSNER, MR. ANDREW OYLER to MISS ANN ELIZA McGEE, both of Adams Co.//On the 14th ult. by the same, MR. CHARLES B. HARRIS, of Adams county, (formerly of Baltimore,) to MISS ELIZA WEBB, of Emmitsburgh, Md.//On the 12th ult., by the REV. MR. ERNST, the REV. C. F. STOEVER, of Milton, to MISS LOUISA VAN HOFF, of Lebanon county, Pa.//In Guilford county, N. C., the 14th ult., by the REV. J. H. CRAWFORD, MR. SILAS C. LINDSLEY, A. M., Professor of Languages in the Caldwell Institute, Greensboro, N. C., to MRS. AMELIA G. LERCH, consort of the late REV. D. B. LERCH.//Wednesday morning last by the REV. MR. WILEY, ZACHARIA HOLLAND, U. S. Navy, to MISS LAURA SOPHIA WILLIAMS, daughter of GENERAL O. H. WILLIAMS, of Hagerstown.//On the 26th ult. MR. GEORGE POFFENBERGER, of Dauphin county, Pa., to MISS RACHEL POFFENBERGER, of Frederick county, Md.//By the REV. MR. ZACHARIAS on Thursday last, MR. GEORGE MILLER, to MISS ELIZABETH YEAST, all of Middletown Valley, Md.//**DIED** Dec. 24th, in Friend's Cove Bedford county, MR. FREDERICK ZIMMERS in the 71st year of his age.//In Hagerstown on the same day, MRS. CATHARINE LITTLE, consort of JOSEPH LITTLE, in the 38th year of her age.// **QUACKERY** DR. FROST, of NY, who was convicted of manslaughter, in causing the death of TIBERIUS FRENCH, by excessive use of lobelia, was found guilty of manslaughter in the fourth degree, after a trial of ten days.//**MONIES RECEIVED** By D.

WEEKLY MESSENGER OF THE GERMAN REFORMED CHURCH

SMALL from JACOB SHAFFER, 2.//**ORATION** delivered by B. CHAMPNEYS, member of the Bar, to the Diagnothean and Goethean Literary Societies of Marshall College, Mercersburg.

131. Jan. 10, 1838//**MARRIED** In Shippensburg on the 5th ult., by the REV. MR. STROB, MR. RICHARD P. RETTICH, Merchant of Wooster, OH, to MISS ANN C. CRESSLER, of the former place.//On Thursday the 28th, ult., in Frederick Md., by the REV. D. ZACHARIAS, MR. HENRY RAMSBURG, to MISS CHARLOTTE GESEY all of Fred'k Co. Md.//On the 26th ult. by the REV. MR. BARE, GEORGE REINECKER to MISS MARY ANN LITTLE, daughter of MR. PETER LITTLE, all of Adams county.//On the 28th of Dec. by REV. J. B. KNIPE, MR. CHRISTIAN WAGNER, to MISS MARY EMORY, all of Pikeland Co., Pa.//By the same, on the 4th of Jan. MR. TAYLOR DILWORTH, to MISS PRISSILLA THOMAS, all of Chester county.//In Green Castle, on the 25th ult. by the REV. J. REBAUGH, MR. DANIEL PIPER to MISS SARAH NICHOLSON, all of Washington county, Md.//In Dauphin county on the 21st ult., by REV. ISAAC GERHART, MR. SIMON FORNEY, to MISS HANNAH, daughter of DOCTOR LONG, formerly of Jonestown, Lebanon county.//On the 26th, by the same, MR. PETER STOUCH, to MISS SUSAN BRESSLER of Licken's Valley.//By the same on the 2d inst., MR. JONATHAN RUPP, to MISS SALOME, daughter of MR. PETER BORDNER of Berrysburg, and MR. ABRAHAM HESS of Gratztown to MISS CATHARINE, daughter of JACOB HOFFMAN, Esq.//**DIED** The 23d ult. MRS. VIRGINIA LUCAS, wife of WILLIAM LUCAS, Esq. of Charlestown, Va., and daughter of the late DANIEL BEDINGER, Esq. of Shepherdstown, Va. //On the 31st ult. in Adams Co., Pa., MRS. MARIA ESSOM, in the 61st year of her age.//On the 19th ult., WM. CLINTON, infant son of DANIEL P. MILLER, in the second year of his age.//MR. JESSE STEINER has accepted a call from the Congregation in Northumberland, Penn'a.//The REV. GEO.A. SMITH, has retired from editorship of the Episcopal Recorder and will be succeeded by the REV.

MESSRS. TYNG, SUDDARDS, J. A. CLARK, and MAY.//
AGENTS for Marshall College. The following will collect subscriptions in their neighborhoods, viz: WM. HEYSER, Esq., Chambersburg, Pa.
M. RICKENBACH, Esq., Hagerstown, Md.
M. HAMMOND, Esq.,   "   "
HENRY COST, Esq., Jefferson, Md.
GIDEON BANTZ, Esq., Frederick City, Md.
by BERNARD C. WOLFF, Gen. agent.//
MISSIONARY EFFORTS. The brig *Himmaleh,* of NY, CAPT. FRASER, returned to this port yesterday, after a voyage among the islands of the Eastern archipelago. MESSRS. OLYPHANT & Co. fitted out the brig and invited the REV. MR. STEVENS, an AM missionary located in Canton, and MR. LAY, an English gentleman well known in the scientific world. The brig left China and arrived here about the beginning of December last. Shortly after her arrival,her commander and the REV. MR. STEVENS were attacked with fever, from which the latter gentleman did not recover. His place was supplied by REV. MR. DICKINSON, a member of the Atmerican (sic) mission here. MR. WOLFF the resident missionary, was a passenger to benefit his health; but on the 28th of April last, he fell ill.--"Singapore Chronicle of June 17, 1837."

132. Jan. 17, 1838//**MARRIED** In Lancaster, Pa., Thursday the 11th inst. by REV. MARTIN BRUNER, REV. DANIEL FEETE, of Middletown, Md. to MISS CHARLOTTE A. HELFENSTINE, of that city, daughter of the late REV. JONATHAN HELFENSTINE, of Frederick city, Md.//On Thursday Dec. 28, by REV. W. D. PAISLEY, DOCTOR DANIEL BROWER of Randolph, to MISS ELIZABETH A. CLAPP, daughter of COL. DANIEL CLAPP of Guilford county, N. C.//On the 10th, by REV. WM. A. GOOD, MR. WM. W. MURPHY to MISS HANNAH, daughter of DAVID FEGLY,all of Mercersburg. //On Tuesday the 9th inst. by the REV. MR. GOOD, of Mercersburg, MR. JOHN CORR, of Bridge Port, to MISS ELIZA JANE COSLEY, of the same place.// By REV. J. HELLER, on the 21st ult. MR. ANTHONY

WEEKLY MESSENGER OF THE GERMAN REFORMED CHURCH

MOURY, to MISS RACHEL MAURY, (sic) both of Pendleton county, Va.//By the same, on the same day, MR. GEORGE ARMENTROUT, to MISS MARY ANN BORER, both of Pendleton county, Va.// By the same, on the 31st ult. MR. EMANUEL REXROAD,to MISS AMELIA PROPTS, both of Pendleton county, Va.//On the 4th inst., by the same, in Franklin, MR. JOHN M. BRADSHAW, of Pocahontas Co. Va. to MISS ELIZABETH ANN EVICK, of the former place.//In Martinsburg, Va. on the 24th ult. by the REV. MR. DOUGLAS, MR. JONATHAN W. McGINNIS, Printer, of Hagerstown, Md., to MISS MARY KINART, eldest daughter of MR. DAVID BALES of the former place. //On Tuesday last, by the REV. D. DENNY, DR. A. H. SENSENY, to MISS JANE DAVIS, all of this place.//**DIED** At Harper's Ferry, Va., on the 8th inst.after a short illness, MRS. ELIZABETH, consort of MR. RICHARD JOHNSON, and second daughter of MR. GEORGE KNODE, of Pleasant Valley, Washington county, Md., in the 24th year of her age. She left a disconsolate husband with whom she lived only the short space of one year in matrimony. On Tuesday the 9th of January, her mortal remains were conveyed to the cemetery near her father's residence in Pleasant Valley, Md.//**TRIBUTE OF RESPECT** From the Diagnothean Literary Society in consequence of the death of JOSEPH E. LANE, a student at Marshall College, dated Dec. 30, 1837.//**A SHOCKING MURDER.** Committed on Saturday night the 6th inst., in the neighborhood of RIPPLE's tavern on the South Mountain in this county. It appears that JAMES McGLINCHY and JOHN MURTAUGH, both Irish laborers, who had been upon bad terms, attracted the attention of MR JOHN TRACY, about 11 o'clock at night, who heard the cry "murder," up on (sic) which he went to the spot, and found McGLINCHY lying on his back with his face horribly beaten, and MURTAUGH standing by, who fled and was pursued by MR. TRACY to RIPPLE's. The inquest found thirteen stab wounds, besides which his face was beaten in by blows with a stone. His trial will take

WEEKLY MESSENGER OF THE GERMAN REFORMED CHURCH

place at the April term.--"Chambersburg Whig."//
FOR SALE. Orders for Catechism and Constitution a neat work either in english or german (sic) may be supplied thro' REV. ROBERT DOUGLAS, Shepherdstown. DAVID WEIDNER, bookseller, No. 107 Race st. Philadelpha, (sic) and VICTOR SCRIBA, Pittsburg, will also fill orders. JOHN SMITH, Chambersburg.//**CHURCH ORGAN FOR SALE.** An uninjured instrument which has been used for several years will be sold low, if immediate application is made to W. HARMON, Professor of Music, Liberty street, Baltimore.//**MONIES RECEIVED.** From REV. D. HERTZ, from W. SHIRK, (Churchtown,) $2; HENRY SHIRK 2, and R. GOSHEN 1; from HENRY BOVEY 1; by REV. H.BASLER, from PHILIP DUTRO 2, JOHN DRECK, (Kulpsville,) 1; from DANIEL HOSLER, JOHN BOWLES (St. Thomas,) each 2; from D. FLEAGLE, (Taney-town,) 5.00; by REV. DAVID WINTERS, from J. W. WOLFF, GEO. KIEFER, (Fairfield,) KOOGLER & BATES, JACOB S. BRENNER, WILLIAM ORAM, MICHAEL BRENNER, H. & A. DEAM, JOHN SHAFFER, JR., JACOB RIKE, ABRAHAM HAWKER, (Dayton,) JOHN GLODFELTER, H. SHANK, JACOB COY, G. GLODFELTER, (Bellbrook,) J.PETERSON, (N. Burlington,) RYAN GRAY, BARBARA HANES, A. FOWLER, ANNA GRAY, BATHSHEBA BULLARD, LYDIA NIMERICK, RACHEL EYLER, JACOB STEEL, SAM'L ANKENNY, JOHN SHANNON, A.H. BAUGHMAN, JACOB HERRING, J.F. MYERS, JOHN ANKENNY, JONATHAN SNYDER, JACOB BOOTS, JACOB PETERMAN, J. WEATHERHOLTZ, J. STEMBLE, W. H. DOWNES, W. R. FIELDS, ADAM RADER, JESSE BOOTS,MARTIN BOOTS, and KETTERMAN & PETERSON, (Xenia,) each, 2; by REV. J.C. BUCHER, from JOHN KELLER, JR., PETER BISER, SEN., HENRY COCHRAN, PHILIP FLOOK, JOHN J. SMITH, JOHN COBLENTZ, (of J.), each 2; and J. P. COBLENTZ, JOHN REMSBERG,JR., DANIEL FLOOK, each, 4; PETER BISER,JR. 6 75; JACOB SHRIVER 5; REV.J. C. HENSEL 1; DAVID SHULTZ 2; and JOHN HOWPE 2.//From MR. JOHN COBLENTZ, (of JOHN P.) for the Missionary Society, one dollar, which was unsolicited.

133. Jan. 24, 1838/**MARRIED** Sept. 19, in Bucy-

WEEKLY MESSENGER OF THE GERMAN REFORMED CHURCH

rus, OH, by REV. F.J. RUTH, REV. A. KUHN, pastor of the Lutheran Church, Reedsburg, OH, to MISS MELVINA RUPP, formerly of York, Pa.//York, Pa., on the 20th ult. by REV. JOHN CARES, REV. JACOB ZIEGLER, pastor of the Reformed congregation of St. Matthews, Chester county, to MISS ANN M. DANNER, of the former place.//On the 8th inst., by the same, MR. SAMUEL ZIEGER to MISS CHARLOTTE DANNER, both of York, Pa.//**DIED** At the Trappe, Montgomery county, Pa., REV. JACOB WAMPOLE, in the 35th year of his age.//In Hanover, Pa., on the 10th inst. MISS MARY D. PYLE, in the 19th year of her age.//In this borough, on the 17th inst., MRS. MARGARET DENNY, consort of the REV. DAVID DENNY, Pastor of the Presby. church, of this place.//Dismissal demand of the endictments now pending in York county Court against NATHAN S. BEMIS, JACOB FORWOOD, EDWARD PRIGG, STEPHEN LEWIS, citizens of MD, for the alledged crime of kidnapping; and modification of the law relating to negroes recognizing the rights of the master. From the committee MESSRS. MAULSBY and ALEXANDER of the House.//**MONIES** From C. BIGLER (Strasburg) $2. JOHN NYCUM, Esq. 5.00. By REV. J. F. LOY, 6, --to be credited we presume to H. FLUCK, G. B. KAY, FRANCIS GROVE. By REV. A. P. FREEZE, from DANIEL ROUSER 3, DANIEL FIROR 4,and JOHN P. ZIMMERMAN,5. By D. SHRIVER, Esq., from GEORGE WILL, LUDWIG STUDY, SNYDER and KREPS, H. GUTELIUS, E. LEFEVRE, JACOB STARNER, JACOB KELLER, M. STEFFY, each 2, D. SHRIVER 3, YOUNG & FELTY 4, and PETER HULL 5. From GEORGE WILLIARD, 2. From REV. J. PENCE, 3, SAMUEL BAKER,2./**LETTER** B. LEHMAN, Esq.

134. Jan. 31, 1838/**MARRIED** The evening of the 28th inst., at MR. SNIDER's Hotel, in Chambersburg by REV. B. S. SCHNECK, MR.SAMUEL CAHOON, of DE, to MISS REBECCA COUFFER, from the vicinity of Mercersburg.//On Tuesday last, by the REV. R. GRACEY, MR. THOMAS G. CRISWELL, to MISS MARTHA G., daughter of the late JUDGE McKESSON, both of Green township.//On Wednesday the 24th inst., by

WEEKLY MESSENGER OF THE GERMAN REFORMED CHURCH

REV. J. CLARY, MR. JOHN D. CRILLEY, to MISS REBECCA SHAFFER, both of Mercersburg, Pa.//Wednesday the 17th inst, by J. HUNTER, Esq., MR. ISAAC CHAMBERLIN to MISS POLLY MAYERS, both of Franklin County.//Thursday evening the 25th, by REV. R. KENNEDY, REV W.A. GOOD, Rector of the Preparatory Department of Marshall College, Mercersburg, to MISS MARY A. MINICH of St.Thomas.//**DIED** On Wednesday the 17th inst., in this place, MRS. MARGARET DENNY, consort of REV. DAVID DENNY, in the 68th year of her age. Sudden was the summons which called the subject of this notice from the theatre of life. She was often visited with bodily infirmity and distress.//On the 19th ult., in Antrim township, Franklin county, Pa., MRS. CHARITY E. HICKS, consort of CAPT. DAVID HICKS, in the 26th year of her age. She left a husband and two helpless children.//Suddenly, in this borough on Saturday last, MR. GEORGE STECH, aged 71 years and several months.//On Monday last, MRS. CADOW, wife of MR. WILLIAM CADOW, of this place.//**DROWNED.** In Cayuga Bay, the 31st ult., JACOB PARTENHEIMER, late of Philadelphia, aged 18. While skaiting on the ice it gave way, and thus he found a grave in the water.//**FIRE!** The large barn of JOHN L. SNYDER, and stabling of the Hon. C. OGLE, in Somerset, Pa., were destroyed by fire, on the 22d inst., together with horses, cows, carriage, stage-harness, and hay.

135. Feb. 7, 1838/**MARRIED** Thursday last in this place by REV. B. S. SCHNECK, MR. HENRY CHRISMAN, to MISS ANN M. FREEZE, both of St. Thomas township, Franklin county, Pa.//In Attica, IN on the 8th of January by REV. J.L. SANDERS, MR. WILLIAM HAWKINS, to MISS HENRIETTA HOFFMAN.//In Lincolnton, N. C., the evening of the 24th ult. by REV. J. G. FRITCHEY, MR.FRANKLIN W. HOKE to MISS MARY second daughter of COL. JOHN ZIMMERMAN, dec'd. //**DIED** On Wednesday the 17th ult. at his residence about 9 miles from Hagerstown, Washington county, Md., MR. JOHN SCHNEBLY, SEN, in the 88th

WEEKLY MESSENGER OF THE GERMAN REFORMED CHURCH

year of his age.//On Friday last, at his residence, after a few hours illness, MR. ABRAHAM RIFE, an aged and respectable farmer of Hamilton township.//On the 22d ult. at the residence of her brother near Green Castle, MRS. MARY VANDYKE in the 31st year of her age.//**MONIES** From FRED. WOLFF (Abbotstown) 5. By REV W C. BENNET, from JOHN FULWILER, 2 50 and SAMUEL PAGUE 3 00. From JOCOB (sic) BRUBAKER (N. Holland) 2. By GEO KEEFER (Clearspring) from DAVID CUSHWA 5, HENRY ANCHONY 6, MICH'L SEIBERT 3, GEO KEEFER 1. GEO WOLFF (Martinsburg) 5. By G SHENEBERGER, from W MARTIN 4. J HASSON 4. G SHENEBERGER, SEN. 2.

136. Feb. 14, 1838/**MARRIED** Woodstock, Va., by REV. J. G. DIEFFENBACHER, MR. FREDERICK DELLINGER to MISS MARY FETZER.//Thursday 8th inst., by REV. D. BOSSLER of Harrisburg, MR. JOHN G. RUPP, of Cumberland co., to MISS ANN ELIZABETH, second daughter of MR. G, MILLEISEN, Dauphin county.// In Greencastle, the 23d ult. by REV. J. REBAUGH, MR. JONAS SPEILMAN, to MISS MARGARET MORRIN, of Washington county, Md.//The 24th ult.near Greencastle,by the same, MR. ISAAC LONG, to MISS MARTHA GILBERT, all of Franklin county, Pa.//On the same day, by the same, MR. MATHIAS CORDMAN, to MISS MARY CHAMBERS all of Washington county, Md. //Thursday, 1st inst., by the same, MR. WILLIAM BROWN. to MISS SARAH MILLER, all of Washington county, Md.//**DIED** Sunday, January 28th ult. at his residence in Berkely Co. Va., MR. JOHN MYERS JR., in the ___ (sic) year of his life. He was cut off in the vigor of youth by the unskillfulness of a pretended physician upon whom he called to let a little blood. As soon as the danger was discovered DR, N. of Smithfield was called to visit him. He left an aged Father and several brothers and sisters.//On the 10th inst., in this place, JOHN,infant son of EMANUEL CROSSLAN, aged 21 months.//On the 11th inst., in Guilford Township, MRS. ELIZABETH KELLER, relict of the late DAVID KELLER, in the 77th year of her age.

WEEKLY MESSENGER OF THE GERMAN REFORMED CHURCH

//DAVID DARBY, formerly assistant Postmaster at Harborcreek, Erie county, Pa. has been convicted of purloining money from the mail, and sentenced to twelve years in the Eastern Penitentiary of PA.//**FIRE in Baltimore.** The Theatre and Circus, in Town, belonging to MR. COOK, together with the the Tailor stand of MR. MURPHY were consumed.

137. Feb. 21, 1838/**MARRIED** On Wednesday week, by REV. DAVID McKINNEY, MR. MOSES THOMPSON, to MISS MARY, daughter of JOHN IRVIN, Esq., all of Penns Valley, Centre Co., Pa.//In Woodstock, Va. on the 8th inst. by REV. JACOB G. DIEFFENBACHER, MR. ISAAC HOTTLE to MISS ANN FRAVEL.//On the same day, by REV. D. HERTZ, MR. JOHN LIGHTNER, to MISS ELIZABETH BENDER, all of Lancaster Co., Pa. //The 11th ult. by REV. ISAAC GERHART, MR. ANDREW FLIEGER, of Clark's Valley, to MISS MARGARET BRIGHT all of Dauphin county, Pa.//On the 8th inst. by the same, MR. JACOB GERMAN to MISS MARTHA SPANG, of Millersburg, Dauphin county, Pa.// On the 8th, by REV. A. P. FREEZE, MR. FREDERICK TROXELL, to MISS SOPHIA BARBARA FIROR, both of Frederick county, Md.//On the 13th, MR. JNO. ZIMMERMAN, to MISS MATILDA WICKHAM, both of Frederick county, Md.//The 6th inst. by REV. D. MOSER, REV. L. G. EGGERS, to MISS LYDIA SHAFER, of Nittany Valley, Centre county, Pa.//**DIED** In Bellefonte, Centre Co., Pa. on the 13th inst, MISS HARRIET SPEESE, in the 22nd year of her age.//In Lexington, Ky, on the 2nd inst., MR. JOHN EBERLE Medical Professor in Transylvania University, formerly of Philadelphia.//On the 3d inst. at York after a short illness, MISS JULIA ANN WEAVER, in the 28th year of her age.//We consider it our duty to decline the offer of a benefit performance by the Thespian Society for our sick poor. We, in return, invite them to an address by PROFESSOR M'CLINTIC, of Dickinson, in behalf of said object. For the Society, M. A. COLHOUN.

138. Feb. 28, 1838/**MARRIED** In Hanover, Pa., on

WEEKLY MESSENGER OF THE GERMAN REFORMED CHURCH

Thursday evening, 22d inst., by the REV. JACOB SECHLER, the REV. SAMUEL GUTELIUS, to MISS HENRIETTA A. PYLE, all of the former place.//On the 13th inst. by REV. WM. SUDDARDS, WM. P. WELLS, Esq. Attorney at Law, Union Town, Pa. to MARY R. daughter of the late ANDREW BYERLY, of the city of Philadelphia.//On Thursday, the 22d inst. by the REV. ROBT. HENRY, MR. ROBERT McMILLEN, of Huntingdon county, Pa. to MRS. DORCAS CULBERTSON of New Derry, Westmoreland county.//On Thursday week, by the REV. J. GEIGER, M. JOHN WEIST, of Paradise, York Co. Pa.,to MISS ELIZABETH, eldest daughter of JACOB MAUS of Carroll Co. Md.//On Thursday last, by the same, MR. JACOB GEIMAN, to MISS JULIA HAINS, both of Carrol county, Md.//In Strasburg, on the 22d inst.by REV. W. C. BENNET, MR. WILLIAM WILSON, to MISS REBECCA SHEARER both of Strasburg, Pa.//**DIED** At the residence of the REV.R. KENNEDY, on the 15th inst. MISS PRISCILLA CUNNINGHAM, in the 19th year of her age.//On the 19th, near Fayetteville, JACOB SHOBER,in the 52d year of his age.//On the 20th at the residence of REV. JACOB GEIGER, in Manchester, Md. after a lingering illness in the 28th year of her age, MISS RACHEL GOBRECHT, third daughter of the REV. JOHN GOBRECHT,late of Allentown, Pa.//On Friday, 2d February, 1838 after an illness of two weeks, REV. WILLIAM F. HOUSTON, M. D., pastor of the Presby. Church at Wrightsville, Pa.//On Saturday morning last, after a short illness, MR. WILLIAM NIXON, of this place, aged about 45 years.// Suddenly, at Jefferson, Frederick Co., Md., on Monday morning, the 19th inst., MRS. ELIZABETH, consort of MR. HENRY KELLER of that place, in the 58th year of her age. For years often infirm and distressed in body, and afflicted in mind, she endured with christian resignation.// **RAIL ROAD ACCIDENT.** The train which left Richmond, Va., at 4 o'clock on Saturday morning, after it had gone about seven miles, encountered an obstruction on the track, which threw the engine off the track. A tree, heavily laden with sleet had been blown down across the track. MR. JOSEPH ANTHONY, the engine man, and MR. ALPHEUS MALLORY, the fireman, were both thrown from the engine--the tender fell upon them, and both were killed.//A letter from the Hon. D. SHEFFER to a gentleman of this place contains the information that JONATHAN CELLY, member of Congress from ME, was killed in a duel between him and WILLIAM J. GRAVES, a member from KY, on the 24th inst. MR. CELLY refused to fight JAMES WATSON WEBB, of NY, on account of remarks made during a debate some weeks ago, on the grounds that he (WEBB) was no gentleman. He agreed to fight MR. GRAVES, bearer of the challenge. The first rifle shot proving ineffectual, an attempt was made to settle the affair, and a second shot deprived CELLY of his life.//**FIRE** at the Bowery Theatre, NY, a little after 2 o'clock on Sunday morning, believed to be the work of incindiaries, destroyed the tavern, and a stable adjoining, the property of MR. HAMBLIN, and a colored man sleeping in it burned to death.//New species of corn, procured by MR. H. L. ELLSWORTH while Indian Commissioner at the "Far West".//**MONIES.** MRS. MARGARET R. RIDDLE 2, JACOB CORT 2 50, DANIEL CORT 2.50, ISAAC WHITE 1 GEORGE W. WILLIARD 2, MATTHEW PATTON 2, HENRY J. SCHREINER, (Gettysburg,)5, A S.E. DUNCAN 5, REV. HENRY WILLIARD 5, ABRAHAM LIND (Canton,) 2, CONRAD PLASTERER 2.--From REV. J. GEIGER 2, LEVI MAXFIELD 2, JOHN KRANTZ 3. By REV. H. WAGNER, from J. B. HIESTER, DOCTOR GLONINGER, H. DEHUFF, ANN RINGEL, DAVID GREENAWALT, DOCTOR LEINAWEAVER JOHN ERMENTROUT, JOHN HEILMAN, W. MOORE and JOHN BEHM, each 2. By REV. JOHN KELLER, (Bnffalo, N. Y.) (sic) from JESSE SHAFER 4, SAMUEL YOUNG 3, JACOB SHIMER (or SCHMECK?) (sic) 2 JACOB KOCH 1. By M. ROUNSAVILLE, from JACOB BARRIER 2, JOHN HEDRICK 1, P. HELMSTETLER, neat 3.65, by J. C. BARNHART, from MOSES FOIL 2, REV. G. BOGER 2, J. GUELICH 2. For "Christliche Zeitschrift," from M. A. BARNAHRT(Greensboro', N. C.) $1 -hereafter to be sent to Mt. Comfort,N. C. For "Der Herold"

WEEKLY MESSENGER OF THE GERMAN REFORMED CHURCH

from REV. A. BAYER, $1. A credit of $2 to MR. KIEHL instead of $1, from REV. MR. BEYER.

139. Mar. 7, 1838/**MARRIED** On the 20th ult., by the REV. ISAAC GERHART, MR. PETER FEID, to MISS ELIZABETH, daughter of DANIEL WIRT.//On the 22nd by the same, MR. JONATHAN KOPPENSHAFER, to MISS MARY UHLER, of Lykens Valley, Dauphin co.//On Wednesday 14th inst. by the REV. R. S. GRIER, of Adams Co. Pa., MR. WM. C. LANDERS, of Franklin MIlls, to MISS SARAH A. youngest daughter of MR. D. ROUZER, both of Frederick Co., Md.//On Thursday evening last, by the REV. DANIEL ZACHARIAS, MR. JOHN HIMBURY, to MISS JULIAN HOOPER, all of Frederick city, Md.//**DIED** Near Reading, Pa., on the 21st ult., MRS. MARY DEININGER, daughter of the Hon. HENRY A. MUHLENBERG, in the 32d year of her age.//In Huntingdon Co. Pa. on the 15th Feb. REV. THOMAS J. KEATING.//Near Salisbury, Md., on the 26th ult., REV. WILLIAM STONE, D. D., Bishop of Protestant Episcopal church of that state.// **MONIES** From MAJ. JOHN NEFF $2. JOHN STOUFFER 2, REV. P S. FISHER 3, JACOB HALLER 2, JAMES HARRIS 2, (Bellefonte) REV. SAMUEL HESS 5, SAMUEL WAGNER, (Juniata,) 2, JOHN HARMONY 2, JOHN LANDIS 1.25, JOSEPH BOGGS 5, WILLIAM FETTER 2, REV. E. HEINER 62 1/2 cts., JOHN B. FREY 2.37 1/2, and J. B. SEIDENSTRICKER 2. Editor of the "Christliche Zeitschrift," please send paper to JONAS DOLL, Abbottstown, Adams county, Pa. From REV. J. SECHLER, (Hanover.) $1, from REV. E. KIEFFER, Bellefonte, Centre county, Pa.,$1.

140. Mar. 14, 1838/**MARRIED** In Lancaster, Pa., by REV. MR. BRUNER, SAMUEL WAGNER, Esq., Cashier of the York Bank, to MISS ELIZABETH REITZELL, of the former place.//Near Green Castle, on the 8th February by REV. J. REBAUGH, MR. THOMAS GILLAND, to MISS SUSAN CONRAD, all of this county.//On Thursday evening,March 1st,by the same, MR. WILLIAM BURK, to MISS ELIZABETH SMITH, all of this county.//Thursday evening last, Green Castle, by

WEEKLY MESSENGER OF THE GERMAN REFORMED CHURCH

the same, MR. HENRY CORWELL, to MISS MARIA BARKMAN, of Washington county, Md.//Near Middletown, Frederick county,Md.,at LIDY's Hotel, on Tuesday evening, Feb.27, by REV. J.C. BUCHER, MR. DAVID WM. OYSTER, of Georgetown, D. C., to MISS ELIZA ANN THOMPSON, of Frederick Co., Md.//At the Parsonage of the GRC, Middletown, Md., on the 1st of March,by the same, MR. AARON YOURTEE, to MISS CATHARINE McDADE, both of Pleasant Valley, Washington county, Md.//At Mount Parnol, on Wednesday the 7th inst. by the REV. THOMAS CREIGH, DR. WILLIAM R. HUMPHREYS of St. Thomas, to MISS MARY M. daughter of THOMAS M'DOWELL, Esqr.//**DIED** After one day's illness in Green Castle MRS. SARAH SHOOK, in the 24th year of her age.//**MURDER** of a pedler in Lycoming county, Pa. Suspicion fell upon a MR. MILLER, who was seen to have articles known to belong to HOFFMAN. The Muncy Telegraph says:--"After he was committed for trial,he confessed to have aided in murdering HOFFMAN. He and a person named FAULKERSON were in the woods near the road chopping, when HOFFMAN was passing by."//**EXECUTED** JAMES READ and THOMAS EVANS were executed for negro stealing, at Edgefield, N. C. on the 9th inst. READ had resided in Philadelphia and Pittsburg, Pa., and left a family in NJ.//GEN. SCOTT was accidentally killed by one of his own men, but in what manner we have not been able to ascertain.--"Franklin Telegraph."

141. Mar. 21, 1838/**MARRIED** In Pittsburg on the 6th inst., by the REV. MR. HACKE, MR. WILLIAM HAGUS, to MISS JULIANA HACKE both of that place. //In Philadelphia, by the REV. J. F. BERG, Feb. 22, MR. JOHN FREAS, to MISS ANN FISHER, both of Whitemarsh township, Montgomery county.//By the same on March 6, MR. STEPHEN D. KIRKNERS to MISS ISABELLA FAMER, both of Plymouth township, Montgomery county, Pa.//On Thursday evening last, by REV. BENJAMIN S. SCHNECK, MR. JOHN W. WHITMORE, merchant, of Dayton, OH, to MISS ELIZABETH R. CRAWFORD, of Franklin county, Pa.//On the 15th,

WEEKLY MESSENGER OF THE GERMAN REFORMED CHURCH

by the same, MR. WILLIAM MURRAY, to MISS CATHARINE HUMMELSTINE, both of this place.//Thursday evening last, by the REV. MR. KELLER, MR. AUGUSTUS WOLF, to MISS ELIZA GILLESPIE, daughter of MR. WILLIAM GILLESPIE, all of Gettysburg.//Near New Chester, on the 1st inst. by the REV. JACOB BARE, MR. GEORGE SPANGLER to MISS NINETTA WOLFF, daughter of MR. FREDERICK WOLFF, all of Adams county.//**DIED** In NY city, REV. GEORGE MILLS, latterly pastor of the German Episcopal church in that city, aged 41 years.//**ERROR** A statement of GEN. SCOTT's death in our last week's paper, which was copied from Baltimore papers, is incorrect.//**MONIES RECEIVED.** From JOHN KILLINGER $4, WM. SEIBERT (Chamb'g) 2 HENRY DIEHL (Bedford) 2. By REV. MR. WOLFF, from W. H. LAWALL, J. CHRISMAN, JR, MRS: DESHLER, ANNA M. BLACK, PETER POMP, GEO. LERCH, each 2, and REV. J. G. WOLFF 5 By GEORGE B. WELTY, From HENRY NYMAN 2, SAMUEL YONTZ 5. HENRY SHRIVER (Leitersburg,) 5.

142. March 28, 1838/**MARRIED** On Thursday last, by the REV. B. S. SCHNECK, MR. WILLIAM VONDERAU, to MISS CATHARINE FINFROCK,both of Franklin co., Pa.//By REV. JOHN WM. HOFFMEIER, near Sharpsburg on the 15th of March, MR. ANTHONY ROWE to MRS. ANN THOMAS McWILLIAMS,both of Washington county, Md.//By REV. JACOB SHOLL, on the 15th, MR. JAMES WELSH, to MISS FANNY MOSSER,--MR. JACOB BARD, to MISS MARGARET MATZER,--MR. HENRY TITZEL to MISS ELIZA NEWCOMER,--on the 13th, MR. JOHN LIGHTNER, to MISS MARY CREE, all of Perry county, Pa.//In Shippensburg, on the 22d ult, by the REV. W. C. BENNETT, MR. WILLIAM EARLY to MISS MARGARET FORNEY, both of Franklin county, Pa.//**DIED** Near Emmittsburg., Md, (sic) on the 27th of February last, after an illness of about five weeks, MR. JOSHUA MORITZ, in the 20th year of his age. It was about two weeks ago before his death that he felt that God had pardoned his sins. In his case we see that God is willing to receive the prodigal, even at the eleventh hour.//In Lancaster,

Pa., on Sabbath morning, 18th inst., in the 79th year of his age, REV. JOHN H. HOFFMEIER, of the GRC. He was born in Anhalt Goethen, in GER.

143. Apr. 4, 1938//**MARRIED** On Tuesday morning, the 3d inst. by the REV. B. S. SCHNECK, the REV. JACOB SECHLER, of Hanover, Pa., to MISS NANCY, youngest daughter of MR. JOHN HARMONY, of Jackson's Hall, Franklin county, Penn'a.//**DIED** Near Womelsdorf, Berks county, of Scarlet fever, JUSTINA ELIZABETH, in the 16th, and SAMUEL R., in the tenth year of life, children of MR. JOHN SEIBERT. They were buried in one grave.//On the 26th ult., in Fountain Dale, Adams county, Pa., in the 37th year of his age, MR. SAMUEL BARKDOLL leaving a wife and seven small children.//On the 20th ult., MARGARET ELIZABETH, daughter of MR. HENRY HEAGY, of Freedom township, York co., Pa., aged 13 years---being the fourth child removed from him by death within a few weeks.//At his residence near Waynesboro,' on Monday last, DANIEL ROYER, Esq. aged about 80.//At his residence in Guilford township, MR. HENRY M'FERREN.//MRS. MATTHIAS, wife of REV. J. J. MATTHIAS, Governor of Liberia, died in January last, as also a MISS ANNESLY, of Albany.//**LETTERS** from REV. J. C. HENSEL, F. RUPLEY, C. H. LEINBACH, F. SPARE, PHILIP BONESTEEL, REV. A. P. FREEZE, W. W. BELL, Esq., DANIEL HERMAN and S. STATLER--you did not pay your postage! J. R. REILY, JAMES COOK, REV. THEOD. L. HOFFEDITZ, REV. DR. RAUCH, REV. JON'A. ZELLERS, D. M. LIVERS, DANIEL HOFFMAN, WILLIAM AUGHENBAUGH, Esq., REV. D. ZACHARIAS, JACOB KROH PROFESSOR S. W. BUDD, HENRY KELLER, JOHN HOSSLER

144. Apr. 11, 1838/**MARRIED** On the 24th ult., by REV. K. ZACHARIAS,MR. DAVID C.STEINER to MISS ELIZABETH WIEST,all of Frederick, Md.//On Thursday last,by the same, MR. WILLIAM STALEY to MISS MARY ANN RAMSBURG, all of Frederick county, Md. //On the same day by the same,MR. SAMUEL NUSBAUM to MISS CATHARINE REESE, all of Frederick, Md.//

WEEKLY MESSENGER OF THE GERMAN REFORMED CHURCH

On the evening of the 29th of March, MR. SIMON BARRICK to MISS ANN CATHARINE BUCKEY, both of Frederick county, Md.//On the 8th inst., by the REV. B. S. SCHNECK, MR. NICHOLAS DOERNBERG, a native of Hesse-Darmstadt, GER, to MRS. MARTHA BACKENSTOSE, of Franklin county, Pa.//On Monday the 2d inst., by the REV. MR BENEDICT, JOSEPH H. PIERCE of Harrisburg, Pa., to MISS JANE M. LAMBERT, of NY city.//**SEMINARY FUNDS.** From Bedford Co., PA - Bedford, Pa.---PETER SCHELL $10, J. H. HOFFIUS 25, PHILIP WIESELL 5, JAMES WIESELL 3, PETER MANN 10, JOHN WIESELL 2, HENRY KOONS 5, ELIZABETH HERSHBERGER 1, DANIEL KOONS 2, JOHN MANN 3, ANN ANDERSON 50 cts., JACOB BOLLINGER $2 HENRY LEADER 5, JOHN YOUNG 5, JOB MANN 5, DAVID MANN 5, DANIEL CRAUSE 5, DANIEL WASHABAUGH 5, WILLIAM BERG 2, MARY MATDORF 12 1/2 cts., WILLIAM STAHL $2, MICHAEL REIMUND 2, JOSEPH WOLF 5, GEORGE W. BOWMAN 5, JACOB SCHERTZER 5, JOHN RYNDELS 5, WILLIAM TODD 5, MOSES DUBBS 2, JOSEPH B. WHITMORE 1, RICHARD SPICER 2, JAMES McVICKERS 50 cts.-- Friends Cove, GEORGE SHOEMAKER $8, HENRY SHOEMAKER 10, JOHN KAGG 5, PHILIP J. SHOEMAKER 10, JOHN DIEHL, JR. 5, JOHN FEUCHT 5, ADAM KOONS 10, NICHOLAS KOONS 2 50, JACOB WHETSTONE 25 cts. SAMUEL WHETSTONE $1, LENHART NICHOME 1, SOLOMON DIEHL, SEN. 6, SOLOMON DIEHL, JR. 8, ELIAS DIEHL 1, JOHN DIEHL, SEN. 5, JONAS DIEHL 2, PHILIP DIEHL 3, DAVID FAUGHT 1, JACOB SHUMAN 50 cts., SAMUEL OPPENHEIMER 25 cts., HENRY FEIGHT 50 cts. JONATHAN NICKCOME $1 50, MICHAEL OTT $2, SOLOMON BIEGEL 2, MICHAEL DIEHL 1, SOLOMON DIEHL 1, JOHN EXLINE 3, JONATHAN DIEHL 2, JOHN MORTIMORE 25 cts., DANIEL EXLINE $2, ADAM H. EXLINE 5, ADAM DIEHL 5, JACOB STANDENOUR 1, FRED'K. SMITH 5, JOSEPH CARIL 2, JOHN SMITH 5, JOHN FOLK, JR. 5, DAVID EXLINE 5. -- Schellsburg, ABRAHAM SCHELL $5, HARBET OTTO 5, JOHN WHETSTONE 50 cts., JOHN HAMMER $1, ISAAC MINGEL 1, JOHN CLARK 1, JOHN S. STATLER 5, GEORGE ROCK 50 cts., ELIZABETH SCHELL $2, BENJAMIN BLYMYER 2, GABRIEL HULL 1, JACOB WALTER 1, WILLIAM ALEXANDER 2, EMANUEL STATLER 5,

WEEKLY MESSENGER OF THE GERMAN REFORMED CHURCH

MARIA SCHELL 2, MICHAEL BASORE 50 cts. JOHN BOWSER $5, FREDERICK HILLEGAS 2, JACOB HILLEGAS 5, JOHN MAURER 1 50, HENRY SCHELL 5,E. D. SCHELL 1, DAVID BORDER 5. -- Babscreek, TOBIAS HEINZERLING $1, JOSEPH RIDDLE 5, IASEAH SILL 50 cts. JACOB FICKES $5, ADAM MOSAS 1, PAUL MACK 5, FREDERICK OSTER 10, WILLIAM BERGHEIMER 2, ANN ANDREWS 50 cts. -- Greenfield cong., MARTIN DIVELY 25 cts., JOSEPH EMLER 25 CTS., ABRAHAM DIVELY $2 50, JACOB LINAFELDER 1, JOHN MARTHER 1, ANOTHONY (sic) HARNER 1, RACHEL LINEFELDER 1, MARGARET DIVELY 1. -- Morrison's Cove, JOHN NICHODEMUS $20, HENRY DAILY 2, FREDERICK FAUSE 5, WILLIAM FOUSE 10, JONAS HAMLINE 5, JOHN SKYLES 1, CHRISTIAN WEINBRENNER 5, JACOB NICHODEMUS 5, FREDERICK NICHODEMUS 8, JOHN SMITH 5, WILLIAM FALKENOR 1, HENRY FLUCK 5, MARGARET NICHODEMUS 5, WILLIAM DUDEN 1, PAUL RHODE 5, MARTIN LOY 5, JOHN R. LOY 5, HENRY NICHODEMUS 2. -- Ray's Hill, CHRISTIAN FELDEN 2, JOHN NYCUM 15, JAMES SPROUT 5, WILLIAM WILSON 1, SOLOMON WILLIAMS 1 SIMON NYCUM 1.//**BEQUEST** CAPT. ISAAC ROSS, of LA, has left to the Colonization Society by will his entire estate. He had about 170 slaves who were to be emancipated and settle in Africa.//STEPHEN HENDERSON, Esq. who recently died in New Orleans, left a bequest of $2000 per annum, to be distributed to the poor of his native town in Scotland.--"Gaz.".

145. Apr. 18, 1838/**MARRIED** In Pittsburg, on Thursday last, by the REV. DAVID H. RIDDLE, REV. HENRY G. COMINGO, of Steubenville, OH, to MISS ISABEL W., daughter of NEVILLE B. CRAIG.//On the same day, at Shafer's Hotel, on the same day, by the REV. B. S. SCHNECK, MR. DAVID SHERTZER, to MISS MARY GROSS, all of Franklin county, Pa.//On Thursday evening last, by the REV. MR. HIGGINS, REV. CHARLES TUCKER, to MISS MARGERY GREGG, both of Centre county, Pa.//In GreenCastle, March 13th by REV. J. REBAUGH, MR. JOHN BREAKBILL, to MISS MARY ANN WEAGLY, all of Franklin county, Pa.//On the evening of the same day, near Green Castle,

WEEKLY MESSENGER OF THE GERMAN REFORMED CHURCH

MR. JOHN HENWIEX, to MISS SUSAN OMWAKE, all of this county. By the same in Green Castle, March 20th, MR. HENRY FRICK, to MISS SUSAN SOUTH, of Washington county, Md.//In Troy, Pa., by REV. E. BRONSON, REV. HENRY MILLER, of the GRC, to MISS SARAH T. COLE, of the former place.//**DIED** On the 1st ult. in Logansport, IN, MR. ADAM YOUNG, consort of MRS. SOPHIA P. YOUNG, aged about 38 years.//On Friday morning the 6th inst., at his residence in Bellefonte, JAMES M. PETRIKIN, Esq. Attorney at Law, in the 37th year of his age.// On the 26th ult. MISS ELIZABETH, eldest daughter of MR. LEWIS WAMPLER of Westminster, Md., in the 15th year of her age.//The religious periodical, "Cyfaill" is issued in N. York in the Welsh language. Its editor is the REV. WILLIAM ROWLAND, of the Calvinistic Methodist (Whitfieldian) denomination.//**MONIES** From DAVID DERR, (Rodrocksville, Pa.) $2. J. R. REILY 3. T. M. K. HIESTER, 1 25. THOMAS GOLDMAN 2. FRANKLIN W. KREMER, 5. From MAJOR HENRY SNIVELY (Green-castle.) 2, JOHN WEAVER, (Up-?????.//**FUNDS** CHRISTIAN HOFFER 15, PHILIP KREIDER 10, JACOB E. STOVER 5, HENRY WITMER 5, JOHN KELLER (of JACOB) 5, HENRY STOUFFER 5, JAMES DUNCAN 20, DR.CHARLES COBURN 5, FREDERICK MAYER 10, ADAM NEIDIGH 15, JAMES ALLISON 5, MA[ink spot]ET SHENEBERGER 1, GEORGE HUBLER 5, PHILIP DINGES5,JOHN HOSTERMAN 5, CATHARINE ABELE 2 50, MICHAEL BOLLINGER 5, JOHN WEAVER 2, JOHN FORSTER 10, S. & F. LINEBACH 5, JACOB WOLFF 1, POLLY HENNY 2,THOMAS KRONMILLER 5,JOHN STOVER 2, ADAM STOVER 2,HENRY HETTINGER 1,ANDREW HARTER 2, JOHN KREMER 10, JOHN WOLF 5, ADAM BAUER 5, HENRY BAUER 5, ADAM STOVER 10, JOHN MOTZ 5,GEO. WEAVER 5, JACOB STOVER 5, JOHN TUTWILER 10, SAMUEL E. SHULTZ 2, JOHN G. WALTZ 1, ELIAS K. WASSER 3 50, DAVID DUNCAN 15, DAVID KAMP 1, HENRY HAUSMAN 5, WILLIAM KREB 10, EMANUEL NOFSKERT 1, JOHN MOYER 1, WILLIAM ALLISON 10, DAVID KELLER 1, WILLIAM McWILLIAMS 1, JAMES M'FARLANE 2.//**LETTERS.** REV. J. G. WOLFF, REV. S. GUTELIUS, SINGLETON MYERS, HENRY HERRING, Esq., THOMAS SHAW, REV. C. GATES,

WEEKLY MESSENGER OF THE GERMAN REFORMED CHURCH

REV. J. C. BUCHER, W. W. BELL, Esq., J. BEAVER, Esq., G. HERGESHEIMER, Esq., J. H. GREER, Esq., MARTIN HOOVER, Esq., J. GLANTZ, Esq., FRANKLIN W. KREMER, J. B. WALLACE, Esq., D. DUNCAN, Esq., L. ALLEMAN, M. KIEFFER, JOHN KILLINGER, Esq., REV. ALBERT HELFENSTEIN, JR., REV. J. REBAUGH, M. SILBER//Two females of Sunbury township Crawford county, Penn., have been charged with poisoning a MR. ISAAC DAVIS.

146. Apr. 25, 1838/**MARRIED** On March 29th, MR. WILLIAM YONTZ, to MISS SARAH ANN KIMES, both of Shepherdstown, Va.//On the 5th of April, inst., MR. GEORGE REYNOLDS, JR., to MISS MARY A. HENSELL, daughter of MR. MICHAEL HENSELL, all of Jefferson county, VA.//The 12th of April inst., MR. WASHINGTON HENSHAW to MISS MARY ELLEN DALGARN, of Jefferson county, VA.//On the 3d inst., by REV. D. DENNY, JONATHAN H. SLOAN, of Hollidaysburg, to MISS ADELINE, daughter of JOHN HUTCHISON, Esq., of Chambersburg.//**DIED** On Tuesday last, at his residence in Waynesboro', JAMES REILLY, Esq., aged 54 years.//At his residence, Saturday the 14th inst. MR. JACOB FRY, a respectable farmer of Green township, aged 79 years.// On the 10th inst., after a short illness, in the 47th year of his age,MR. ABRAHAM THOMAS of Washington county, Md.//At York, on Monday the 9th inst., MRS. HENRIETTA EICHELBERGER, wife of MR. BARNITZ EICHELBERGER and daughter of MARTIN DANNER, Esq., aged about 24 years.//On Friday, 13th inst., in York, MRS. CLARRISSA EBERT, relict of the late MR. ADAM EBERT, in the 72d year of her age.//**FUNDS** ?? KNAUSS 10, JOHN FISHER 1, GEORGE DRIESBAUCH 1,50, DANIEL BECKLEY 2. New Berlin, Union county, Pa.--MICHAEL CLEN[ink spot] $1,75, ISAAC PETERS 2, ABRAHAM SCHOCH 2, JOHN KLINE 1, JACOB SMITH 1, MICHAEL BENFER 5, WILLIAM FISHER 3, G. E. LASHELLS 2, JOHN BAKER 1, JACOB WETZELL 5, HENRY WETZELL 5, JOSEPH WETZELL 1.50, GEORGE DAUBERMAN 2, JOHN BENFER 2, HENRY ERDLE 1, JACOB ERDLE 1, JOHN ERDLE 1,HENRY WETZELL 5. Freeburg,

WEEKLY MESSENGER OF THE GERMAN REFORMED CHURCH

Union county, Pa.--GEORGE GLASS 5, PHILIP MERTZ 5, PETER MERTZ 10, F. C. MEYER 5, JOHN MEYER 5, HENRY HILBESH 5, JOSEPH PONTIUS 3, JOHN HILBISH 8, WILLIAM WALDSCHMIDT 5. Seliusgrove, Union county, Pa.---CHRISTIAN HAUTZ $20, JOHN BASKIN 5, JOHN FISHER 10, JACOB WAGENSELLER 10, WILLIAM P. WAGENSELLER 1, PETER RECHTER 10, GEORGE ADAMS 1, JACOB ALBERT 1, PHILIP GEMBERLING 10, ISAAC HOTTENSTEIN 5, LEONARD APP 5, CHARLES RHOADES 2,50, WILLIAM GAUGLER 1, GEORGE BERGSTRESSER 2,50, CHRISTIAN KAUTZ 2.

147. May 2, 1838/**MARRIED** Recently, at Dayton, (OH) by REV. D. WINTERS, MR. JACOB WITT, formerly of Chambersburg, to MISS MARY DARST, of Dayton.//**DIED** Communicated.--In York, on the 16th ult. MRS. HENRIETTA EICHELBERGER, consort of MR. BARNITZ EICHELBERGER, and daughter of MR. MARTIN DANNER, in the 26th year of her age. Her sickness was of a lingering nature. For some time, she was in great darkness and distress of mind; weeks before her death, however, light burst on her soul.//On the 20th ult. MRS. MARY W. BROWN, consort of REV. MATTHEW BROWN, D. D., President of Jefferson College, Cannonsburg, Pa.//On Monday in this place, MR. GEO. MARQUART, aged 43 years.//On the same day, in this borough, CAPT. JOHN CLUGSTON, at an advanced age.//**WHAT NEXT?**-MR. JOHN COCKERILL of Kottbus, has introduced a method at Berlin of reducing old cloth back to wool and re-weaving it. He has 300 men employed in the process.//**TREPANNING**. On a morning visit last week, to MA General Hospital, we saw REV. E. W. SEWELL, of Situate, a patient of the institution who had been in more or less constant pain for twelve years, due to a diseased condition of the bones of the skull on the left and upper surface of the head. Under these circumstances he came to Boston for advice. DR. GEORGE HAYWARD after examining all the circumstance was convinced that the mode of relieving an obvious pressure on the brain which was causing seizures

WEEKLY MESSENGER OF THE GERMAN REFORMED CHURCH

was to take out a portion of the bone. He took out a button of bone about three-quarters of an inch in diameter. The pain from the operation was intense, but there has been no return of the pain or the epilepsy.//**CHANGES** REV. JONAS DODGE from Lockport, Niagara county, N. Y., to Elmira, Chemung county.--STEPHENS TRUAX, from Ulster, Bradford county, Pa., to Ann Arbor, Washtenaw county, MI. Discontinuances.--THOMAS FULLERTON, Reading, S[age spot]ben county, N. Y.//**BANISHED IN CANADA.** On Wednesday, 18th inst., GEN. SUTHERLAND was banished for life to New South Wales. MR. JOHN G. PARKER pleaded guilty; it is feared he will be among those banished to New South Wales, and on the 12th the court was occupied with the trial of DR. HUNTER, who was finally acquitted. SAMUEL LOUNT, executed at Toronto on the 12th, was upwards of six feet in height, and aged about 47 years, and is said to have been a very good looking man. He was a native of PA, and has been in Canada since 1812. He married a daughter of MR. SOLES, a wealthy farmer who resides a few miles north of Toronto; he has left a widow and seven children.//Four--THELIER, ANDERSON, MONTGOMERY, and _____, (sic) are to be executed on the 30th.--"Toronto Colonist, April 12th."//**ESCAPED PRISONERS.** The sheriff and high constable of Lancaster, Pa. have been in quest of three prisoners who made their escape from jail about three o'clock on the morning of the 21st inst., by sawing through the bars, letting themselves down by blankets and scaling the wall by means of planks torn off the pig-pen. The names of the rogues are JAMES WAITE, who was on his trial for breaking open and robbing cars, and THOMAS SANDS and ROBERT BRICELAIN, (the latter known by the nickname BALTY,) who were confined for passing counterfeit money.//MR. GEORGE HARRIS, whilst engaged in quarrying Limestone for REV. DANIEL ZOLLICKOFFER, near Uniontown, Md., was deprived of life on the 11th ult., by the falling in of a bank of earth.//We learn

WEEKLY MESSENGER OF THE GERMAN REFORMED CHURCH

from the Watchman that the Baptist Mission in India has been deprived by death of the services of REV. LEVI HALL (husband of MRS. HALL, whose death was noticed) and MRS. ELHIRA BROWN OSGOOD, wife of MR. SAMUEL M. OSGOOD, printer. The first died in August, the last in October.//A man named THOMAS, Post Master at Broad Mountain, (Pa.) was arrested a few days since for opening letters and purloining money. He was brought to Philadelphia for trial, and is now confined in Moyamensing Prison.--"Philad. Herald."//**AN AWFUL ACCIDENT.** By a slip from the Pittsburg Gazette of Saturday last, (copied from an extra of the Cincinnati Whig of Wednesday night,) we learn of a most awful occurrence which took place within sight of Cincinnati, the afternoon of that day. The steamboat, *Moselle,* CAPT. PERRIN, left the wharf, for Louisville and St. Louis. About one and a half miles up the river, the boiler burst only thirty feet from shore, scattering the mangled limbs of the wounded, the dying and dead in every direction.//MR. BUCKINGHAM, the Oriental Traveler, to repeat his Lectures on Egypt &c. in Philadelphia city this week.//DR. COLLIER, Professor of Phrenology, visited our town some time last summer or fall and manipulated the Crania and surplus shin-plasters of some of the people in Hagerstown. The Doctor has left town without satisfying some of his creditors. Editors will confer a favor by giving the above a place in their papers--"Hagerstown Torch Light."

148. May 9, 1838/**MARRIED** At Baltimore on Thursday evening, April 26th, by REV. ROBERT BRECKINRIDGE, REV. RICHARD WEBSTER, of Mauch Chunk, PA, to ELIZABETH, daughter of the late WILLIAM CROSS of Baltimore.//At Morristown, NJ, on the 24th ult. by the REV. O. L. KIRTLAND, REV. GEORGE W. WOOD, Missionary of A. B. C. F. M. destined to Singapore, to MISS MARTHA MARIA, daughter of MR. SILAS JOHNSON, of Morristown.//**DIED** On Friday the 20th ult., after a long & severe illness,

WEEKLY MESSENGER OF THE GERMAN REFORMED CHURCH

MRS. CATHARINE E., consort of MR. P. L. HUYETT, Merchant of Funkstown, Md., third daughter of GEO. STONEBRAKER, Esq. in the 26th year of her age.//A young man, named HENDERSON, at one time employed in one of the Departments at Washington, has been arrested in Baltimore charged with forging Treasury Notes. He's suspected of theft at the US Hotel in Philadelphia.//**DISASTER.** The Steam boat *Moselle*-Nearly all on board (with the exception of those in the ladies' cabin,) were killed or wounded, principally Germans bound for St. Louis. Many have not been found. MR. WATTS merchant of Springfield, Mass., was driven head foremost through the roof of a house, on the OH side, about half his body inside. The body of CAPTAIN PERIN, was found under the bow of a new boat. The brother of CAPTAIN PERIN is alive, much bruised and scalded, not likely to recover. The second engineer, HALSEY WILLIAMS, is dangerously scalded. The pilots, first engineer, MR. MADDEN, clerk; second mate, deck hands and firemen, were all killed, as they are missing. MR. JAMES LYNE, of Henderson, Ky., had his left leg and arm broken, and his side much injured, not likely to recover. The list of the living, the dead and missing is from the Gazette slip of the 27th April: <u>DEAD</u> ELIJAH NORTH, Alton, Ill. W. PARKER's daughter MARY found drowned. B. FURMAN, Merchant,Middletown, O. barkeeper, B. MITCHELL, Cin. JOB JONES, Loudon co. Va. CAPT. PERIN, J. CHAPMAN, second clerk. T. C. POWELL, Lou., Ky. H. B. CASEY, Cin. JAMES BARNET, Mo. CALVIN R. STONE, Shrewsbury, Mass. JAS. DOUGLASS, Fort Madison, W. T. J. WILLIAMS, (colored.) HENRY STOKES, 2d steward. J. MADDEN, first engineer, HOLLY DILLON, fireman. ROBERT WATT, deck hand. E. DUNN, chambermaid. JAS. B. McFARLAND, Knox county, OH. MR. THOMAS, first mate MISS DUNHAM, 2MR. WATKIN's of VA. (sic) A. BURNS, Philadelphia. <u>WOUNDED</u> WM. H.INSKEP, St. Clairsville, OH. ____ (sic) SHERWOOD, Cincinnati. BENJAMIN BOWMAN, first clerk, HALSEY WILLIAMS, second engi-

WEEKLY MESSENGER OF THE GERMAN REFORMED CHURCH

neer. JAMES TURRELL, deck hand. _ (sic) DE JAUNE fireman, STEPHEN BAILY, carpenter. D. HIGBEE, Cayuga county, NY. ISAAC VAN HOOK. CAPT. PERIN's brother. __ TEED, (sic) Worcester, Mass., EDWARD SEXTON. __ FRANKLIN, (sic) 2d cook. JAMES FRY, 3d do. (sic) D. HIGBEE, NY state. <u>MISSING</u> GEO. KRAMER's two children, WM. PARKER's wife & two children. DR. W. HUEY, U. S. Army. JOSEPH SWIFT, Buffalo, N. Y. JOSEPH FOTLER, Boston, Mass. FILBIN FOTLER, do. GREKE FOTLER, do. JACOB FOTLER, do. JACOB BEAVER, do. JOHN BEAVER, do. EAVER BEAVER, do. MARY BEAVER, do., children of JOSEPH and EVE BEAVER. PETER TRAUTMAN's child 2 1/2 years old. MICHAEL KENNEDY's wife and two children. THOS. WATT, deck hand. MR. ARMSTRONG, mate. MR. WHITE, engineer. MR. PATTON, lawyer, Portland, Me. S. POST, wife and two children. J. FLEMING, pilot, Angelica co., N. Y. MR. D. HIGBEE's wife and two children. E. RAYMOND's wife and child, Baltimore, Md. JOHN EUDIG and JOHN SEIM, with each a wife and child. <u>SAVED</u> J. COULTER, Licking co., O. F. M. TOBIN's wife Lawrenceburg, Ky. G. KRAMER's wife and 6 children. W. PARKER, Pa. ___ WHITE, (sic) of Cin., wife and sister. ROBT. GIBSON & JAMES GIBSON, Louisville. JASPER HAMER, M'Cain co., Pa. W. B. PARKER, Cincinnati. ___ GATES, (sic) Franklin co., O. J. KEAN, Quincy, Ill. ___ THOMPSON, (sic) Cincinnati. J. C. RICHARDSON, Holden, Mass. SAMUEL DELLENGER. D. W. VISTTMAN, Canton, Ill. J. M. MANN and A. M. MANN, Portage, N. Y. C. and S. OSBORN, Cuyahoga co. N. Y. LAW. L. MINER, Green co.,.Pa. JOHN POOL deck hand. JOS. BEAVER and EVE his wife, and 3 boys. WM. HARRIS, ISAAC DAVIS. MICHAEL KENNEDY. FREDERICK DWIGHT, Springfield, Mass. JOHN PATTNAN and family, Canton, O. JONAS REMICK, MRS. HURST and child. A. BURNS, mother. __ FERRIS, (sic) Lawrenceburg, Ia. ELIZA FOTLER, J. FOTLER, SUSAN FOTLER (mother.) J. CADWELL, Wheeling, Va. T. O'NEAL, New Brunswick. PETER TRAUTMAN, wife and small child, Cin. J. PHELIM, Green co., Pa. D. O'NEAL, wife and 2 children

WEEKLY MESSENGER OF THE GERMAN REFORMED CHURCH

F. STEIN, wife and 2 children, New Philadelphia, O. JOHN SEIME and child. MRS. ANDERSON and one child. MRS. WEBBER and 4 children. GEORGE BROWN steward. EUGENE BAPTIST, do. EDWARD FLEMMAN, do. BENJAMIN LEWIS, do. LONDON ALLSON, cook. WM. HUSTON, deck hand. J. MENNICKEN, Mt. Vernon, O. J.D. ATHERTON,Sunbury, O. JOHN LYTLE, Ross co.O. JAS. THOMPSON, Cumberland co.,Pa. WM. SMITH, do. ADAM WEAVER, Canton, O. The Cincinnati Whig slip of 26th April: We have just returned from the scenes of horror, and the account above published, falls far short of dreadful reality. Fragments of human bodies are lying scattered all along the shore. Only four bodies have to-day been taken from the boat. One young man by the name of EDWARD SEXTON, from CT, we saw, dreadfully scalded; but his physician thinks he will get well. The lower deck is yet underwater, and when the boat shall be raised, a large number of persons, it is expected, will be found. MR. BROADWELL, the Agent of the boat, says positively there were one hundred thirty passengers on board, exclusive of the very large number who took passage at this place. In addition to those mentioned:--DAVID JAMES, Loudon county, VA. JOHN G. FREEMAN, Middletown, OH. GEORGE GLASSER, Cincinnati. JAMES BARNET, Rolls county, MO. JAMES B. McFARLAND, Knox county, OH. ROBERT WATTS, a young man whose father resides in Newport, Ky. We saw the father weeping over the corpse. JAMES DOUGLAS, merchant of Chillicothe, OH. COLLY DILLON, boat hand. MR. BURNS, boot binder, from Philadelphia. We saw his mother weeping over the body. Two of the Engineers--one named JAS. MADDEN a boy learning the business, was near the others but escaped. The Chief and second Clerk-the latter is stated to have escaped--but this proves to be erroneous--he has since died. The name of one of the clerks is BOWMAN, but we have not ascertained which. CALVIN R. STONE, Shrewsbury, MA. MISS DUNHAM, daughter of a Methodist clergyman living on the Miami. MR. CHAPMAN, a young man---saddler--Cincinnati. HENRY CASEY, a young man--boot maker,Cincinnati. B. MICHELL,bar keeper of the boat.//**ANOTHER** steam-boat accident is also noted in the Whig. "The *Oronoko,* CAPT. YOUNG, collapsed a flue near Vicksburg and forty to fifty persons were scalded. The Louisville Gazette of the 27th ult. states the explosion occurred opposite Princeton, Miss., on the 21st ult.; and that twenty persons were killed.//**YET ANOTHER!** The mail boat *Eutaw* between Wheeling and Steubenville, collapsed a flue on the morning of the 20th ult., by which one fireman was killed and thrown overboard--the engineer badly scalded--the clerk and a MR. NEAL, slightly.// **JAIL BREAK** The jail of Henrico Co. Va. was broken on Wednesday night last, and all prisoners escaped except DR. VAUGHN, confined for shooting MR. PLEASANTS. He would not leave.//**FIRE!** On the night of the 3d ult. in a block of frame buildings, on the main street in New Lisbon, OH, owned by MR. DAVID P. GRAHAM. The loss falls on MR. JOHN ARMSTRONG, CASPER & HARRISON, druggists; S. S. CLARK, hatter; DAVID MILLER, grocer; and J. & H. JANNEY, shoe store.//**MURDER** In Rockingham county on the 19th ult. While MR. WM. COMER (overseer for ABNER WEBSTER) was sitting on a stump calculating the number of hills made in a tobacco field, one of the negroes came on him in the rear and gave him a blow on the head which bro't him to the ground, when Mr. C. received many other blows inflicted by four negroes. The negroes have all been arrested and lodged in Jail.--"Greensboro' (N. C.) Patriot." //During the late meeting of the Carlisle Presbytery the REV. MR. DENNY asked for and obtained leave, to withdraw from his congregation in his declining years. REV. RICHARD WYNKOOP, late pastor of Hagerstown, was stricken from the roll. Mr. W. had complained of grievances which were decided against him,---and latterly has applied to the NY presbytery of the Associate Reformed church (commonly called Seceders).//**FIRE** Nearly all merchants on King street in Charleston, were burnt out. The fire broke out in a paint store last night at a quarter past 8 o'clock. PARISH, WILLEY and Co., G. H. KELSEY & Co., BORHEM & Co. and MILLER, RIPLEY and Co. were lost.//**MONIES** By REV. A. P. FREEZE, from MARTIN EICHELBERGER, $5. JOHN P. FREEZE, 1.25, REV. A.P. FREEZE, 3.75. By REV. S. R. FISHER, from H. MANAHAN, 2, MARTIN NEWMAN, 2, PETER TROXEL, 2, ELIZA RIFE (IN,) 2. ANDREW DONALDSON, (alias BOLDWIN,) 6, MRS. DR. DIEFFENDERFER and T. S. HUBBARD, each 2, REV. E. HEINER, 1. PETER WHITEHEAD, (Adamsburg) 2, G. & L. M. TROUTMAN, 2, C. GAST, 1, G. METZGER, 1, JACOB SLEMMER, 2, ELIZABETH WEBER, (Warren,) 2. By W. AUGHINBAUGH, from GEORGE SHEETZ, GEORGE PHILIPPI, B. COUNTRYMAN, each 2. By D. WEIDNER, from MRS. M. THOMAS, 2, HANNAH GIRVAN, 4, and AUGUSTUS WAGNER, 2. GEO. CHAMBERS, Esq. 2. By J. INGOLD, from HENRY SMITH, (St. Thomas,) 4, JACOB MILLER,JOHN NEWCOMER, each 2, JOHN LONG (Loudon) 4, JOHN BEAVER, 4, JACOB MILLER, 2. For Christliche Zeitschrift from FREDERICK DRYER, (Emmitsburg,) $1 to be discontinued.//**LETTERS** HENRY C. BEAM, SIMON DRUM, R. E. LINEBACH, H. LEAS.

149. May 16, 1838/**MARRIED** In Lebanon, on Tuesday evening last, by the REV. MR. RUTHRAUFF, E. W. HUTTER, Editor of the "Independent Republican" of Allentown, to MISS ELIZABETH E. SHINDEL, of Lebanon, Pa.//At Sunbury, on Monday the 30th of April, by REV. JAMES KAY, MR. CHARLES PLEASANTS to MISS ELIZA P., daughter of HUGH BELLAS, Esq. all of that place.//On the 6th ult., by the REV. MR. BIBIGHOUSE, the REV. JACOB ALLEBORN, to MRS. CATHARINE DEDECKER, both of Philadelphia.// In Harrison, IN, on the 18th March, by REV. W. C. RANKIN, MR. JOSEPH F. DOLL, to MISS ELIZABETH M. FRAVEL, daughter of MR. BENJ. FRAVEL, formerly of Woodstock, Va.//Tuesday, the 1st inst. by REV. A. KIRKPATRICK NELSON, MR. WILLIAM BLAIR, formerly of Carlisle, to MISS ELEANOR COYLE, all of Perry county, Pa.//At Hancock, MD, on Thurs-

day, 3d inst., by the REV. DR. KNOX, the REV. J. McELROY, D. D., of NY, to MISS SARAH McLANAHAN, of the former place.//**DIED** In Harrisburg on the 10th inst., SIMON SNYDER, Esq. aged about 74 years. The dec'd. was a native of Lancaster, Pa. He removed to Northumberland county. On division of the county, he held office in Union county.// Saturday morning last, MRS. SUSAN HARRIS, wife of MR. THOS. J. HARRIS of this place.//In Philadelphia on Wednesday morning last MRS. MIRA HALL in the 25th year of her age, wife of MR A. M. HALL, daughter of the Editor of the Franklin Repository.//The New Orleans True American in an article relating to the explosion on board the steamboat *Oronoko*. Among the victims was a known black-leg, who in the extremity of agony, confessed himself the incendiary who fired Pinkard House, in hope of burning Vicksburg! He denounced another gambler DR. SAUNDERS, as his partner in the intended sack of the city.

150. May 23, 1838/**MARRIED** In Mifflinburg, on the 3rd inst., by REV. J. H. FRIES, MR. SAMUEL SMITH, of Venango, Pa., to MISS CHRISTIANA LENHART, of Mifflinburg, Union county, Pa.//On the same day, in Mifflinburg, by the same, MR. JACOB SHAFFER of Venango county, Pa., to MISS MARY ANN CAMP, of Mifflinburg, Pa.//On the 14th inst., by REV. HENRY R. WILSON, SEN., REV. ROBERT W. DUNLAP of St. Augustine, FL to MISS MARTHA B. MAHON of Shippensburg, Pa.//In Lykens Valley, Pa., May 15., (sic) by REV.I.GERHART, MR. GEORGE RECKS of Southbend, IN, to MISS HENRIETTA, third daughter of THOMAS HARPER, Esqr.,recently of Lebanon Co., Pa.//In Lancaster, OH, May 3d, by REV. H. WILLIARD, MR. GEO. GRIM, of Tarlton, to MISS MARIA STROUSE, of Fairfield co, OH.//On the 3d inst., in Fayetteville, by REV. GEO. St. C. HUSSEY, MR. SAMUEL MITCHELL, of Mt. Rock, Cumberland, co., Pa. to MISS PRISCILLA SHREADER, of Green Castle, Franklin co., Pa.//**DIED** Monday morning, May 7th at the residence of her father in Easton, MISS

WEEKLY MESSENGER OF THE GERMAN REFORMED CHURCH

LETITIA HESS, in the 21st year of her age; after a consumptive illness of about four months. She connected herself with the GRC when she was sixteen, under the pastoral care of REV. T. POMP.// The Buffalo Journal of Saturday says the Circuit Court yesterday decided BENJAMIN RATHBURN may be released on bail in the sum of $5000 upon each indictment, three in this county and two in Genesse.//MR. MATTHEW CRAIG, a paper maker, in the paper mill of WM. WALLACE, in Somers, Tuesday of last week, attempting to pry the fly wheel, the mill accidentally started, crushing his arm and skull, producing instant death. He left a wife. -Sing Sing paper.//REV. J. D. KNOWLES, professor in the Newton (Baptist) Theological Institution, died on the 9th inst. at his residence, of varioloid. He had just returned from NY, where it is supposed he contracted the disease.---"Boston Mercantile Journal."//The Little Rock Gazette states that CAPT. De HART, of the U. S. Army, reached Fort Towson the morning of the 31st ult. //**HIMMALEH MOUNTAINS.** A letter from New-England clergyman REV. JAMES WILSON to the Boston Herald describing scenery.//**FOR MISSION BOARD** Per REV. B. S. SCHNECK 2 90 in Shippensburg. From REV. S. GUTELIUS: DAVID SHRIVER, BARBARA SPANGLER, HENRY SHRIVER, each 10 00; REV. JACOB BEAR, JOHN HORN, GEORGE HARN, GEORGE WILL, Esq., each $5 00; JOHN THOMAS 1 00; ISAAC KREPS 3 00; JACOB MYERS 2 00; //**MONEYS RECEIVED.** From REV. D. WILLERS $2, and P. PETERS 2; REV. JACOB BEAR 2, JOHN CASHMAN 2, JOHN WOLFF 2; MRS. C. & R., donation of 4; MYERS & WOLF, (New Oxford) 2; by REV. S. HELFENSTEIN, from ABRAHAM YOST, MRS. HUNT, ADAM RUMER, each 2; REV. S. HELFENSTEIN 1, MARTIN HOOVER, Esq. 4, SAMUEL HEBERLIG 2; PETER TRITT 1.12 1/2, by F. A. RUPLEY, from JOEL B. DANNER, (Gettysburg,) 5.75; S. S. FONNEY 3, JAMES HEAGY 4, CHRISTIAN DOBLER 2, DR. JESSE GELBERT 2, JOSEPH MATHIAS 1 25; WM. SMITH, (Bellefonte,) 2. JACOB (alias CHARLES) COONTZ, (Martinsburg, Va.,) 2.50, MISS SUSAN GROVE 2, C. EVERSOLE 25 cts. JOHN D. KEEDY (now OH,) 2, SAMUEL S. MORITZ (Emmitsburg) 2, JOHN OVER, (Marion, Pa.) 2, JACOB SNIDER, Esq. (Shippensb.) 1, CONRAD ZODY 2, REV. JAMES BLACK [OH,] 5. Received for "Christliche Zeitschrift" from REV. D. WILLERS, Fayette, N. Y., $1, JOHN NOLL, Millersburg, Dauphin Co., Pa., $1, CHRISTIAN HOFFMAN, Berrysburg, Dauphin Co., Pa., $1.

151. May 30, 1838/**MARRIED** On Tuesday evening, 1st inst. in Reading by REV. J. PERRY,MR. GEORGE E. LUDWIG, to MISS MATILDA H. KEIM, daughter of BENNEVILLE KEIM, Esq., all of Reading.// On the 15th inst., by REV. DANIEL GOTTWALD, REV. JOHN ULRICH, pastor of the Lutheran Church of Carlisle, Pa., to MISS SUSAN CATHARINE, only daughter of MR. HENRY GROVE of Allen township, Cumberland county, Pa, formerly of Baltimore.//May the 3d, by REV. D. G. BITTLE, REV. JOHN J. REIMENSNYDER, pastor of Zion's Church, to MISS SUSAN M. BRYAN, daughter of CAPT. BENJAMIN BRYAN, Augusta county, Va.//On Thursday evening last, by REV. MR. HELFENSTINE, MAJ GEORGE KEALHOFER, to MISS MARY ELIZABETH, daughter of the late DR. HANENKAMPF, of Hagerstown, Md.//On Tuesday last, by REV. H. R. WILSON, DR. ROBERT T. YOUNG, to MISS ANNETTA CULBERTSON daughter of STEPHEN CULBERTSON, Esq., of Shippensburg, Pa.//On Thursday the 14th inst. by REV. O. H. BORGESS, MR. JEREMIAH DONAVIN, to MISS MARY BROWN, all of Cambersburg (sic).//**DIED** At his residence near Wellsville, OH, the 2d of May, 1838, REV. THOMAS EDGAR HUGHES, formerly of York county, Pa.//In Green Castle, Pa., Tnesday (sic) the 15th inst., MISS MARGARETTA WALKER, aged 32 years.//On Wednesday last, MR. WILLIAM DOUGHERTY, in the __ (sic) year of his age. The dec'd. bore the character of an up-right, honest man. This tribute is more readily given as he belonged to a religious communion(RC) from whose tenets we widely differ.//THOMAS BRADFORD, Esq., successor to DOCTOR FRANKLIN, oldest printer and editor in the Union, died in Philadelphia in the ninety-fourth year of his age.//**MONIES** By C. H.

WEEKLY MESSENGER OF THE GERMAN REFORMED CHURCH

LEINBACK, from CATHARINE DAVENPORT (Sink Spring) $2, N. and A. DICK 2, ADAM LEIS 2.

152. June 6, 1838/**MARRIED** February 8th, by the REV. J. HELLER, MR. ELIAS WAGONER, to MISS JULIA ANN DYER, both of Pendleton county, Va.//Somerset, Pa., on the 10th ult., by C. FORWARD, MR. JOHN J. HENNEBERGER, of Hagerstown, to MISS JULIAN COFFROTH, of the former place.//On the 20th ult., by REV. ISAAC GERHART,MR. ISAAC WINGERT to MISS HANNAH SMELTZER, both of Millersburg, Dauphin county, Pa.//On the 24th, by the same, MR. CHRISTIAN SHEIDER, to MISS SUSAN MILLER, of Armstrong Valley.//On the 29th, by the same, MR. FRANCIS WENNIG from Perry county, to MISS MARIA, youngest daughter of ADAM LIGHT, Esq., of Millersburg.//On the 31st, by the same, MR. JOSEPH WILLIER to MISS ELIZABETH MATTER, both of Lykens Valley.//In Easton, Pa., May 29, by REV. BARNARD C. WOLFF, REV. JOHN G. WOLFF to MISS SUSAN YOUNG all of that place.//The 24th ult., by REV. PETER M'ENALLY, MR. G. W. BOWMAN, Editor of the "Bedford Gazette," to MISS EVE ANN, daughter of MAJ HENRY LEADER of Bedford township.//Thursday last by REV. JOHN N.HOFF ,MAN, (sic) MR. PHILIP EVANS to MISS ANN BANKERD all of this place.//**DIED** In NY, on the 27th ult., REV. F. W. GEISSENHAINER, SEN., in the 66th year of his age for many years pastor of the Lutheran Church in that city.// **MONIES RECEIVED.** By J. EBBERT, from HENRY FLUCK (Bloody Run)2, From JOHN BORTNER 2, F. SHEARER, (Cookstown) 3. By REV. J. G. WOLFF, from JACOB BAKER, (Mt. Bethel) MISS MARY STEM, each 2. By REV. B.C. WOLFF, from MR. BOYER, MARIA HUBER, S. W. FOGEL, each 2,REV. ZUILCH 5. By REV. J. ZEIGLER, from JOHN BROWNBACH 5. By REV. G. GLESSNER, from D. HOTTEL, (Woodstock) 5, GEO. HOTTEL 2, and H. EMSCHWILLER 2. By REV. J. HELLER, from JOHNSON and DYCE, ABR. LOUGH, J. W. SEMER, each 2. SAM'L STAMBAUGH 1. D. HELLMAN (Jackson Hall) 2; JACOB GORNER (Maytown) 3; ROBERT FILSON 2. The Editor of the "Christliche Zeitschrift," is

WEEKLY MESSENGER OF THE GERMAN REFORMED CHURCH

requested to send his paper to REV. CHRISTIAN WINEBRENNER, Martinsburg, Bedford Co., Pa.,

153. June 13, 1838/**MARRIED** In Middletown, Md. on the 7th of June by the REV. J. C. BUCHER, MR. WILLIAM SAVOY, to MISS SUSAN, only daughter of the late MICHAEL HOFFMAN all of Frederick county Md.//On Thursday, the 7th inst., by REV. A. P. FREEZE, MR. SAMUEL CRAMER, to MISS SUSAN BUCKEY, both of Frederick county, Md.//**DIED** Near Middletown, Frederick county, Md., the 20th of May, MR. CHRISTIAN NEYSWANGER, aged 79 years, leaving widow and twelve children.//Near Burkettsville, Md., the 29th May, CORDELIA, youngest daughter of DR. JOHN D. GARROTT, aged 1 year 1 month, and 25 days.//In Green Castle, on Friday night, June 1st, WILLIAM M., son of CONRAD and CATHARINE HERR, in the 9th year of his age. On Saturday afterwards the corpse was conveyed to the GRC cemetery.//Wednesday last in this borough, MRS. CATHERINE HOFFMAN, wife of FREDERICK HOFFMAN, dec'd. late of this place, aged 76 years and 7 months.//Tuesday morning last, MR. JACOB MAWRER, respectable citizen of Hagerstown leaving a wife and several small children; formerly a citizen of Chambersburg.//A gentleman from Oswego says that ten pirates have been arrested. The Watertown Jeffersonian says that three are in jail in that village. Of those arrested are NATHAN LEE, of Clayton, in Jefferson county; BATES, HUGH SCANLON, and two brothers WARNER--all Canadiand (sic) except LEE.//E. HEINER, Agent received these sums pledged on the Theological Library Debt.

REV. J. C. BUCHER,	$20
" S. R. FISHER,	20
" MR. FREEZE,	15
" E. HEINER,	35
" G. W. GLESSNER,	20
" R. DOUGLAS,	15
" J. F. DIFFENBACHER,	10
" J. W. HOFFMEIER,	10
" J. C. HENSEL,	5

WEEKLY MESSENGER OF THE GERMAN REFORMED CHURCH

154. June 20, 1838/**MARRIED** In Frederick city, on the 10th of May by REV. DANIEL ZACHARIAS, MR. R. J. W. POLK, of Woodstock, Shenandoah county, to MISS SARAH J. SOMERVILLE of Winchester, Frederick county, Va.//On the 5th inst., by the REV. SAMUEL SMITH, REV. WM. M. REYNOLDS, (Principal of the Preparatory Department of PA College,) to MISS ANN M. SWAN, both of Gettysburg.//**DIED** At York on the 17th ult., MRS. MARY AUSTIN, consort of MR. MARTIN AUSTIN, in the 26th year of her age.//On the 10th inst., in Guilford township, WILLIAM COOK, son of GEORGE COOK, JUN., aged 21 years. In the field, the horses became unruly, ran off and caused the plough share to enter his body, which terminated in death.//In Philadelphia, one of the watchmen, named JOHN BATTS, of the District of Southwark, was murdered abut two o'clock on Friday morning, 8th inst. at Third and Shippen streets by a coloured man. The murderer has been arrested, and is proved to be in a state of frantic lunacy, that he escaped the previous day from the lunatic apartment of the Philadelphia alms house. A young man, FRANCIS KEARNEY, aged about twenty-two years, died Sunday morning, 10th inst. at the PA Hospital by a wound in the abdomen inflicted by a mulatto man with whom he had quarrelled on the day before.// **MONIES.** By REV. W. COLLIFLOWER, from ISAAC HOTTEL, JACOB ROSENBERGER, R. J. W. POLK, each 2, and SAMUEL RINKER 1. JAMES DUFFIELD 2. By GEO. BESORE Esq. from GEO. PENCE, 2. ELIZ. ALLSWORTH, (Greensb'g)2//**LETTER** J. KULP, THOS. H. BURROWES.

155. June 27, 1838/**MARRIED** On Thursday last, by the REV. B. S. SCHNECK, MR. HENRY FRANCISCUS, to MISS MARTHA JANE BESORE, both of Letterkenny township, Frankl. Co.//Monday morning, the 11th inst., in the GRC, Philadelphia, by the REV. J. F. BERG, WM. H. TODD, Esq., of Louisville, Ky., to MISS AMANDA MELVINA, daughter of HENRY DERRINGER, Esq. of that city.//On Tuesday evening, 12th inst., by REV. MARTIN BRUNER, MR. LUTHER

WEEKLY MESSENGER OF THE GERMAN REFORMED CHURCH

RICHARDS, junior editor of the Lancaster Examiner and Herald, to MISS ELIZABETH, daughter of the late, JOHN REITZEL, all of Lancaster, Pa. //DIED On the 14th inst., in Shippensburg, in consequence of an injury received on the railroad, about three weeks previous, MR. ADAM WOLF, in the 64th year of his age.//At Princeton, NJ, Saturday, the 16th inst., after a lingering illness, MRS. MARGARET BRECKINRIDGE, wife of REV. JOHN BRECKINRIDGE, D. D., professor of Pastoral Theology in the Seminary at Princeton, NJ, and daughter of the REV. SAMUEL MILLER, D. D.//REV. M. ROTER, D. D., Superintendent of the Methodist Mission in TX, died on the 15th ult.

156. July 4, 1838/**MARRIED** In Lincoln county, N. C., Thursday evening, the 7th inst., by REV. J. G. FRITCHEY, MR. HENRY F. RAMSOUR, to MISS SARAH E., daughter of MR. PHILIP SHUFORD.//**WRECK OF PULASKI.** We give the following particulars from two passengers who survived. Copy from the Balt. Chronicle and other papers. A short time previous to the explosion it was remarked to MAJOR HEATH the guage (sic) showed thirty inches of steam. The engineer replied it would bear with safety forty inches. Hearing the noise of the explosion, the Major got under the steps, as did MR. LOVEJOY of GA, and they were shielded. MR. AUZE, a French gentleman, of Augusta was crushed by the mast. The boat now broke in two. At daylight he found that there were twenty-two on the wreck with him, among them CAPT. PEARSON, who had been blown out to sea. After five days the schooner *Henry Cameron,* bound from Philadelphia to Wilmington, N. C. took them on board. During the morning another portion of the wreck was seen. On this wreck were MRS. NOAH SMITH of Augusta,MISS REBECCA LAMAR, MASTER CHARLES LAMAR of Savannah, and MR. ROBERT HUTCHINSON, also of Savannah. MR. HUTCHINSON had lost his wife and child. His wife was the daughter of MR. ELLIOTT formerly US Senator from GA. When the prominade

deck separated from the hull, MR. G. B. LAMAR of Savannah, and two children, the REV. MR. WIRT and lady of FL, a child of MR. HUTCHINSON, and the 2d mate took refuge on it. On Saturday, the mate proposed to take the boat which they had secured to the deck, and with five of the most able on the raft to endeavor to reach shore. On Wednesday they reached New River Inlet. Those remaining died from exhaustion---among them the REV. MR. WIRT and lady. The body of MR. PARKMAN of Savannah floated to the raft. Also dying, JUDGE ROCHESTER, of NY, formerly of NC. By slip from the Wilmington Advertiser, thirty more have been saved. The following are the persons taken from the wreck. A. LOVEJOY, Camden county, GA ; MR. GREENWOOD, Augusta, GA; MR. O. GREGORY, ditto; MRS. NOAH SMITH, do.; MISS REBECCA LAMAR, do.; MR. A. HAMILTON, do.; __ (sic) CHICKEN, 1st engineer ; E. JOSEPH, NY; D. WALKER, and THOMAS DOWNING, Charleston; MAJOR HEATH, Baltimore; PATRICK and BILL, deck hands ; MAJOR TWIGGS and son, Richmond co., GA; CHARLES LAMAR, Savannah; ROBERT SEABROOK, Edisto Island, S. C.; MASTERS T. and W. WHALEY, do.; MR. EDINGS, do.; MR. HUTCHISON, (sic) Savannah, MR. C. WARD, do.; C. W. CLIFTON, Canton, Miss.; CAPTAIN PEARSON, Baltimore ; WARREN FREEMAN, Macon, GA ; JOHN CAPE, fireman, Baltimore; RHYNA a negro woman.//**MONIES** By JAMES POTTER, from D. WISE, J. POTTER, W. HEWES, A. McCOY, JONAS FROM, each 2, and JACOB KRISE 2.50. From J. H. ALEXANDER (Balt.) 5. By D. WEIDNER, from MRS. C. WEISER (al. ENGARD) 2, A. M. WAGONER 50 cts. From GEORGE MILLER, JR., (York) 2, JEREMIAH SNIDER (Chamb.) 6, JOHN MILLER (Jackson-Hall) 2, HEN. SCHNEIDER (N.Hanover) 5.50, REV. LEWIS C. B. HERMAN 4.50. By J. MYERS (Marietta) from JOHN KLINE and H. SULTZBACH each 6.50. By REV. J. HENSEL, from JOHN SHUTZ (Va.) 7, MRS. MARY COYNER 2 and REV. J. HENSEL 1. From GEO. NEWMAN (VA) 1. By REV. D. ZACHARIAS, from CATH. HEITSHU, MARY SHOLL, and J. REYNOLDS, each 2. By J. COULTER, from JACOB RAMSOUR, JOHN HOKE,

WEEKLY MESSENGER OF THE GERMAN REFORMED CHURCH

JOHN MOTZ, JR., SAMUEL LANTZ, DR. A. RAMSOUR, DAVID RAMSOUR, (Tanner) SOLOMON RAMSOUR, MICHAEL FINGER, ABEL A. SHUFORD, WARLICK and FINGER, J. COULTER, DANIEL and J. RAMSOUR, JOHN RAMSOUR, MISS ALVIRA WILSON, each 2. By J. J. SHUFORD, from ROBERT P. EDWARDS, ISAAS (sic) DOUGLAS, WM. EDWARDS and J. J. SHUFORD, JOHN EDWARDS, each 2. By REV. J. G. FRITCHEY, from SUSAN SHUFORD, D. RAUCH, (Evesville) REV. J. G. FRITCHEY, LAWSON REINHARDT and F. W. P. REINHARDT, each 2. By REV. G. A. LEOPOLD, from J. ROLLER, 5, and KIRSH and WISE, 4. For the Christl. Zeitschrift. MR. DANIEL LANTZ, new subscriber, $1. From REV. J. B. ANTHONY 50 cts., and for the "Religoese Zeitschrift" 1.50 to the credit of FATHER HINTSH.//**A FLOOD** Hollidaysburg, June 18, Letter to the Editors of the Philadelphia Spirit of the Times. It commenced raining last night about 11 o'clock until about 4, when the waters of the Juniata were rising with fearful rapidity. MR. BARRACK, wife two children and servant girl attempted to escape. Mrs. B. and the children were drowned, Mr. B and the girl narrowly escaped, being rescued, the former by PATRICK SMITH and another, and the latter by J. C. BATES. MR. JOS. KEMP, of the Pilot Line, also narrowly escaped. The store of MESSRS. CULBERTSON & CHAMBERS was carried entirely away.//**LIBRARY DEBT** From the REV. MR. GERHART, the following sums, viz:

	REV. J. H. FRIES,	$22 00
"	D. WILLERS,	20 00
"	P. S. FISHER,	21 00
"	D. GRING,	15 00
"	R. DUENGER,	13 55
"	R. A. FISHER,	5 00

From REV. JOHN BROWN, Harrisonburg, Va, through REV. J. HENSEL, $10.00.//**LETTER** ABR. HORN.

157. July 11, 1838/**MARRIED** On the 17th June, by the REV. W. F. COLLIFLOWER, MR. MICHAEL SMITH to MISS ELIZABETH LINDAMOOD, both of Rockingham co., Va.//On the 28th of June, by the same, MR.

WEEKLY MESSENGER OF THE GERMAN REFORMED CHURCH

CHRISTOPHER HICKLE, to MISS ANN BENDER, both of Shenandoah co., Va.**//DIED** In this borough, after a lingering illness, Saturday morning last, MR. THOMAS SCOTT, aged about 35 years**//THANK YOU** to CAPTAIN DAVIS of the schooner *Henry Camerden,* (sic) and the citizens of Wilmington adopted by the survivors. MR. J. H. ELLIOTT and MRS. PHILLIPS, whose names were published in this list of passengers, left the *Pulaski* at Charleston, and consequently did not perish.**//LETTER** June 26, from Attica, IN. Last Sabbath we concluded the services of a protracted meeting. MR. SANDERS was assisted by the REV. MESSRS. CRAWFORD and KINGSBURY of the Presby. church. There was an uncommon degree of indifference exhibited on the part of the people, until Sabbath day.**//MONIES.** From D. DUNCAN, (Centre co.,) 5, JAMES ALLISON 2.50. By J. HADE, Esq., from CONRAD HERR 2.

158. July 18, 1838**/DIED** Friday last, in Green township, MR. ADAM HECKMAN, aged about 60 years. The death was occasioned by the bite of his own dog in the arm, whilst engaged in holding him.**//** It is said the LAMAR family, lost in *Pulaski,* were all going to England to see the coronation. The young LAMAR that survived has gone raving mad.**//MOURNFUL** One day last week MR. DOYLE, of Pine Grove, left this town on a visit to Emmitsburg, with his wife and two small children in a gig. The wheel passed over a stump, by which they were all precipitated from the gig - and their youngest child, aged 3 months, was so injured as to cause its death in a few minutes.--- "Gettysburg Whig."**//**The Sheriff of the County has been in possession of MURTAUGH's death warrant, designating this day (Friday, July 13,) for execution. The prisoner, however, continuing in a state of derangement, the Governor has forwarded a reprieve until Friday the 12th of October next, unless the mind of the prisoner should become sufficiently "right" to justify execution. --"Chambersburg Whig.".

WEEKLY MESSENGER OF THE GERMAN REFORMED CHURCH

159. July 25, 1838/**DIED** On Thursday morning in this place, after a short illness, MRS ETTER, wife of MR. CHRISTIAN ETTER, at an advanced age //On the 15th inst., MR. JOHN CHRIST, of Hamilton township, aged 23 years.//On the 16th inst., MR. JOHN SHETRON of Hamilton township aged about 83 years.//Suddenly, at the house of JAMES DIXON in St. Thomas township, on the 10th inst., CATHARINE STOHRM, in the 22d year of her age. The dec'd. was at work in the Harvest field of M. M. WAGNER, apparently in good health, and in a few hours was a corpse.//In Mercersburg, on the 10th inst. after a lingering illness, MARGARET McDOWALL, wife of DOCTOR JOHN McDOWALL, in the thirty ninth year of her age.//**REVOLUTIONARY** soldier, JOHN CAMPBELL, lying dangerously ill in Piqua on the Fourth asked that the procession of citizens should stop at his dwelling as he wished to see the American Flag. His wish was complied with, and during the day, he expired.--"Columbus (OH) Journal."//**MURDER!** The night of the 16th, a man named GEORGE COLLINS living on the Magothy River in Anne Arundel County, while under the influence, as is supposed, of ardent spirits, shot his sonRICAHRD, aged 18 years, and killed him on the spot; had another of his sons named JOSHUA, up in one of the rooms of his house, but he escaped by breaking through the window, and while in the act of running from the house was fired at by his father, and severely wounded in one arm.--"Balt. Am."//**MURDER!** Three years ago last April, MR. JOHN McDUFFIE, formerly from VT, who had been long known in the vicinity of Sing Sing as a pedlar and school teacher left the residence of MR. SAMUEL KIPP, where he was then boarding to go a few miles on business. He was never heard of. He left at MR. KIPP's a quantity of clothing, at MR. R. WILLIAM's he left a horse, wagon and some goods. Last week as persons were cutting a new road near the "Furnace Woods," his body was discovered buried in a sitting position. The verdict of the jury was, that he was

murdered by a person or persons unknown. "Hudson River Chronicle."//**MONIES RECEIVED.** By REV. J. ZELLER, from DR. HOUTZ, JOHN HUYETT, H. SPIESE, JOHN KELLER, (of JOHN,) (Yellow Springs,) HENRY HUBLER, and DR. W. SWOOPE, each 2. By REV. B. C. WOLFF, from MISS COOPER, JULIA LEVAN, JOSEPH SHEIMER, MARIA YOHE and REV. B. C. WOLFF each 2.

160. August 1, 1838/**MARRIED** On Thursday evening last by REV. B. S. SCHNECK, MR. THOMAS JAMES to MISS MARGARETTA RAMSEY, both of Chambersburg. //By REV. J. REBAUGH, in Green Castle, on Thursday afternoon July 5, MR. LEWIS CHEANEY, to MISS MARY ANN DODD all of Williamsport, Md.//**DIED** In this borough on the 12th ult., MRS. JANE COOPER, consort of MR. SAMUEL COOPER, aged 62 years.//On Saturday last near Hagerstown, MR. DAVID MIDDLEKAUFF, in the 35th year of his age. //In Frederick, on Thursday last, MR. CHRISTIAN GETZENDANNER, late editor of the Frederick Times, aged 47 years.//A few weeks since near Mercersburg, Pa., MRS. HORNBAKER, aged one hundred and ten years. //On Monday morning last, DR. SAMUEL YOUNG, one of the oldest inhabitants of Hagerstown, Md., in his hundredth year.//In Berlin, Somerset county, Pa., on the 14th ult. WILLIAM GELLERT, son of REV. S. K. DENIUS, aged 7 years, 6 months, and 12 days.//**A FIRE** in Harrisburg, Pa. on the 20th inst. in a stable belonging to MR. J. OSTLER, on Strawberry alley, between Market and Walnut. It destroyed the stage stable of MESSRS. COLDER and WILSON, stable belonging to MR. ROBERTS, lumber yard of MESSRS. HOLMAN and SIMMONS, dwelling and bindery of MR. C. MUENCH, dwelling of MR. JOHN SHANNON, and injured MR. JENNINGS' residence on Market street.//**MONIES** By C.F. HOFFMEIER,from P. METZGER 1, JACOB BUSHONG, $2. From ISAAC SMITH, (Up. Mt. Bethel) 1. By GEORGE BESORE, from HENRY HERBAUGH, 2. JAMES LEIBY, (Newburg,) 1.25.// **LETTERS** SAMUEL G. FRAVEL, PATRICK YEATZ.

161. Aug. 8, 1838/**MARRIED** By the REV. P. SAHM,

WEEKLY MESSENGER OF THE GERMAN REFORMED CHURCH

in St. Thomas, MR. JOSEPH ALSOP, to MISS SARAH CRUMMEL formerly of Marietta, Lancaster co., Pa.

162. Aug. 15, 1838/**DIED** On Thursday last, MISS RACHEL BESORE, daughter of MR. PETER BESORE, of Letterkenny township, aged 23 years.//The same day, ELIZABETH, daughter of MR. FREDERICK ROEMER of Green township, aged about 6 years.//At his residence in Green township on Monday last, ANDREW THOMPSON, Esq., aged about 70. His remains were intered (sic) at "Rocky Spring."--"Whig."// In Philadelphia, on the 1st of August, after a lingering illness, COMMODORE JOHN RODGERS, of the US Navy. Obit from National Intelligencer. **//HORRID MURDER.** From the AR Gazette of June 27th: Particulars of the murder committed in Pope county by WM. BROWN, on the person of his wife. BROWN, according to the testimony of his children, had threatened her on the morning of the murder, the 15th inst. In a few minutes she looked in the direction of the house to see the muzzle of a rifle pointed at her, she received the contents (2 balls) between her breasts. The children fled to the neighbors at Dardanelle, about three miles from the house. When they arrived back at the scene, the brutal murderer had laid the victim on the bed, washed the blood from her, and drank himself stupidly drunk. His weapons were secured, himself seized and bound. The body was buried at Dardanelle, followed by the manacled murderer who showed no remorse. Both were from the neighborhood of Concord, NC, and were the father and mother of five children, the oldest 14 and the youngest 2 years old.--- From the "New Yorker."//**DEATH** of MR. and MRS. PERRY, Missionaries at Ceylon, on the 10th and 13th March, of Cholera. Mrs. P. (formerly HANNAH JOANNA LATHROP, of Norwich, CT) watched her husband to the last, and followed him within two days. Three of the four missionary sisters have thus gone.//New York, August 1. About half past three o'clock this morning a fire broke out in

WEEKLY MESSENGER OF THE GERMAN REFORMED CHURCH

the soap factory of BAURMEISTER & SCHEPELIN and a major portion of the block destroyed. SAMUEL KILPATRICK, an aged man residing at No. 146 Hammond street, was burned to death.//**TEMPERANCE** A convention will be held in Chamb'g, on Friday the 7th of September next. FRED. SMITH, PHILIP BERLIN, RICHARD BOND, JAMES MORROW, JOHN SMITH, Committee.//**WANTED.** Steward of moral worth with small family in Marshall College. GIDEON BANTZ, Frederick, Md. JOHN SMITH, Chambersburg, Pa. WM. McKINSTRY, DANIEL SHAFFER, WM. METCALFE, Mercersb'g.//**MONIES.** By REV. J. HELLER, (Virg.) from JOHN EYE 2, JOHN W. DAVIES 2, SAMUEL MILLER 1.25. By REV. J. G. WOLFF, from BENJ. WEBER 2, MISS MARTINS 2, (Worcester,) REV. J. STRASBERGER 4. From ANDREW WHISLER 1, REV. GEO. LEIDY 2.

163. Aug. 22, 1838/**MARRIED** In Shippensburg, on Thursday the 16th inst., by REV. WILLIAM C. BENNET, MR. JOHN JAMES BENNET, of New Utrecht, Long Island, N. Y., to MISS KEZIAH CRISWELL, of Shippensburg, Cumberland county, Pa.//In York, Pa., on the 4th inst., by REV. JOHN CARES, MR. ROBERT C. WOODWARDof Cincinnati, OH to MISS SARAH ELLEN SPANGLER, youngest daughter of MR. PETER SPANGLER, dec'd.//In Greencastle on the 12th inst. by REV. J. REBAUGH, SAMUEL OTT, to MISS MARY BROWN, all of Washington County, Md.//**DIED** On Saturday last, in this place, MR. THOMAS LINDSAY, at an advanced age.//On Saturday afternoon 11th inst., a man named ALLEBON, near Shippacksville, Montgomery co., Pa. was killed by lightning.//**SEMINARY FUND** From Agent REV. JACOB MAYER, in Montgomery county, Pa. congregation of REV. HENRY S. BASSLER. BENJ. REIFF, Esq. $10.00; HENRY FREIER, 2 50; BERNHART FREIER, 1 00; PETER FREIER, 1 00; BENJ. WEIL, 1 00; ISAAC KRUPP, 50 cts; JACOB C. OVERHOLSER, 5 00; FRED. WARMPOLE, 10 00; ANDREW KRIEBEL, 1 00; BENJ. KRIEBEL, 5.00; SARA ANDRES, 1 00; GEORGE ANDRES 10 00; JOSEPH KRIEBEL, 1 00; ABRAHAM KRIEBEL 1 00; REV. DAVID KRIEBEL, 5 00; MICHAEL REIFF, 2,00; REV. H. GERHART, 5 00; DR.

WEEKLY MESSENGER OF THE GERMAN REFORMED CHURCH

SAMUEL YOUNG, 5 00; ANDREW REED 5 00; WILLIAM K. STAUFFER, 3 00; HENRY LANDIS, 5 00; REV. JOHN C. BECHTEL, 3 00; PETER NEIMAN, 5 00; C. K.SCHULTZ, 10 00; AMOS SCHULTZ, 5 00. DANIEL STEARLY, 1,00; DR. W. B. HAHN, 5 00; ADAM HILLEGASS, 6 00; JOHN KOONS, 1 00; ISAAC LINDERMAN, Esq. 5 00; JOSEPH BOYER, 2 00; JACOB BOYER, 2 00; JOHN YOST, 1 50; JACOB SCHLI?HTER, 2 00; MICHIAL DECKER,1 00; JOSEPH GROVE, 50 cts; HENRY BAREMAN, 3 00; SAMUEL GRUBB, 5 00; AARON MULL, 10 00; BENJ. B. YOST, Eqs. (sic) 5 00; PETER SHAFFER, 5 00; JACOB SERVER 5 00; GEORGE SCHWENK 2 00; BENJ. BRAND 2 00; HENRY GRUBB 1 00; JOHN GRUBB, 1 00; HENRY GRUBB, JR. 1 00.//Donation to the Education Society of MD Classis, of $16 00 from the Female Education Society of Emmittsburg.' per hands of MISS M. L. BAUGHER.//Four Americans, the rest British subjects, have been sentenced to be hung on the 28th. The Americans are LINIUS WILSON MILLER, NORMAN MALLORY, GEO. COOLEY, and WM. REYNOLDS.

164. Sep. 19, 1838/**DIED** At Fairbreeze, in this county, on Tuesday last, MRS. ELIZABETH DUNCAN, late of Erie.//On Wednesday morning, 5th inst., at his residence in Southampton township, MR. JAMES BRACKENRIDGE, (of JOHN,) in the 33d year of his age.//On the 5th inst., of the Dysentery, WILLIAM SHARP, aged about 10 years; and on the 12th inst., of the same disease, AGNES MARGARET SHARP, aged about 7 years, children of MR. ROBERT SHARP, of Green township.--"Franklin Repository."//On Monday morning, 10th inst., at the residence of ___ (sic) HAMBRIGHT, Esq., near this place, MRS. ELIZABETH SHIRK, in the 79th year of her age. She had but a short time ago, left her home for the purpose of visiting her daughter and son-in-law in this county. Instead of returning to her earthly home (New Holland, Pa.,) she returned we trust, to Heaven. Tuesday morning, interred in the GRC cemetery of this place. //September 7, 1838, of a lingering and afflictive disease, MRS. SUSANNA, consort of MR. PETER

WEEKLY MESSENGER OF THE GERMAN REFORMED CHURCH

KEPHART, of Middletown Valley, Frederick city, MD, agad (sic) 32 years and 22 days. She left a husband and six children.//At York, Pa., on the 4th inst., very suddenly, MR. GEORGE SMALL. He left a consort and four children.//At his residence in Gettysburg, Adams county, Pa., Tuesday evening, August 28th, DR. JESSE GILBERT, in the 32nd year of his age. A native of Adams county he has left very circumspect parents, brothers and sisters, a young and tender widow, and two young daughters, unconscious of his departure, to mourn him. The disease which terminated his existence, was painful and severe; he first took to his couch on the 13th ult.//MR. SAMUEL CROUSE of Taneytown, Md., is appointed an Agent for the Messenger, in conjunction with BR. FEETE. MR. JOHN HEIMER, JR., former agent at above place, having removed to Indianapolis, Ind., requested to act in the same capacity in the latter place.
//**MONIES** By REV. S. B. LEITER, from JAMES LANGHAM $2, SAM'L DOME 2.50, S. B. LEITER 50 cents; by H. COST, from P. SOUDER 5. JOHN FEASTER, SEN. 2, MARIA KELLER 2, H. COST 3; from JACOB WEAVER, GEORGE SHAFER, JOHN COBLENTX, SEN. (sic) (Middletown, Md.) each 2, REV. J. C. BUCHER 1; from GEORGE GRIMES, (Taneytown) 2; by J. BANKS, from NANCY KNODE, A. NEFF, MARY EAKLE, each 2; JACOB RAMP, (Newville) 1.25. MRS. NANCY McCLEERY 2, REV. T. OSBORNE 2.50, & MRS. C. ROOP 2.50; from MESSRS. KOONS, BROWER, and GRATER, (Schwenks) 5; ALEXANDER JAMIESON, (Pittsburg) 2, HENRY HECKERMAN 2, SAMUEL SNYDER, (D?dotsburg,) 2. WILLIAM VONDERAW, (Green-castle) 5; by REV. J. WOLFF, from JACOB MOORE, PETER SNYDER, REBECCA SAEGER, (Allentown,) REV. A. L. HERMAN, (Reading,) each 2. DR. A. J. HERMAN 5, C. J. FABER 5, REV. W. PAULI 7, MRS. JOS. GOOD, (Reading,) 2 50, JOHN HOFFMAN, Esq. 5; W. LOTZ 5, by REV. B. WOLF from E. NEWLAND 2.50, and MRS. S. SNYDER 2; from DR. YOUNG, (Montgomery co.) 2, REV. DR. HENDEL 3, I. & D. SHULTZ 2, DANIEL BOYER, Esq. 4, D. HERR. *We acknowledged $2 to B. C. WOLFF, which he now

WEEKLY MESSENGER OF THE GERMAN REFORMED CHURCH

requests transferred to MISS J. OBERLY. MR. JOSEPH SPRINGER, Hillegass P O Montgomery Co., Pa. wishes to subscribe to Christleche Zeitschrift. //**SEMINARY FUND** Per REV. JOHN G. WOLFF, JACOB LERCH Allen towns'p, Northam'n co., $10. JACOB LERCH, do. do. 4. GEO. WOLFF, Esq., Martinsburg, Va. in full $75.

165. Sep. 26, 1838/**MARRIED** On Wednesday evening last by REV. MR. GRACEY, DR. ROBERT M. DENIG of McConnellsburg, Bedford county, to MISS JANE K. HARRY, daughter of MR. SILAS HARRY, of Chambersburg.//On the 19th ult., by REV. J. ZIEGLER, MR. JESSE AMOLE, to MISS SIDNEY DAVIS, both of Coventry.//**DIED** At his residence in Westpensborough, near Carlisle, Pa., on the 21st of August, REV JOSHUA WILLIAMS, D D in the 71st year of his age.//A correspondent at Monmouth, (IL) date of the 12th inst. says: "On Thursday last, about 6 A.M. near Bowling Green in this (Warren) county, lightning struck the house of MR. OTHO CARR and struck down MRS. CARR and four children, killing three of the latter. The children were about 5, 7, & 9."--"Peoria Register Aug. 25."//The daughter of MR. RISINGER, in Ripley county, OH, was shot a few days ago by her father. He was hunting with his brother, and shot what he thought was a deer. He found it was his own daughter who had come to hunt the cows.//MR. ASAHEL COLLINS, of Ulster Village, N. York, has made application for a patent for an apparatus to improve supplying air to furnaces and forges.//The Toronto Patriot states that JACOB BEAMER, JOHN W. BROWN, SAMUEL CHANDLER, BENJAMIN WAITE, ERASTUS WARNER, and ALEXANDER M'LEOD, sentenced to be executed on the 31st ult. have been respited to the 1st of October//A fine specimen of gold found on the land of MR. THORNTON ASH, Fauquier county, Va.

No marriages or deaths in Oct. 3, 1838 edition.

166. Oct. 10, 1838/**MARRIED** On the 6th ult., by

WEEKLY MESSENGER OF THE GERMAN REFORMED CHURCH

REV. JACOB ZEIGLER, MR. ELI KNOWER to MISS SAVILLAH HOUCK both of Chester county.//By the same on the 23d ult.,MR.CHARLES A. SPIESE, of Chester county,to MISS MARY SNYDER, of Berks co.//On the 27th ult., by REV. D. FEETE, MR. DANIEL DANNER to MISS DEBORRAH ECKER, all of Carroll county, Md.//**DIED** In Hilltown, Montgomery co., Pa. on the 22d ult., MR. JOHN LEIDY,in the 59th year of his age.//Near Middletown, Md., MRS. HAPE, consort of MR. JACOB HAPE, in the 47th year of her age.//On the 21st of August last at his residence near the Newville, REV. JOSHUA WILLIAMS,D.D., aged about 70 years.//Petersburg (Va.) Intelligencer chronicles the death of PLEASANT BUTTERWORTH, aged 19. Six or seven weeks previous, he was bitten by a dog belonging to the family, having symptoms of being rabid. He applied one of the "celebrated Mad Stones". After a week, he was induced to submit to a mercurial course until he salivated. He enjoyed good health, until last week, (Frday,) (sic) when he was taken with a pain between his shoulders and a chill. Saturday spasm after spasm succeeded each other, until death.//**FUND**. In aid of the Building Fund collected by REV. JACOB MAYER, Trappe Congregation, Montgomery county.--REV. J. C. GULDIN $5, HENRY WEICKEL 1, SAMUEL CHRISTMAN 2, PETER LONGACKER 5, SALOME RONDEBUSH 1.50, SAMUEL ROUDEBUSH 1, HENRY SHADE 2, GEORGE BUCKWALTER 1.50, HANNAH PAUL 1, HENRY LOUCKS, Esq. 1, WILLIAM CASSELBERY 1, MARGARET MOSER 25 cts. WM. BUCKWALTER3, LYDIA FREY 50 cts ABRAHAM REED 50 cts. HENRY E?PENSHIP 5, DAVID BEARD, Esq. 2 50, JACOB HISER 1, AARON WANNER 50 cts. HENRY NETZ 50 cts. JACOB FREY 3, ABR'M KOONS 5, JAMES KOONS 2.50, JULIAN FOX 50 cts. MARY FOX 1,JACOB PETERMAN 1, ISAAC LANGEKER 1,ROBERT UNMSTEAD 1.50, JONAS TYSON 5, ELIZABETH SCHRACK 50 cts. JACOB WEICKEL 75 cts. VALENTINE KRATZER 50 cts, PHILIP WACK, D.M. (sic) 1, BARBARA WACK 1, JOHN EISENBERG 2, SAMUEL SCHLEIFER 50 cts. Wenses Congregation, Montgomery county.-HENRY FRICK $2, LEDIA BOYER 5, HENRY FRICK 2.50,

WEEKLY MESSENGER OF THE GERMAN REFORMED CHURCH

ANNA FRICK 50 cts. FRONICA FRICK 2, ELIZABETH A. WACK 50 cts. PHILIP S. GERHARD 5, JACOB HEISLER 5, ABIGAIL P. GERHARD 5, PHILIP HOOT 2.50, PETER HOOT 5, BARBARA BEAVER 1, CATHARINE WANNER 1, FREDERICK BEAVER 1, JESSE FRAUTZ 1, MARY DANCHAUER 1, SARAH MARTIN 1.25, MARY MARTIN 1.25, MARY ANN SNYDER 1, HENRY HEEBNER 2.50, SALOME SCHULTZ 5, JOHN ANDERS, SEN. 5, JOHN ANDERS, JR. 2, JACOB ANDERS 3, ABRAHAM KRIEBLE 2, BENJAMIN ANDERS 2, JOSEPH KRIEBLE 2, PETER WANNER 5, DEWALT WANNER 2, MICHAEL ZILFING 1, GEO. SCHULTZ 2, ABRAHAM HEEBNER 5, ANTHONEY HEEBNER 5, JOHN and PHILIP STONG 2, BARBARA STONG 1, HENRY STONG 2, RICHARD STONG 25 cts. FREDERICK STONG 1, JOHN WEBER 5, MELCHER KRIBBEL 3, ELIZABETH WEBER 1, MICHAEL BRUNNER 5, JOHN FRICK 3, N SCHLA?CH 3, REV. BALSER HEEBNER 5, DAVID S. HEEBNER 1, FREDERICK ANDERS 1, GEORGE SEIPT 1, MICHAEL VANFOSON 2, JOHN WANNER 2, MARIA M. WEBER 50 cts. EMALINE M. WEBER 50 cts. BENJAMIN WEBER 5, REV. GEORGE WACK 10, ADAM KERN 50 cts. ELIZABETH WACK 5, N. PANEBECKER 5. Hilltown Congregation Bucks county GEO. SCHEIB $10, GEORGE WEISEL 10, JOHN SCHEIB 5, MICHAEL SCHELLENBERGER 5, BARBARA SCHEIB 1, JONATHAN GERHARD 5, JOHN GOTSCHALL 1, JACOB REED 2.50, HENRY FUHRMAN 2.51, MAGDALENA MOYER 1, JACOB RENDER 1, HENRY BRUNNER 5, SAMUEL CONVER 1. From different persons.--JACOB LEIDY $10, SAMUEL LEIDY 12.50, LEIDY WORMAN 5, JOHN WEAVER 5, JOHN STEINER 5, JOHN H. STEINER 1, JOHN RICHNER 1. New Goshenhoppen Congregation, Montgomery county additional - REV. CHRISTOPHER SHULZE $10, SAMUEL HILLEGASS 5, CHARLES HILLEGASS 5, CHARLES REED 1, JOHN WOLFFARD 2, CASPAR SCHULTZ 1, GEO. KOLP 1.50, REBECCA HILLEGASS 5, JOHN SASSEMAN 5. In Centre county.--PHILIP REITZEL $5, JOHN WALKER, SEN. 10, JOHN W. EHRHART (sic) 2.50, N. KAUFFMAN 2, MICHAEL HACKMAN 7; by W. REIFF, from BALTZER HEIDRICH, Montgomery co., 5//**MONIES RECEIVED** By REV. A. P. FREESE, from D. V. MILLER 2, CHARLES D. SMITH 7--(deduct $1 for coll.) DANIEL PANNEBAKER 2, PHILIP REED 5, JOHN HARTRANFT 2, (by

WEEKLY MESSENGER OF THE GERMAN REFORMED CHURCH

REV. WEISER.) At Synod - from PHILIP REITZEL, (Centre county) 4, CHARLES TROXEL (Reading) 2, ROB. S. LODER (Cherryville) 1.25, JOSEPH SNAVELY 2, JOSEPH LAUBAUCH 2, JOHN WOLFERSBERGER 2, JOHN BRUNER (Jonest'n) 2, PHILIP VONEADA 2, HORACE LEET, (Somerville, N.J.) 2, REV. B. C. TAYLOR (do.) 2, MRS. C. MOSER (Philad.) 2, MRS. OAT 2, H. RILE 2, JOHN RILE 2, JOHN SCHLATTER 2, JOHN FITZGERALD 2, WILLIAM REIFF 2, WILLIAM FRUTCHEY, 2, A. LONG, (alias A.& J.L.) 2, REV. J. H. SMALTZ 2, DANIEL LONGENECKER (Lanc.) 2, DAVID DAVIS (St. Mary's) 2, JOHN SHIMER 2, WILLIAM BROWNBACK 3, JOHN P. COBLENTZ (Middletown, Md.) 2, ROBERT SCHAEFFER 6, DANIEL BISER, SEN., 3, JOHN MICHAEL 4, HENRY COCHRANE 2, and REV. J. C. BUCHER 1. By REV. J. MAYER, from AARON WANNER (Trappe) 2, SAML. EBERT(Worcester) 2, ZACHARIAH LEIDY (Line Lexington) 1;MRS. KING 5.//**LETTER** M. M. STONER.

167. Oct. 17, 1838/**MARRIED** On Wednesday evening, Sept. 5th, by REV. W. F. COLLIFLOWER, MR. BENJAMIN ZIRKLE, of Dandridge, Jefferson co., East TN, to MISS SUSAN PENNYWITT, of Shenandoah co., Va.//On the 16th of Sept. by the same, MR. MOSES FREY to MISS MARY MOHLER, both of Shenandoah co., Va.//The 9th inst. by REV. E. HEINER, MR. CHARLES DIFFENDERFFER to MISS MALINDA ANN NEFF, all of Baltimore.//The evening of the 7th inst., by the same, MR. JOHN W. HOLLAND to MISS ANN MARIA CRULLE, all of Baltimore.//In Middletown, Md. on the 30th ult. by REV. J. C. BUCHER, MR. JOHN MILES to MISS LYDIA GAVER, all of Burkettsville, Md.//The 11th inst., by REV. JACOB HELFFENSTEIN, MR. LEWIS ANDREW to MISS CATHARINE BROWN both of Fayetteville, Franklin county.//On the 21st ult. by REV. J. F. BERG, MR. ARCHIMEDES HECKMAN to MISS CATHARINE W., daughter of the late ANDREW STEWARD, Esq.,all of Philadelphia.// On the 21st of August, by the REV. J. REBAUGH, MR. PETER MOWER, of this county, to MISS REBECCA RENNER,of Washington county, Md.//On the 23d, by the same in Green-castle, MR. WM. SHAFER to MISS

WEEKLY MESSENGER OF THE GERMAN REFORMED CHURCH

ELIZABETH BOWMAN, all of Hagerstown, Md.//By the same, MR. JACOB BOHER to MISS JANE LAUTON all of Franklin county.//On the 6th ult., by the same, MR. JOHN WACHTER to MISS ELIZABETH POWERS, all of Washington co., Md.//**DIED** Tuesday the 31st of July, at Timberville, Rockingham county, Va., after a long and severe illness, which confined her for eleven months, MRS. SARAH THOMPSON, consort of WM. E. THOMPSON, leaving a husband.//On Monday, the 24th September, after an illness of about eight months, SAMUEL D. son of REV. JOHN BROWN, aged 29 years, 5 months and 10 days of consumption.//On the 9th inst., at his residence in Harmony, N. J. leaving a widow and four children, REV. ROBERT LOVE, pastor of the Presby. church of that place in the 32d year of his age. //In Westminster, on Thursday morning, the 27th ult., MRS. HANNAH WAMPLER, relict of the late J. LEWIS WAMPLER, dec'd., in the 58th year of her age.//At Reading, Pa. on Friday, 5th inst., MRS. SUSAN D. B. REEVE, wife of SAMUEL REEVE, and daughter of GEORGE D. B. KEIM.//On Monday evening, September 24th, MR. UPTON BRUMBAUGH, third son of MR. HENRY BRUMBAUGH, aged 26 years and 8 day. Some months previous he left home with a friend for the West, with the rose of health on his cheek. His remains were deposited in the family burial ground on Tuesday following.

168. Oct. 24, 1838/**MARRIED** On Wednesday evening, 17th inst. near Chambersburg, by REV. B. S. SCHNECK, REV. FREDERICK RAHAUSER, of Tiffin, OH, formerly of this place, to MRS. HANNAH KIEFFFER, of Franklin co., Pa.//On the 30th ult., by REV. S. R. FISHER, MR. WM. FERGUSON to MISS CATHARINE WILLIARD, both of Washington township, Franklin county, Pa.//On the 7th inst. by the REV. DANIEL HERTZ, MR. DANIEL STARK to MISS AMANDA RUP, both of Lancaster county.//On the 11th inst., by the same, MR. ISAAC RANK, Teacher, to MISS CATHARINE RUTH, both of Lancaster county.//The same day by the same, MR. SAMUEL FRANTZ to MISS MARIA SCHNI-

WEEKLY MESSENGER OF THE GERMAN REFORMED CHURCH

DER, both of Lancaster county.//In Harrisburg, the 4th inst., MR. JOSEPH LEIB, of Pottsville, to MISS ROSANNA KELKER, daughter of FRED'K. KELKER, Esq. of the former place.//**DIED** After a painful illness of five days in Vincent, Chester co., Pa., HENRIETTA FREDERICA THERESA, daughter of REV. JOHN C. GULDIN, and his wife, HENRIETTA CATHERINE, aged 6 years and 10 months.//Suddenly near Tiffin, OH, Sept. 6th, MRS. SARAH KROH, consort of MR. JACOB KROH, of that place. MRS. KROH was originally from Washington county, Md. //In Harrisburg, on Saturday last, MISS MARIA GROSS, daughter of the late ABRAHAM GROSS, aged about 21 years.//**ABDUCTION**. The captain of the Madison steamboat on Lake Erie, is in prison at Pittsburg on the charge of abducting MISS HAMOT, of Erie, some months since.//**MONIES**. REV. E. RAHAUSER $1, DAVID ROSENBERGER 2.50, MRS. SUSAN BUCHER, (Harrisburg,) JOHN ZELLER, (Leacock) 2; by J. FOLCK, (Rainsburg) from JAMES RAWLIINGS 5, THOMAS OLIVE? 5, I. LINGENFELTER 5, JACOB STEUDEN?OWER 2.50, and FRED'K. HISSONG 2, (ded. 1.50 p.c.) by J.B. WELTY,from JOS. WEAST, J.B. WELTY, HENRY NYMAN, each 2.//**LETTERS** CHARLES LEVY.

169. Oct. 31, 1838/**MARRIED** On the 23d inst. by REV. J. HELFFENSTEIN, MR. DANIEL AUGER to MISS CATHARINE BROADRIP, both of Franklin co., Pa.// On the 25th inst. by the same,MR. THOS. HARRISON to MISS MARY LEIDY, both of Franklin co.//On the 6th ult., by REV. D. G. BRAGONIER, MR. ROBERT M. SMALL, of Clearspring, to MISS J. E. M. daughter of MR. D. HOWER.//On the 14th ult, by the same DENTON J. McCOY, proprietor of McCOY's Ferry, to MISS SUSAN MILLER, both of Washington co., Md.// **DIED** In Sharpsburg, on the 12th ult., after a few days sickness, JOHN CALVIN, eldest son of REV. JOHN W. HOFFMEIER, aged 2 years, 14 months and 12 days.//On Saturday, the 7th ult., in the 49th year of her age, MRS. ELIZABETH BLACKFORD, consort of COL. JOHN BLACKFORD, of Ferry Hill, Washington county, Md. Interred on Tuesday, in

the family burying ground, in Jefferson county, Va. The complicated disease was less than three days duration. She left a husband and children.//On Wednesday, the 24th inst., in Bedford, Pa., MR. JOHN REYNOLDS. Conversing with an individual, he dropped down and expired as he fell.

170. Nov. 7, 1838/**MARRIED** On the 1st inst., by REV. J. HELFFENSTEIN, MR. AUGUSTUS REINEMANN to MISS HARRIETTA JARRETT, both of Chambersburg.// On the 30th ult., by REV. J. SECHLER, MR. JOHN CASHMAN to MISS SUSAN THOMAS both of Adams county.//On the 10th ult., by REV. C. G. M'LEAN, MR. EBENEZER WADE, of Montgomery county, OH, to MISS ELIZABETH, daughter of MR. JOSEPH WALKER, dec'd. of Adams co., Pa.//On Thursday evening, the 11th ult., by the REV. MR. ZOCCHI, DR. DAVID DILLER, of Huntingdon county, Pa. to MISS ELIZA ANN, daughter of JACOB MATHIAS, Esq. of Westminster, Md.//On the 10th ult., by REV. SAM'L SPRECHER, MR. WELLS COVERLEY, of Houston's Place, Centre county, to MISS MARY ADALINE COLDER, of Harrisburg.//**DIED** In Guilford county, NC, on the 30th ult., in the 20th year of his age, NATHANIEL B. CLAPP. Two years ago, after a protracted meeting at the Brick Church, under the care of REV. MR. CRAWFORD, he attached himself to the GRC.// In Chambersburg on the 31st ult. MR. HUGH GREENFIELD, aged about 50 years.//In Baltimore on the 31st ult., MRS ARMSTRONG consort of MR. JAMES ARMSTRONG, (Holliday street.) leaving a husband with two infants.//On Wednesday 17th ult. CHRISTIAN FRANKLIN, son of DANIEL KEMP, Esq., near Buckeystown, Md.,in the 15th year of his age. He had returned from college about two weeks, during which time he complained of a slight cold.// Suddenly, on Monday afternoon, COL. JOHN FINDLAY, Postmaster of Chambersburg. He was highly esteemed as a friend & neighbor.//**MONIES** GEORGE MILLER, (Strasburg, Frank. co.,) 2; HEN. SNYDER, (Pickering,) 2; STEWARD & ETCHBERGER, 2; by JOHN HOUCK, from SAM'L McLEAN, 2.50; JOHN W. EDWARDS,

WEEKLY MESSENGER OF THE GERMAN REFORMED CHURCH

2; and JOHN HOUCK 50 cts.; by SAMUEL LEIBY (Newport) from GEO. CARL, 2; HENRY SWITZER, 2; and JACOB YOHN, 3.25; by REV. D. GRING, from JOHN BALLIET, PHILIP FOLMER, JACOB BOUSH and JAMES LEWARS, each 2; from ISAAC CLUGSTON, 2; HENRY K. HENNIGH, (Gettysburg,) 2; by D. H. DOLL, from MICHAEL SEIBERT, BERNARD DOLL, DANIEL H. DOLL, ROSANNA DOLL, and JOHN C. CUSHWA, each 2. For Christliche Zeitschrift from HENRY DIEFENBACHER, North'd co. $1.25 JOHN DEIFENBACHER, do. 1.25.//
SUNK We learn from the Baltimore Transcript of Saturday, that on the night of Wednesday last, the schooner *American Trader* CAPTAIN DOLBY, from Fe??y Landing, when off the river Wicomico, in Chesapeak Bay was sunk by a Dutch galliot, about two o'clock in the morning. There were on board nine persons, three of whom were saved--the captain, MISS SUSAN KEILER, and MISS EMILY PALMER, daughter of COL. PALMER, of the Eastern Shore.

171. Nov. 14, 1838/**MARRIED** By REV. GEO. GLESSNER, MR. SAMUEL STONER to MISS SUSAN BOWDEN, all of Waynesburg, Franklin Co. Pa.//Thursday last, by REV. A. HELFENSTEIN, MR. JOSEPH FIERY of this County, to MISS MARIA NEWCOMER, of Hagerstown.// On the 18th of October, by REV. A. HELFENSTEIN, MR. GEORGE KNODLE to MISS MARGARET SPIELMAN.//On Thursday morning last by REV. WILLIAM T. SPROLE, ALFRED ARMSTRONG, of Harrisburg, to MISS ANN, daughter of THOMAS CAROTHERS, Esq., of Carlisle. **//DIED** In Funkstown, Md., on 31st October, ANN ROSINA VIRGINIA, daughter of H. J. & MR. (sic) A. SHAFER, aged 4 years and 11 days.//On Sunday afternoon at the Hotel of MR. N. SNYDER in this place, HENRY WHEELER, in the prime of life.

172. Nov. 21, 1838/**MARRIED** By REV. J. REBAUGH in Green Castle October 11th MR. JACOB CROSS, to MISS MARY A. STROCK,of Washington county Md.//By the same on the 17th MR. SAMUEL LESHER, to MISS SARAH A. YOUNG, all of this county.//By the same on the evening of the 17th MR. SAMUEL HOUSER, to

WEEKLY MESSENGER OF THE GERMAN REFORMED CHURCH

MISS MARY HARRISON, all of this county.//By the same, on Thursday last MR. WILLIAM REED, to MISS SARAH NISEWANDER, all of this county.//By the same on Thursday last,MR. WILLIAM NEEDY, to MISS ELIZABETH PORKELT, all of Washington county, Md. //On the 4th inst. in Springfield, OH, MR. WILLIAM COMEGEYS, of Urbanna, OH, to MRS. JANE BRADLEY, daughter of WM. W. BELL, Esq. of Gettysburg.//On the 1st inst. at Tansey-town, (sic) by the REV. MR. FEETE, MR. WILLIAM OTTER, JUN. of Emmittsburg, to MISS ELIZABETH LATHAM of Tanneytown. (sic).//On the 4th ist. (sic) by REV. MR. ALBERT, MR. SAMUEL T. ATLAND, to MISS ELIZABETH HILDEBRAND---both of Berlin, Adams Co., Pa.//On Thursday evening, Nov. 1st in Lincoln Co., N. C. by REV. J. G. FRITCHEY, MR. F. D. REINHARDT, to MISS MARTHA S. youngest daughter of COL. EPHRIAM PERKINS, dec'd.//On the 8th inst. by REV. N. P. HACKE, MR. JOHN KNERE of Grapeville, to MISS ANN MAGDALEN, daughter of GEORGE BENDER of Westmoreland Co, Pa.//On the same day, by the same, MR. JACOB GRIFFITH to MISS MARGARET FELLBAUM both of Mountpleasant, Westmoreland Co, Pa.//**DIED** The 28th of October, at his residence in Attica, IN, MR. MICHAEL HINDES, formerly a resident of this place, in the 45th year of his age; leaving a widow and three children.//About the same time, SANES HINDES, son of MICHAEL HINDES, dec'd., in the 12th year of his age.--"Hag. Torch Light."// In Pittsburg, October 25th of scarlet fever, after 24 hours illness, JOHN BRENEMAN, infant son of CHRISTIAN and ELIZABETH SEICHRIST, in the third year of his age.//In new Holland, Pa. on the 10th inst. SOLOMON GOSHER, son of RICHARD GOSHER, of that place, in the 20th year of his age.//At Mercersburg, on Sunday evening the 4th inst. MR. JOHN CROOKS, aged 36; years (sic) leaving an affectionate wife and three children.

173. Nov. 28, 1838/**MARRIED** On the 1st of Nov. by the REV. D. WEISER, DR. SAMUEL YOUNG of Colebrookdale, Berks county, to MISS ANNA MARIA,

daughter of DR. CHARLES DICKENSHIED, of Upper Milford, Lehigh county, Pa.//**DIED** On Thursday evening, the 1st inst., the clothes of REBECCA ADELAIDE, daughter of HENRY and ANN ELIZA EMSCHWILLER, caught fire, how no one knows; she was so severely burnt that she died on the following evening. She was aged 2 years, 2 months and 18 days.//On Thursday night last, MR. CHRISTIAN WINTER, of this place, accidentally shot his eldest son, a boy about 8 years of age, thro' the head. The ball entered, on the left side, in front of the ear, and passed out the back of the head, carrying a portion of the brain and scull (sic) with it. Mr. W. was examining a pistol, which accidentally went off, the ball passing through a thin part of his hand, and the child's head, slightly wounding a man in his employ, and lodged in a partition.--"Hagerstown Torch Light, Nov. 22."//A tribute of respect from the Diagnothian Literary Society of Marshall College, adopted on 13th November, to the family of MR. CHRISTIAN F. KEMP. Signed WM. MAYBURRY, Speaker. THEO. C. W. HOFFEDITZ, Secretary.//Appointed to the Ex. Com. of the Board of Domestic Missions.-REV. J. HELFFENSTEIN, BARNARD WOLFF, JOHN SMITH, LEWIS DENIG, W. HEYSER, and PETER COOK, Esqs.

174. Dec. 5, 1838/**MARRIED** In Hagerstown, Oct. 16,by REV. JOHN REBAUGH, MR. JACOB IRWIN,formerly of Cumberland co., Pa., to MISS LAVINIA BOWERS, of Sharpsburg, Md.//Oct. 25th, by the same, in Greencastle, MR. ANDREW NEVIN, of Adams co., Pa., to MISS MATILDA, daughter of LEWIS RIPPLE, Esq. of Franklin county.//Nov 22nd, by the REV. D. HERTZ, MR. ABRAHAM KURTZ, of Berks county, to MISS ANN SHARK, of Conestoga, Lancaster county, Pa.//**DIED** In Guilford county, N. C., on the 2nd Nov., in the 93rd year of her age, MRS. ELIZABETH CLAPP, relict of GEORGE CLAPP, long since dec'd.,leaving one hundred and thirty-six living (28 dead,) descendants. She was a daughter of CHRISTIAN ALBRIGHT of Berks co., Pa., from when-

WEEKLY MESSENGER OF THE GERMAN REFORMED CHURCH

ce A. D. 1765, she emigrated with her husband to the place where she spent the remainder of life. //On Friday week, in Frederick, Md., MRS. SUSAN, wife of HENRY RHODES, in the 36th year of her age, leaving a husband and four small children. //On Saturday week, near Frederick, MR. MICHAEL JEFFERSON GETZENDANNER, in the 37th year of his age, leaving wife and eight children.//**SEMINARY FUND** Collected by REV. JACOB MAYER, Agent, from Behms' Congregation Montgomery county. MARGARET RILE 50 cents, JOHN RILE, Esq. $10, MARY GREENAWALT $1, JOHN LAYBOLD 50 cents, ABLE TOMPKINS 50 cts, HENRY H. RILE $5, SARAH SAUTMAN 2.50, JACOB SHIVE 5, PHILIP HOOVER, Esq. 10, SAMUEL LINTON 1, JOHN SCHLATER 10, ANN HARNER 50 cents, ROSANA HARNER $1, LOUISA BODEY 50 cents, HENRY BODEY, SEN. $1, FREDERICK MUSS 2, FREDERICK DULL 5, ULRICH SCHLATER 75 cents, WILLIAM SCHLATER 1, HENRY SCHLATER 75 cents, HENRY BODEY, JR. $1, SAMUEL HOFFMAN 75 cents,JOSEPH T. FITZGERALD $1, ELIZABETH ST?I?? [wrinkled] 1.50, WILLIAM EARNST 1, CATHARINE EARNST 50 cents, MARY AMBLER 50 cents, JOHN FITZGERALD $3, JOHN SCHLATER, JR. $1, JOHN REX 2, ANN CHOYCE 50 cents, CATHARINE FREEZE $1, SAMUEL ZEARFASS 1, JOSEPH SHEARER 1, ELIAS JONES 75 cents, JOHN JONES 75 cents, ABRAHAM YOST 10, MARY YOST 5, SARAH YOST 5, PETER ACKER 1, JACOB HOOVER 5, JESSE CASTNER, JR 3, ABRAHAM GREGER 3 ADAM RUMER 1, GEORGE WERTSNER 2, GEORGE GEATRELL 1, CONSENTINE VANDERAW 50 cents, SAM'L DAVIS 1, BENJAMIN HILL 2 JOHN F RUMER 1 Indian Creek Congregation, Montgomery county. ABRAHAM GERHART $5 JOHN GERHART 5,JACOB SCHOLL 5, SAMUEL LEIDY, JR. 5, WILLIAM LEIDY 2, GEORGE SCHWANCK 5, MICHAEL SCHOLL 2, SAMUEL SCHOLL 1, MAGDALENA GERHART 1, PHILIP GERHART 5,REV. J.A. STRASBERGER 30. Hilltown Congregation, Bucks county. GERRET C. WACK $10, EMELINE B. WACK 2, HENRY LEIDY 1, BENJAMIN WEIERBACH 1, WENDEL WEISE 50 cents, GEORGE LEIDY 1, LEVI LEIDY 2, JOHN ALTHAUS 50 cents. For the Committee, JOHN SMITH.//**MONIES.** By REV. JONA. ZELLERS, from LEWIS KNODE, JAMES McCLURE, JOSEPH

WEEKLY MESSENGER OF THE GERMAN REFORMED CHURCH

STRUNK, JOHN REBER, REV. J. ZELLERS, each 2; by DR. HOFFIUS,from SAMUEL WHETSTONE, 5; by REV. D. WILLERS,from PHILIP DENLER 2, PETER HOLBEN 2,and PHILIP PETERS 1; by REV. J. MAYER,from P. and G. HOOT, AARON MULL, JOHN WEBER, JACOB LEIDY, JESSE CASTNER, each 2, and J. BOILEAU, GARRET C. WACK, REV. G. WACK, each 1; by M. RONDEBUSH,from JACOB WEIKEL 2, LAWRENCE EISENBERG 2, BENAIAH THOMPSON 1; by REV. D. ZACHARIAS, from MRS. MARY SCHLEY, JOHN CRONISE, JACOB REESE, DAVID DUTROW, ABRAHAM KEMP, each 2; by REV. D. HERTZ, from DAVID STONE 2, JACOB BRUBAKER 2, D, HERTZ 1; HENRY STICKEL 2 JOHN COOK 1, ADAM VANDERAU 2. By M. RICKENBAUGH, from SAMUEL MIDDLEKAUFF, DANIEL ZELLER, S. J. DOWNEY, JOHN WOLFERSBERGER, DAN'L MIDDLEKAUFF, SEN., JOHN TICE, JOHN SCHLEIGH, each 2, and W. HEYSER 4; SAM'L BRANDERBERG 2; HARRIET BENTZ 2.

175. Dec. 12, 1838/**MARRIED** In Dauphin county, on the 27th ult., by the REV. MR. GERHART, MR. CHRISTIAN HEY to MISS LEAH, daughter of the late JOSEPH NOVINGER.// on the 13th ult., by the same, MR. JOHN KELLER of Lancaster co., to MISS CATHARINE RUNK, of Lykens Valley.// on the 29th ult.,by the same, MR. ANDREW SHITZ,to MISS CATHARINE STREHER, all of Pauls Valley, Dauphin co. //In Rowan co., N. C., on Thursday evening the 22d ult.by REV. JOHN G. FRITCHEY, MR. DAVID CORRELL to MISS FRANEY, youngest daughter of SAMUEL FREEZE, dec'd.//On the 29th ult., near Middletown, Frederick county Md.,by REV. J. C. BUCHER, MR. HENRY SLIFER to MISS CATHARINE ANN, daughter of MR. JACOB LEIGHTER, all of Middletown Valley, Md.//Thursday, the 29th ult., by REV. R. GRACEY, MR. DAVID ETIMIRE, of Huntingdon county, to MISS JANE, daughter of MR. DAVID FERGUSON, of PathValley, Franklin county.//Thursday the 22nd ult, near the Burnt Cabins, Bedford county, by REV. A. A. McGUINLEY, MR. JAMES CREE of Chambersburg, to MISS ELIZABETH WALKER, of the former place.// On the 5th inst., by REV. J. HELFFENSTEIN MR. CHRISTIAN H. SENSENY to MISS ISABELLA N. BARNITZ

WEEKLY MESSENGER OF THE GERMAN REFORMED CHURCH

both of this place.//On the 5th ult., by REV. T. H. LEINBACH, MR. GEORGE KRUM to MISS LUCY ANN ARTZ, both of Shafferstown, Lebanon co., Pa.//On the 11th ult. by the same, MR. BENJAMIN PFEIFFER to MISS LAVINIA ARNOLD, of Berks county.//On the 18th ult., by the same, MR. ISAAC YINGST to MISS MARIANNA MATIS of Lebanon co.//On the 25th ult., by the same, MR. JONATHAN ROYER to MISS LUCETTA STEWART both of Meyerstown.//On the 4th inst. by the same, MR. JOHN GERHEART,to MRS. MARTHA REED, of Lebanon county.//**DIED** In Carlisle on Tuesday evening last the 4th inst. MRS. JANE SPOTTSWOOD, relict of the late JAMES SPOTTSWOOD, in the 57th year of her age.//**MONIES.** JACOB WIRT 2, WILLIAM HANES 2, REV. J. S. DUBBS 4, JOSIAH DUFFIELD 2. By REV.J. ZIEGLER,from LEVI NYCE 2, D. McFARLAND (Pottsgrove) 2,and LEWIS SPEECE (do.) 2. By REV. W. COLLIFLOWER, from COL. LEVI RINKER 1, SOLOMON PRINTZ 2 50, P. PRINTZ 2 50, MICHAEL KOONTZ 1. By REV. D. FEETE, from JOHN GROFF 2,and D. FEETE 1, REV. JOEL OSBORN, (Spencertown, N. Y.) 2; by REV. A. BERKY, from J. DENNISTON 2, JACOB GLACE 2, and J. WELSH 1. For "Christliche Zeitschrift" by REV. I. GERHEART, from JACOB SPATZ, Dalmatia, Pa $1 00, MICHAEL RUNK, Elizabethville, Dauphin co., Ps. (sic) 1 00. Send the paper to ABRAHAM KRIEBEL, MELCHION KRIEBEL, and BALTZER HEIDRICH, all to Worcester, Montgomery co., Pa.//**BOY TAKEN BY A BEAR.** About 7 o'clock in the evening MR. ISAAC SAUNDER's son JAMES, who is about eight years old, was sent to the barn to feed cattle. On returning to the house he met a bear, gave a loud screech and ran towards the barn. The bear seized the boy, and started for the woods. The men from the house pursued the bear armed with axes. One went back for a gun and returned to the woods. The bear was shot, the boy escaped unharmed. MR. DAVID ROLLIN has lost two fine cows to wild animals.//CAPTAIN MOODY writes that the coldest weather experienced in twenty three years has occurred during this month.--"Portland (ME) Advertiser Nov. 26."//**LETTERS** N. M. GROVER,

WEEKLY MESSENGER OF THE GERMAN REFORMED CHURCH

J. TURNER, STEPHEN WILSON, REV. A. BERKY.

176. Dec. 19, 1838/**MARRIED** Wednesday 5th inst. by the REV. R. BOND, MR. CHARLES H. ALBERT, to MISS SARAH ANN daughter of MR. JACOB HEART of this place.//On Tuesday 4th inst. by the REV. J. N. HOFFMAN,MR. WILLIAM SLYDER, to MRS. CATHARINE DENIG.//On the 4th inst. by the REV. MR.KIEFFER, MR. MICHAEL WHEELAND, to MRS. SPIESE, of Bellefonte, Pa.//On the 14th inst. by REV. J. HELFFENSTEIN MR. JOHN COOK, to MISS CATHARINE KING, both of this place.//**DIED** On Thursday last, in Green township, MRS. CATHARINE KAHL, wife of MR. JACOB KAHL, aged 51 years, leaving a husband and large family of children.//Thursday night last, in this place,after an illness of several weeks, MR. JAMES KINNEARD, Inkeeper, aged 65 years.//At York, Pa. the evening of the 11th inst. DR. BENJAMIN JOHNSTON, in the 33d year of his age. The 3d inst. he received slight injury to his little finger while in the act of putting coal into his stove. After some time it began to swell. The afternoon of the next day he went in the cars to Baltimore to attend to some business but suffering a great deal of pain during the night, he returned the next day. He suffered the most excruciating pain in his hand and arm, which had become so greatly swollen as to be relieved only by making incisions into it. He was a graduate of Washington Medical College of MD. He left a mother, brothers and sisters.//The Miner's Journal mentions a fire in Pottstown which destroyed a new untenanted house owned by MR. DEBERG.//A fire broke out near Market and Adams streets, in a house occupied by MR. WOMELSDORF as a saddlery about 8 o'clock on Thursday morning. The corner grocery store of MR. CRAMER, and the Flour and Feed store of MESSRS. WOLLISON & LERCH were totally lost, with damage to two buildings, owned by N. J. MILLS.//The following was formerly an Attorney at Law and editor of a paper at Lancaster, in this state. He removed to WI some years

ago. "The Iowa Gazette states that a recontre recently took place in that town between CYRUS S. JACOBS and MR. DAVID ROHRER, which resulted in the death of the former, by pistol shot from the hands of the latter.//From a correspondent in Penns Valley, Centre county, Pa., on Saturday afternoon Dec. 1, the house of MR. WILLIAM GENTZEL near Spring Mills, burnt. A hired woman had occasion to go to the field in search of cattle, previous to which she bolted the door from the outside, leaving two children within, who burnt to death! The parents were both from home.//A **STEAMBOAT DISASTER.** The New Orleans Courier the 28th ult. publishes an account of the disaster. From CAPTAIN STRADER, of the steamer *Tiber*, from Louisville, we learn that he passed the wreck of the steamboat *Gen. Brown*, (late) CAPTAIN CLARK, at St. Helena, at which place she collapsed a flue the 25th inst. <u>Dead.</u> SAMUEL CLARK, master; BASNIL BRONSTUTE,(sic) first mate; WILSON,of New Albany, first engineer; FELIX UNDERWOOD, pilot; carpenter, bar-keeper. Passengers: D. L. DAVIS, from Louisville for Natchez; ELISHA LIBBEY, from Louisville for Port Hudson; W. A. MILLER, from Louisville for Natchez;DR. PRICE,from Louisville for Vicksburg; BLANCHARD,from Louisville; EDWARD HUBBARD, from Louisville for New Orleans; ROBERT JOHNSON, from Louisville for New Orleans; JAMES BALL, from Louisville for New Orleans; JOHN CONLEY, of Philips county, AR; SILAS DRURY, of Helena; J. C. LONG; T. D. LEWIS. <u>Missing.</u> J. R. GARTHWAITE, of Newark, N. J.; THOMAS TEWE; BARNEY GAFFENEY, from Madison. <u>Wounded.</u> ELIJAH ENSIGS, of New Albany, second engineer -- life despaired of; ELI JOHNS, of Maysville, KY, third engineer -- life despaired of; HAMILTON McCRAE, from Louisville, KY, pilot, leg and arm broken; BENJAMIN HANDY, (black)of Louisville, KY, second cook,severely scalded; DAVID APPLEGATE, do (sic) of Louisville, KY, fireman, badly scalded; JEREMIAH McCASSEL, do. of Louisville, KY, fireman, badly scalded; GEORGE MYERS, from Pittsburg, first cook, severely scalded; HENRY McFINLEY, do. from New Albany, fireman, severely scalded; J. K. LONG, from Louisville for New Orleans, legs and arm broken; JOHN S. WARNER,from Westchester, Penn'a, for New Orleans, very badly scalded; MR. GEORGE, of Vicksburg, slightly injured.

177. Dec. 26, 1838/**MARRIED** On the 10th inst. by REV. WM. F. COLLIFLOWER, MR. DANIEL H FRAVEL, to MISS MARY, only daughter of the late CAPT JACOB RINKER, both of Woodstock, Va.//In Middletown, Frederick county, Md. the 17th of December by REV. J. C. BUCHER, MR. ISAAC B. ROWLAND of Washington county, to MRS. SUSAN UPDEGRAFF, of Hagerstown.//**DIED** At Philadelphia, on the 12th inst., WASHINGTON W. FETTERMAN, Esq. a member of the Pittsburg Bar, in the 37th year of his age. //MISS SARAH E. NORTON, of Edgartown, NY died a a few days since very suddenly. She was to have been married on the following day.// A family of twelve persons named ZIPPAR were murdered by Seminoles about the 10th ult. in FL twenty miles from Black Creek in a North West direction.//**A SUICIDE.** When ROBINSON was tried for the murder of ELLEN JEWETT, ROBERT FURLONG was his principal witness and procured his acquittal, swearing that on the night of the murder, ROBINSON was at FURLONG's Store. In October last, he took passage on the brig *Wexford,* CAPTAIN MUNDAY bound to Puerto Cabello, and when 3 days out was attacked with delirium tremens. He told some persons he had since come to believe that he had sworn untruly. He refused to go below and stated that ELLEN JEWETT was sitting there. The second day he became violent. To avoid confinement FURLONG leaped on the gunwale and into the sea. A seaman jumped overboard, and laid hold of him, but life was extinct.---"Journal of Commerce."//MR. JOHN ZIEGLER, son of MR. JOHN ZIEGLER, of New Berlin, Union county, Pa., and a younger brother of REV. DANIEL ZIEGLER, of York, and REV. JACOB ZIEGLER, late of Chester county, died in Cave-

WEEKLY MESSENGER OF THE GERMAN REFORMED CHURCH

town, where he had been teaching school.//**MONIES** By S. RINKER, from B. COBE,2,and LAWRENCE KELLER 6; from MRS. JOSEPH GOOD 2; GEORGE COOK, (Upton) 4; JOSIAH DUFFIELD 2; by J. F. LOY, from G. B. KAY2, F. GROVE 2, J. F. LOY 4, and DANIEL RIEGEL 2; by REV. J. C. BUCHER, from JOHN J. SMITH 2, REV. BUCHER 2, HENRY LEIGHTER 6, ELIZA A. MARIS 1.25.//**SEMINARY FUND.** From DANIEL BISER SEN. & Son $50, (per REV. J. C. BUCHER.) Also, from JACOB FICKES, by PHILIP MANN Bedford co. $10.00.

178. Jan. 2, 1839/**DIED** MR. JOHN ZIEGLER, 18th of December. Tribute of Respect from the Diagnothian Literary Society. WM. MAYBURRY, Speaker, THEOD. C. W. HOFFEDITZ, Sec ty.(sic)

179. Jan. 9, 1839/**MARRIED** In Harrisburg, on Thursday evening,27th ult.,by REV. J. H. SMALTZ, MR. PETER BLACK to MISS SARAH ANN PEFFER all of that place.//On the 25th ult. by REV. J. GEIGER, MR. BENJAMIN YINGLING, son of DAVID YINGLING, to MISS MARY BARD.//On the same day,by the same,MR. ABRAHAM BANKER, to MISS SUSANNA BISH, of Carroll county,Md.//**DIED** At Mercersburg,on the 16th day of December, MRS. MARY ANN, wife of REV. WM. A. GOOD, aged 22 years, the only child of the late GEORGE MINICH, born on the 7th of April, 1816, near St. Thomas, Franklin county. When but two weeks old, her father was suddenly removed, and she left an orphan. She connected herself with the Presby. church under the pastorage of REV. J. McKNIGHT. Her marriage took place the 25th day of January, 1838. On the 2nd day of December, returning from worship, she complained her throat and head were affected by cold. Her disease was one of those fearfully afflictive dispensations. One thing is remarkable---she took sick on the same day of the week--continued for the same length of time (precisely two weeks)--- consequently died on the same evening, and was afflicted with the same disease of her father.// St. Vincent, in Switzerland, Oct 26, ELIZA, wife

WEEKLY MESSENGER OF THE GERMAN REFORMED CHURCH

of VINCENT RUMPFF, Minister Resident at Paris for the Hanse Towns, and daughter of JOHN JACOB ASTOR,Esq., of NY.//On the 13th ult, MRS. MAGDALENA SNECK, near Manchester Va.,aged 92 years.// On the 15th,MARIA ELIZABETH,daughter of MR. GEO. EVERHART of Manchester, Md. age 4 years 4 months 12 days.//On the 24th, near Uniontown, MR. PETER SLAMAKER, aged 81 years, 9 months and 2 days.// Near Middletown, Md., on the 25th of December, after an illness of a few hours, SOLOMON, son of MR. PETER BISER,JR., in the 3rd year of his age. **//THEOLOGICAL FUND.** By REV. J. MAYER, from REV. JACOB ZIEGLER, through J. H HOFIUS, Esq. From JACOB BOLLINGER $4.--By SAMUEL HARNISH, Esq. Waterstreet--from CHRISTIAN HARNISH $6, JOHN HYLE $15, PHILIP WALTERS $4.--By JOHN SWOOP,Esq. from JOHN SWOOP $25, JOHN RIDENOUER $10, JOHN HEAFNER $6, ISAAC VANDERANDER $2.**//SEMINARY AGENTS** *Bedford county, Pa.* DOCTOR HOFIUS, Bedford. PHILIP J. SHOEMAKER, Friend's Cove. Hon. PETER SCHELL, Schellsburg. PHILIP MANN, Bobb's Creeks. ABRAHAM DIVELY, Greenfield. REV. C. WINEBRENNER, Morrison's Cove. *Huntingdon county, Pa.* SAMUEL HARNISH, Water Street. HENRY KNODE, Hartslog Valley JOHN SWOOPE, Woodcock Valley. *Centre county, Pa.* REV. P. S. FISHER, Penn's Creek and Aaronsburg. JOHN KELLER, SEN., Boalsburg. PHILIP REITZELL, Esq., Brush Valley. JAMES POTTER, Esq., Potter township. JOHN KOOKEN, SEN., Pinegrove. REV. E. KIEFER, Nittany Valley. *Northumberland county, Pa.* REV. D. GRING, Milton and Paradise. REV. R. A. FISHER,Sunbury. *Union county, Pa.* JOHN REBER, Lewisburg. JACOB WETZEL, New Berlin. FREDERICK PONTIUS, Mifflinburg and Dreisbach congregations. REV. SAMUEL SEIBERT, Selinsgrove. *Montgomery county, Pa.* REV. DAN'L WEISER, Goshenhoppen and Great Swamp congregations. REV. H. S. BASLER, Limerick congregation. BENJAMIN REIFF, Esq., Towamensen congregation. REV. GEORGE WACK, Wense's congregation. HENRY WEICKEL, Trappe congregation *Bucks county, Pa.* GEORGE SCHEIB, Hilltown congregation. REV. J. A. STRASBERGER, Indian Creek

WEEKLY MESSENGER OF THE GERMAN REFORMED CHURCH

congregation. JACOB MAYER General Agent.**//MONIES** From JESSE SHAFER (Lockport,) $3, SAM'L YOUNG, (Niagra.) 2;HENRY WELSHANS,(Va.} 2, EYE & SHAFER 2, W. LOUGH 2, DR. W. HERMAN 1; JOHN HEBERLIG 2; JOHN BUCK, (Greencastle) 2.50, by J. MOTTER,from HARRIET MOTTER, PETER TROXEL and LUCINDA HENKEL, each 2; by REV. J. ZIEGLER, from SAMUEL HARNISH, SEN., 2, JOHN AURANDT, Esq. 2, A. SANGREE 5, W. FOLKNER, 3.75, JOHN SWOOPE 2; from D. ALBRIGHT, (N. C.) 2.50; by REV. J. GEIGER, from J. KRANTZ, L. MAXFIELD, GEO. ORNDORF, REV. J. GEIGER, and GEORGE EVERHART, each 2; by REV. ? DOUGLAS, from J. WOLFORD, A. SUMMER, H. STAUB, MARGARET REINHART and MISS P. KILMER, each 2; by REV. J. C. BUCHER, from JOHN COBLENTZ, (of J.) 2, and J. A. MAHN 2; by GEORGE WELKER, from PHILIP RENN 4, MISS C. DERING 1, DAVID WILSON 2, D. WASHABAUGH 1.75, R. VAN PELT, (N.Y.)2, J. GUELICH 4. Credit given to MR. HENRY LEIGHTER for $6--should have been PETER LIGHTER. Error acknowledging $2 from J. K. BOYER, (Bethel)--not paid. REV. J. HELLER requests "ZEITSCHRIFT" sent to the following: JOLM PROPTS, (sic) Franklin, Pendleton co., Va. F. REXROAT, do. do. do. DAN'L SIMMON, Crabbottown, do. do.

180. Jan. 16, 1839**/MARRIED** On Thursday evening last, by REV. MR. MOODY, MR. WILLIAM M. MATEER, of Mechanicksburg, Cumberland county, to MISS JANE A. JOHNSTON, of Franklin county.//Wednesday morning the 26th ult. by REV. THOMAS CREIGH, MR. BENJAMIN HAMILTON, of Peters township, to MISS MARGARET DEAN of Mercersburg.**//DIED** On Thursday the 27th ult., at his residence on Beaver Creek in Washington co., Md., MAJ. PETER SEIBERT, in the 66th year of his age.//Suddenly, on Wednesday of last week, MR. DAVID DENNY, son of REV. DAVID DENNY of this place.**//MONIES.** By REV. D. WINTERS, from HENRY BATES, (alias KOOGLER&BATES, Dayton) JACOB S. BRENNER, JOHN SHAFFER, JR. ABR. HAWKER,JOHN RIKE, CHRISTIAN RIKE,A. Y. McPHERSON (sic) JOHN PRUGH, JOHN SHROYER, MAJ. P COBLENTZ,

WEEKLY MESSENGER OF THE GERMAN REFORMED CHURCH

VALENTINE WINTERS, ABR. ARTZ, GEO. KIEFER(Xenia) RYAN GRAY, A. FAWBER, ANNA GRAY, BARABARA HANE?, SAM. ANKENNY, JOHN SHANNON, JACOB STEELE, ANDREW H. BAUCHMAN, JACOB HERRING, ISAAC GENTIS, JACOB F. MYERS, JOHN ANKENNY, JONATHAN SNYDER, RACHEL EYLER, JACOB BOOTS, JACOB STEMBLE, JOEL WEATHERHOLTZ, ADAM RADER, MARTIN BOOTS, JESSE BOOTS, KETTEMAN & PETERSON, WILLIAM HALLEY, JOSEPH A. CRAIN, JONATHAN KEAFAUVER, (Alexanderville) ABR. HIVLING, JOHN GLOTFELTER, (Bellbrook) MICH. HALL JACOB COY, JACOB RIKER, GEO. GLOTFELTER, MICHAEL LONG, STEPHEN HAGENBUCH, (Fairfield) JOHN COST, W. WILSON, JOHN WOLF, JR., JACOB PETERSON, (N. Burlington,) JOB CRITS, each $2, in advance, and JOHN ALLEN, $1. From DANIEL MAY (York) 3; SAMUEL LEIBY 50 cts.; SINGLETON MYERS 1, JACOB MILLER, (Juniata,) 4.50; GIDEON RAHAUSER 2; GEO. KELLER, (Jackson Hall) 2; by LEWIS JORDAN (IN) from JOHN RICE 2, A. ROSENBERGER 2, JOHN RICE 2, CATHARINE JORDAN 4, D. G. MERKEL 3, JACOB DOLL 4, L.JORDAN 3, B. FRAVEL 1,and REV. W. C. RANKIN, 1. By JOS. SNAPP, from ROBERT McCAYAND, F. COLHOUSER, ELIAS FREEMAN, S. GILPEN, and JACOB B. SNAPP, each 2; by REV. JOHN LANTZ,from JACOB SHOLLENBERGER, DAVID CORRELL, JOHN CORRELL, JOSEPH FISHER, JACOB LINGLE, PAUL KLUTZ, GEO. KLUTZ, each 2, and REV. J. LANTZ 5.40; by M. RICKENBAUGH, from M. HAMMAN JOHN M. SPIELMAN, A. KERSHNER, JOHN SHAFER, JR. MARTIN KING, SAM. SPIELMAN, DANLEL (sic) M. MIDDLEKAUFF, SAM. PRETZMAN, SAM. J. DOWNEY, HENRY SHAFFER, DAN. SCHNEBLY, Esq. and M. RICKENBAUGH, each 2; by REV. A.. HELFFENSTEIN, from MISS L. LENTZ, JOHN HINKLE, SAM. EARNEST (Chestnut Hill) A. HELFFENSTEIN, each 2. To Editor of "Christliche Zeitschrift" from REV. JOHN LANTZ, (N.C.) 60 cts. Send the Zeitschrift to JACOB HOSSINGER, Valley P. O. Mifflin county, Penn'a.

181. Jan. 23, 1839/**MARRIED** In Guilford co., N. C. on the 6th ult., by REV. J. H. CRAWFORD, MR. DANIEL F. CLAPP to MISS SARAH, eldest daughter of MR. DANIEL FOUST.//The 20th ult. by the same,

WEEKLY MESSENGER OF THE GERMAN REFORMED CHURCH

MR. FREDERICK SMITH to MISS ELIZA, daughter of COL. D. CLAPP.//On the 27th ult., by the same, MR. JOEL SWING to MISS CHARLOTTE KOLLE.//On the 16th ult., in Lancaster co., Pa., by the REV. D. HERTZ, MR. FREDERICK SCHNEIDER, of New Holland, to MISS ADELINE RETTUE, of Adamstown.//On the 1st inst., by the same, MR. SEBASTIAN MILLER, JR., to MISS MARIA, eldest daughter of MR. H. RICHARD.//At the same time by the same, MR. JOHN MOSER, to MISS CASIA, daughter of MR. SEBASTIAN MILLER, SEN., all of Adamstown.//On the 3d inst. by REV. W. F. COLLIFLOWER, MR. WILLIAM PRINTZ to MISS LYDIA COFFELT, both of Shenandoah county, VA.//On Thursday the 17th by REV. B. S. SCHNECK, MR. GEORGE NULL, of Cumberland county, to MISS MARY REIFF, of Franklin county.//On Tuesday, the 8th, by REV. ROBERT DOUGLAS, MR. JACOB MILLER to MISS EVELINE, daughter of CAPT. JAMES MASON, all of Berkely county, VA.//**DIED** On the 30th ult. in Harrisburg, MRS. SUSAN BUCHER, consort of the late JUDGE BUCHER, aged 64 years.//On the 30th ult., in Brecknock township, Berks co., MARIA BEALER, aged 8, and on the 1st inst., WILLIAM BEALER, aged 5 years--both children of MR. JOS. BEALER.//The 8th ult. near Pinegrove Mills, Centre county, Pa., MR. JOHN PATTON, in the 74th year of his age, an affectionate parent and husband.//Near Bakersville, Md., on the 13th ult., MRS. ELIZABETH, consort of MR. JACOB HAMMOND, dec'd., in the 48th year of her age leaving nine children.//Friday, the 18th inst., SAMUEL LEWIS, son of MR. JACOB GARVER, JR., aged 16 months.// At Philadelphia, on the 8th inst., MRS. MARIA JOHNSON, wife of REV. STEPHEN JOHNSON, who has been for the last six years engaged in the Mission to Siam, established by the A. B. C. F. M. and recently returned to this country on account of the health of Mrs. J.//The Grand Inquest of the county of Franklin at the January term 1839, adopted the following, viz: Whereas, Intemperance is acknowledged to be the fruitful source

WEEKLY MESSENGER OF THE GERMAN REFORMED CHURCH

of crime...Resolved, That we entirely discountenance the habit of exacting from Grand Jurors, sitting for the first time, a *Tribute,* usually denominated a *Treat* and that we earnestly recommend abandonment of the practice. Foreman JOSEPH SNIVELY.//A request to correct the mistaken impression introduced into the paper by Brother TRUMAN OSBORN of Germantown, that "instead of no Sunday School at all, we now have three." Every one would infer that there was nothing of the kind in existence when I left the charge. This I deny. The first, before death deprived us of superintendant MR. LEONARD NUTZ, numbered nearly 200 scholars. ALBERT HELFFENSTEIN, JR., Hagerstown.//Plan to relieve the Parent Board from its present pecuniary embarrassment, pledged by:
  MRS. ELIZ. REBAUGH, Greencastle, $5.00
     R. R. SCHNECK, Chamb'g. 5.00
     ANN CARES, York, 5.00
     ELIZA BESORE, Waynesboro', paid 5.00
     B. M. SMITH, do. do. 5.00
     MARGARETTA MAYER, Chamb'G, 5.00
     C. Z. ZACHARIAS, Frederick, Md., 5.00
  Plan for Gentlemen.
    MR. WILLIAM HEYSER, Chamb'g, $ 5.00
    MR. JOHN SMITH, do. 10.00
    REV. J. H. SMALTZ, Harrisburg, (paid) 5.00
    MR. GEORGE BESORE, Waynesboro, (paid) 5.00
Per MRS. M. L. BAUGHER, Treas, $7.00 from Female Education Society of Emmittsburg.//**MONIES.** By REV. J. C. BUCHER, Esq, from MISS S. HOYER and MISS A. GOLDMAN, each 2; by REV. B.C. WOLFF,from B. APPLE, 5 (advance) CAPT. WOODRING, SUSAN INNES, MARG'T BEIDLEMAN, and PETER STEM, each 2; by REV. J. G. WOLFF, from MISS M. EYERMAN and W. REWALT, each 2; by REV. D. HERTZ,from JOHN BEARD 2, PHILIP VONNEADA 2, and D. HERTZ 1; FREDERICK KARPER 2; By REV. P. NEWHARD, Esq., from MRS. M. ROMIG 5, EDW. KERN 5, MRS. A. PRETZ 5, MRS. R. SAGER 4, REV. D. ZELLER 4, E. FRAMER 2 12 1/2, JOSEPH WEISS,C. DAVIS, W. WEAVER, HANNAH WEAVER, J. JAMESON, SOLOMON WINT, each 2, and P. NEWHARD

WEEKLY MESSENGER OF THE GERMAN REFORMED CHURCH

1; V. PENTZER (OH) 2; by JESSE BANKS, from HENRY STONEBRAKER, D. H. SCHNEBLY, JOSIAH DAVIS, ELIAS HOUSER, and JAMES GRIMES, each 2; by REV. J. C. BUCHER, from ADAM KELLER, HENRY COBLENTZ, JOHN KEFAUVER, each 2; By REV. F. KIEFFER, from JACOB HALLER 3, F. KIEFFER, 2; by M. ROUNSAVILLE, from HENRY BARRIER 2.50 JACOB LEONARD 2.50; by REV. E. HEINER, from P. BAKER, J.J. MYER, M. SHAW, T. & P. BALTZELL, CHAS. BALTZELL, C. DIEFFENDERFFER, G. RICHSTEIN, JUCAS DEAVER, each 2, JACOB SMITH 4 By REV. R. DOUGLAS, from JOHN HOFFMAN, JOHN MILLER, MICHAEL HENSEL, JOHN N. SHELL, and A. ROSENBERGER, (Smithfield,) each 2. From WM. DEAN, (Liberty,)2, JACOB GREENAWALT, (Marion,)2. //**SEMINARY FUND.** Received, by REV. E. KIEFFER, from VALENTINE MEYER, (Nittany Valley, Centre co.) $10, JACOB CANDY $5, subscription obtained by REV. J. MAYER. For the Committee, JOHN SMITH.

182. Jan. 30, 1839/**MARRIED** Wednesday last, by REV. J. N. HOFFMAN, PHILIP BERLIN, Esq. to MRS. ELEANOR SUESSEROTT, all of this place.//On the 13th inst. by REV. L. EGGERS, MR. HENRY GRAEB to MISS SUSAN, daughter of MR. PETER BEST, of Nittany Valley, Centre county, Pa.//On the 19th ult., near Green-castle, by the REV. J. REBAUGH, MR. JACOB HADE, JR. to MISS MARY SELLERS, all of Franklin county, Pa.//By the same, on the 17th inst , near Green-castle, MR. GEORGE HOCKE, of Baltimore, to MRS. CATHARINE KEEFER, of Franklin county, Pa.//In this place, by REV. J. N. HOFFMAN,MR. GEORGE ETCHBERGER,of Lebanon co.,to MISS ELIZABETH MINICH, of Chambersburg.//On the 23d ult. by REV. S. R. FISHER, MR. JOSEPH McCULLOUGH to MISS MARY MILLER, both of Harbaugh's Valley, Frederick county, Md.//On the 16th inst., by the same, MR. ELI SMITH to MISS MARGARET KETRON both of Fountain Dale,Adams co.,Pa.//On Tuesday evening the 8th inst,by REV. THO. CREIGH, MR. ATCHESON RITCHEY,to MISS ELIZABETH RHEA,near Mercersburg.//The evening of the 16th inst,by the same, MR. WILLIAM McKINSTRY, of Mercersburg, to MISS

WEEKLY MESSENGER OF THE GERMAN REFORMED CHURCH

ROSANNA COOPER, daughter of THOMAS COOPER, dec'd. of Peter's township.//On the __ inst., (sic) by REV. MR. BOND, MR. JOHN GROVE, to MISS REBECCA E. HERSHBERGER, all of Chambersburg.//**DIED** On Wednesday last 23d inst., after a lingering illness, MR. VOLNEY SMITH, aged about 30 years. A native of VT, he came to this place about a year since, and was engaged as a teacher, at the same time pursuing the study of Law under JUDGE THOMSON. His health was delicate when he came here. He was a member of the Episcopal church.//On Thursday night last in this place, AUGUSTUS CULBERTSON, son of DR. S.D. CULBERTSON, in the 19th year of his age.//In NC on the 7th inst, whither he had been on a visit, REV. THOMAS D. BAIRD, in the 56th year of his age. He was, until recently, editor of the "Pittsburg Christian Herald." //On Friday evening the 11th inst., at his residence in Mercersburg, CAPT. JOSEPH GRUBB, in the 75th year of his age. He was born in Lancaster county but resided in this county for upwards of fifty years.//On the 30th ult., RACHEL, youngest daughter of HENRY WERTZ, of Liberty, Adams county, Pa., aged 5 years, 5 months and 22 days.//On the 10th inst., in the city of Baltimore, ALEXANDER FRIDGE, in the 74th year of his age.//The estate of GEORGE LAW, who resided in Middletown, Pa., has been in law, and is not yet settled. He left a large estate for an Orphan House for members of the Lutheran Church.//A trial in Philadelphia, has resulted in the conviction of DR. CHAUNCEY (a Botanic physician) for murder in the second degree of a young woman (named SOWERS) living in Manayunk.//**MONIES** By REV. C. ZWISLER, from C. SILBERT, M. TROUTMAN, J. KEISER, J. FELGER, (Waynesburg) C. ZWISLER, each 2; W. BUSH, (Chester co.) 2; WILLIAM STREBIG 3 50; CHRISTIAN WOLFF, (Pittsburg) 4; JACOB SNIDER (Chamb'g,) 2; by REV. E. HEINER, from BOYER & DIEFFENDEFFER, G. DECKER, JACOB WOLFF, H. BAKER, D. BUCKEY, F. ACHEY, H. HABLISTON, J. RODENMAYER, G. ELLIOTT, each 2, MRS. R. ROMIG, 1; by REV. S. R. FISHER,

WEEKLY MESSENGER OF THE GERMAN REFORMED CHURCH

from JACOB SHOVER, GEO.TRENKLE, ELI SMITH, CATH. TROXEL, S. R. FISHER, each 2. For "Christliche Zeitschrift." From DR. ROMIG,(Baltimore,) $1 00.

183. Feb. 6, 1839/**MARRIED** On Thursday last, by REV. J. SECHLER,MR. GEO. SPANGLER, of Cumberland county,to MISS NANCY MYERS, of Adams county.//On the same day,by the same.MR. FREDERICK PALMER,to MISS LYDIA UNGER both of Adams county.//At Hampstead, Md. on Tuesday evening,Jan. 24th, by REV. JACOB GEIGER, MR. WESLEY W. GARNER, (firm of J. GARNER & Son) of Manchester, Md. to MISS HARIET, daughter of JOHN MURRAY,Esq.dec'd, of Hampstead, Md.//**DIED** On Wednesday last, of Catarrh fever, BENJAMIN, infant son of REV. B. S. SCHNECK.//On Saturday last, near St. Thomas, in the 63rd year of her age, ELIZABETH,consort of MR. JOHN BAUGHMAN.//In Albany, N. Y. on the 26th ult., STEPHEN VAN RENSSELAER, at an advanced age. He died at the Manor House on Saturday afternoon from a fit of coughing which produced strangulation. He served in several distinguished public offices. From "NY American."//The dwelling of DAIEL (sic) S. BISER, member of the House of Delegates from Frederick county, was destroyed by fire Saturday night 19th ult.//In Erie, Pa., a fire originated in the barn of MESSRS. BIRD & HART stage proprietors, and enveloped the Mansion House, kept by MRS. WM. H. CHAMPLIN, situated in front of the barn.//Appointed by the Governor: JOEL B. DANNER Clerk of the Court, and JACOB LEFEVER, Register, Recorder, and clerk of the Orphans' Court, Adams county.//By a Philadelphia paper it appears that R. T. W. DYOTT, the great Druggist, and Free Banker, is an applicant for the insolvent laws.

No marriages or deaths in the Feb. 13th issue.

184. Feb. 20, 1839/**MARRIED** On the 1st ult., by the REV. J. S. DUBS, MR. HENRY LOB to MISS PHEBE TRAXELT all of Southwhitehall,Lehigh county, Pa. //On the 13th ult.,by the same,MR. ELIAS GUTH to

WEEKLY MESSENGER OF THE GERMAN REFORMED CHURCH

MISS SALLEY ANN TRAXELL, all of Southwhitehall, Lehigh co.//On the 20th ult., by the same, MR. CHAS. FREYMAN, of Southwhitehall, to MISS ELIZABETH JEHL, of Northwhitehall, Lehigh county.//On the 24th ult., by the same, MR. EPHRAIM FENSTERMACHER to MISS JULIA BACHMAN, both of Lehigh township, Northampton county.//On the 26th ult., by the same, MR. GIDEON GUTH to MISS SARAH WENNER, all of Southwhitehall.//At the same time, by the same, MR. SANFORD STEPHEN, of Upper Saucon, to MISS SARAH STECKEL, of South White Hall.//On the 5th inst, by the same, MR. JONAS KNERR to MISS SUSAN MILHOUSE, both of Low Hill.//At the same time by the same, MR. JOHN JERG, of Northwhitehall, to MISS HELENA WEAVER, of Saltsburg, Lehigh county. //On the 27th ult., by REV. J.B. KNIPE, MR. RODY DOUGHERTY, of Penn township, Philadelphia co., to MISS MARGARET KELLEY, of West Vincent, Chester county.//On the 31st ult., by the same, MR. ANTHONY KELLER to MISS ELLEN QUAY, all of West Vincent, Chester county.//On the 7th inst., by the same, MR. SAMUEL MARCH to MISS REBECCA FEDENIC, all of Chester county.//On the same day, by REV. J. BEAR, MR. JOHN NOEL to MISS MARY CHRONISTER, all of Adams county, Pa.//On the 14th inst by REV. J. HELFFENSTEIN, MR. HUGH McKANE to MISS MARGARET STEWART, both of Fayetteville, Franklin county, Pa.//On the 7th inst, by the REV. E. KEEFER, MR. BENJAMIN BOWERS to MISS MARY OHL, both of Centre county, Pa.//Near Middletown on the 31st ult, by REV. J. C. BUCHER, MR. JACOB KEAFAUVRE to MISS LEONORA, youngest daughter of MR. J P COBLENTZ, all of Middletown valley.//On the 3d inst, by the same, MR. JOHN HUTZELL, of JOHN, of Washington co., to MISS SARAH ANN, eldest daughter of CAPT. JOHN L. SMITH, of Middletown valley.//In Baltimore, on the 12th inst, by REV. E. HEINER, MR. HENRY RICHMOND to MISS ANN SEESNOP, all of that city.//On the 24th ult., near Sharpsburg, by REV. J. W. HOFFMIER, MR. JAMES HARPER to to MISS ELLEN HARPER.//On the 31st ult, by the same, MR. JACOB KEFFEY to MISS [wrinkle distorts

WEEKLY MESSENGER OF THE GERMAN REFORMED CHURCH

the print].//[Wrinkle] same, MR. JOSEPH PARKS to MISS MARY FINFROCK.//At York, on the 5th inst., by the REV. MR. ZEIGLER the REV. MICHAEL EYSTER to MISS JULIA ANN EICHELBERGER, both of York.// On Tuesday last, in Mercersburg, by the REV. T. CREIGH, ROBERT M. BARD, Esq. Att'y at Law of Chambersburg, to MISS ELIZABETH LITTLE, daughter of DR. P. W. LITTLE, of the former place.//**DIED** On the 5th inst, in Sharpsburg, GEORGE HENRY, infant son of REV. J. W. HOFFMIER.//On Thursday last,at Pine Grove,Centre county,MR. ANDREW CURTIN, merchant, a native of IRE, aged about 40 years.//Of fever, in the Spring of 1838, (sic) in the city of Honston, (sic) TX, ROBERT MONTGOMERY,M. D., formerly of Milton, Northumberland county, Pa., in the 2?th year of his age.//Additions of Pledges for Parent Board Plan:

MRS. SARAH DENIG, Chambersburg,paid		5.00
" DAVID SCHNEBLY, Wash.co.Md.,p'd,		5.00
" CATH. SMALTZ, Harrisburg,		5.00
MISS ELIZA REINHART,Shep'town,Va.	p'd,	5.00
" MARGARETTA REINHART, do.	do.	5.00
MRS. ANN E. SHRIVER,Car'll co.,Md.	do.	5.00
" ARIANA RIDDLE, Chambersburg,	do.	5.00
" ROEMER, Roemer's mills,		5.00
A. B., Philadelphia		p'd,$5.00
C. D., do.		p'd, 5.00
MRS. MARY SWOOPE, Huntingd. co.	do.	5.00
" B. WOLFF, Chambersburg,	do.	5.00
" SARAH SHRIVER, Littlestown,	do.	5.00
" ANN SECHLER, Hanover,		5.00
MISS LOUISA SHRIVER, Littlestown,	p'd,	5.00
REV. H. WILLARD, OH,	p'd,	5.00
MR. J. U. GIESY, do.	do.	5.00
" H. KNODE, Huntingd. co.	do.	5.00
" S. HARNISH, do,	do.	5.00
" J. KNODE & H.SWOOPE,do.	do.	5.00
" A. LAYMAN, VA.	do.	5,00
COL. D. SCHNEBLY, Wash.co.,Md., paid,		5.00

[See #180 for original article on list. BAM]// **SEMINARY FUND.** Collected in BROTHER DUBBS'Congregation. Lehigh County, Pa. Allentown Congre-

WEEKLY MESSENGER OF THE GERMAN REFORMED CHURCH

gation. MICHAEL D. EBERHART $20, ELIZABETH KUGLER 5, CHRISTIAN PRETZ, Esq. 20, WILLIAM ECKERT 20, JOHN ROMIG 15, THOMAS HARTER 5, WM. ECKERT, JR. 5, ELIZABETH FREY 3, BENJAMIN LUDWIG 3, EDWARD KERN 3, JONATHAN SAEGER 2, JOSEPH HARIMAN 1, PAUL KNAUS 3, EDMAN STICKEL 5, JACOB FRICK 50 cts JOHN STRASBURGER 5, PETER NEWHARD, ESQ. 3, WM. H. BLUMER 2, C. SAEGER 5, THOMAS H. WILSON 3, PETER HABER 5, JOSEPH STETLER 5, JOHN FREY ?, JOSEPH SAEGER, Esq. 3, CHARLES DAVIS, Esq. 10, SAM'L L KEEK 3, JACOB GEISSINGER 20, CHRISTIAN GEISSINGER 10, DAVID SCHOLL 2, ABRAHAM SPINNER 1, DAN'L SCHOLL 1, JOHN SPINNER 1, PETER LUDWIG 1, JACOB TRAXEL 5, MARY EISENHARD 1, JACOB E?H?LMAN 10. Jordon Congregation. WOLBERT & GUTH 20, DANIEL A. GUTH 25, PETER TRAXEL 3, JOHN TRAXEL 4, G??INE GUTH 10 HENRY GUTH 50 cts JOSEPH GUTH 4, (Wrinkle through two names, two unreadable) JOHN MOYER 2, LEONARD MOYER 1, LO?S??E GETH 25 cts, THOMAS KERN 10, PETER GROSS 50 cts, JOSEPH KERN 1, JOHN HOFFMAN 3, THOMAS VOUST 1, JOHN VOUST 2, HENRY KERN 50 cts, JONES G?TH 2, JOHN TRAXEL 50 cts PETER TRAXEL 1, STEPHEN TRAXEL 1. Union Congregation. PAUL HALLIET 20, STEPHEN HALLIET 2 50, PETER POMICH, JR. 2 50, WM. KLAUSER 2, PETER SHIDY 2, PETER H?TZ 15, ABRAHAM S?EFF 75 cts WM. LINTZ 1 50, PETER ROMICH, SR. 5, JONATHAN MOYER 1, GEORGE KENNEL 1, STEPHEN SCHOSSER 1, DANIEL PETER 50 cts MICHAEL WOODRING 1, MICHAEL WOODRING 4, (sic) HENRY JACOB 50 cts. HENRY PETER 1, NATHAN PETER 50 cts DANIEL PETER 25 cts, (sic) DAN'L REBER 2, GEORGE REBER 50 cts, JOHN PETER 50 cts, CASPER PETER 1, GEO. KERN 74 cts, CHARLES KERN 75 cts, JOHN KERN 2 50, JAMES KERN 1, DAN'L ANDREW 50 cts GEORGE REMAILY 1, ISIAH REMAILY 1 50, JOHN REMAILY 25 cts JACOB KENNEL 1, HENRY WOODRING 50 cts [Seven unreadable names in Union List.]//**MONIES** From JOHN BODINE 4, JACOB SHANTZ 2, MICH'L D EVERHART (Allentown)2, JOHN WAGGONER (Chamb'g)2, JACOB KUKIN, (St.)2; (sic) by REV. D. WINTERS, from W. DOWNEY 2, and P. BINKLEY(Xenia) 2; from H. LEONARD, (Basel) 2, H.

WEEKLY MESSENGER OF THE GERMAN REFORMED CHURCH

COSS 2; by J. C. DIEFFENDERFER, from JOHN HALL 2 JOHN DIEFFENDERFER 4, W. BASH 3, and JACOB DIEFFENDERFER 1; by REV. HENRY WILLIARD (OH) from JACOB ASHBOUGH, D. MUSSER, HENRY RUBLE, MUSSER & STEWART (Brewen,) J. U. GEISY, DAN'L WOOLAM, J & S. CRAMPTON)Lancaster) (sic) H. ANESHENSLY, J. WESSENBERGER, JACOB SHAFER, JOHN LYSINGER, ISAAC MEYER,REBECCA ELY,SAM'L SPOHR (Rushville) Hon.J. STUCKEY (Sugar Grove) JACOB KLINGLER (Somerset) each 2, JOSEPH BURY and REV. H. WILLIARD 1; by REV. J. BOMBERGER,from L. H. KNODE, HENRY KNODE, E. EISENBERG,SAM'L HARNISH, JR. and CATH. PATTON (Woodenck) (sic) each 2; from HENRY C. BEAM 2; by D. H. DOLL, from LYDIA STEPHENS, POLLY MILLER HENRY J. SEIBERT (Hedgeville) W. A. CUSHWA and SAMUEL KEEFER, each 2; by REV. T. L. HOFFEDITZ from D. EILENBERGER 2, H. EILENBERGER4, TAYLOR & MESSENGER 2, JOHN KERN 1.25, and T. L. HOFFEDITZ 75 cts; by REV. A. BAYER, from B. KIDD 2, JAMES KICHLE 2, and REV. A. BAYER 1; by H. ECKERT 2, from MRS. C. LEAMAN 2 50, H. ECKERT 2 50, J. K. ECKERT 2, J.P. McILVAINE 2, and GEORGE L. ECKERT 1; by REV. J. HOFFMEIER, from DANIEL THOMAS 4, JOHN MILLER (of JOHN) 2, and J. W. HOFFMEIER 4. Christliche Zeitschrift: Send paper to JONATHAN STORK, JOHN ROOPERT, EVERHARD HAFER,all of Chambersburg Pa. MRS. CHRISTIAN SNIDER, Jackson Hall Frank. co. Pa.,($1 received); from REV. DR. HENDEL, Womelsdorf $1.

185. Feb. 27, 1839/**MARRIED** On the 20th inst., by REV. J. F. DIEFFENBACHER, MR. JACOB DIEFFENTHALER, to MISS BARBARA STOUCH, all of Erie, Pa. //On Tuesday morning, 19th inst , by the REV. J. SECHLER, MR. MATTHEW EICHELBERGER to MISS SARAH ICKES both of Abbottstown.//On the 14th inst, by REV. D. FEETE MR. HENRY G. BRENDEL of Hagerstown to MISS MARY A. FEETE, of Middletown.//Thursday last by REV. D. ZACHARIAS, MR. JOSEPH FAUHLE, to MISS MARGARET REYNOLDS, both of Frederick city. //**DIED** Near Chambersburg, on Saturday last,JOHN STREALY, in the 78th year of his age.//The Cum-

WEEKLY MESSENGER OF THE GERMAN REFORMED CHURCH

berland (Md) Civilian records the death of the daughter of DANIEL ALBRIGHT, in her fifteenth year. Alone in the house with younger children, her clothes caught while putting a kettle on the fire, and she burnt to a crisp.//**MONIES.** HENRY MYERS, (Chambersburg) $2, C. WOLFF, Esq. 2, JOHN HART 2, M. PATTON 2, J. M. McILVAIN (Hanover) 2, S. STOUFFER 6, W. BERRY 2, W. OTT, (Utica Mills) 5; by HENRY FETTER, from B. SHEIBLY, S. WAGNER, B. SMITH, CATH. WAGNER and H. FETTER, each 2; by REV.S.B. LEITER, from J. LANGHAM 2, DAVID LEITER 2, and S. B. LEITER 1,; by DR. HOFFIUS, from J. WEISEL, J. G. MARTIN, Esq., W. STAHL, F. OSTER, each 2; by J. G. MILLER, from J. CLOTFELTY 2, PETER BAKER, (L.Crossings,) 2, and C. COMPTON 1. Christliche Zeitschrift. Send paper to ABSALOM MOYER, Zelienople, Butler county, Pa.-JOHN BUTT, Erie county, Pa.//From MR. JAMES M. McILVAIN for the Parent Board, $3.00.//From HENRY KUHNS, $5, EVE NYCUM, 2, obtained by the REV. J. MAYER, in Bedford county, for the Seminary.

186. Mar. 6, 1839/**MARRIED** On the 20th ult., at the residence of MR. JOHN CARMACK, by REV. A. P. FREEZE, MR. JOHN FULTON to MISS SARAH CARMACK both of Frederick county, Md.//On the 14th ult., by the REV. D. G. BRAGONIER, MR. JOSEPH TROUP to MISS SARAH, second daughter of BENJ. CUSHWA,Esq. //On the 14th ult., near Middletown, Md, by the REV. J. C. BUCHER, MR. DEWALT WILLIARD to MISS ELIZABETH, eldest daughter of MR. JACOB FLOOK, of JOHN, all of Middletown Valley, Md.//On the 21st ult,by the same, MR. JACOB S TOMS, of Washington county, Md., to MISS ELIZABETH SHOEMAKER, of Frederick county,Md.//By the same on the same day, MR. HENRY K. HILTON to MISS MARGARET KNOUFF all of Frederick county,Md.//On the 14th ult.,by the REV. D. ZACHARIAS, MR. JOS. D FAUBLE to MISS MARGARET REYNOLDS, both of Frederick city.//On Tuesday last, by the same, MR. SAMUEL KEYSER to MISS ANN C. POOL,both of Frederick county, Md.// On the 24th ult., by REV. E. KIEFFER, MR. JOHN

WEEKLY MESSENGER OF THE GERMAN REFORMED CHURCH

OHL to MISS NANCY BROWNLEE, both of Centre co., Pa.//On the 19th ult., by REV. DANIEL HERTZ, MR. JACOB KELLER to MISS ELIZABETH ANDERSON, both of Lancaster co.//On the 28th ult, by the same,MR. WM. D. STAUFFER to MISS HANNAH KONIGMACHER, both of Lancaster county//**DIED** Near Emmittsburg, Md. the 22d ult, JOEL SENTZ, aged 8 years,2 months, and 3 days. He left home in company with his elder and only brother. They came to a place where a man was blasting rock. Several other boys were present. The moment a blast was about being fired, they ran in different directions. An only stone of about seven pounds struck the deceased, though upwards of forty yards distant from the blasted rock on the back part of the head fracturing it exceedingly.//The 25th ult., in East Earl township, Lancaster co., MRS. ELIZABETH JOHNS, aged 84 years.//**MONIES.** By JOHN WILLIARD, from DR. J. D. GARROT, JOSHUA BISER, PERRY FLOOK, DANIEL GROVE, each $1, and DANIEL S BISER 4, ADAM TRUMBLE 4, JOHN KELLER 6, GEORGE COST 10; from JACOB THOMAS (Middletown, Md.)2, C. NOECKER 3 37 1/2; from REV. A. FREESE, RAPH. JONES, L. CRAMER, MICH. ZIMMERMAN and FRED. BARRICK, each 2, REV. E. HEINER 50 cts, MRS. JANE ARMSTRONG 50 cts. M. EICHELBERGER 2, JACOB COOK 2, JACOB SHITZ (Sloucksb'g) 1, REV. GEO. LEIDY 2, JOHN ROCK 2, PHILIP WEISEL 2, WM. NYCUM 1, HERMAN ALRICKS, Esq. 1, JOHN PAUL (Chester co.,) 2, JACOB SMITH (Chamb'g) 2; by REV. D. GRING, from SOLOMON ESHBACH 4, SAM'L MORRISON, JR. 2, SAMUEL LERCH 2; H. SMITH (Chamb'g) 4, A. DONAT 2, GEO. H. BUCHER 2,---by same, for MRS. M. A. HALDEMAN (Marietta)2. To Christliche Zeitschrift from DAVID EXLINE, Bedford co.,Pa., $1.25. Send paper to WM. LOHR, Salona, Centre co.,Pa.

187. Mar. 13, 1839/**MARRIED** On the 28th ult. by the REV. MR. BOND, MR. GEORGE KEYSER, to MISS ELIZABETH, daughter of MR. JACOB KELTNER, all of this borough.//By REV. B. S. SCHNECK at Snider's Hotel, on Tuesday last, MR. JOSEPH BRENDLE, of

WEEKLY MESSENGER OF THE GERMAN REFORMED CHURCH

Tulpehoccon, Berks county, to MISS MARTHA ROUCH, of Franklin county.//In Green Castle, on Tuesday evening, January 29th, by REV. J. REBAUGH, MR. ADAM SHIREY to MISS EVELINA FERREN, both of this county.//By the same, on the 21st of February, MR. DANIEL DOLLINGER to MISS SUSAN CLEEN, all of this county.//On the 26th ult., by REV. JOHN H. HOFFMIER at the house of CHARLES MANTZ (Antietam Furnace) MR. GREENBERRY FOUT, of Frederick county, to MISS ANN ELIZABETH POST, daughter of JOHN GROVE, of Sharpsburgh, Washington co., Md.//**DIED** In Middletown, Md. on the 26th ult, ALFRED HAMILTON, youngest son of MR. HENRY COCHRAN, in the 3d year of his age.//At the residence of her son near Mount Jackson, Shenandoah co., Va., on the 27th of Feb'y, MRS. ELIZABETH WILL, in the 84th year of her age.//In Mercersburg, the 20th of February, MRS. JANE B., wife of MR. ELLIOTT T. LANE and sister of the Hon. JAMES BUCHANAN. She was born July 17th, 1793, and united with the church in 1813. Though suffering from a pulmonary disease a great part of her life, she was of a cheerful disposition, and she was a kind and tender mother.//At his residence in Lancaster, OH, on the 20th ult. MR. JOHN POORMAN, formerly of this county.//At Pittsburg, on the ___ (sic) ult. MR. ADAM ROEMER, recently of this place.// Additional pledges for the Parent Board:

```
  MRS. S. MILLER, Berlin, Pa,.         paid  $3.00
   "   DR. SPANGLER, York,              do.   5.00
   "   J. B. HIESTER, Lebanon, Pa.      do.   3,00
   "   WAGNER              do.          do.   5.00
   "   R. GEORGE,                do.          5.00
  MISS M. DOLL,                   do.         3.00
   "   A. C. RAHOUSER, Buffalo, Pa,  do.      3.00
  MRS. E. W., Gettysburg,                     5.00
   "   CATHARINE SMALTZ, Harrisburg,          4.00
   "   M. HADE, Greencastle,                  5.00
  MR.  W. HIESTER, Lancaster co.,  paid,$20,00
   "   JACOB THOMAS, Middletown, Md.,do.  5.00
   "   JOHN DARBY, Fayetteville,    do.   5.00
   "   J. MILLER,    Berlin,        do.   5.00
```

WEEKLY MESSENGER OF THE GERMAN REFORMED CHURCH

" G. H. BUCHER,Cumberland co, do. 5.00
" W. A. WILT, York, do. 5.00
" JOHN SMITH, Chambersburg, do. 5.00
" WILLIAM HEYSER,Chambersburg, 10.00
[See articles 180 & 183. BAM]//The N. Orleans Observer states that the REV. MR. FINLEY, Colonial Agent of the MS Colonization Society was put to death at the town of Fishman in Africa, a few miles from the MD colony, in Sept. last. He was on his way from Greenville to Bassa Cove. Natives, it appears,killed him to get his money. --"Obs. & Teleg."//**MONIES.** By REV. J. REBAUGH, from H. J. RAUCH, J. FUSS JOHN WEAVER, C. DEITRICH and JOHN McLANE, each 2--JOHN SCHARFF (Leetown) 5; G. and L. M. TROUTMAN 2; ABR. LEFEVER, (Paradise) 2; JOHN STAMBAUGH 5; W. MAYBURRY 2; JAMES WRIGHT, Esq. 2; SAMUEL MAXWELL 50 cts; by REV. W. COLLIFLOWER, from A. WISE, 3rd, and A. WISE, JR., J. PENNYWITT and W. DOSH, each 2; by REV. J. C. BUCHER, from DAVID BRANDENBERG 2, ADAM KELLER 2, and HENRY LEIGHTER 6. F. ROEMER, GEORGE THOMAS, JR. J. D. COLDSMITH, D. MILLER, each 2, HENRY LEADER 2, AARON GROVE 2.//**SEMINARY FUND** From DR. HOFFIUS, obtained by REV. J.MAYER, in Bedford county: WILLIAM BERCKHEIMER, $4.00, DAVID KUHNS, 2.00, FRED'K BERKHEIMER 3.00, HENRY KUHNS, JR. 2.00.//**LETTERS** DANIEL CORT, JR.

188. Mar. 20, 1839/**MARRIED** On the 26th ult., by REV. A. P. FREEZE, MR. JACOB DUDRAW to MISS AMELIA GRINDER both of Frederick county, Md.//On the 14th inst., by the same, MR. JACOB KEYSER to MISS CATHARIN ZIMMERMAN, (sic) both of Frederick co., Md.//On Thursday the 7th inst., by the REV. MR. KIEFFER, MR. WILLIAM GRAHAM to MISS SOPHIA SMITH, both of Bellefonte, Pa.//By the same, on the 12th inst., MR. JONATHAN KREIS to MISS LYDIA WINGARD,both of Centre co. Pa.//At Whitehall, on the 21st ult., by the REV. J. CARES, MR GEORGE KEENER to MISS ELIZABETH PATTERSON both of Chanceford, York county, Pa.//On the 25th ult., by the same, MR. JOHN KING to MISS CHRISTIANA HEIN-

WEEKLY MESSENGER OF THE GERMAN REFORMED CHURCH

DEL, both of York county, Pa.//On the 5th inst. by the same, MR. CHRIST. BESHORE to MISS ELIZABETH KNAAB, both of York county.//By the same, on the same day, MR. EDW'D BRIDGER to MISS SARAH WOLF, both of Hanover, York county.//**DIED** February 18th at Lebanon, Pa., MRS. ANN FOULK, aged 43 years 8 months and 6 days. She became a member of the GRC about 8 years ago under REV. H. KROH. Her husband died before her.//On Tuesday the 5th inst., JOHN MELVILLE, son of REV. DANIEL G. and MRS. M. E. BRAGONIER, aged 1 year, 10 months and 11 days. Ere the tears had ceased to flow, God called away their only child, a lovely infant daughter. On the 9th inst., ELIZABETH SHINDLER BRAGONIER departed this life, aged 2 months and 2 days. [Communicated Shepherdstown, Va. March 9.//Suddenly, March 8th, in Meadville, Pa., MRS. MARY, consort of JOHN STEWART RIDDLE, Esq. She has left two children, scarcely conscious of their loss, besides her husband.//The annual meeting of the Chambersburg Temperance Society to be held Monday evening. WILSON REILLY Sec'ty.//MR. POTTER, of IL, has successfully erected earthen houses.//Additional Pledges for the Parent Board: [See 180, 183, 186. BAM]

MISS ALEPH,	Harrisburg,	paid,	$5 00
MRS. J. A. STEHLEY,	do.	do.	5 00
" GEO. MISH,	do.	do.	5 00
MR. J. ZIMMERMAN, SEN.	Franklin co.	do.	5 00
" Y. R.,	Baltimore	do.	5 00
REV. J. G. FRITCHEY,	Lincoln co,N.C.	do.	5 00
MR. J. COULTER,	do.	do.	5 00
" SOL. RAMSOUR	do.	do.	5 00
" D. RAMSOUR,(Tan.)	do.	do.	5 00
" SOLOMON WARLICK,	do	do.	5 00

//**MONIES.** W. WISE, (Mercersburg,) $7, MRS. JANE MAY, (N. Cumberland) 2, MRS. N. REMSHART (Harrisburg,) 2, W. HOFFMAN (Attica, Ia.,)2,M. HINDS 3, JACOB STAUB (formerly of VA) 6, PHILIP FELLTY 2,W. WENNER 2,JOHN YAKEY 2, JONA. WENNER 1, MRS. WAMPLER 4, GEO. BARRICK2, JOHN COOK1, J.S.MARTIN (Hampstead) 5; by JOHN COULTER, Esq,, from ALVI-

WEEKLY MESSENGER OF THE GERMAN REFORMED CHURCH

RAH WILSON, JACOB RAMSOUR, JOHN HOKE, JOHN MOTZ, JR. S. LANTZ, JOHN RAMSOUR, (Tanner,) ANDREW RAMSOUR, SOL. RAMSOUR, MICH. FINGER, WARLICK & FINGER, D. & J. RAMSOUR, and D. RAMSOUR, (Tanner,) each 2, and J. COULTER 1. The Christliche Zeitschrift. REV. J. H. SMALTZ, paid $1.00. Send paper to GEO. FREEZE,Mechanicstown,Frederick co. Md., WM. BOLLAR, SEN.,Graceham,Frederick co. Md.

189. Mar. 27, 1839/**MARRIED** On the 7th inst., by REV. W. F. COLLIFLOWR, MR. ISAAC RINEHART, of Shenandoah county, to MISS SUSANNAH KROTZER,of Rockingham county, Va.//**DIED** Suddenly, at the house of his brother in this place, on Saturday last, MR. ANDREW CALHOUN, of MO, formerly merchant in this borough--leaving a wife.//On Sabbath morning, the 3d inst., near Woodstock, MRS. MARIA CATHARINE HOTTEL, consort of GEORGE HOTTEL, Esq.,in the 61st year of her age. She was confined one year and two months. She called to her bedside her husband, children and her grand children and exhorted them to make preparation for eternity.//HENRY R. WARFIELD of Frederick, was found dead in his bed on Monday morning of apoplexy. He was for a number of years a representative in Congress.//The last Louisianian contains intelligence of the death of GENERAL ELEASAR W. RIPLEY, native of NH, for many years a resident of LA and Representative in Congress. //The Evansville Journal of the 6th inst. states that GEORGE H. DUNN, while on his way home from Congress had both ankles broke in an overturned coach. He had a similar accident last year.--- "Madison Courier."

190. Apr. 3, 1839/**MARRIED** On the 14th ult., by REV. E. KIEFFER, MR. HENRY KOONS to MISS JULIAN RAUSH, both of Boalsburg, Centre county, Pa./On the same day, by the same, MR. DAVID YOUNG to MISS SAPARA REAM, both of Boalsburg,Centre county.//On the 19th ult., by the same, MR. SOLOMON MANN to MISS MARGARET HOOVER, both of Centre

WEEKLY MESSENGER OF THE GERMAN REFORMED CHURCH

county.//On the 14th inst., by REV. S.R. FISHER, MR. WM. BELL to MISS MARY ANN DERR both of Adams co., Pa.//On the 12th inst. by the same, MR. ARMER BIGHAM to MISS ELIZABETH HAHN, both of Adams county.//The 16th inst., by the same, MR. SAM'L KEDDLE to MISS ANNA KROM, all of Frederick county, Md.//The 20th ult. by the REV. MR. GUTELIUS, MR. GEO. E. BUEHLER to MISS JULIA ANN WAMPLER, both of Gettysburg, Adams county.//On the 14th ult., LEVI DAVIS, Esq. of Seneca county, OH, to MISS JULIANNE, daughter of ISAAC SHRIVER,Esq. of Westminster Md.//The 26th inst. by REV. J. HELFFENSTEIN, MR. LEWIS KORUB to MISS MARY McGIGHEN, both of Franklin county, Pa.//On the same day, by the same, MR. CHRIST. MICHALS, of Lebanon, Pa., to MISS HARRIET REED, of Chambersb'g.//The 29th inst., by the same, MR. WM. WESTON to MISS MARY SNYDER, both of Franklin county.//The 13th inst., at Middleberg, by REV. DAN'L FEETE, MR. HANSON CARMAOTH to MISS HARRIET, third daughter of JOHN CLABAUGH, Esq. all of Carroll co., Md.//
DIED In Penn's Valley, Centre county, Pa., on the 19th of February, MRS MARGARETTA SHANNON, in the 84th year of her age.//On the 16th ult., in the same house, MISS MARTHA HANNA, in the 39th year of her age.//The 1st ult., in Dauphin county,Pa., near Harrisburg, MR. PETER HECKART, aged about 63 years.//On the 23d ult., MISS MATILDA MANTZ of Frederick city, in the 31st year of her age.//On the 19th ult., in Philadelphia, JOSEPH R. FRIEDLANDER, founder of the Philadelphia Institute for the Blind. He was born in Breslau, GER.//On the 7th ult., at the residence of THOS. ANDERSON, in Letterkenny townshiy,(sic) BENJAMIN FRANKLIN HAY, son of JOHN HAY, formerly of Westmoreland county, aged 7 years and 7 days.//On the 23d ult., near Taneytown, MRS. CATH. RECK, at an advanced age.//After a short illness, on Monday evening last, MARY JANE, daughter of MR. SAMUEL McILROY, of Green township, aged 5 years. //The coal mine of MR. DOUGHERTY, near Pottsville, which caught fire in January, continues

WEEKLY MESSENGER OF THE GERMAN REFORMED CHURCH

to burn.//The Grand Jury for the city and county of Philadelphia has returned a true bill against DR. DYOTT for fradulent insolvency.//**MONIES** MRS. LYDIA VAN DYKE $2, S. ALLISON,(Centre co.) 2, F. MIESS 2. C. ALLEMAN2, J. HICKS2, R. SHULTZ,(Ky.) 2, T. S. HUBBARD,(Balt.)2, J. SNIDER,Esq. (Shippensb'g) 1, G. AUDENREED2, S. WINT 2, J. DARBY2, G. H. BUCHER (change) 40 cts., G. MOWER (Waynesboro')2, J. HARMONY (of P.) 10; by REV. J. CARES from M. GARDNER 4, J. STAHL 4, and REV. D. ZIEGLER, W. JOHNSON, W. WAGNER, J. SPANGLER, Esq. G. SMALL, M. DANNER, S. WAGNER, Esq, D. WEAVER, D. RUPP, DR. H. McCLELLAN, J. DIETZ, J. HARTMAN, D. SPANGLER, J. GLESSNER, Esq. G. W. LAUCKS, G. KING, G. WELSH, P. SHULTZ, each 2. [Spaces added as the original list had few separations between the names. BAM]//Additional pledges to Parent Board: [See 180, 183, 186, 187. BAM]

  MRS. JULIANN HOFFEDITZ,Richmond, Pa. paid $5 00
" SARAH SAYLOR, Hamilton,Monroe co.,do. 5 00
" ELIZ. KELLER do. do. do. 5 00
" CATHARINE ALLGART,Mt. Bethel, do. 5 00

//**SEMINARY FUND** By the REV. MR. HOFFEDITZ, from MR. JACOB FRASS, Northampton county, $25.00; by REV. J. G. WOLFF, MR. J. FISTER, $25.00, MR. J. DARNER, 20.00, MR. G. MAHN, 25.00, all of Middletown Valley, Md., and J. STAUB, 10.00, Shepherdstown, Va. Per DR. HOFFIUS, from PETER PENSIL $5.00 in Bedford county. From REV. S. HELFENSTEIN,JR. $5 for Building Committee.//Christliche Zeitschrift. Send paper to

JOHN LEIDY, Lower Saucon, Northampton co, Pa.
PETER LAUBACH, Weaversville, do. do.
GEO. WEBER,Esq.,Kreidersville, do. do.

Received $1 00 from the following
W. BARTHOLOMEW, Nittany, Centre county,
G. ULRICH,Heidelberg, Berks county
    (probably Womelsdorf R. D.)
J. LAMM, do. do.
P. KLOPP,SR. do. do.
P. KLOPP,JR. do. do.
JOHN LEIDY, Lower Saucon, Northampton co.,

WEEKLY MESSENGER OF THE GERMAN REFORMED CHURCH

From ABR. MOYER, Zelienople,
From JOHN BUTT, Erie,

191. Apr. 10, 1839/**MARRIED** Near Bakersville, on the 26th of March, by REV. JOHN W. HOFFMIER, MR. JOHN C. SNIVELY, of the State of IL to MISS MARIA, eldest daughter of JOSEPH STONEBREAKER, of Washington county, Md.//By the same, on the 27th, MR. JOHN F. KNODE, near Funkstown, to MISS HESTER ANN, second daughter of JOSEPH STONEBREAKER, both of Washington county, Md.//By the same, on the 30th near Sharpsburg MR. ELIAS WE?K to MISS BELINDA UNCLESBY, both of Washington county, Md.//**DIED** At St. Croix (West Indies) on the 4th of March, DR. JOHN D. SHIVELY, son of MR. JOHN SHIVELY, of Guilford township, in the 24th year of his age. He had just become a member of the profession. Laboring under laryngitis or disease of the throat, he left but a few months ago to take advantage of the curative effects of a sea voyage. His remains were deposited in the church yard of St. Pauls, (Episcopal,) the service was performed by the REV. MR. PERKINS of Montreal. He was connected with the "United Brethren in Christ."//JAMES JOHNSTON, Esq. of Peach Bottom township, was killed Wednesday last by being thrown from his horse. He was about 60 years of age.//We learn from the Salem Register, that REV. OZRO FRENCH and lady--REV. DAVID W. HUME and lady--REV. EBENEZER BURGESS and lady, and MISS CYNTHIA F????, were to embark from Salem on Monday, in the brig *Waverly*, CAPT. WARD, for Bombay under the direction of the AM Board. //CAPT.JEWETT, of the ship *Harriet R??* of Portsmouth, N. H. on his way to Boston from Liverpool experienced bad weather, was swamped and drowned with his 2d officer, and four men.//**MONIES** MRS. HAGAN 6; JAS. McMAHAN 2; DANIEL BUCHER 8 MRS. N. McCLEARY 2; F. WOLF (Abbitst.)2; HENRY SHIRK 3; SHESHB?ZZER BENTLEY 2; W. WILSON (Bath)2.50; OHN (sic) WEAVER (Weaversville) 1.25 and S. WEAVER 1.25; by D. H. DOLL, from HENRY MYERS, JACOB

WEEKLY MESSENGER OF THE GERMAN REFORMED CHURCH

COONTZ, and SUSAN GROVE, each 2, and D. REED 4; from REV. E. KUHNS, (OH)4; JOHN BAUM, JOHN DRAYER and JOHN MAUS, each 2; by REV. J. C. BUCHER, from JOHN KELLER 4, and H. COST 50 c.--from COL. JACOB CRAMER 2; MRS. MARGARET R RIDDLE 2; ANDREW SNIVELY2; CHRISTIAN BIGLER 2; by M. RICKENBAUGH, from W.H. BOYD, MICH'L MILLER, HENRY McLAUGHLIN, W. STONEBRAKER, SAM'L WELTY, and HENRY FENKE, each 2; by D. WEIDNER, from G. TROUTMAN, SEN., P. GRIM, MRS. CLAPP, MRS. OAT, MRS. MULLEDOR and J. G. ALBERGER, each 2. Christliche Zeitschrift. Send paper to REV. A. P. FREEZE, Walkersville, Fred. co., Md, paid $1.-- Received from DAN'L MIDDLEKAUFF, SEN., Hagerstown $1.//**SEMINARY FUND** Per ANDREW SNIVELY, Esq. Forty Dollars from MRS. CATHARINE MOREA near Greencastle. Per MR. D. H. DOLL, from MR. HENRY WELSHANS, Martinsburg, Va., $10--per REV. J. C. BUCHER, from J. A. MAHN, his subscription to the Second Professorship, $25.

192. Apr. 17, 1839/**MARRIED** On the 21st inst., by the REV. MR. ADAM, DOCTOR WILLIAM YOUNG, of Mount Vernon, IN, to MISS ANNA MARY DEAN of this place.//On the 13th ult.,by REV. J. REBAUGH, MR. GEORGE MITCHELL to MISS RACHEL PAULDING, all of Franklin co.//On the 14th,by the same, MR. PETER YOUNG to MISS DOROTHY BARNHARD, all of Franklin County.//On the 21st,by the same,MR. JACOB MASSY to MISS CATHARINE CURFMAN, of Wash.co., Md.//The 28th, by the same, MR. RUDO'PH HEIGHERT to MISS MARY SHELLER.//By the REV. R. DOUGLAS,on the 4th inst., MR. JOHN N.SHELL, to MISS MARGARET ERNST, all of Shepherdstown, VA.//**DIED** The 5th April, 1839, in Littlestown, Adams co., Pa., JAMES MONROE M'ILVAINE, son of ROBERT M'ILVAINE dec'd, aged 20 years,10 months and 25 days. When young he lost his father, and soon after became the support of his feeble mother until her death two years ago. A year ago he entered college, but through intense application, his health was much impaired and he returned to his friends with a broken constitution which baffled medical skill.

WEEKLY MESSENGER OF THE GERMAN REFORMED CHURCH

He left his estate to the Board of Missions and Beneficiary Education Society of the GRC, but as he was not legally of age, his wishes cannot be complied with unless by voluntary consent of his relatives.//STAFFORD H. PARKER has been elected Register of the Land Office, State of VA, vice WILLIAM SELDEN, resigned.//**APPOINTMENTS** by the Governor--DANIEL SHEFFER, of Adams county, JAMES P. BULL,of Bradford county, and WM. M'CREERY, of Washington county, to be Appraisers of Damages. //**MONIES** ARCHIBALD BEARD 1, ADAM HOKE 3, SAMUEL SMITH (Greencastle) 6, SAM. WITMIRE 1 25, MISS MARY SMITH (Park Head) 2, MICHAEL REED (Shellsburg) 3 and AB. SCHELL 2. HOLMES CRAWFORD 2, DR. A. SENSENY 4, JOHN CHRISSMAN (Valley) 2, and JACOB KRISE 2 50, D. SHOOTS (Balt.) 2, by REV. H. BASLER, from AND. REED 2, JOHN SHEIB 2, and DANIEL HUFFERT (Dublin) 1, by REV. S. R. FISHER, from SAMUEL FLEGEL JOHN HARBAUGH (Sabillasville) and W. WINROTT (Fairfield) each 2, by H. COST, from L. RODRICK 2 CAPT. W LEAKIN 2, H. STOCKMAN 2, JNO. SHARER 2, by D. HUYETT, from JACOB HUYETT 2, D. HUYETT 2, JOSEPH FLEMING 7, A. H. LAPPON 4, ABR. GARVER 2, JOSPEH WOLFERSBERGER 2, DAVID HAMMET 2 50, by REV. R. DOUGLAS, from JOHN SMURR 2, ELIZABETH BLACKF RD (sic) 2 ELIZA HOFFMAN 2, and ELIZABETH KEARNEY 4, by REV. D. ZACHARIAS from JONATHAN GETZENDANNER 2, JOSEPH FLEMING 2, and SOPHIA MICHAEL (Buckeystown) 2. For Christliche Zeitschrift send paper to
   MARTIN YOST, Dublin, Bucks Co , Pa.
   GEORGE SINE, do. do. do.
Received from JONATHAN STRACK, Chambersburg, $1. You will see that MR. JACOB GUELICH, of Cincinnati (please see if you have his name correct) has paid $1.//**SEMINARY FUND.** By REV. ROBERT DOUGLASS, $75 from MR. JOHN MAYER, Smithfield, VA.//**LETTERS.** J. HERGESHEIMER, JACOB HARBAUGH.

193. Apr. 24, 1839/**MARRIED** In Mercersburg,Pa., on the 11th inst., by the REV. DR. RAUCH, REV. J. H. A. BOMBERGER, pastor of the GRC in Lewis-

WEEKLY MESSENGER OF THE GERMAN REFORMED CHURCH

town,to MISS MARION HOUSTON, of Mercersburg.//At Newburgh, NY, on Wednesday evening, April 10, by the REV. JOHN JOHNSTON, the REV. JOHN M. KREBS, of the city of NY, to MISS ELLEN DE WITT CHAMBERS, daughter of JOHN CHAMBERS, Esq. of Newburgh.//**DIED** In Philadelphia, on Sabbath the 14th inst., the REV. ALBERT JUDSON,pastor of the First Presby. Church in Southwark.//Proposal to raise money for Mission Board by B. S. SCHNECK, BARNARD WOLFF, JACOB MAYER, JOHN SMITH, LEWIS DENIG, Committee.//**MONIES.** JOS. MENSER 1.50; FELIX BECK 4; JACOB OMAWAKE 1; GEO. NAGLE 7.50; C. & J. REBUCK 2; MICHAEL SHOFF 2; (Gebhart's,) MRS. M. McDOWEL, (St. Thomas,) 1; SARAH ABRAHAM (Carlise) (sic) 2; by J. C. BARNHART, from REV. P. STROBEL, REV. G. BOGER, COL. G. BARNHART and HEN. MOOSE, each 2; by A. CLAPP, from P. FOUST, DANIEL FOUST, JOHN CLAPP, SEN., W. FOUST, J. G. CLAPP, H. FOUST, MR. McCULLOCH, and A. CLAPP, JR., each 2; and JOSHUA CLAPP 4, and CHRISTIAN FOUST 4; REV. J. FENE?, OH, 1; S. BAKER 2; DR. T. KINDELBERGER 2; HENRY SEIBERT 2; SIMON SHUMAN 4 68; HENRY J. BROWN 2; PHILIP STOEHR 2.--Dednct (sic) per ct.2.37 1/2, J. G. BARNHART 2.

194. March (sic) 1, 1839/**DIED** Near Bakersville ABRAHAM D. M. HOUSER, aged 11 years, 11 months and 5 days.//In Mercersburg, the 25th of April, MRS. LYDIA W., wife of DR. A. SPEER, aged 41, a member of the Presby. church for the last twelve years. Suffering from a lingering and distressing nervous disorder, she has left a bereaved husband. [Communicated.//The dwelling of JOHN B. COOKE, Esq., near Winchester, (Va.) was entirely destroyed by fire on the 11th ult.//The death of the Hon. LUTHER LAWRENCE, Mayor of Lowell, by an accident, is related by the Lowell Patriot. MR. LAWRENCE, with a friend went into a planing mill which is now fitting up for a grist mill, caught his foot in a rope and was precipitated into the wheel pit.--"Boston Transcipt of Thursday."//A daughter of JACOB ORT, of Derny Township, Miff-

lin county, in this state, two years of age, was burned on the 6th ult., by her clothes taking fire, so much as to occasion her death.//**MONIES.** By GEO. C. WELKER, from S. REILAND $2, FRANCIS BUCHER 2, CATH. DERING 1; By REV. J. ZELLER, from PHILIP FREDERICK 2, SAMUEL REBER 2 and JOHN ZELLER, (Lewisburg,) 1; By S. LEIBY, from GEORGE ZINN 2, from S. LEIBY 3; By REV. B. C. WOLFF, from EVE FABER, MARY STEM, BERNARD ODENWELDER, JOSEPH SHIEMER and JACOB BAKER, each 2. By REV. S. R. FISHER, from E. EBBERT 2, MARTIN NEWMAN 2; from JACOB MILLER (St. Thomas) 2, P. COOK, [Fayetteville,] 2; from REV. D. WILLERS 2, and P. PETERS 1. To Zeitschrift. By E. KIEGGER, from JACOB BROWN, Salona, & GEO. SNYDER, Kitany, each 1.//**LETTERS** D. LYNCH, JESSE BANKS.

195. May 8, 1839/**MARRIED** On March 21st, by the REV. D. G. BRAGONIER, MR. GEORGE SNYDER, to MRS. ANN TROUBTMAN.//On the 22d ult. by the same, MR. GOTTLIEB WORNER, to MISS FRANCISCO KERBLE.// On the 30th ult.,by the same,at Rocky Fountain, MR. EDWARD G. W. STAKE, of the firm of STAKE and HOLLIDAY, Williamsport, to MISS ANN E., daughter of CAPT. SAMUEL MILLER.//**DIED** At his residence in Franklin county, Pa., MICHAEL COOK, SEN'R, aged 84 years, 1 month, and 6 days. He was one of the few remaining veterans who was actively engaged in our Revolutionary struggle in 1776. About this time he also joined the GRC. For the last fifteen years he had been deprived of his natural sight.//**APPOINTED** By the Governor, JOHN KLINGENSMITH, of Westmoreland county, to be Secretary of the Land Office. JACOB SALLADA, of Berks county, to be Surveyor General. GEORGE R. ESPY, of Venango county, to be Auditor General. //ZERA COLBURN, who was so distinguished in his childhood for his powers of calculation, died at Norwich, Vt., in the 35th year of his age. He was a Methodist clergyman.//MR. THOMAS TYRELL, of Mo., advertises that a cancer upon his nose, which had been treated without success by DR.

WEEKLY MESSENGER OF THE GERMAN REFORMED CHURCH

SMITH, of New Haven, had been cured by the use of strong potash, made of the ashes of red oak bark, boiled down to the consistency of molasses to cover the cancer with it and in about an hour to cover with a plaster of tar, which must be removed in a few days, and if any protruberances remain, reapply the above; then heal the wound with common salve.--"N. Y. Com. Adv."//The house of MR. GEORGE THORNBURG, in the Western part of Hagerstown, was struck by lightning Tuesday afternoon last. Some members of the family were stunned and there was damage to the gable end and the chimney.//**MONIES** At Hanover, from JESSE HIPPLE 5, VALENT. SMITH, Ickesburg, 2, ABR. ALBERT, Oxford, 2, REV. J. BEAR 2, HENRY WIRT, JACOB GROVE, JACOB FORNEY, JOHN FLICKINGER, REV. J. SECHLER, DANIEL FLICKINGER, each 2, DAVID HOFFMAN, Berrysburg, 4; A. RAIGUEL 4, JOHN KILLINGER 2. By REV. J. CARES, from HEN. SMALL, JACOB KING, HENRY KING, JOSEPH SMALL, (Coachmaker) and PETER CARES, each 2. By REV. MR. HOFFEDITZ, from AARON MESSINGER 2, PETER EMERICH 2, and JOSEPH STALY 1. By J. G. MILLER, from M. ZIMMERMAN 2, PHIL. CUSTER 2, and D. COMPTON 1. From F. W. HOOVER 2, and PHILIP HOOVER 2. By GEO. KELLER, from ROB. HEAGY 2.50, GEO. KELLER, 2, and B. HAVERSTICK 4, JOHN CROSSEL, Ephrata, 2. J. L. LIGHTNER, Intercourse, 1, REV. D. HERTZ 50 cts., JACOB KULP, Trappe, 5. By REV. J. G. FRITCHEY, from J. COULTER 1, and ELKANAH SHUFORD, F. & P. REINHARDT, L. REINHARDT, and J. G. FRITCHEY, each 2. By REV. D. ZACHARIAS, from GEO. GITTINGER, E. THOMAS, E. DOUB, DAN. BENTZ, and MARY SPECHT, each 2. Last week, we should have credited WILLIAM SEIBERT for $2, instead of HENRY. MR. SAMUEL LEIBY is informed he has paid $7.50. BROTHER FEETE is informed that MR. SLICK'S money was credited. BROTHER WOLFF is informed that MR. S's paper was ordered sent to Mt. Bethel---then to Martins Creek. We changed his paper as requested, but the late address was not Lower Mt. Bethel, but Martin's Creek--is this right?

WEEKLY MESSENGER OF THE GERMAN REFORMED CHURCH

To the Christliche Zeitschrift. By REV. ISAAC GERHART, from JOHN WEBER, $1. By REV. D. HERTZ,* from JOSEPH GURGIS $1; from J. GRAY and D. MARKLY, (to be discontinued,) 50 cts. By REV. J. G. FRITCHEY, from PETER HARMAN, SEN., NC, $1. Send paper to PHILIP SCHWALM, Womelsdorf, Berks co., Pa. *Please correct your acknowledgment of DAN MOHR, into DAN'L MOON.//**PRINTING ESTABLISHMENT SUBSCRIPTIONS.** JACOB HEYSER, $100.00 WILLIAM HEYSER 100.00 LEWIS DENIG, 50.00 BARNARD WOLFF, 50.00 R. H. 50.00 P. C. 30.00 J. C. 15.00 PETER COOK, SR., 30.00 D. SPANGLER 20.00 PHILIP NITTERHOUSE, 20.00 J. LOGAN SMITH, 10.00 JEREMIAH SNIDER, JR., 5.00, all of Chambersburg, Pa. REV. JOHN CARES, York, Pa., 25.00, REV. J. SECHLER, Hanover, 25.00 REV. J. REBAUGH, Greencastle, 25.00 B. S. S., 25.00 DR. F. A. RAUCH, 25.00.

196. May 15, 1839/**MARRIED** On the 2d inst., by the REV. THOMAS CREIGH, MR. JOHN SWIGART,to MISS ISABELLA SMITH,daughter of FREDERICK SMITH, Esq. all of Mercerburg.//On Thursday last,at the Parsonage of the Ev. Reformed Church, by the REV. DANIEL ZACHARIAS, MR. JESSE MAYOR, to MISS LYDIA SMITH, both of Frederick.//On the evening,of the same day by the same, MR. JOHN RANDOLPH NICHOLS, of Frederick, to MISS CATHARINE MYERS, of Frederick co. Md.//On the 1st inst., by REV. SAMUEL R. FISHER, MR. ELIJAH CLOSE, of Frederick co., to MISS SUSAN, daughter of FREDERICK BIGGS, of Carroll co. Md.//On the 7th inst., by the same, MR. JOSEPH MARTIN, to MISS HENRIETTA STEVENSON, all of Frederick co. Md.//In Bellefonte, Centre co., Pa., Tuesday evening, May 7th, by the REV. MR. LINN, WILLIAM E. MORRIS, Esq., Principal Engineer on the West Branch Canal, to MISS MARY, daughter of the Hon. THOMAS BURNSIDE, of that place//In Washington City, on the 16th ult., by the REV. W. McLEAN, REV. H. G. O. DWIGHT, Missionary at Constantinople, Turkey, to MISS MARY LANE.//**DIED** Near Emmittsburg, Md., on the 30th ult., MRS. SARAH FEEZER, wife of JACOB FEEZER,

WEEKLY MESSENGER OF THE GERMAN REFORMED CHURCH

aged 39 years, 2 months and 15 days.//In Guilford township, Franklin county, on Friday morning, JACOB SNIDER SEN., at an advanced age.//On Friday evening last, in Guilford township, MRS. CATHARINE KOLBY, wife of GEORGE KOLBY, a member of the Evang. Reformed Church.//Near Bellefonte, of a lingering illness, MRS. CAROLINE, consort of MR. EDWARD McGARVEY, in the 30th year of her age.//At Pensacola, FL, the 28th of March, JOHN O. YATES, Esq., formerly of Jefferson County, Va., in the 25th year of his age.//On the 17th ult, MR. THOMAS GILL, JR., of Mill Creek, Berkley County, Va., aged 33 years.//At Jersey City, on Friday evening, the 19th ult., COL. AARON OGDEN, an officer of the Revolutionary Army, and President General of the Society of Cincinnati, aged 84 years.//At Shepherdstown, Va., on the 18th ult., MISS SARAH W., daughter of JOHN T. COOKUS, Esq., of that place, in the 18th year of her age.//At the residence of his father on Friday morning the 3d inst. MR. CONRAD LEISENRING, Merchant of this place, aged 24 years 1 month and 21 days. He had been a member of the GRC at Easton.--"From the Mauch Chuck Courier."//It is stated in the New Orleans Bee that JAMES PERRY and THOS. F. McKINNEY, have subscribed $3000 per annum for five years for a female academy in TX.

197. May 22, 1839/**MARRIED** On the 14th inst. by the REV. J. HELFFENSTEIN, MR. JESSE COOKSTON, to MISS CATHARINE PEPLE, both of Washington county, Md.//In this place, on Tuesday the 14th inst.,by REV. DAVID DENNY, MR. ABRAHAM K. WEIR, of Mercersburg, to MISS SUSANNAH, second daughter of MR. WILLIAM LAURENCE, of Green Castle.//On the 14th inst., by the REV. JAMES WATSON, DR. JOHN M'DOWELL of Mercersburg, to MISS NANCY M'PHERSON of Gettysburg.//The citizens of Franklin county met in Mercersburg, the 4th of May, to express a preference for the route surveyed for the railroad. MR. DAVID DUNWOODY was called to Chair, and A. K. WEIR appointed Secretary.//The barn of

WEEKLY MESSENGER OF THE GERMAN REFORMED CHURCH

MR. PETER CULP near Gettysburg was struck by lightning and burnt on Wednesday evening last week.//The Gettysburg Sentinel of Monday week says:--Saturday last, MR. PETER MARSHALL,of Berwick township, went out with his gun. A short time afterwards, he sent home a lad to request his wife to come to him. As she hurried out she heard the report of his gun. She found him on the ground dead, the load having passed through his head. He was about 50 or 60 years of age and had been in an unhappy state of mind occasionally.//**MONIES.** REV. P. S. FISHER 3; DAVID NEIDIG 5; JOHN SHROCK 1, AND C. HOFFERT 1. From JOHN HOUCK 3 and MATTHEW TRUMAN 2. ADAM VONDERAW 2; WILLIAM FETTER (Strasburg)2; DR. JOHN REAM 2. By M.RICKENBAUGH, from JOHN TROUB 2, DAVID TROUP 2, and JOHN YOUNG 5. From J. P. FREEZE (N. Y.)1. //**EDUCATION FUND.** From MRS. GEISY, Lancaster, OH, per REV. H. WILLIARD, (paid,)$5.00.//**LETTERS** MR. TROUP's paper forwarded to Beaver Creek, Md.

198. May 29, 1839/**MARRIED** Near Middletown, Md. on the 25th of April, by REV. J. C. BUCHER, MR. PETER SCHENCK, to MISS SARAH ANN HESSONG, all of Middletown Valley, Md.//On the 16th inst.,by the same, MR. JETSON ECKTON, to MISS SARAH ANN GALWITH, all of Burkittsville, Md.//By the REV. C. G. HERMAN, DAVID LEVAN to LYDIA GERET,of Maccungie, Lehigh co., Pa.//By the same, BENNEVILLE LESHER, to MARIA HEINLY, of Berks county.//By the same, GUELIAN BRAUCHER, to HETTY BIEBER, of Cootstown.//On the 24th ult., by REV. MR. DUBBS, AARON BUCHECKER, of Upper Saucon, to SUSAN OAKS, of Allentown.//On the 31st ult., by the same, GEORGE METZGER,to POLLY HAUSMAN, both of Heidelburg.//At the same time, by the same, HILARY KEHNEL, to JUDITH HAUSMAN, both of North White Hall.//On April 14th, by the same, WILLIAM PETER to SARAH HANDWERK, of Heidelburg.//On the 11th ult., by the same, ELIAS SCHNEIDER, to CATHARINE BAEHR, of Heidelburg.//On the same day, by the same, ABRAHAM KRISCHNER, to POLLY BUTZ, of South

WEEKLY MESSENGER OF THE GERMAN REFORMED CHURCH

White Hall.//On the 24th ult., by the same, MR. HENRY ZIMMERMAN to JULIA KELCHNER, both of South White Hall, Lehigh county.//On the 12th inst., by the REV. D. ZACHARIAS, MR. GRAFTON SHAWEN, to MISS CHRISTINA BENTZ, both of Frederick, Md.//On the same day, by the same, MR. HENRY BRANE, to MISS MARGARET LAWMAN.//In Cherryville, Northampton county, Pa., by the REV. W. T. GERHARD, DR. CHARLES HUMPHREYS to MISS ELIZA STANTON.//By the same, on the 11th ult., COL. JOHN SENT to MISS JULIAN BERNITZ.//By the same, on the 14th ult., MR. DANIEL OBLINGER to MISS SAVINA SEIP.//By the same, on the 23d, MR. JOHN KERN, to MISS LYDIA BEST.//By the same, on the 28th ult., MR.. LEWIS SCHUMACHER, to MISS ABBY KINER, all of Nothampton (sic) co.//**DIED** At her residence in Chambersburg, on the 21st inst. MRS. CRAWFORD, widow of the late EDWARD CRAWFORD, Esq.//[The following had been forwarded in due season, but was mislaid.] Near Millerstown, Adams county, Pa.,on the 18th of February last, MRS. CATHARINE WORTZ, wife of LEWIS WORTZ, and daughter of CHARLES DONALDSON, aged 22 years, 11 months and 8 day. But seven short weeks previous to her death, she was called to witness the consignment of the remains of her interesting little sister-in-law to the tomb. At the funeral she contracted the disease that resulted in her own dissolution.// In Frederick city, on Sunday morning last, after a lingering illness, MR. JOHN MANTZ, aged 71 years, 9 months, and 5 days.//At Middletown, Md. on the 20th of April, ALPHEUS, only son of MR. JOSEPH WISE. He was precisely one year of age on the day of hs death.//Also, at the same time, on the 1st of May, after a painful and distressing illness, ANN REBECCA, eldest child and only daughter of MR. JOHN WEAVER-aged 3 years 1 month and 1 day.//Also, near Middletown, on the 15th of May, EUGENIA CLEANTHA, daughter of MR. HENRY COBLENTZ, aged 1 year, 4 months, and 1 day.//On the 5th inst., of a lingering pulmonary disease, at the residence of her father in Mercersburg,

WEEKLY MESSENGER OF THE GERMAN REFORMED CHURCH

Pa., MRS. SUSANNAH L. PORTER, eldest daughter of DR. P. W. LITTLE, and wife of REV. G. D. PORTER, lately pastor of the Presby. church, Williamsport, Washington co., Md. Parents, brothers and sisters, and a husband have been called to mourn and a promising son has been doomed to an early orphanage.//In Bedford, on the 5th inst., MARY, daughter of REV. JACOB ZIEGLER, aged 7 months and 15 days.//On Sabbath evening the 19th inst., MRS. ANNA REWALT, wife of WM. REWALT, Esq., and a daughter of DANIEL HERSTER, of Easton, in the 38th year of her age. She was stricken with a slow wasting disease from which she was never to recover.//MR. DANIEL S. MONTGOMERY, of Danville, Penn., has willed to the REV. DR. PROUDFIT in trust for the Colonization Society, the sum of $500.//We learn from the Boston Advocate, PROFESSOR LEONARD WOODS, JR., of the Bangor Theological Institution, has been elected President of Bowdoin College.//REV. A. A. PHELPS has resigned as a member of the Board of the MA Anti-Slavery Society as it has beome a woman's rights non-government Anti-Slavery Society.//MR. KENNARD, an agent of the MD Colonization Society, has obtained in Anne Arundel county, subscriptions towards the purchase a vessel between Baltimore and Cape Palmas, Africa, the site of the Colony.//A little daughter of MR. ELLIS, of Willet, Cortland Co. lost her life on the 2d ult. by prataking (sic) of Muskrat weed (Cicuta Maculata,) which is a deadly poison. It was eaten supposing it to be Spikenard.//A case in the Superior Court on Monday may serve as a caution. WM. P. HALLETT, Esq. was sued for recovery of a judgment which had been obtained against a MR. CHARLES MORRIS, in consequence of having overlooked a previous judgment against MR. MORRIS. MR. HALLETT was sued for $4,000, and before the case was submitted to the jury, consented to the payment with costs.---"N. Y. Transcript."//The schr. *Atlas* of Dexter, CAPT. WESCOTT, went down under a close reefed mainsail within sight of

WEEKLY MESSENGER OF THE GERMAN REFORMED CHURCH

Oswego, Lake Ontario, on the morning of the 4th inst. Seven person drowned.//**MONIES** By REV. D. GRING, from JONATHAN LENTZ, W. H. POMP, W. FREIMYER, D. FOLLMER, (Limestone,) and GEO. STAHL, each 2; from C. LEISENRING (M. Chunk) 5, FRED. KELLER, [Mt. Pleasant, Md.] 2, MARG. KETRON 2; REUBEN STEM (Fount. Dale) 2; by CHARLES H. LEINBACH, from ISAAC ECHERT, Esq., N. V. R. HUNTER, Esq., DR. GEO. N. ECHERT,(Swatara) PETER ECHERT, Esq., JOSEPH LEVERS, (Cherryville,) B. YODER, (Tre?lerstown,) W. STEWART, (Stouchburg,) each $2, and DR. A. J. HERMAN 1 25, WASHINGTON RYON, 2 25, REUBEN MEYER, (Allentown,) 1, A. G. STEIN, (Stouchburg) 1, and JACOB JONES, (Kreidersville) 1 25. From JOS. BRUBAKER, (Berlin, Pa.,)2. By REV. W. F. COLLIFLOWER, from REV. JOHN BROWN 5, JOSEPH FUNK 5, JONAH JORDON 2, GEO. HOTTEL, Esq. 2, and W. F. COLLIFLOWER 1. By REV. J. C. HENSELL, from JOHN HAWPE, SR., DAVID SHULTZ, and J. C. HENSEL, each 2. From PAUL HAUGH 2, BURKHARDT MYER, (Balt.) 2, JOHN ZIMMERMAN, (Emmittsburg,) 2, TUNIS J. STIVES,(N.J.)2,ABRAHAM CLAPP, (N.C.) 1, BARBARA H. CLAPP 2, and J. HENRY CLAPP 2. By WM. RUSSEL, from HENRY KEEN, JR. 5. From GARRET CLARK, (Hoguestown,) 2, HENRY CHRI??MAN, (Town,) 2, JAMES HOLLAND 2, DANIEL HA[spot] 50 cents, JACOB CRIDER 50 cents. MASTER SAMUEL S. MORITZ is informed that 50 cts. will pay the balance. MR. PAUL HAUGH is informed the $5 were acknowledged. MR. JOHN ZIMMERMAN (Emmittsburg) is informed he commenced with No. 1., vol. 1. (Aug. 1835) he now has credit for three years.

199. June 5, 1839/**MARRIED** In York, on Wednesday the 22nd ult., by REV. JOHN CARES, MR. MARTIN AUSTIN, to MISS CATHARINE GILL, both of that place.//On the 21st ult., by REV. J. SECHLER, MR. JAMES FIESER,to MISS ANN MARIA KING, both of Carroll county, Md.//On the 12th ult., by the REV. MR. ZEIGLER, MR. JOHN RUTH, to MISS CASSANDRA LAUBOTH,of York county.//On the 16th, by the REV. MR. GEIGER, MR. JOHN GITT, to MISS JULIA

WEEKLY MESSENGER OF THE GERMAN REFORMED CHURCH

RENNOLL, of York co.//At York, on Friday Morning, 10th ult., by REV. B. J. WALLACE, the REV. JOSIAH B. CLARK, of Rising Sun, IN, to MISS MARY J. LINSLEY, of that borough.//On Thursday last, by the REV. HENRY AURAND, MR. MICHAEL SCHLEY, to MISS CATHARINE E. REISENGER, both of Cumberland county.//April 18th, by the REV. MR. COWEN, MR. HIRAM R. SMITH, (Merchant) to MISS ANN C. LEITER both of Mansfield, OH.//On Thursday evening, 30th ult., by the REV. MR. BOWEN, MR. CHARLES W. HEART, to MISS MARIA KERR, all of Chambersburg. **//DIED** On Wednesday last, near Shippensburg, after much pain and affliction for two years past, MRS. CATHARINE TICE, consort of MR. PETER TICE, in the 56th year of her age. She was a member of the ERC.//On Tuesday morning May 28th, after a lingering illness, MR. JAMES WEISEL, of Bedford, Pa.//In Mifflinburg, Union co., Pa., on the 30th ult., MR. ___ (sic) GUTELIUS, father of the REV. SAMUEL GUTELIUS, in the 73d year of his age.//A meeting of the American Sunday School Union was addressed by REV. MR. IDE of Philadelphia, of the Baptist Church, REV. MR, KAVANAUGH, of IL, of the Methodist Church, and REV. DR. BETHUNE of the Dutch Reformed.//**MONIES RECEIVED.** From HENRY BITTINGER, York Springs, for 3 years, 7; GEORGE SHAFFER, do. 7; JACOB EBBERT 2; ABRAHAM FLUCK 2; by JOHN SMITH, from REV. H. BIBIGHOUSE, 4; JOS. & N. KIEFFER, GEORGE CHAMBERS, Esq.,JACOB BESORE, each 2; M. GROSSMAN, (W.Run,) 5; by C. F. HOFFMEIER, from DANIEL HELM 2, ABR. PETERS 1, and MR. BUNDLE 1; By H. O. WALLACE, from C. HOLSHOUSER, JOHN MOOSE, WILLIAM FISHER, HENRY SECHLER, ELIJAH SHOLLENBERGER [Selma,Ala.] each 2; by REV. J. HELLER, from J. H. WILL, F. MUMMA, G. HAMMER, A. LOUGH, and JOHN DAVIS, each 2. REV. W. CONRAD (for vol 3 & 4) 5; by REV. S. B. LEITER, from F. KAYLER 2.50, LEPPO, WISE & LEITER 3, J. APPLEGATE 4.50; by REV. S. GUTELIUS from JOHN HERMAN (Gettysb.)2, JOHN RUBY (Hellam) 2,and HENRY RUBY 2. We were requested to credit DANIEL BESORE with $2--which should have been to

WEEKLY MESSENGER OF THE GERMAN REFORMED CHURCH

F. KAYLER. To Christliche Zeitschrift. Received from REV. JOHN LANTZ, N. C. $1.

200. June 12, 1839/**DIED** At his residence in Davidson county, N. C. on the 14th of February last,MR. CASPER BRINKLE, aged 88 years, 7 months and 11 days, leaving an aged companion with whom he had lived nearly 63 years, eight children, 57 grand children, and 58 great grand children.// The Natchez Free Trader states that in the Circuit Court of Copiah county on the 10th inst., ALVA CARPENTER was put on trial, charged with the murder of MR. KELLER, late Judge of Probate. The Jury returned a verdict of manslaughter. As the officer was on the eve of taking the prisoner back to jail, the lights were put out, and CARPENTER was stabbed in three or four places, one of his hands cut off, and he fell a corpse. //**POISON** ELLEN GRAVES, residing at NY, on Friday night last, took what she supposed to be salts, and died in great agony. It was ascertained she had taken in mistake oxalic acid.// The Pottsville Journal Saturday states a child belonging to MR. PAYNE, aged about ten months, was so severely burned as to survive only a few hours; another child of MR. J. KOHLER's near three years of age, while playing about the fire of a plumber in the street, had her clothes burned off, and lived but a short time.//A man by the name of WILLIAMS, died recently at Catskill, from drinking on a bet, five half pints of spirits.//We regret to hear the HOWITTS, of Nottingham, will settle in Australia. WILLIAM will stay home, but DR. GODFREY and RICHARD with numerous relatives and a few scientific friends are emigrating to South Australia.-"Sheffield (Eng.) ??is."//We saw in operation the other afternoon the newly invented printing press of the MESSRS. SCHNEBLY of Hagerstown, Md. at the machine factory of WILLIAM M. HARTSHORNE, on the Willow street railroad, near 13th st..--"The Philadelphia Herald and Sentinel."//**MONIES** From JOHN D.

WEEKLY MESSENGER OF THE GERMAN REFORMED CHURCH

APPLE [Sumnyt.] 5; J.H. GEYER 7; WM WAGNER, York 1; JAMES DUFFIELD 2; JOHN MILLER, JR. 2; by C.F. HOFFMEIER, from P. HEITSHU, W. HEITSHU, C. GAST, B. CHAMPNEYS, H. MARKLEY, each 2, G. BOMBERGER 3.25, JOHN LENHERR 3, GEO. LEFEVER, Paradise, 2, D. MUSSELMAN 2; by JOHN C. BUCHER, from G. MISH, E. GREENAWALT, MRS. H. WIESTLING, S. ZACHARIAS, G. Z. KUNKLE, each 2; by T. S. GISINER, from J. KEEDY, SAMUEL KEEDY, SAM'L PRY, SAM'L COST, each 2, H.B. ROHRBACK 1, A MOSTELLER 4.50, J.H. MYERS 1.50; by REV. J. MAYER, from DANIEL STECKEL [N. Whitehall] 2, REV. J. ZUILCH 1, REV. L.C. HERMAN 2, BENONI BATES 2, and CHARLES HILLEGAS 4; by J. POTTER, Esq. from C. PETERS 5, JANE McCORMICK 2, JOHN BLOOM 4, J. POTTER 2, W. HEWES, Esq. 2, A. McCOY 2, JOHN KELLY,SEN., 4.25. Credit was given to JOSEPH FLEMING---should have been JAMES FLEMING. MR. CHARLES HILLEGAS commenced with second volume--has paid for four years. To Christliche Zeitschrift. Rec'd f'm JACOB HEILMAN (Shepherdstown, Va.) adv.$1. NICHOLAS FLEEK (Jackson Hall, Frank co. Pa.) 1.**//SEMINARY FUND.** On account of subscriptions obtained by REV. JACOB MAYER,Brush Valley, Centre county,Pa. By PHILIP REITZEL,Esq. from ANTHONY WOLF $20, PHILIP REITZEL $5, JNO. WOLFORT $10, JOHN WALKER $10, PAUL WOLF $3, JOHN REITZEL $2.**//LETTERS.** JAMES PEACOCK; JAMES POTTER; REV. BENJAMIN SCHNEIDER, from Asia Minor.

201. June 19, 1839/**MARRIED** In Baltimore by the REV. MR. HEINER, MR. C. K. THOMAS, of Frederick co. Md. to MISS EVELINE VIRGINIA, second daughter of DANIEL BUCKEY, Esq. of that city.//On the 5th inst., by the REV. A. P. FREESE, MR. GEO. T. ZIMMERMAN, to MISS ANN McNAIR, both of Frederick county, Md.//**LOST BOY** On Thursday the 5th inst. JOSEPH BRIGGS, of Mercersburg, Franklin co. Pa., aged 15 years, was sent by his parents in the direction of Cove Gap to find a cow, since which time he has not been heard from, altho' diligent search has been made. Whether he is lost or eloped intentionally is a mystery. When he left

WEEKLY MESSENGER OF THE GERMAN REFORMED CHURCH

home he had on a dark mixt cotton roundabout, a grey mixt Cassanet vest, coarse hemp pantaloons, a brown hair cap, tore in front, no shoes--He is of the ordinary size(of that age) with dark hair and dark eyes.//**ADVERTISEMENT** Now cultivating 20,000 genuine Chinese Mulberry Trees for sale. Persons wishing to engage in the Silk Business are assured these trees are grown from cuttings, and not fsom (sic) seed. D. GILBERT, June 19, Gettysburg, Pa.//**VARIOUS SUBSCRIPTIONS.** By MR. JOHN KELLER, SEN., Boalsburg, Centre co., Pa., from HENRY MOYER, $25, HENRY HUBLER's estate 20, C. DALE 5, JACOB MOYER, JR., 5, HENRY MOYER JR. 5, JACOB HURST 5, JOHN ELDRES 3. By JAMES POTTER, Esq., Potter's Mills, Centre co., Pa., from JONAS FROMM $10, JACOB KRYDER 5, JACOB ROAN 1. From REV. GEO. GLESSNER $10, JOSEPH FRAVEL, 5; REV. GEIGER, 22; REV. FRIESE, 20; per REV. J. C. BUCHER, 15, per REV. HENSEL, 10; JOSEPH SNAPP, per REV. COLLIFLOWER, 5; ANN E EMSEWILER, 5; ISAAC HOTTLE, 3; D. HOTTLE, 1; MARY WALTERS, 50 cts. Acknowledgments of monies from the REV. J. MAYER shall appear next week.//**FUND FOR PROPOSED PUBLICATION OFFICE** for the Mission Board. B. S. SCHNECK, BARNARD WOLFF, JACOB MAYER, JOHN SMITH, LEWIS DENIG, Committee. WILLIAM HEYSER $100.00 JACOB HEYSER, 100.00 LEWIS DENIG, 50.00 BARNARD WOLFF, 50.00 R. H. 50.00 P. C. 50.00 J. C. 50.00 PETER COOK, SR., 30.00 PHILIP NITTERHOUSE, 20.00 D. SPANGLER, 20.00 J LOGAN SMITH, 10.00 JEREMIAH SNIDER, JR., 5.00, all of Chambersburg, Pa. REV. J. REBAUGH, Green-Castle, 25.00 REV. JOHN CARES, York, 25.00 REV. J. SECHLER, Hanover, 25.00 REV. DR. RAUCH 25.00 and REV. W. A. GOOD, 25.00, both of Mercersburg, S. S. B., 25.00 GEO. BESORE, (Waynesb'g--p'd $25) 50,00 "ALPHA," Baltimore, 100,00.//**MONIES.** By M. ROUNSAVILLE, from JOHN YONTZ 3, D. SHOAF 3, P. HELMSTETLER 1.65, SOL. LEONARD 3.50, [netto. $10] (sic) DAVID KEIPER 5, REV. J. A. LEIS 4, REV. JOHN PENCE 1, REV. J. DESCOMBES 4; by J. B. WELTZ, from SUSAN SMITH 2, and JACOB NICODEMUS 2.50; by REV. J. C. BUCHER,

WEEKLY MESSENGER OF THE GERMAN REFORMED CHURCH

from G. KEEFAUVER 2, JOHN COBLENTZ, SEN. 2, JOHN REMSBURG 4;from COL. GEORGE WEBER 2, P. AUNEWALT 6, and MRS. W. WEBER 1. Christliche Zeitschrift Received from REV. J. C. BUCHER, Middletown, Md. $1, JOHN P. COBLENTZ, do. 1. MR. CHRISTIAN GEIB, Lebanon, wishes his paper to be sent in future to St. Thomas, Franklin co., Pa.

202. June 26, 1839/**MARRIED** On Thursday last by the REV. B. S. SCHNECK, MR. CONRAD NEWROTH, to MISS MARIA MERCER, both of this place.//On the same day by the same, MR. FRANCIS WARNER to MISS ELIZABETH BENDER, both of this county.//**DIED** At Emmittsburg, Md., on the 13th of May, last, MRS. REBECCA ZIMMERMAN, aged 48 years 5 months and 16 days, of a protracted sickness, leaving a husband and a large family of children.//**LIGHTNING.** The wife of HENRY AGER, residing opposite Palmer on the St. Clair River, was killed by lightning a few weeks age. Three children in the room escaped unhurt. Deceased was nursing her infant at the time she was struck, and the child was only burnt a little about the eyebrows. MR. ISRAEL P. SLATE of Ellisville, Fulton co., Ill. was killed by lightning a few days ago, passing from a store to his house. It passed through his hat and down his breast, melting his watch-chain.//The Senate of this State have confirmed the nomination of ALEX'R M'CALMONT, Esq. of Venango county, to be President Judge of the 18th Judicial district. The confirmation of ALMON H. READ had been refused by the senate.//The Evening Post states that GERRIT SMITH, Esq., of Petersboro, made a donation of $10,000 to the AM Anti-Slavery Society.--"Jour. of Com."//**VALUABLE HORSE.** The Louisville Journal states that "Grey Eagle" was sold for $6,000, to MR. SHOTVILLE, of Georgetown, Ky.//The Richmond Whig says that a strawberry was gathered from the garden of MR. JAMES WINSTON, on Church Hill, measuring upwards of five inches in circumference. It was said to be the largest ever raised in VA.//**A FIRE** broke

WEEKLY MESSENGER OF THE GERMAN REFORMED CHURCH

out the afternoon of the 11th inst., in the city of New Orleans in the "cotton pickery" of MR. J. C. JONEY, and is said to have been caused by a careless segar (sic) smoker.//SAMUEL SHOCH, Esq. of Harrisburg, has been elected Cashier of the Columbia (Pa.) Bank and Bridge Company, in place of PRESTON B. ELDER, resigned.//**SEMINARY FUND.** partial collection by REV. JACOB MAYER. <u>Forks Township, Northamp. co., Pa.</u> JONAS LERCH 5, JOHN LERCH $10, THOMAS LERCH 10, PETER ANGLEMEYER 3, PETER KEMMERER 10, MICH. ABEL 3, JAC. P. MESSINGER 5, JOHN METZGER 50 cts. MICHAEL FREY 50 cts. VALENTINE UHLER 4, ELIZABETH GROSS 1, CATHARINE HAUSER 1, MARTIN SEIPEL 2, CATH. KOEHLER 25 cts. ABRAHAM BABP (sic) 1, JOS. MESSINGER 1.50, GEO. MESSINGER, SR. 1, GEO. MESSINGER, JR. 1, JOS. BROWN 1, JOHN KEMMERER 10, JOS. ROESLE 2, JOHN ROESLE 1, GEO. ABEL 10, WM. DECK 50 cts., MARIA ABEL 3, PETER CORRELL 5, MICH. FRASE 5, ANDREW UHLER 1, PHILIP SANDT 1, GEORGE SHERP 1 50, WM. SCHUG 2, SANDT SCHUG 5, JACOB SNYDER 5, JACOB FRAUNFELDER JR. 2, PETER FRAUNFELDER 2, JACOB FRAUNFELDER, SR. 2, HENRY SCHUG 12, MARY M. SANDT 5, CHARLES SANDT 3, ADAM SANDT 1, LEONARD SANDT 2.50, AARON KICHLINE 1, WM. BECKER 1.50, JACOB BREIDENBERGER 50 cts, MICH. MESSINGER 2, WM. N. WOODRING 5, E. L. EVANS 5, JOHN EVANS 1, DAVID HELLER 1, JESSE KEMMERER 10, BERNHARD STOCKER 50 cts., JACOB MILLER 2 50, JACOB HELLER 2, HENRY WEITZELL 5, MICH. FRAUNFELDER 1.50, JOHN KELLER 1, CHAS. BROWN 1, JOHN KNECHT 1, DANIEL ADAM 25 cts. SAM'L SCHUG 25 cts., JOHN STOFLIT 1, CHRISTIAN KNECHT 2, ABRAHAM KNECHT 1.50, JOHN STOFLIT 1, PHILIP ABEL 2, JONAS SANDT 1, GEO. G. MESSINGER 1, CHRISTIAN LERCH 5, JACOB SEIBERT, SOLOMON KNECHT 50 cts., DAN'L B. LERCH 1, THOMAS PERLMER 5. In <u>Allen township, Northamp. co. Pa.</u> BENONI BATES 5, CHESTER CASE 5, JONAS SNYDER 5, ADAM KOCH 50 cts., CHA'S HEINEG 2, NATHAN REEN 2, JOHN MILLER 3, G. W. SMITH 2, REUBEN BECK 50 cts., GEO. BECK 1, JOHN BACHMAN 5, JOHN KOH 50 cts., WM. STEWART 3, SAM'L STEMM 50c., G. W. BEER

WEEKLY MESSENGER OF THE GERMAN REFORMED CHURCH

50c., JONAS NEWHARD, JR. 50c., JOHN BACHMAN 50c. JOS. NEWHARD 5, JACOB SCHWARTZ 50c., JNO. YOUNG 50c., MICH. YOUNG 50c., SUSAN NEWHARD 1, JACOB BOYER, SR. 1, MARGARETTA DRIESBACH 1.50, JONAS KNAUS 3, MARY BEER 50c., CHRIST. LAUB 50c., AB'M HEISTAND 5, PETER AUNAWALT 5, DAV. HEISTAND 2, JONA. FENSTERMACKER 1, CONRAD REYER 1, THOMAS FATZINGER 1, AB'M. STEMM 5, JOHN LAUBACH 5, ADAM LERCH 10, JOHN J. GEISER 1, THOMAS STEWART 50c., GEO. NEWHARD 50c. In St. John's Congregation, Northamp. co., Pa., SUSAN BECKER 5, JOHN MERTZ 50c., SAM'L SHMEIER 50C., GEO. HOWER 5. In Lower Saucon Congregation, Northamp. co., Pa., CHRIST. RUCH 1, CHAS. CHRISTMAN 1, JOHN JACOBY 1, HENRY UNANGEST 2, ANTHONY OBERLY 5, JACOB RICHLINE 1, JOHN LUTZ 1, CHAS. FRANSOE 50C., ABRAHAM REICH 1, JACOB K. REIGEL 2.50 JESSE SHIMER 2.50, JESEE (sic) OBERLY 1. In Towsaminsing congregation WM. F. NAGEL 2, JACOB SNYDER 5, SIMON SNYDER 5, JOHN OLEWINE 1, PETER SNYDER 10, JOHN D. BOWMAN, SR. 10, GEO. ZIEGENFUSZ 2.50, CONRAD MEHRCOM 1.50, JACOB MEHRCOM 1, DAN'L BELTZ 1, NICH. STROHL 1, SAM'L P. TENPLIN 5, JOHN A. BOYER 50c., JONAS BYCK 50C., JOHN BIAC 50c., MARY SNYDER 1, JOSEPH BROWN 1, DANIEL KUCHNER 40c., THOMAS ARNER 50c., JONA. HAINTZ 1, GEO. WAGNER 1, JOHN SALT 5, JOHN D. BOWMAN; JR. 5, JOST DRIESBACH 1, DANIEL BLOSE 1, CHARLES SNYDER 50c. St. Paul's Congregation, FREDERICK BACHMAN 1, RUBEN PARSON 25c., JOSEPH KUNTZ 50c., WM. REYER 1, WM. WEATHERHOLD 3, JOHN WENTZ 25c., JONAS BACHMAN 50c., JOHN KUNTZ 3, DAN'L KUNTZ 1.50, JACOB WENTZ 50c., S. C. KUNTZ 50c., PETER KRATZER 50c., RUBEN JANTZ 25c., JOHN SHEFFER 1, PETER SHEFFER 2.50, MICHAEL DRIESBACH 50c., WM. S. ARNEMAN 2, DAVID SEIPEL 75C., DAN'L BEST, (sic) JOSEPH SHEFFER 25c., ROBERT LODER 1, JONAS SEIBENGUTH 1, WM. SHOEMAKER 1, SAM'L REPH 2, JOHN HENRICH 50c. Mauch-Chunk--in part. GEO. FEGLEY 5, PHILIP DEYOUNG, M. D. 5, JOHN LEIZEN-RING 5,--**//MONIES** D. P. LANGE, Hanover, 2; JOHN DOUGHTY 5. REV. W C. BENNET 1.75; SAM'L HEBERLIG 1.25, and B. HEBERLIG 2; CHARLES VAN READ, Reading, 2; by REV. H. WAGNER, from J. B. HIESTER, Esq., W. MOORE, DAVID GREENAWALT, MRS. RINGEL, DR. LINEWEAVER, H. DEHUFF, J. HEILMAN, P. KOONS, C. GREENAWALT, J. SNAVELY, J. KARCH, D. SHIRK, each 2, REV. WAGNER 1 ; by JOSEPH SNAPP, from F. COLHOUSER 2, ISAAC SUMPTION 1.25, T. ROSSEN 1.25 and JOSEPH SNAPP 50 cts.; by REV. S. R. FISHER, from HENRY WORTZ, ELI MOORE, JOSEPH MARTIN, M. ZACHARIAS, each 2, and GEO. WEAVER 8.

203. July 3, 1839/**MARRIED** On the 16th ult., by the REV. MR. HOFFEDITZ, MR. JOSEPH ADDISON BROWN Merchant of Stroudsburg, to MISS RACHEL SHAW, of Hamilton, Monroe co.//On the 28th, by the same, MR. DAVID KELLER, Esq., of Hamilton, to MISS ELLEN BROWN, daughter of the Hon. JUDGE BROWN, of Stroudsburg, Monroe co., Penn.//On the 9th ult. by the REV. MR. ALBERT, MR. GEORGE FRYSINGER, JR., Editor of the Hanover Herald, to MISS SARAH BARNITZ, both of Hanover, Pa.//**DIED** Near Middletown, Md., on the 17th, of a protracted and very painful illness, MRS. CATHARINE CRONE, relict of the late MR. CONRAD CRONE, in the 65th years of her age. She left six children and a number of grand-children. On the 18th her remains were borne to the cemetery of the GRC.//On Wednesday, 18th ult. at the Shade Gap, Huntingdon county, MRS. RACHEL BLAIR, in the 85th year of her age.//We understand that proceedings will commence this morning against C. S. RAFINESQUE, founder and perpetual treasurer of the Divitual Savings Institution of North America, in Vine street above Fourth, Philadelphia.-"Phila. North American."//**MONIES.** REV. H. G. IBBEKEN 75 cts. JACOB LAMBERT 3. MASTER SAML. S. MORITZ 50cts. CHARLOTTE HERR (Safe Harbor) 2. By REV. R. DOUGLAS from MRS. M. FAHNESTOCK 4, MRS. S. B. SHEA 4, F. LORENTZ 4, EDWARD FABER 5, D. W. RAHOUSER 5, MRS. K. T. FRIEND 3, A. JAMIESON 2, REITER & Co. 2, WM. HUGUS 2, FRED'K. WHITMORE 1, ANDREW REITER: By REV. J. C. BUCHER, from J. FEASTER, SEN.2, JOHN KELLER, JR. (Middletown) 2 and JACOB

WEEKLY MESSENGER OF THE GERMAN REFORMED CHURCH

WEAVER 1: By J. G. MILLER (Berlin) from PETER ZIMMERMAN 2, J. G. MILLER 3, and REV. H. IBBEKEN 9.25. J. H. ALEXANDER (Balt.) 5 REV. CHARLES W. SCHULTZ 5, PETER TICE, (M'Conn'g) 2, M. SULLIVAN (Westminster) 2. To Christliche Zeitschrift.
From J. YONTZ, Lex N.C.for 2d & 3d vols. $2.00
" DAVID SHOAF, do   do $2.00
Above was, by mistake, credited for Messenger. To Der Herold. From JOHN YONTZ and D. SHOAF, Lexington, N.C. per MISS ROUNSAVILLE, each 2.

204. July 10, 1839/**MARRIED** On the 2nd ult., by REV. JOHN LANTZ, MR. JOHN HALEMAN, of Cabarrus, to MISS MARGARET EDLEMAN, of Rowan, N. C.//Near Green Castle, by the REV. J. REBOUGH, on Thursday the 13.h, (sic) MR. JACOB SCULLY, to MISS ELIZABETH GARDNER, of this county.//By the same, on Thursday 29th, MR. JOSEPH HISSONG, to MISS REBECCA GARDNER of this county.//By the same, on Thursday 29th, MR. JOHN BEAVER to MISS ELIZABETH ANN DRILL, of Washington county, Md.//**DIED** Departed this life, in Washington county, Md., on the morning of the 21st of June, of a very painful illness, MR. JACOB VANDEROW, in the 45th year of his age. The deceased left a widow and six children, and a number of friends and relatives. On the 22d his mortal remains were borne to the cemetery of the GRC, of this place, Green Castle.//On the 19th ult., PETER, aged about 17 years, on the 26th ult., ELLIAS, aged about 11, and on yesterday evening, CYRUS, aged about 15-- all sons of our worthy fellow citizen MR. GEO. CHORPENNING of this borough.--"Somerset Herald." //It is with no ordinary grief that we announce the death of MRS. SUSAN A. SAVAGE, wife of the REV. DR. THOMAS SAVAGE, Missionary of the Protestant Episcopal Church, at Cape Palmas, West Africa, eldest daughter of JOHN METCALF, Esq. of this town. With full knowledge of the trials which awaited her in Africa, she gave her hand in marriage to the REV. DR. SAVAGE, in September last, and in about two months, embarked for her

future home. The voyage was long and disagreeable. She arrived in Cape Palmas on the 29th January, and until the 22d February, was in good health, when she was seized by the acclimating fever. At the moment when the prospect of her full recovery was brightest, she relapsed, suffering from irritability of the stomach, and expired at Mount Vauham, on the 27th April, in the 26th year of her age. Her remains were interred on the Mission premises.-"Fredericksburg Arena, July 2."//**STEAMBOAT ACCIDENT.** The night of the ? ult., says the Wheeling Gazette, the steamboat *N. M'Farland*, CAP. D???ETH, from Cincinnati, to New Orleans, was run into by the *Danube*, at Walnut Bend. The following named individuals were missing: JAMES BROMBAUGH, of Wellsburg, Va. (cabinboy), JOHN THOMAS, of PA, RICHARD MILLS, of KY, JOHN ?????, OH, (printer). There was an individual belonging in Helena, OH. name unknown and a German.--"Torch Light."//**SEMINARY FUND** In Centre county, per REV. J. MAYER, viz: By J. KOOKEN, SEN., from R. F. BARRON,$5, JOHN PATTON, dec'd, $5.//**MONIES.** By J. KOOKEN, from JAMES M'KIM, 3.25, J. PATTON, dec'd. 2, MICH'L ULRICH 2; by REV. S. HELFFENSTEIN, JR., from MISS SARAH DOLL (Barren Hill) 2, and MISS A. SCHLATTER 2; from JOHN FORSTER, JR., 5, WM. HOFFMAN (Ind.) 3, JACOB YOUNG (do.) 2; by REV. G. SCHLOSSER from ANTH. SCHNEIDER (OH) 2,and JAMES ROSS, (Fayetteville)2; DR. DELLERBACH (Georgetown) 3, from W. AUGHINBAUGH 1, and CHRISTIAN CRAMER 4; by REV. MR. HOFFEDITZ, from P. SHAW,Esq.2, GEO.ECKERT 2, and JOSEPH STALY 1; by REV. H. KROH (IL,) from P. SNIDER 4, A. HEDRICK, S. HEDRICK, and G. HEDRICK, each 2; from JUDGE SCHELL 5. Christliche Zeitschrift from REV. S. HELFFENSTEIN, JR. Gwynnedd, Montg. co., Pa. $1. The $2 each from N. Carolina for 'Der Herold' last week, should have been $1 each.

205. July 17, 1839/**DIED** On the 21st of June in Brooklyn, Susquehanna county, Pa. JESSE LONG, a

WEEKLY MESSENGER OF THE GERMAN REFORMED CHURCH

a young man who had scarcely attained the 22d year of his age. He was the son of MAJ. ABRAHAM LONG, of Upper Mt. Bethel, Northampton county. In March last he returned from NJ, where he had been engaged in the mercantile business, to his parents, with impaired health. He left home on the 12th of June, with his uncle with a view of purchasing cattle. On the 19th, at Brooklyn, he complained of sickness in his stomach. The next afternoon he had a slight attack of Epilepsy, followed by a severer one. He was deprived of his mental faculties until about noon, when he suddenly awoke. He made an effort to speak, in vain, and soon after, between 11 and 12 o'clock, closed his eyes in death. Several of his relatives from Wallsville, Luzerne co., removed his remains from Brooklyn to the former place, where he was interred. According to the declaration of the physicians, his death proceeded from an ulceration in the stomach, which had supperated. //In Huntingdon, Pa., on the 29th ult. MR. PETER SWOOPE, SEN. merchant, at an advanced age.//Near Roemer's Mill, Franklin co., on Thursday last, MRS. SUSAN THOMAS, consort of MR. GEORGE THOMAS. Her sufferings were protracted and of an exceedingly painful nature.//The Gettysburg Sentinel, of Monday week, says:--It is our painful duty to state, MAJOR JOHN ASH, Coroner of Adams county, was killed by a fall from his horse, on Thursday afternoon last. He was on his return from Gettysburg to Marsh creek (his place of residence,) taking MR. HERR's tavern on his route. He had just left the latter place, when his horse ran off with him, and he was thrown and killed.//**A CASUALTY** During the gust on Thursday afternoon, MR. JACOB HISS,SEN'R. residing about seven miles from Baltimore on the Harford Turnpike was killed by lightning within a few yards of the door, as he hastened towards his house. He was in the seventy eighth year of his age.--"Balt. Am. of Saturday."//The vessel *Burlington* left the city about nine o'clock for Bordentown and when oppo-

site the Five Mile Point, the *Salem,* bound down the river, struck her. As DR. SWAIN, a worthy resident of Bristol, was missing on the arrival of the boat at Bristol, it is to be supposed he met his death by the accident. [Confirmed] (sic) **//MONIES** MARTIN HOOVER 2; R. HARTMAN (Leitersb.) 2 25; L. HAWK (Newscomerst., O.) 2; JOS. LEITER 2 75; By REV. HERTZ, from JACOB SODER (Churcht.) 2, and J. RINGWALT 1; AMELIA MIDDLEKAUFF 2; S. S. MIDDLEKAUFF 2. To Christliche Zeitschrift:
From J.&C. BENTZ (Addamstown,Pa.) $1 00
EPHRAIM BEAR (New Holland) 1 00
HEN. CLOTH (new sub.) Bedington,
Berkely co.Va. 1 00
MR. B. SWARTZ of Addamstown, (sic) Pa. don't receive the paper.

206. July 24, 1839/**DIED** On the 13th inst., at his residence in Frederick county, Md., MR. JACOB BARRICK, in the 84th year of his age. The deceased was the son of JOHN BARRICK, who was among the earliest settlers in this part of the county. He left 6 children, 37 grand children and 23 great grand children. It is remarkable that he never changed his place of residence until Sunday the 18th inst., when his remains were deposited in the cemetery of the GRC. Since the death of his aged companion, seven years before, he still, with a single servant girl, lived by himself.//On the evening of the 13th inst., in Mercersburg JOSEPH B. infant son of FRED'K WALK. //On the 5th inst., JOHN M. KNODE, Esq. in the 59th year of his age; an old and respectable citizen of Sharpsburg.//**CASUALTY.** On Wednesday morning, MISS MARY MACNAMARA, a daughter of COL. MACNAMARA of our town, started to her father's plantation; when her horse became unmanageable, and despite the exertion of the gentleman riding with her--whose horse threw him--after running into the woods, struck her against a tree. After reviving a moment she sunk in the slumber of death.--"Salisbury (N. C.) Carol. July 12."//**A**

WEEKLY MESSENGER OF THE GERMAN REFORMED CHURCH

MELANCHOLY OCCURRENCE took place on Friday last near Port Deposite about 2 o'clock, resulting in the death of two young men, says the Chronicle of Monday. DR. A. C. TATE, CORNELIUS J. SMITH, JR., HENRY ARCHER and JOSEPH QUARLE left Havre de Grace in a schooner for Port Deposite. At the head of Watson's Island, the wind lulled. MR. SMITH left the schooner and in the effort to get into the small boat, in tow of the schooner, fell into the water; DR. TATE leaped overboard to his rescue, and both sank. MR. ARCHER also sprang into the water to save them, and it was only by an almost superhuman effort that he disengaged himself from the death-grasp of SMITH. MR. ARCHER would probably have been drowned but for the plank thrown to him.--"Torch Light."//On Friday evening of last week, MRS. MILLY HOUSE, living a few miles from this place, in Hampshire county, Va., on her return home from Cumberland, and in crossing the Potomac, the current being much swollen, the body of the wagon capsized and MRS. HOUSE was carried beneath it. Her body was found the next day.//**HYDROPHOBIA.** The Pennsylvanian of last week, says:--Two brothers named SMITH, residents in Fayette township, Pa., died on the 7th inst. at which time two other members of the family were suffering from the disease.// MISS FRANCES FLEMING of Lewistown, N. York, aged 22, was burnt to death at Fort Wayne, OH, a few days since by her clothes taking fire.//[Portion of a letter published in an article. BAM] "My child having labored under this kind of deformity (club foot) causes me to feel deeply interested for this class of the afflicted. Eight or nine weeks ago we took our little girl to Phila. DR. MUETTER performed the operation as stated in his Lecture. Nine or ten days ago I brought home my child perfectly cured."//**MONIES** WILLIAM BEAR (Hanover) 2, A. KOONS (Md.) and J. LESHY 2. From DETWILER & POE 2. By REV. ?. GERHART, from H. GRUBB 6, JACOB KEAGY 2, JOSEPH MILLER [Gratzt] 2. By REV. J. C. BUCHER from JACOB WEAVER 1, JOS.

WEEKLY MESSENGER OF THE GERMAN REFORMED CHURCH

WISE 2, PHIL. FLOOK 2, ANN R.POOL 2 DANIEL FLOOK 2, PETER SCHAFFER 10.00. By REV. J. W. HOFFMEIER from CATH. MILLER (of JACOB) 2, SAM. COST 2,50, SAMUEL KEEDY 2 50,DAVID RUSSEL 6.**//LETTERS** S. J. HEWES, GEORGE A. ACKENBACH, R. F. KELKER.

207. July 31, 1839/**DIED** On the 16th inst., at his residence in Green Castle, CONRAD SMITH, in the 87th year of his age. He was a soldier of the Revolution, and has resided in Green Castle 55 years.//On the same day, in Antrim township, DANIEL EBERLY, in the 77th year of his age.//In Bedford, July 23, PETER DECHERT HOFIUS, son of DR. J. H. HOFIUS, aged 16 years, 2 mos. and 7 days. But a few weeks since he was in the vigor of youth.//**A SECT** has appeared in the metropolis calling themselves "Christian Israelites," being followers of JOHN WROE, of Tong, in the parish of Bristall, near Bradford. He intends to visit London to announce the day of the great millenium. Some of his proselytes intend to proceed to Australia.//**AD** P.S. VAN PATTEN, Dentist of Chambersburg performs all operations on Teeth with professional skill and least possible pain, at the Boarding house of MRS. FINDLAY.//**MONIES.** By REV. B. C. WOLFF,from MARIA HUBER, JULIAN BOYER, LACTITIA HESS, JULIAN OBERLY, CHAS. HELLER & P. MEIXSELL,each 2, and B. ODENWELDER 50 cts. From JACOB DAGGY (Ind.) 2 50, M. DAGGY 2.50.--JOSEPH BOUCHER(Pa)5.//**LETTER** JONATHAN NYCE, JOHN STRUNK

208. Aug. 7, 1839/**MARRIED** On Thursday morning, in the Second street Church, by REV. E. HEINER, JOHN GABLE, merchant, to LOUISA M. BENNIMAN,both of Baltimore.//On Saturday morning 27th ult. by REV. E. HEINER, LEON HEFFELK to JOSEPHINE SWIFEL both of NY.//On the 25th July, in Sharpsburg, by the REV. MR. HOFFMIER, JAMES A. BUCHANAN, M.D., to MISS ELEANOR - daughter of COL. JOHN MILLER, both of Sharpsburg, Wash'n co. Md.//By the same, MR. ELIAS PIPER, to MISS BARBARA THOMSON, both of Washington county, Md.//On the 1st inst. by

WEEKLY MESSENGER OF THE GERMAN REFORMED CHURCH

REV. J. HELFFENSTEIN, MR. DAVID ZEIGLER to MISS SARAH SWISHER, both of Fayetteville, Franklin county, Pa.//**DIED** Wednesday, the 16th July, in Green Castle, MRS. MARGARRETTA R. wife of COL, DAVID DETRICH, and daughter of MRS ELENORA CORNMAN, of the same place. She was a member of the Presby. Church.//On the 5th of July, in the 61st year of his age, MR. ROBERT FILSON, a tender parent and kind husband. The following day, his remains were taken to the cemetery of the GRC. [Communicated.//ARTHUR WALL, living at Raleigh, N. C., is 119 years of age.//The brig *America*, sailed ?0th July from St. John's River, East FL, having on board nearly 100 free colored and some white passengers of that neighborhood, for Hayti intending to settle near Port au Plate under the patronage of MR. KINGSLEY, a FL planter, wishing to transfer their industry to his own lands in Hayti.//Christliche Zeitschrift. Send the paper from next No. to GEORGE HOYER, Harrisburg, Pa.//
PRINTING ESTABLISHMENT FUND DONATIONS.
MATTHIAS FLOOK, Middletown Valley, Md. $10 00
REV. P.S.FISHER, Spring Mills,Centre co. Pa. (sic)   25 00
  HENRY STICKEL, Franklin co. Pa.   30 00
  SAMUEL FREDERICK,   -   -   (paid) 5 00

209. Aug. 14, 1839/**MARRIED** On Wednesday the 31st ult., by REV. THOS. CREIGH, MR. ARCHIBALD SKINNER, near Dayton, OH, to MISS MARGARET ANN, eldest daughter of MR. JOSEPH DUNCAN, near Mercersburg, Pa.//On Thursday last, by REV. W. C. BENNET, REV. JACOB BEAR, of New Chester, to MISS ELENORA AMELIA ENTLER,of Berlin, Adams county.// On Wednesday morning last by REV. D. ZACHARIAS, MR. WILLIAM GITTINGER to MISS ANN R. BRENGLE,all of Frederick city.//On the 31st ult., by the REV. MR. JACOBS,MR. LANCELOT BELL,to MISS ELIZABETH REITZEL.//**DIED** On the 30th of July, MR. JOHN FREDERICK WISE, of Frederick, in the 48th year of his age.//On the 4th of August, MRS. SUSAN REYNOLDS, consort of MR. JAMES REYNOLDS, in

WEEKLY MESSENGER OF THE GERMAN REFORMED CHURCH

the bloom of her days.//On the 30th ult. WILLIAM COST,infant son of COL. THOMAS JOHNSON,near Jefferson, aged 4 years 6 months and 15 days.//Monday last, at the residence of MR. JOSEPH RENTCH, in Hagerstown, MISS MARY ANN, daughter of MRS. HANNAH MIDDLEKAUFF, of the neighborhood of Clear Spring, Md., aged 22 years.//DR. F. M. ROBERTSON of Augusta, Geo., reports, in the July number of the Southern Medical and Surgical Journal, two cases of erysipelas, successfully treated by external application of raw cotton.//**MONIES** BENJ. REIFF, Esq. 3,ANDREW KRIEBEL 2, MRS. SUSAN SLOAN 2, W. H. SEIBERT (Womelsdorf) 1, D. M. LIVERS 2. By REV. J. CARES, from P. CARES, WILLIAM BEITZEL, and G. MILLER, each 2, J. P. MILLER, (NY)2. To Christliche Zeitschrift: Send paper to GEO. PHIPHER, Brownstown,Jackson co.IN. (Will act as Agent for you.)//**OFFICERS** elected for Franklin Rail-Road Company: President--DR. S. D. CULBERTSON. Managers--GEORGE CHAMBERS, THOMAS McCAULEY, GEORGE A. MADEIRA, JOHN F. DENNY, DAVID G. YOST, THOS. CHAMBERS. Re-appointed: DAVID FULLERTON Treasurer, and J. E. BRADY Secretary. THOMAS CHAMBERS,Esq.declined re-election to Presidency.

210. August 21, 1839/**MARRIED** On Thursday the 8th inst. by REV. D. BOSSLER, MR. SIMON HESS, to MISS SARAH WERT, both of Dauphin county//On the 11th inst. by the REV. MR. CARES, MR. HENRY HAHN to MISS CATHARINE FREY, both of York co.//On the same day, by the same, MR. H. D. MORRIS, to MISS SARAH JANE COLLINGS, both formerly of Baltimore county, Md.//**DIED** Near Jefferson, on the 8th of July, MARY JANE, youngest daughter of MR. JACOB FLOOK, aged one year, seven months and seventeen days.//At his residence in Frederick county, Md. on the 13th ult. MR. JACOB BARRICK, in the 84th year of his age. The deceased was the son of JOHN BARRICK.//On Wednesday last, EDWARD LAUMAN, infant son of MR. JACOB DIETZ, of York.//At his residence in York, on Friday last, MR. CHAS. STUCK, in the 74th year of his age.//**EMANCIPATED**

WEEKLY MESSENGER OF THE GERMAN REFORMED CHURCH

Twenty one blacks passed through Dayton on Tuesday last on their way to a settlement in Mercer county. They were freed by R. I. HALE and BENJ. KNOX of NC, both Presby.--"Dayton (OH) Journal." **//FATAL MISTAKE.** The Baltimore Post of Friday afternoon states that MRS. MORRISON of Hillen street, Tuesday evening, before retiring, mixed some laudanum with brandy, which was intended to be administered in drops to a restless infant. In the night, however, an elder child, of about two years, desired water. The father, in the dim light of the room, not perceiving the previous contents of the cup, poured water into it and gave the whole dose to the child. Severe spasms ensued, and the little sufferer was released by death before morning.**//ACCIDENT** In Carlisle, on Monday last, MR. JOHN FLEMING, (of the firm MURRAY & FLEMING) met with an accident which resulted in his death in a few hours. The train going west, had attached to it five burthen cars, which were to stop at his Store House. As they approached, he sprang upon the baggage car and uncoupled the burthen cars. He jumped off, but fell upon the track, and was unable to recover himself before the burthen train came upon him. Two cars passed over his leg and arm. To his widow, family and friends, this sudden stroke has carried deep affliction.**//MONIES.** JOHN BESORE (Waynesboro) 2. JOHN C. BUCHER(Harrisb.) 2, JACOB ZEIGLER 2, JOHN HAUSER 2, FRED'K KELKER 2, and MISSES KELKER and STEES (Ind) 1,GEO. FAYMAN, (Va.) 5, LEWIS WAMPLER 2, By D. KROH, from D. SHAFFER, Esq. 6, W. METCALFE 2, C. HERR 2, GEO. ASHWAY 4.50, JONATHAN KIEFFER 4, JOHN BEAVER, SEN. 2, P. KUNKLEMAN 2 00, D. HOSSLER 2, WILLIAM BURK (Loudon) 2, GEORGE KRAMER (Bridgeport) 2, STEPHEN KIEFFER 8, MICHAEL STINE(Greencastle) 2. By REV. E. KIEFFER,from DAN'L and JONATHAN KRISE 4,JOHN HOOD (Stoughstown) 2, JAS. D. SCOTT 2 50. To Christliche Zeitschrift: Send paper to ISAAC BRALL, Greencastle, Pa., MARY SAHM, Shippensburg, Pa., JACOB RAMP, Newville, Pa. paid $1 00,

WEEKLY MESSENGER OF THE GERMAN REFORMED CHURCH

also to FIDEL WIRTH and MARTIN MIESS,both Bellefonte, Pa. From FREDERICK MICHTLY, Nittany, Pa. 1 00. Also, direct W. BARTHOLOMEW's and FREDERICK MICHTLY's paper to Hublersburg, instead of Nittany.//**SEMINARY FUND.** In Centre county, Pa.-- per REV. E. KIEFFER: JOHN FURST $5 00 GEORGE FURST 5 00 BENJAMIN SNYDER 3 00 SAMUEL ALLISON 1 00 MRS. ALISON (sic) 50 GEORGE OHL 75.//**PARENT BOARD** From J. C. BUCHER, Esq. Harrisburg $20 00. //**PRINTING ESTABLISHMENT FUND** JACOB HADE, Greencastle, $25 00 DANIEL CROUSE, Waynesboro, 10 00.

211. Aug. 28, 1839/**MARRIED** On Tuesday morning of last week, by REV. B. S. SCHNECK, MR. WILLIAM RAWN, of Adams county, to MISS REBECCA ANN OVERKERSH, of St. Thomas, Pa.//At the Parsonage of the GRC, Middletown, Md. on the 15th inst. by REV. J. C. BUCHER; MR. JACOB YOUNG to MISS ANN ELIZA ITNIRE, of HENRY, all of Washington county, Md.//On the 14th inst. by the REV. MR. HELFENSTEIN, MR. JOHN SCHLEIGH to MISS CATHARINE LOUISA MITTAG, all of Hagerstown://**DIED** Near Jefferson, Frederick countyy, (sic) Md., on the 8th July, MARY JANE, youngest daughter of MR. JACOB FLOOK.//At the same place, ROBERT JOHNSON, infant son of MR. JOHN LAMAR.//**MISSIONARIES** The REV. MR. ROBERTS of the Baptist church, who went from KY to China a few years since, writes that he, BRO. SHUCK and MRS. SHUCK are commencing a school. DOCTOR LOCKART, to practice medicine, and two young ladies, to teach, have arrived from England. BEN YOUNG, a Baptist missionary from Batavia arrived from NY on the *Morrison.*

212. Sep. 4, 1839/**DIED** On the 24th of August, in Baltimore, SAMUEL JAMES, son of THOMAS S. and SARAH ANN HUBBARD, aged 4 years 10 months and 2 days.//On the 16th July, at Franklin, Robinson county, TX, the REV. ROBERT RROTHERTON, (sic) of the Presby. church. A native of Greencastle, Penn., he had spent several years in the South, principally in MS. At the beginning of the pre-

WEEKLY MESSENGER OF THE GERMAN REFORMED CHURCH

sent year he came to TX. Since May 1838, the Gospel ministry has been called to mourn the departure of a RUTER, a JOHNSON, a FRAZIER, a STRICKLAND and now a BROTHERTON from their scattered ranks.--"Morning Star,Houston,TX."

213. Sept. 11, 1839/**MARRIED** At Green Castle, on the 1st ult. by REV. JOHN REBOUGH, MR. JEREMIAH CARPENTER to MISS SUSANNA CROSS---and MR. SAMUEL RUSH to MISS MARY HUFFEET,all of Washington county, Md.//In Philadelphia, on the 27th ult. by REV. J. F. BERG, MR. DANIEL H. HOUZELOT to MISS MARY BEACKLEY, both of Northern Liberties.//On the 22d ult. by REV. JOHN REBOUGH, MR. SAMUL MILLER to MISS SARAH A. HUFFER, of Franklin county.//**DIED** In this borough, of scrofula, on the 4th inst., DANIEL SMITH HECK, in the 16th year of his age, oldest son of MAJ. JACOB HECK. For the last five months his condition was peculiarly distressing. To the most severe pain was added the prostration of his bodily powers and loss of sight and hearing.//In this borough, on the 3d inst, CHARLES WRIGHT, only child of JAMES NILL, Esq., aged 19 months.//In Washington county, Md. on the 14th ult., MR. SAMUEL WEAVER, in the 41st year of his age. He went forth to his labor in health but scarce had the meridian of the day appeared before the Hand of death was on him.//In Emmittsburg, Md., on the 4th of August last, MRS. ELIZABETH WEAVER, consort of MR. JOHN WEAVER, aged 62 years.//On the 5th of July, in the 59th year of his age, of apoplexy, MR. JOHN M. KNODE, long a respectable citizen of Sharpsburg, entombed in the cemetery of the GRC, leaving a widow, brothers and sisters. //On the 19th of August, MR. HENRY SHARER, in the 76th year of his age, a repected inhabitant of this county. His remains were conveyed to the burying ground of the GRC followed by his surviving friends and neighbors.//Extract of letter from Fort Gibson, from Fort Gibson, July 24th, 1839.--"There is a prospect of settlement of the difficulties among

the Cherokees. Both the old party and the new, headed by JOHN ROSS, are in council. We had the misfortune to loose LT. BOWMAN, of the Dragoons, who died on Sunday last. He has served a long time on the southwestern frontier."-"AR Gazette, Aug. 7."//The Galena Advocate of August 1st contains a letter from REV. EZEKIEL T. GEAR, U. S. Chaplain at Fort Snelling, confirming the massacre of Chippewas, women and children, by Sioux, at the Fall of St. Anthony.// **MONIES** By REV. J. REBOUGH, f'm MRS. NANCY KNODE (Sharpsburg,) 2. ABR. FELKER (State Line) 2, GEO. COOK (Mt. Hope) 4, JACOB LINE 2;by REV. J. C. BUCHER, from JACOB FLOOK, of JOHN, 6, CAPT. J. KEAFAUVER 6, MRS. CATHARINE BOWLES 4, JOHN J. SMITH, Esq. and JOHN DARNER each 2; by REV. S. R. FISHER, from SAM'L. MARTIN (Fountain Dale,) 5, WM. FERGUSON (Zero,) and MICH. HELMAN (Emmittsourg,) (sic) each 2; by GEO. BESORE, Esq. from CHR. WELKER 4, MRS. BARBARA M. SMITH, REV. G. W. GLESSNER, D. BESORE, SEN., MRS. MARY NEWCOMER, and JACOB BESORE, each 2; by H. ERMENTROUT, Esq. (Reading,) from MISS C. ERMENTROUT, E. DECHERT, Esq. HESTER HIGH, WM. BEECHER, CATHARINE COLEMAN, N. & A. DICK, JACOB FRICKER, G.& D. M. BUSHAR, and CATHARINE DAVENPORT (Sinking Sp'g,) each 2, HENRY ERMENTROUT 1; by M. RICKENBAUGH, from MISS A. SPRIHLMAN, JOSHUA HOFFMAN, D. ZELLERS, ELIAS CHANEY (Funkstown,) CHAS. LOCHER (do.) J. BROGUNIER, D. M. MIDDLEKAUFF, D.RICKENBAUGH (Tiffin, O)each 2; A. TROUP (Clearspring,) 3, J. C. MIDDLEKAUFF 1; by REV. HENRY SONNENDECKER, from JOHN BRINKER, JOHN FOX, ANDREW BRINKER, H. & J. ZIMMERMAN, PETER HECK, NEIDIG & DEHOFF, each 2; DAN'L HECK, and REV. H. SONNENDECKER, each 4; by REV. W. CONRAD, from E. RIDGELY 2 50, JOSEPH GLODFELTY 3, and WM. CONRAD 50c.; by D. KROH, from M. SEIBERT 6, JOHN SCHNEBLY 3 25, BENJ. CUSHWA 9 50, HENRY ANCHONY 4, ADAM TROUP 3, ELIZA LOOSE 5, GEORGE KIFFER 5, CATHARINE SEIBERT 1 75, DANIEL H. TICE 4, GEORGE HELLER 2, GUSTAVUS KERSHNER 2, OLIVER ZELLER (Hancock) 2, SUSAN BRENTLINGER 2, GEORGE

WEEKLY MESSENGER OF THE GERMAN REFORMED CHURCH

LIPPY (Greencastle) 4, MICHAEL STICKEL 9 50, WM. EAKLE (Funkstown,Md.)3, PETER LOOSE (State Line) 2, by GEORGE BESORE, from LEWIS S. FORNEY 10. To Christliche Zeitschrift. From REV. S. R. FISHER [Emmittsburg,] 1; by REV. H. ERMENTROUT, from HENRY WERNER $1. Send to JOHN FELKER and PETER LOOSE, each one copy State Line, Franklin co. Pa.--MICHAEL WACHTER,Utica Mills,Carrol co., Md.

214. Sep. 18, 1839/**ACCIDENT**. We learn from the Maysville Eagle, that on Thursday last, whilst REV. P. L. McABOY and others were standing on the first floor of the steam-mill of MESSRS. HOW & Co. at Murpheysville, the third floor, which contained a large quantity of wheat, gave way, the whole mass burst through the second floor and buried Mr. McA. and others to a considerable depth. The victims were rescued, but Mr. McA. was found dead. The Eagle speaks of deceased as a young Presby. clergyman.//The Mount Pleasant Register of Westmoreland county, Pa. reports the family of MR. JOSEPH HOPLER, in South Huntingdon had an especially severe visitation of dysentary in which the mother and five children were carried off. Four of them died on the same day.//A **FIRE** in St. Louis, MO on the 31st ult. resulted in the death of BENJAMIN L. TURNBULL, Esq. JAMES HAYDEN, Esq. and MR. ARTHUR BREWER when gun powder blew up, throwing a brick wall on the unfortunate individuals.//On Monday week, WILLIAM GROVER, aged about 18, was killed by lightning in Aurelius. He was at work on a load of hay. MR. SAMUEL GOULD, who was engaged in pitching hay up to him was unhurt.--"Auburn Journal."//A committee of the Vicksburg City Council have reported Mayor R. J. M'GINTY guilty of habitual drunkeness, misdemeaners, neglect of duties, and other charges which should be sufficient for his removal.//**PRINTING FUND** WM. A. WILT, York 5 00. Cash, W. A. WILT, 5.//**MONIES**. By PETER SWIGART, from HUGH SCOTT (Cashtown) 2, J. R. DANNER 2.50, S. S. FORNEY (Gettysburg)2, J & D.N. MARK 7, WM.

WEEKLY MESSENGER OF THE GERMAN REFORMED CHURCH

Mc LELLAND2 (sic) DAVID BEECHER 4.50 H. GUTELIUS 2, HENRY SCHRIVER (Littlestown) 2, DAVID SCHRIVER 2, SNIDER & STALSMITH 2, J. STUDY 2, W. DUTERER 2, JOSEPH FISHER 5, JACOB KELLER 2, GEORGE WILL 2, JOHN ARNDORFF (Westminster)2, ROBERT CRAWFORD (Union Mills) 8 PETER EICHELBERGER (Utica Mills) 8, HENRY STIMMEL 2,50, JOHN KING 4,50, CONRAD KOONTZ (Taneytown) 2,25, WILLIAM FISHER 2,50, THOS. B. CORN (Sabillasville) 2, WM. HINEA 2, MICHAEL ZIMMERMAN (Creagerstown) 1,50, JOHN P. ZIMMERMAN 4,50, DANIEL KRISE 8, JOHN KUHNS (Manchester) 1,25, and D. CRUMBERGER (Woodborough)2. From PHILIP BEAMER3,50, JOHN HEAGY (Newville) 2. By JOSEPH LEITER, Esq. from JACOB HOUSER 5. From REV. J. H. CRAWFORD per JACOB CRAWFORD 2,50. By REV. D. FEETE, from JOHN COOVER (Middleburg) 5. From THOMAS GILLAN 2. By REV. JOHN CARES, from WM A. & P. WILT M. AUSTIN, JACOB GOTTWALT, and MISS ELIZABETH SPANGLER, each 2; by WILLIAM AUGHINBAUGH, Esq. from HENRY SHAFF and PETER PUTMAN each 2, WM. AUGHINBAUGH 1; by REV. GEORGE WACK, from MICHAEL VONFASSEN 2 and GEORGE WACK 3; by the Editor, from HILARY GRAFF, JONATHAN SAEGER, PETER J. KERN, (Saegerstown) and PHILIP KLECKNER (Rockville) each 2. Christliche Zeitschrift. By REV. REV. J. F. DIFFENBAUCHER, from WM. BOLLIS, Zelienople, Butler co. Penn. $1---to whom send Zeitschrift,--please name ABRAHAM MAYER, of Harmony, Butler co. Pa., as Agent for that place.

215. Sep. 25, 1839/**MARRIED** On the 8th inst. in Crab Bottom, by the REV. J. HELLER, MR. MICHAEL HIVELY, to MISS MARY HAMMER, both of Pendleton co. Va.//**DIED** Saturday the 7th of Sept. inst. the sanctified spirit of MARY KERN left its clay tenement, in Allentow, (sic). Her husband, EDW. KERN, had been preparing a handsome dwelling house for himself, his wife and children. MARY SAGER (for that was her maiden name) was a lovely and affectionate woman, and a Sabbath-school teacher until she married. She was ill one week.//**MISSION BOARD** The REV. MR. HAND, General

WEEKLY MESSENGER OF THE GERMAN REFORMED CHURCH

Agent for the Northern District of New England has resigned; also the REV. MR. BARDWELL of the Southern district. REV. C. EDDY and REV. F. E. CANNON continue in NY and REV. W. M. HALL in NJ, PA, DE, MD. REV. W. H. FOOTE, Secretary of the C. B. F. M. resigned as General Agent for VA and NC. REV. W. J. BREED was appointed last spring General Agent for the Western States but was detained by ill health. REV.MR.COE has labored in the Western Reserve; REV. E. N. NICHOLS in MI. **//NOTICE.** JOHN MYERS, late of Upper Mt. Bethel township county of Northampton, deceased, by his last will and testament dated 14th day of December, A. D. 1829, bequeathed to the children of his sister SARAH the sum of $500; to the children of his sister RACHEL the sum of $500; part of which is in the hands of the subscribers. The residence of said legatees is unknown, as they left their place of residence some forty years, (Kingswood or Amwill township, NJ) and went to MD or VA. Come forward on or before the 3d day of October, 1841. PETER FRUTCHY JOSHUA HAGERMAN, Executors Williamsburg, Northampton county, Pa.**//THEOLOGICAL FUND** From JACOB MAYER, Agent, in <u>BROTHER HOFFEDITZ's congregation</u>, Upper Mount Bethel, Northampton county, Pa.: JACOB MESSINGER, $10; FERDENAND MANN $5, PETER EMERICH 1; HENRY ALGERT 5; MATHIAS FRUTCHEY 3, GEORGE HERTZEL 10; PETER OTT JR. 4, GEORGE GO?? 3, SAMUEL SMITH 2 50; PHILIP PEARSON JR. 10, JOSEPH STEHLY 1, SAMUEL RAESLEY 3; JACOB RAESLEY SEN. 12; DANIEL RIEGEL 5; SOLOMON HELLER 5, FRANTZ HILGERT 2, ISAAC HILGERT 2; JACOB RAESLEY JR. 10; PHILIP PEARSON SEN 10; SAMUEL STEM 2 50; JACOB PEARSON 1; JOHN HILGERT 5; GEORGE HOUCK 2; JEREMIAH HESS 5; PHILIP WH?TMAN 2; ANDREW HERTZEL 5; ABRAHAM LONG 3, JOHN A. LONG 1; WILLIAM RIEGEL 1, PHILIP RIEGEL 1; J. HAGERMAN 1; JACOB YONSON 5, ANDREW KURTZ 5; ADAM KURTZ 1; EMANUEL N. LEWIS 1; PETER FRUTTCHEY Eqr. 5; JOHN GR?DER JR. 2; JACOB RIEGEL 1; ABRAHAM MANN 5; JOHN G. MANN 5, SAMUEL RAESLEY 2, JACOB RAESLEY 2; JACOB

WEEKLY MESSENGER OF THE GERMAN REFORMED CHURCH

BEST 4; JACOB WEAVER 1; GEORGE BAKER 2 CHRISTIAN FOLLMER 3, ADAM KELLER Eqr. 10; ROBERT E. JAMES 1; THOMAS MICHLER 5; LENHART KERN 10; ADAM TEEL 5; JOSEPH KIEFFER 5; PHILIP KELLER 5; FRIDLICH ANGER 1, JOHN ROESDLEY 3; JOSEPH ENGLER 5. Hamelton Congregation, Monroe County Pa. in part. (sic) PETER SHAW Eqr. 5; CHARLES SAYLOR Eqr. 5; HENRY FENNER Esq. 10; JOSEPH KURTZ 5; CHARLES J. MESSINGER 3; ADAM LAUBACH JR. 5; BROTHER POMP's Congregation, Planefield Northampton Co Pa. JOHN H. KELLER Eqr. 10; GEORGE HAHN 5; FREDERICK GERMANTOWN 4; THOMAS HUPPEL 2; HENRY METZ 10; ARON DREISBACH 1; JACOB RUTH 6; GEORGE HAHN JR. 1 50; FREDERICK ACHENBACH 5; PHILIP ACHENBACH 1; JACOB ACHENBACH 1; DANIEL ACHENBACH 5; CHARLES ENGLER 1; GEORGE DOUBT 00 50; J. T. ROGERS 1; WILLIAM ENGEL 3; GEORGE METZGER 1; LEWIS MICKE Eqr. 3; THOMAS GOLD 1; STEPHEN HESS 1; ALFRED SCHNEIDER 3; JACOB S. HELLER 2; CONRAD HAHN 6; DANIEL WARG 1; CONRAD METZ 10; JOHN STORY 1; JACOB DREISBACH 2; PHILIP UNANGEST 00 50; JACOB BAUER 3; CONRAD BENDER 5; JOSEPH BENDER 2; PHILIP HAHN 2; GEORGE WERNER 3; SIMON SIEGEL 2; JACOB BENDER 3; THOMAS METZ 1;JACOB KELLER 5; ENOS LEHR 2; PETER SCHUCK 2;JOHN NYCE 2; PETER METZGER 2 50, JOHN BENDER5.

No Marriages or Deaths in issues of Oct 2 or 9.

216. Oct. 16, 1839/**MARRIED** In Gettysburg, on the 25th ult., by REV. S. GUTELIUS, REV. EMANUEL HOFFHEIN, Pastor of the GRC, in Beaver township, Union county, Pa., to MISS JULIA ANN, daughter of MR. ADAM SWOPEof Gettysburg.//**DIED** On Monday of last week, in Hagerstown, in the 82d year of her age, MRS. MARY HUMRICKHOUSE, relict of the late PETER HUMRICKHOUSE, Esq.//In the N. Y. Observer we find the following extract of a letter from REV. W. T. HAMILTON, of Mobile, formerly of Newark, N.J., dated Sept. 15th: "For the past five or six weeks the yellow fever has prevailed here....P. was attacked about three weeks since. T. was taken ill the next day after P., but less

WEEKLY MESSENGER OF THE GERMAN REFORMED CHURCH

severely; yet P. is recovering more rapidly than T. MRS. HAMILTON was attacked with considerable severity; she is now recovering slowly. J. was taken next, but is well again. You may suppose, therefore, that with all this sickness in my house and sickness all around me, I have had but little leisure. This morning I preached in town ..at 5 o'clock, I attended the funeral of LIEUT. KIBBE, late of the U.S. Army, at Summerville, 3 miles out of the town. Mr. K. died last night, in horrible agonies, of yellow fever."//The Cumberland, Md., Civilian of the 5th inst. says:--- Early in the morning of Wednesday last, MR. HENRY FOLCK of Pleasant Mills was found dead in his mill, shot through the head,... the gun, from all appearances, having accidentally gone off whilst Mr. F. was in the act of returning the ram-rod. MR. FOLCK left a young wife and several small children.//Additional particulars of the Philadelphia conflagration noticed in our last. The National Gazette of Sunday afternoon says: About eleven o'clock last night, a fire was discovered in the basement story of W. J. STROUP's Provision Store, No. 14 South Wharves. The Gazette then gives detail of the buildings, &c. destroyed which we omit.//We learn that MR. THOMAS FORWOOD, of Harford co. in this state, was mortally wounded Thursday morning at the residence of MR. TURNER, Spesutia Island, by the accidental discharge of a gun. He lingered until Saturday morning.--"Balt. Chron."//**MONIES** By the Editor from A. DIVELY & H. REIMUND (Bedford)each$2: J. STEWART RIDDLE2; N. CALENDER 4; REV. C. KNOUSE(N.Y.) 2; F. W. HOOVER 2; JOHN LEADER (Nanticoke) 4. Through REV. HEINER, from JOHN DOHM, P. ENTLER, MISS.C. COST, MRS.DR. DIEFFENDERFER, M. HOFFMAN, C. SUTER & MRS. O. SPEER, each 2.--Thro' REV. J. HELFENSTEIN, JR., from ABR. YOST 2, & ANN SCHLATTER 2.--JOHN BRUNER (Leb.) 2, & JOHN ERMENTROUT 2. KOONS, GRATER & BROWER, 5.--ANN M. BREECHBILL (Cumberl.co.) 2 50.---Thro' REV. B. WOLFF, from DR. DEICHMAN (Mart. Creek) SOPHIA SNYDER, JACOB

WEEKLY MESSENGER OF THE GERMAN REFORMED CHURCH

MOORE,MRS.YOHE,each2, J.CHRISMAN,4, JONA. JAEGER (Berrysb.) 2; DANL.E. MUENCH 4; PETER SNYDER 2; JOHN REIFSNYDER (Liverpool) 1.--Thro' REV. HOFFMEIER, from MRS. MARY MILLER(Sharpsb.) H. NYMAN, ELIZ. SMITH, & ELIAS DAVIS, each 2.--Thro' REV. HOFFEDITZ, from GEO. BECKER (Richmond) 1; ISAAC MESSINGER2,& JOS. LABAUGH 2.-MISS ELIZABETH LEONARD (Lanc.)4; B.SPEAR (Norrist.) 2.--Thro' REV. KNIPE, from SAML. ACKER, SAML. RIXSTINE, & HEN. SNYDER, each 2; H. SHERBURN (Lanc., OH) 1 25; REV. H. GERHARD 2 50; DR. C. DICKENSHIED 2; MISS CHARLOTTE FLUBACHER (Phila.) 2, & CAROLINE BEALE (do)2; REV. W.CORNWELL 2 50.-D.BENDER (Williamsburg)2,REV. D. RIEGEL 2; CHRISTIAN BARR (Lancaster) 2; JOS. LABAUGH (Middlet'n) 2. Thro' REV. COLLIFLOWER, from JACOB STOUT, JOS. SWENEY & H. WYNANT, each 2. Thro' JOHN WILLIARD, from GEO. GROVE4; EMANL. FINK 2, A. TRUMBLE 2 & HEN.SHAFER 6. Thro' REV. J MAYER, from MISS SARAH MARTINS (Worcester) 2, & WM. REIFF 2. Thro' REV. J. G. WOLFF, from ADELINE WILLIS 2, DAVID HOFFMAN 7;& J.G. WOLFF2; W. RAFFELSBERGER 2 50; J.S. GISINER (Middleway)2; JACOB SHAFER (York) 5; J. HECKMAN, (Rainsburg,) 7.50. Replies to Correspondents: REV.J. BROWN paid to 312. MR. JOS. FUNK to 208. DANIEL HOTTEL paid 3 years; owes past & present.

217. Oct 23, 1839/**MARRIED** Tuesday evening the 15th, inst. by the REV. MR. KLINE, MISS REBECCA, second daughter of ROBERT CROOKS, Esq. of Franklin co. Pa. to MR. JAMES P. MAYHUGH of Washington co. Md.//At Ephrata, Lancaster co., on the 8th of September, by REV. D. HERTZ, MR. HENRY MARKLEY,to MISS MARGARETTA KLEIS,both of Lancaster city.//**DIED** In this place on the 8th inst., of bilious fever, ARCHIBALD I. FINDLAY, Attorney at Law, and son of WILLIAM FINDLAY, Esq., former Gov. of PA.//**BURNT** The paper mill, belonging to MR. BIRKENN?YER, a few miles from Louisville, (Ky.) was destroyed on the 4th inst. The engineer, named YORKE, is also said to have perished in the flames.//A large brick factory belonging

WEEKLY MESSENGER OF THE GERMAN REFORMED CHURCH

to STEPHEN SALSBURY, Esq. at Worcester, Mass. was destroyed by fire on the morning of the 6th inst.//The York, Pa. Republican, of the 16th inst. says--On the evening of Wednesday last, about 6 o'clock, the cry of FIRE alarmed our citizens, and...flames shot high and bright from the stable of MR. JACOB DIETZ. The members of the Engine companies....rushed to the scene. It was not quelled....until it had consumed the stable and...barn of MR. DIETZ-the stable on the ??? belonging to the estate of ABRAHAM DANNER, dec'd.-the ?ides of THOS. KELLY, Esq. and THOMAS TAYLOR--the barn of JAMES JOHNSON, Esq. and that belonging to the estate of JAMES B. WEBB, dec'd. on the corner of the alley and King street.//We were invited, by MR. DE SELD?N of the Museum, to view the progeny of the large rattlesnake which has often attracted the notice of visitors. We are told that during the two months it has been in MR. DE SELDING's possession it has not eaten. --"Balt. Am."//**MONIES** By D. BECKLEY, from HENRY BOVEY 2, MRS. LOUISA ALLEMAN 2, F. PONTIUS 5; D. P. MILLER (Clear Spring) 2; JOHN SHELTON (Greenfield. Md.) 2; from REV. D. HERZ 1 and H. MILLER (Leacock) 2. Christliche Zeitschrift from DANIEL WAGNER (Churchtown) $1 00 BENJ. SCHWARZ (Adamstown)...1 00//MR. EMANUEL THOMAS is informed the money for MISS K. was not paid. The amount sent for MISS A. C. T. pays up to No. 261.

218. Oct. 30, 1839/**MARRIED** On the 24th inst. by REV. J. HELFFENSTEIN, MR. SAMUEL MITCHELL, of Green Castle Pa. to MISS REBECCA ISENBERGER, of Chambersburg.//On the 27th inst., by REV. BENJAMIN S. SCHNECK, MR. EMANUEL MEYER,to MISS HANNAH FLORY, both of Guilford township, Franklin co., Pa.//On Thursday the 17th inst., by the REV. J. SECHLER, MR. MARTIN SMITH, to MISS MARIA BUCHER, both of Carroll co., Md.//On Sunday last, by the same, MR. JOSEPH HERMAN, to MISS SUSANNA HINKLE, both of Carroll county, Md.//On the same day, by REV. J. ALBERT, MR. JOSEPH ALBON,to MISS SUSANNA

WEEKLY MESSENGER OF THE GERMAN REFORMED CHURCH

SHAFER, both of Carroll county.//In Orange county N. C., on the 12th ult. by REV. J. H. CRAWFORD, MR. HENRY A. SHARP,to MISS CATHARINE A. FINDLEY. //In Guilford county N.C. the 17th inst. by the same, MR. LEVI FOUST,to MISS MARTHA. M. WHARTON. //On the 1st inst. by REV. MR. CLARK, MR. JOHN S. RICHARDS, Editor of the Reading "Journal," to MISS NANCY D. O'BRIEN, of Philadelphia city.//On the 17th inst.by the REV. MR.MILLER, MR. JOHN J. COCHRAN, Junior Editor of the York "Republican," to MISS CATHARINE BAUMGARDNER,--all of York.//On the 22d inst. by the REV.MR.BRUNNER, MR. JOHN W. FORNEY, Editor of the Lancaster "Intelligencer and Journal," to MISS ELIZABETH MATILDA REITZEL, daughter of PHILIP REITZEL, Esq.--all of Lancaster.//**DIED** On Thursday last, in St. Thomas, Franklin co., Pa. in the 53d year of hs age, MR. DANIEL HOSLER. The bereaved widow, eight sons and daughters mourn his departure.//**REVOLUTIONARY SOLDIER GONE** On Friday night 18th inst., in the 79th year of his age, CAPT. CASPER SNIVELY. He was one of the oldest and most respectable inhabitants of Washington co. Md.//On Monday the 7th inst. at his residence near Welsh Run, MR. HENRY BUTTERBAUGH, in the 79th year of his age. //At her residence near Booth's mill in Washington co. Md. the 10th inst. MRS. DORCAS E. MYERS, wife of MR. ABRAHAM MYERS, in the 29th year of her age.//On Tuesday the 15th inst., in the 4th year of his age, CHARLES, son of MR. DANIEL M. MIDDLEKAUFF, of Hagerstown Md.//On Sunday night the 29th ult., CAPT. WILLIAM ALBRIGHT, of Guilford county, N.C.---A soldier of the Revolution. //On the 2nd inst. REBECCA LOUISA CLAPP, daughter of CAPT. J. H. CLAPP.//On the 18th, MR. HENRY FOUST of Orange co. N.C.//Sunday morning last at the residence of her son (MR. S.H.BUEHLER) in Gettysburg, MRS. MARY RUDISILL, in the 76th year of her age.//**LETTER** to the Am. Tract Society to increase the variety of tracts issued in Asia Minor in Armenian and Greek. MR. RIGGS arrival strengthened the mission's book-making depart-

WEEKLY MESSENGER OF THE GERMAN REFORMED CHURCH

ment. Signed by DANIEL TEMPLE, HOMAN HALLOCK, ELIAS RIGGS, JOHN B. ADGER.//**A FIRE**. The Mobile Journal of the 11th gives details of the fires of the 7th and 8th, and account of an additional fire on the 9th inst.: Wednesday evening, about 7 o'clock a wooden tenement on Church street was discovered to be on fire. It rapidly communicated to the adjacent houses, and burnt the handsome dwelling of MR. G. G. HENRY to the ground.

No Marriages or Deaths in the issue of Nov. 6.

219. Nov. 13, 1839/**MARRIED** Near Middletown, Md. on the 20th ult. by REV. J. C. BUCHER, MR. BENJAMIN PATTINGALL, to MISS ELIZABETH daughter of MR. OTHO CASTLE, all of Middletown, Valley, Md. (sic)//On the 24th ult., by the same, MR. PHILIP, youngest son of MR. JOHN PHILIP COBLENTS to MISS MARY ANN, daughter of MR. GEORGE KEAFAUVER, all of Middletown, Valley, Md. //On the 29th ult., by REV. R. DOUGLAS, MR. CHARLES HUYETT, to MISS ELIZABETH NOLAND, all of Jefferson co. Va,. (sic)//On the 30th ult.,by the same,MR. SAMUEL HUYETT, of Jefferson co. Va., to MISS SIDNA JONES, of Clark co. Va.//On the 31st ult., by the same, MR. JOHN GEORGE WILHELM AUCKER, to MRS. SOPHIA KRISLER, all of Sheperdstown, (sic) Jefferson co., Va.//On the 3d inst. by the same, MR. BARNEY OTT, to MISS MARGARET WELSH, all of Jefferson co. Va.//On the 29th ult., by the REV. A. P. FREEZE, MR. JNO. W. BARRICK, to MISS CATHARINE SOPHIA, daughter of CAPT. GEO. DIVELBISS, all of Fred.county Md.//On the 29th ult., by the REV. WILLIAM PAULI, MR. HENRY ERMENTROUT, Merchant,to MISS AMEILIA C. SMITH, both of Reading. //**DIED** ON the 19th of October after a short but distressing illness of "congestive typhus" fever MR. JOHN KELLER, eldest son of DAVID KELLER, of Middletown Valley, Md., in the 30th year of his age. He has left a widow and two little daughters. A resolution of sympathy for the family from the Consistory of the GRC Middletown, to be

WEEKLY MESSENGER OF THE GERMAN REFORMED CHURCH

published. JOHN KEAFAUVER, of GEO. Secretary pro tem.//Near Jefferson, Md. on the 30th ult. after a severe illness of Typhus Fever, MR. GEORGE NELSON STOCKMAN, aged 22 years and 1 month and 8 days.//At Natchez, of yellow fever, MR. DAVID BELTZHOOVER proprietor of the City hotel of that place, formerly of Hagerstown, aged fifty five years.//In Frederick, on Thursday last, the 31st ult., MR. CASPER MANTZ, in the 63d year of his age, after lingering some time, from an attack of the TyphusFever.//In Lancaster,on Monday week last, DR.M. LECHLEITNER, in the 55th year of his age.//In Somerset, Pa., on the 5th ult.of inflamation of the stomach, the Hon. CHAUNCEY FORWARD aged about 45 years.//In Bellefonte, on Monday night week last, Hon. WILLIAM W. POTTER, member of Congress from the fourteenth district, aged 45 years.//On Tuesday afternoon last DR. ALBERT G. WALTERS, of this place, performed a surgical operation for club feet.--"Pittsburg Visitor."// On the evening of the 30th, as SAMUEL C. MOTT, in company with five boys, attempted to cross the river from Theller's point to Sing Sing, the boat was upset by a passing steamboat. MR. MOTT and three of the boys, one of them his grandson, another the son of JOHN S. METTICK, and a third the son of DR. N. J. GREEN, of Sing Sing, were drowned. The bodies have not been recovered.---"N. Y. Evening Post."//**IMPRUDENCE.** Monday evening, about 7 o'clock, a young man, named MICHAEL WELSH lost his life while walking near the Rail Road track with WM. GRIFFIN. GRIFFIN warned him not to walk on the track as the locomotive came along very rapidly but WELSH suffered the engine to approach very near, and instead of jumping away, whether from fear or mistake, threw himself in the way of the locomotive. His head was crushed to pieces and almost every bone in his body broken. The testimony at the inquest was sufficient to exculpate the conductors.--"N. Y. Express."//MR. JOSEPH D. COE, of this city, from an ounce and a quarter of seed, raised 40 Rohan

WEEKLY MESSENGER OF THE GERMAN REFORMED CHURCH

potatoes, weighing 18 lbs.--"Newark Daily Adv."
//**FEVER** Advice from Houston to the 21st October have been received in New Orleans. Yellow fever deaths include the Hon. HENRY HUMPHREYS, Chief Justice of that county; the Hon. ROBERT BARR, Post Master General; DR. A. A. ANDERSON, late of Vicksburg.//The printing and drying machine of MR. THOMAS FRENCH is now in opeation in Hanover, N. J. producing a roll of paper seventy feet in length, printed on both sides.--"Philad. North Am."//The District Court of Philadelphia awarded WILLIAM PLEASANTS 11,800 dollars in suit against the Commercial Bank of Cincinnati. The plaintiff who had found one hundred thousand dollars in Post Notes, applied for the ten thousand dollar reward which the bank had offered, but then refused to pay once the notes were recovered. Counsel for the plaintiff, MESSRS. MEREDITH and SHARSWOOD; for defense, MESSRS. CHARLES INGERSOLL, CHARLES J. INGERSOLL and JOSEPH INGERSOLL.
//Romeo, an Irish greyhound, owned by COL. HARNEY, which he had brought from MO, had formed an attachment to MR. DALLAM, owner of the trading establishment at Caloosahatchie. Fourteen days after the massacre of the men at that post, the troops arrived and found the dog, barely able to stand, emitting a feeble howl over the remains of his friend. The devoted animal was taken to the garrison at Tampa Bay.--"St. Augus. News."//
PRINTING FUND SUBSCRIPTION ALLEXANDER H. LAPPON $30 00   ELIZABETH WINTERS, 15 00   JACOB HUYETT, 10 00 JOHN WINTERS, 5 00 JACOB CRAUSE, paid 5 00 PETER CRAUSE, 5 00, DANIEL HUYETT $50 00, all of Cavetown. SUSAN S. KENNEDY, 20 00 CHRISTIAN DIENER, 10 00   JOHN J. KEEDY, 10 00   JOHN B. WELTY, paid, 5 00   SAMUEL R. COST, paid, 5 00, all of Boonsboro.   DANIEL MIDDLEKAUFF, 10 00   DANIEL ZELLER, 25 00   DAVID ZELLER, paid, $15 00   25 00 SAMUEL ZELLER 25 00, all of Hagerstown.//**MONIES** GEORGE SHOLL 2. JOHN BROWN (Waynesb.) 2. JACOB RITTER 1,25. GEO.KING(York)2. REBECCA ANN K?SLER (Md.) 2. By G. C. WELKER, fom MISS E. DERING 2.

WEEKLY MESSENGER OF THE GERMAN REFORMED CHURCH

JOHN BOGAR 4. W. WEITZEL 8,12 1/2. By REV. P.S. FISCHER, from MISS ACHENBACH (Orangeville) 2, H. STAMM 2 and JOHN KELLER, SEN. 1.--By REV. J. C. BUCHER, from J. P. COBLENTZ, S. BRANDENBERG, DR. GARROTT, JOHN COBLENTZ, (of JOHN P.) each 2 and JACOB LIGHTER 1. By REV. J. G. FRITCHEY, from HENRY CHORPENNING, JONA. KNEPPER, GEO. SHAFFER, MICHAEL SHAFFER, GEO. PILE, J. SPEICHER, JOHN C. KURTS, J. F. COX, J. HERR (all of Somerset) and G. CHORPENNING (Stoyst.) each2. GEO. KYLE (Va.) 5. JACOB OSTER (St Clairsville)2. D. BURK, 1,25. JOHN GROVE 2. DR. W. SWOOPE 2. H. HARRIS (Pottsville) 75 cts. E. WEITZEL (sub.) 4,00 (sic). The $6 acknowledged from D. J. WEISER, was intended for REV. D. WEISER. For JESSE CASTNER, instead of CASTINI. To the Christliche Zeitschrift: from J. P. COBLENTZ, Middletown,Md. $1.00.

220. Nov. 20, 1839/**MARRIED** On Tuesday week, at Snider's Hotel, by REV. B. S. SCHNECK, MR. HENRY BIRKINBINE of Perry county to MISS HANNAH YOCKEY of Franklin county, Pa.//At Shaffer's Hotel, on Thursday week, by the same, MR. JACOB KELLER, to MISS CHRISTIANNA, youngest daughter of MR. PETER SYNDER, SEN. all of Guilford towns'p, Franklin county.//**DIED** On Tuesday morning, 5th inst. at Ferry Hill, his residence in this county,after a lingering illness, at an advanced age, COL. JOHN BLACKFORD one of the oldest inhabitants of Washington county,Md.//In Simsbury, Conn. Aug. 20th, CAPTAIN ASA CORNISH, aged 64; on the 27th, MR. ELISHA CORNISH, aged 57--(brothers) on the 31st, MR. ELAM CORNISH, aged 29, on the 17th September MR. NORTON CORNISH,aged 27; on the 18th,MR. NEWELL CORNISH,aged 25; on the same day, MR. NATHAN CORNISH, aged 22; all sons and only children of the said ELISHA CORNISH; on the 8th of Oct. MRS. LIDIA CORNISH, widow of the said ELISHA CORNISH, all of typhus fever. Thus the whole family, in a few weeks were called to eternity not leaving a near relative bearing the family name.//Sunday morning at 1 o'clock,in the 81st year of his

age, LUKE TIERNAN, Esq., one of the oldest, most opulent, respectable inhabitants of Baltimore.//Near Waterstreet, Huntingdon county, on the 4th inst., in the 51st year of his age, of fever and affection of the lungs,SAMUEL HARNISH, leaving a large family.//On Sunday week, the trunk of MR. ALEXANDER KING, a passenger from the West, in a Juniata boat, at Harrisburg, was broken into and robbed of $1,900. Two men belonging to the boat were arrested.//WEAVER was acquitted at Frederick, on Thursday last, for causing the death of M'CARTY, at Emmitsburg.//A fire broke out in the store of BROWN & HATCH, in Chicago, Oct. 18th, destroying nineteen buildings.//**MONIES.** By REV. HERTZ, from W. WITTY and SEB. MILLER (Adamst.) each 2. JOHN LANDIS 50 cts. By C. H. LEINBACH 2, from J. H. KNABB 2, C. H. LEINBACH 2, W. RYAN 2, J.BREITENBACH2, FREDERICK HARNER (viceJ.K.BOYER) 2, T. VANDERSLICE, M. REED, A. G. STEIN, JOHN HARPER (E. Han.) G. HARNER, each 1. By H. HOFFMAN, from THO. HAWK 2.50, D. HOFFMAN, JR. 2, and GEORGE HOFFMAN (Vincent) 2, REV. S. R. FISHER 3, REV. E. HEINER 2, HARRIET BENTZ 2, J. McNULTY 2, HERMAN NISSLEY 1.25, PHIL. MANN 2.50, PETER MANN 2.50, W. ROFFELSBERGER 2 50. Christliche Zeitschrift: from DAVID ROYER, Ephrata. Pa. $1 00

221. Nov. 27, 1839/**MARRIED** On Thursday,the 7th inst., by the REV. S. GUTELIUS, MR. JONAS REBERT to MISS MARY ANN HARTMAN-both of Adams county.//On Tuesday evening 5th inst., by REV. E. KELLER, L. F. COPPERSMITH, Esq. of Columbia, Ia. to MISS MARIA LOUISA daughter of MR. ISAAC BAUGHER (Merchant,) of Emmitsburg, Md.//On the 19th inst. by the REV.J. HELFFENSTEIN, MR. JOHN RITTER to MISS LEAH WOLFKILL both from the neighborhood of Fayetteville Franklin co.//On Thursday evening last 21st inst., by the REV. ELIAS HEINER, THOMAS D. SULTZER to ELEANORA R. C. COOK, daughter of JOHN F. COOK, all of Baltimore.//**DIED** On the 11th inst., MRS. ELIZABETH SCHEIBLY, wife of MR. JOHN SCHEIBLY, of Strasburg, Franklin co. in the 49th

WEEKLY MESSENGER OF THE GERMAN REFORMED CHURCH

year of her age. Before her departure, she exhorted her husband to be a pious example to her remaining children.//On Saturday of last week in the 81st year of his age in McKeansburg, Schuylkill Co., Pa. the Hon. DANIEL YOST, for twenty five years Associate Judge.//On Friday the 8th inst., in Adams county, MRS. CATHARINE DEYSERT, aged 62 years.//The Lynchburg Virginian says MR. HOPKINS, of Abingdon, has discovered a cure for cancer.//**MONIES.** By DR. HOFIUS, from W. NYCUM 2, REV.G. LEIDY2, JOHN MILLER 1.--JOHN B.COOK 4, JOHN SMALL (Chamb.) 2, ALFRED SCHNEIDER 2, J. H. KELLER (Windgap)2, MRS. MARY McCLURE, GEO. CARL, REV. J.SHOLL, each 2, JACOB SHEARER 4. By W. LAKIN, from H. GROSS, SEN., S. REMSBERG, W. LAKIN, L. RODRICK, H.STOCKMAN, D. STOCKMAN, JACOB REMSBERG, W. HOLTER, P. SONDER, MARTHA A. M. LAKIN (Petersv.) each 2. By REV. R. FISHER, from MRS. S. ALLEN 2, D. EBERT 2, E ZIMMERMAN 1. Send the Christliche Zeitschrift to MICHL. EVERT,Sunbury, Pa.//**LETTERS** LAWRENCE EISENBERG, DAVID LUPFER.

222. Dec. 4, 1839/**MARRIED** On the 10th ult. by the REV.J.A.STRASSBURGER,CAPT. ELIAS HARTZEL, of Hilltown Bucks co. to MISS LOUISANNA, oldest daughter of REV.J. A. STRASSBURGER.//On the same day,by the same, MR. S.ROUDENBUSH to MISS HANNAH CRESSMAN, all of Rockhill,Bucks county.// On the 19th inst., by the same, MR. JAC. FRETZ to MISS SUSANNA BEITLER, all of Belminster,Bucks county. //On the 22d,by the same, MR. ISAAC DRUMBORE, to MISS HANNAH MARKEL, of Rockhill,Buck (sic) county.//On the 19th ult., by REV. A. P. FREESE, MR. ERA E. BARRICK to MISS HARRIET CRAMER, all of Frederick County, Md.//On the 24th ult., by REV. J. REBAUGH, MR. JOSEPH CONRAD, to MISS MARY A. OVER of Franklin county.//On the same day,by the same, MR.JOHN STILT, to MISS MARGARET WILT.//On the 5th ult., by the same, SAMUEL C. WEAGLY, to MISS CATHARINE A. BIGHAM.//On the 14th, by the same,GEORGE SHRADER to MISS ROSE ANNA MYERS.//On the 21st, by the same, near Greencastle, MR.

WEEKLY MESSENGER OF THE GERMAN REFORMED CHURCH

JOHN MILLER, to MISS CATHARINE MILLER.//On the 28th, by REV. B. S. SCHNECK,MR.JOSEPH SHEELY, to MISS MARY BYERS, both from the vicinity of Green Castle, Pa.//On the 25th ult., near Mercersburg, Pa., by REV. DR. RAUCH, REV. AMOS H. KREMER, of Shippensburg, to MISS REBECCA, daughter of MR. STEPHEN KIEFFER, of the former place.//**DIED** At Morristown, N. J. on the 19th ult., of a protracted consumption,MRS. SARAH ANN, wife of REV. O. L. KIRTLAND.//At Salem, Mass. CAPT. JOSEPH WINN, an aged citizen of that place. He died in REV. DR. EMERSON'S church soon after the commencement of the morning services. A grandson, observing something unusual in his appearance, called attention to the fact, and he was immediately removed.//The Burlington (IA) Patriot announces the death, in that place, on the 6th of November, of the Hon. WM. B. CONWAY, Secretary of the Territory.//On Monday last, near Schuylkill Sixth and Lombard street, (sic) a lad fourteen years of age named PALLOCK, in getting over a fence, while playing with other boys, accidently (sic) fell upon a sharp upright cornstalk, which entered his groin, and caused his death in twenty-four hours after.-"Philad. U.S. Gazette."
//**MONIES.** JOHN STEVER 5; REV. J. STRASBURGER 3 DANIEL HOFFERT 2; ABR. DONAT 2.50; JAMES LEWARS 2, DAVID ESHBAUGH 2--TREAT BENSON 2, JACOB MAISH 2. MRS. JANE DENIG 5, C. WOLFF, ESQ.2, F. ROEMER 2, RAPHAEL JONES 2.

223. Dec. 11, 1839/**MARRIED** On the 18th ult., by the REV. G. W.GLESSNER, MR. CHARLES MINER, to MISS AGNES JONES, both of Franklin county.//On the 3d inst. by the same, MR. JACOB GARVER, to MISS SARAH MENTZER, both of Washington co.,Md.// On the same day, by the same, MR. GEORGE LEIDY, to MRS. SUSAN BEAVER, both of Franklin county.// Cumberland, Md. Nov. 30, 1939. On the night of the 20th inst., the dwelling house of MR. JOSEPH FRIEND,of JOHN,in the Western part of the county was destroyed by fire, and two of his children, REESE aged about 8 and JOHN aged about 5 years, perished. The particulars are described in a letter received from the brother of the bereaved father MR. ELIJAH FRIEND. The fire was discovered by his eldest daughter, HARRIET. She gave the

WEEKLY MESSENGER OF THE GERMAN REFORMED CHURCH

alarm and returned to rescue her younger brothers, urging her brother FREEMAN to help her rescue the little ones. They were forced to drop their little brothers, and jump from a window thro' which another little brother had made his escape. MISS HARRIET FRIEND was so severely injured as to leave it doubtful whether she will recover.--"Civilian."//Another fire in Mobile on the morning of the 21st of November in the residence and shop of MRS. CLARE, corner of Conception and St. Michael's, destroyed the residence of FRANK MOSLEY, Esq., buildings of MR. N. G. STEBBINS and MR. JAMES ZURCHER, all uninsured.// A little child of MR. SOLOMON LEEPS, about two years of age, was so injured by its clothes taking fire on Thursday last, that it died on Saturday.---"Hagerst. T. Light."//JAMES L. MAGUIRE, keeper of the Alms House, has instituted a suit against the REV. MESSRS. BREEKENRIDGE and CROSS, publishers of the Religious Magazine for libel. --Baltimore paper.//A sensation was created at Lancaster, by accidental meeting of MR. R. W. MIDDLETON, Editor of the Lancaster Examiner, and MR. JAMES CAMERON, Superintendant of the Philadelphia and Columbia Rail Road, at the house of a third person. Violence was avoided when MR. MIDDLETON was recognized as his guest by the gentleman of the house. MR. MIDDLETON proceeded to his office, followed by the other, and was as believed, with the intent to assault the Editor. Thus MR. MIDDLETON provided himself with a pistol and discharged it while his antagonist was in the act of striking him. The Philadelphia US Gazette of this morning says: We learned last night that MR. CAMERON was dead.//We learn from New Orleans papers that the steamboat *Wilmington* on her voyage from that port to St. Louis, burst her boilers on the morning of the 18th ult. near the mouth of the Arkansas river. Among the sufferers, we find the following names: ANDREW HELMS, pilot, blown overboard and lost; JULIUS FISK, first engineer, killed; PAUL ___, do, 2d do, (sic) mortally wounded; and four others, including one of the cooks died. It is reported twelve or fifteen received serious injury.//A distressing casualty occurred on Monday night. MRS. KNOWLES, wife of MR. FREDERICK KNOWLES, and

WEEKLY MESSENGER OF THE GERMAN REFORMED CHURCH

MRS. EDWARDS, wife of MR. SAMUEL EDWARDS, residents of Belle Isle, near this city, visited a sick family on this side, and set out to return to the Island about 8 o'clock in a boat managed by a negro men belonging to the works. It would appear the boat began to leak; it is inferred that the negro, finding his boat sinking, landed the ladies upon a small island in the river and made his way to shore for assistance. It would seem that in his anxiety to afford relief, he failed to give the alarm, and took out another boat; but the poor fellow failed in his efforts; and it is believed was drowned, as both boats were found together in the morning. What is more distressing, the ladies perished, their bodies having been found yesterday. Each of them leaves two young children. MR. KNOWLES is up North.---"Richmond Whig."//REV. JOSEPH D. TYLER, Principal of the Deaf and Dumb, DR. J. C. M. MERRILAT, Principal of the Blind, and MR. WM. GRAHAM, Teacher of the Blind arrived to occupy temporary buildings of the Institution, which is to go into operation immediately.--"Staunton Spectator." //A plea for funds to support missionaries, from the Missionary Society, headquartered in Philadelphia. The requested donations may be remitted to PAUL BECK, JUN., Treasurer, or either of the subscribers, ALEXANDER HENRY, Pres. or FREDERICK W. PORTER, Cor. Sec. at 146 Chestnut st., Philadelphia.//**MONIES** By REV. J.C. HENSELL, from JOHN SHEETZ (Mt. Sidney) 5, DAVID SHULTZ 2, REV. J.C. HENSELL 2--By REV. D. BRAGONIER, from M. BOVEY (Clear Spr.) 2, S. P. STONER 2, GEO. ZIMMERMAN (Hancock)2. By REV. S. R. FISHER, from E. EBBERT (Fairfield) 1, S. EIKER (do) 2, ABIAH MARTIN 2, WM. KROM (Mechanicst.) 2--GEO. PEARSON 2, JACOB BESORE 2. By M. RICKENBAUGH, DANIEL MIDDLEKAUFF, JOHN WOLFELSPERGER, MICHAEL MILLER, JOHN ADAMS, (Funkstown), JOHN KENNODE, HENRY McLAUGHLIN, F. BRYAN, JOHN SCHLEIGH, M. RICKENBAUGH, each 2. J. ZWISLER JR., 2.50. Rec'd from REV. J. C. HENSELL, Middlebrook, Va. $1 for the Christliche Zeitschrift.//**LETTERS** J.GLATZ,P.M.; JOSEPH GOULBOURN; N. VALLENDER; REV. S. HELFFENSTEIN, JR.

No issue is available for Dec. 18 or 25, 1839.

INDEX

The number appearing after each name is the number assigned to the date, NOT the page number. Most courtesy titles were omitted in the index.

Where it was impossible to determine whether the single name was the surname or the given name, it is indexed in both ways. An asterisk (*) indicates the same name appears more than once in the same issue.

Unusually spelled, but seemingly related surnames appear in parentheses.

B, A 184
B, S S 195 201
B, V 17
C, Mrs 150
C, J 195 201
C, P 195 201
D, C 184
H, R 195 201
K, Miss 217 Mr 216
M, D 166
N, Dr 136
R, Mrs 150
R, Y 188
S, Mr 195
S, B S 195
S, H 7
T, Capt 119
T, Miss A C 217
W, Mrs E 187

Alligator 88
Alpha 201
Balty 147
Bill 156
Black Hawk 123
Emannel 41
Fanny (sore neck) 22
Rev George 56
Harvey 106
John (printer) 204
Jumper 88
Keokuck 123
Lewis 22
Pat 22
Patrick 156
Paul 223
Powell 88
Rhyna 156
Solano 20

__ER, William 28
ABEL, Geo 202 Maria 202 Mich 202 Philip 202
ABELE, Catharine 145
ABERCROMBIE, Gen 55 Sir Ralph 110
ABRAHAM, Sarah 193
ACHENBACH, Miss 219 Daniel 215 Frederick 215 Jacob 215 Philip 215
ACHEY, F 182
ACKENBACH, George A 206
ACKER, Peter 174 Saml 216 Samuel 72
ADAM, Rev 192 Daniel 202
ADAMS, Mr 55 Rev 121 George 146 John 117 223*
ADER, Peter 38
ADGER, John B 218
AGER, Henry 202
AIKEN, J 107
ALBACK, Catharine 93
ALBAUGH, __ 74
ALBERT, Rev 116 124 172 203 Abr 195 Charles H 176 George 123 Rev J 218 Jacob 146 Rev John 75
ALBON, Mr Joseph 218
ALBRIGHT, __ 74 Christian 174 D 86 179 Daniel 14 185 Jacob 106 Capt William 218
ALBURGER, John 128
ALCOCK, Dr Edward 81
ALEBERGER, J G 191
ALEPH, Miss 188
ALEXANDER, Capt 50 Mr 133 Mrs 109 A 109 Ann 50 Elizabeth 86 J H 156 203 J T 53 Jacob 41 86 88 James M 101 Mary M 88 Moses 67 Nancy C 67 Susannah 41 William 144
ALGERT, Henry 215
ALISON, Mrs 210

ALLAN, Rev 77
ALLBURGER, John G 32
ALLEBON, __ 163
ALLEBORN, Rev Jacob 149
ALLEMAN, C 190 Mrs L 57 L 145 Louisa 217
ALLEN, James 71 John 180 Mrs S 221
ALLGART, Catharine 190
ALLISON, James 145 157 Maj Robert 51 S 190 Samual 210 William 145
ALLSON, London 148
ALLSWORTH, Eliz 154
ALRICKS, Herman 186
ALSOP, Joseph 161
ALTER, David M 98
ALTHAUS, John 174
ALYMINE, Joseph 38
AMBLER, Mary 174
AMMONS, W Miley 120
AMOLE, Jesse 165
ANCHONY, Henry 135 213
ANDERS, Benjamin 166 Frederick 166 Jacob 166 John Sr 166 John Jr 166
ANDERSON, __ 147 Mr 72 Mrs 148 Dr A A 219 Ann 144 Cunningham 86 Elizabeth 186 Frances Julia 72 Rufus 1 Thos 190
ANDRECK, Joseph 15
ANDRES, George 163 Sara 163
ANDREW, Dan'l 184 Lewis 167
ANDREWS, Col 88 Ann 144 Rev Charles W 79 Dr Seth L 79
ANESHENSLY, H 184
ANGER, Fridlich 215
ANGLEMEYER, Peter 202
ANKENNY, John 132 180 Sam 180 Sam'l 132
ANKENY, Henry 96 Martha 96
ANKONY, Mary A 87

ANNESLY, Miss 143
ANSPACH, Rev J G 71
ANTHONY, Rev J B 156 Joseph 138
APP, Leonard 146
APPLE, B 181 John D 200 Philip 19
APPLEGATE, David 176 J 199
APPOLD, Geo 105
ARCHER, Henry 206*
AREY, Amelia 124 Peter 124
ARMENTROUT, George 132
ARMSTRONG, Mr 148 Mrs 79 170 Alfred 171 Alfried 100 James 64 170 Mrs James 70 Jane 186 John 148 Mary 100 Samuel 19
ARNDORFF, John 214
ARNDT, Jacob 79 John 14
ARNEMAN, Wm S 202
ARNER, Thomas 202
ARNOLD, Lavinia 175
ARNSPERGER, Hiram 54
ARTHUR, Peter 97
ARTZ, Abr 180 Lucy Ann 175 Peter S 85
ASH, Maj John 205 Thornton 165
ASHBOUGH, Jacob 184
ASHWAY, Geo 210
ASTON, Esther 56 Owen 56
ASTOR, John Jacob 179
ATHERTON, J D 148
ATLAND, Samuel T 172
ATLEE, Julia De Haven 81
AUCKER, John Geo Wilhelm 219
AUDENREED, G 190
AUGER, Daniel 169
AUGHENBAUGH, Philip 48* William 143
AUGHINBAUGH, Geo 125 W 148 204 William 214 Wm 19 214
AUMILLER, Jacob 86

AUNAWALT, Peter 202
AUNEWALT, P 201 Capt Peter 107
AURAND, Rev H 59 79 92 Rev Henry 59 64 97 103 199
AURANDT, Jno 74 John 179
AUSTIN, Mrs 8 M 214 Martin 64 154 199 Mary 154
AUZE, Mr 156
AVERY, Mrs 37 Jonas B 37
AYRES, J B 21
BA__RIER, Maj Jacob 28
BABCOCK, D N 37
BABP, Abraham 202
BACHMAN, Conrad 97 Frederick 202 John 202 Rev John 26 Jonas 202 Jonas D 16 Julia 184
BACKENSTOSE, Martha 144
BACKESTOW, George Jr 88
BACON, Rev Leonard 77
BADGER, Mr 110
BAEHR, Catharine 198
BAILEY, Edward 79
BAILY, Stephen 148
BAIRD, Judge 99 Robert 4 Rev Thomas D 182
BAKER, ___ 108 Rev 111 Frederick 17 George 82 215 H 182 H W 57 Isaac 55 Jacob 152 194 John 77 146 P 181 Peter 185 Philip 17 S 193 Samuel 17 133
BALES, David 132 Mary Kinart 132
BALL, James 176
BALLIET, John 170
BALTY, ___ 147
BALTZELL, Chas 181 Elizabeth C 83 P 181 Wm 83
BANGHER, Dan 32
BANKER, Abraham 179
BANKERD, Ann 152

BANKS, Mr 128 164 Jesse 181 194
BANNAN, Samuel D 38
BANTZ, Gideon 17 24 131 162
  Gideon Jr 17 Gideon Sr 50
  Theodore S 16 Uriah S 17
  William S 16
BAPTIST, Eugene 148
BARCLAY, Dr F B 65
BARD, Archibald 95 Jacob 142
  John 86 Mary 179 Robert M 95 184
BARDWELL, Rev 215
BARE, Rev 131 Rev Jacob 141
BAREMAN, Henry 163
BARKDOLL, Samuel 143
BARKMAN, Maria 140
BARNARD, William M 101
BARNES, Rev A 32
BARNET, James 148*
BARNHARD, Dorothy 192
BARNHARDT, Christiana 88
  George 53 J C 53 John C 117 Col John C 28
BARNHART, Col G 193 Col Geo 38 J C 138 193 J G 193 John C 76 103* M A 138
BARNHEISEL, Wm 125
BARNITZ, Mr 100 Alexander H 94 Alexander M 16 Rev Charles 77 Charles J 16 George 94 Gideon 131 Isabella N 175 M'Pherson 16 Rebecca 94 Sarah 203
BARR, Ann 15 Catharine C 97 Christian 216 Henry 89 Jacob 26 John 97 Col John 82 Robert 219 Sarah 89 Wm 106
BARRACK, Mr 156 Mrs 156
BARRICK, Era E 222 Fred 186 Fred'k 66 Geo 84 188 George 17 Jacob 51 206 210 Jno W 219 John 206 210 Simon 144

BARRIER, Henry 75 78 181 Jacob 78 117 138 Jacob Jr 38 M 53 Philip 38 Phoebe 48
BARRON, R F 204
BART, Jonas 38 77
BARTEE, N 53
BARTER, A R 53
BARTGIS, M E 17
BARTHOLOMEW, W 190 210
BARTLETT, Samuel 121
BASH, W 184
BASHOAR, Jacob 124
BASKIN, John 146
BASLER, Rev H 132 Rev H S 179 Rev Henry 16
BASORE, Michael 144
BASSLER, Rev H 84 Rev Henry 94 Rev Henry S 162
BAST, Elias 97
BATCHELDER, Capt Henry 73
BATES, __ 132 153 180 Benoni 200 202 Henry 180 J C 156
BATTS, John 154
BAUCHMAN, Andrew H 180
BAUER, Adam 145 Henry 145 Jacob 215
BAUGHER, Isaac 221 M L 163 M L 181 Maria Louisa 221
BAUGHMAN, A H 132 Elizabeth 183 John 183
BAUM, John 32 191
BAUMGARDNER, Catherine 218 Henry 16
BAURMEISTER, --- 162
BAUSMAN, Andrew 28
BAYER, Rev A 138 184*
BE___MAN, Mrs M 28
BEACKLEY, Mary 213
BEALE, Caroline 216
BEALER, Jos 181 Maria 181 William 181
BEAM, Henry C 148 184
BEAMER, Jac 165 Philip 13 214

BEAR, Ann 17 24 David 87 Rev J 122 127 184 195 Jacob 16 Rev Jacob 118 127 150* 209 John 58 128 John Jr 76 Dr John Y 87 Magdalena 87 William 206

BEARD, Archibald 192 Daniel 94 David 166 John 181

BEATTY, James 91 Juliet C 51

BEAVER, Barbara 166 Eaver 148 Eve 148* Frederick 166 Henry 28 J 145 Jacob 148 John 61 148* 204 John Sr 210 Joseph 148* Mary 148 Susan 223

BECK, Geo 202 Paul Jr 223 Reuben 202

BECKER, J C 70 Rev J C 70 Samuel 110

BECKHART, Lewis 116

BECKLEY, D 217 Daniel 146

BEECHER, Mrs 15 19 Jacob 5 6 Rev Lyman 72 Wm 213

BECHLER, A 77

BECHTEL, David 81 Rev John C 163

BECK, Felix 193 Geo 202 Paul Jr 223 Reuben 202

BECKER, C 8 Geo 216 Samuel 24 Susan 202 Wm 202

BEDINGER, Daniel 131

BEECHER, David 214 Rev Lyman 72

BEER, G W 202 Mary 202

BEHM, John 138

BEIDLEMAN, Marg't 181

BEITLER, Susanna 222

BEITZEL, Henry 56 William 63 209

BELL, Lancelot 209 Thomas 99 W W 143 145 Wm 190 Wm W 172

BELLAS, Eliza P 149 Hugh 149

BELTZ, Dan'l 202

BELTZHOOVER, David 219

BEMIS, Nathan S 133

BENDER, Ann 157 Ann Magdalen 172 Conrad 215 D 216 Elizabeth 137 202 George 172 Jacob 215 John 215 Joseph 215

BENEDICT, Rev 144

BENFER, John 146 Michael 146

BENNER, John 32

BENNET, John James 162 Samuel 86 W 28 Rev W C 28 70 75 90 91 121 135 138 202 209 Rev William C 163 Rev Wm C 53 70 99

BENNETT, Rev W C 38* 48 142 Wm C 11 Wm T 67

BENNIMAN, Louisa M 208

BENOLIET, Judah 95

BENSON, Treat 222

BENTLEY, Sheshb_zzer 191

BENTLY, Thomas 68

BENTZ, C 205 Christina 198 Dan 195 Daniel 17 Harriet 174 220 J 205 John 127

BERCKHEIMER, William 187

BERG, Prof 99 Rev 59 70 93 Rev J F 34 37 70* 99 128 141 155 167 213 Rev Joseph L 43 William 144

BERGER, Christian 107

BERGHEIMER, William 144

BERGSTRESSER, George 146

BERKEY, Rev 67 Rev A 175

BERKHEIMER, Fred'k 187

BERKY, Brother 116 Rev A 175

BERLIN, Adam 99 Catharine 99 P 95 Philip 162 182

BERLUCHY, Dr 122

BERNHEISEL, Mrs 11

BERNITZ, Miss Julian 198

BERRY, W 185 Wm 121

BESHLER, Dr 128

BESHORE, Christ 188 David 17
John 34
BESORE, D Sr 213 Daniel 120
199 David 24 78 Eliza 181
Geo 13 19 42 48* 121 154
201 213 George 10* 11 24 62
99 110 111 160 181 213
Jacob 24 110 199 213 223
John 210 Martha Jane 155
Peter 162 Rachel 162 Samuel
24
BEST, Dan'l 202 Jacob 215
Lydia 198 Peter 182 Susan
182
BETHUNE, Rev 199
BETZ, Henry 82 128
BEYER, Rev 138 William 124
BIAC, John 202
BIBIGHAOUSE, Rev L 19
BIBIGHAUS, C H 101 Rev H 15
Thomas M 16
BIBIGHAUSE, Rev 90
BIBIGHOUSE, Rev 149 Rev H
199
BICKEL, Edward 128
BICKELL, Susan 116 Tobias 26
76
BIEBER, Hetty 198
BIEDELMAN, Mrs M 18
BIEGEL, Solomon 144
BIEGLE, George 644
BIEGLY, Daniel 11 Jacob 11
BIERY, Joseph 113 Mary 113
BIGGS, Frederick 196 Susan 196
BIGHAM, Armer 190 Cath A 222
BIGLER, C 133 Christian 191
BINKLEY, P 184
BIRD, Mr 183
BIRELY, Ann M R 50
BIRKINBINE, Henry 220
BIRKENN_YER, Mr 217

BISER, D S 86 Daiel S 183
Daniel 24 Daniel S 186 Daniel
Sr 166 177 Fred'k 11 24
Gideon 128 Jacob 11 24*
John 11 24 Joshua 32 86 186
Peter 11 24 41 86 92 Peter Jr
132 179 Peter Sr 86 Solomon
179 Sophia 92
BISH, Susanna 179
BISHOP, Mr 107 Sarah 47
BITTINGER, Rev D G 151 Henry
75 95 199 Juha Ann 95
BITTLE, D F 26 124
BIXLER, David 72
BLACK, Anna M 141 Rev J 70
Rev James 150 James S 110
Joseph 118 Martha L 50
Matthias 30 Peter 179
BLACKF_RD, Elizabeth 192
BLACKFORD, Elizabeth 169
Franklin 74 Col John 169 220
BLAIR, Elizabeth 127 Jas T 110
John Sr 127 Martha 113
Rachel 203 William 149
BLAKE, Thomas 28*
BLANCHARD, ___ 176
BLECHER, John 17 24
BLISS, Rev Isaac 79
BLOCKER, Mr 128
BLOOM, John 200
BLOSE, Daniel 202
BLOW, Miss 128 Mr 128
BLUMER, Wm H 113 184
BLYHOLDER, Dorothy 73
BLYMER, Benjamin 144
BOAS, D 37 Frederick 34
BOAZ, Samuel 124
BOCHER, Geo H 34
BODEY, Henry Jr 174 Henry Sr
174 Louisa 174
BODINE, John 15 184

BOGAR, John 219
BOGER, Daniel 14 Rev G 138
    193 Rev Geo 72 99 Rev
    George 76 108
BOGGS, Joseph 139
BOHER, Jacob 167
BOILEAU, J 174 John 99
BOLDENHAMER, Peter S 38
BOLDWIN, Andrew 148
BOLLAR, Wm Sr 188
BOLLINGER, Christian 24 Jacob
    144 179 Michael 145
BOLLIS, Wm 214
BOMBERGER, G 102 200 Geo
    15 18 George 102 Rev J 184 J
    H 37 J H A 74 Rev J H A 193
    John H A 16
BOND, Rev 182 187 Rev R 80
    176 Richard 162 Rev Richard
    95 99 118
BONESTEEL, Philip 143
BOON, Catharine 80
BOOTH, James 91
BOOTHE, J B 8 Wm 26
BOOTS, Jacob 132 180 Jesse
    132 180 Martin 132 180
BOOZER, Henry 71
BORDEN, Joseph 15
BORDER, David 144
BORDNER, Peter 131 Salome
    131
BORER, Mary Ann 132
BORGESS, Rev O H 151
BORHEM, ___ 148
BORNFF, John 70
BORTNER, John 152
BORUFF, John 70
BOSSLER, Brother 116 D 17 Rev
    D 90 136 210 Rev David 24
BOUCHER, Joseph 207
BOUDINOT, Elias 108
BOULDEN, Wm 19

BOUSH, Jacob 170
BOVEY, Henry 132 217 M 223
BOWDEN, James 108 Susan 171
BOWEN, Rev 199 Elizabeth C 99
BOWERS, Benjamin 184 Lavinia
    174
BOWIE, Dr J 109 Maria Louisa
    109
BOWLES, Widow 11 Abraham 62
    Cath 213 John 28 62 132
BOWLUS, Grandiston Livingston
    108 Samuel 108
BOWMAN, ___ 148 Lt 213
    Benjamin 148 Elizabeth 167
    G W 152 George 103 George
    W 144 John D 202 John D Jr
    202 Joseph 13 William 103
BOWSER, John 144
BOYD, Rev Geo 43 Mary 96 W H
    191
BOYER, _ 44 128 182 Mr 152
    Daniel 164 David 86 Henry
    109 J K 179 220 Jacob 163
    John A 202 Jonas 202 Joseph
    163 Julia Ann 90 Julian 207
    Ledia 166 Louisa 69
BOYERS, William 118
BOYLIN, Mary 36
BRACHE, Sarah 118
BRACKENRIDGE, James 164
    John 126 164 Mary Jane 126
BRADFORD, E G 55 Thomas 151
BRADLEY, Jane 172
BRADSHAW, David 69 John M
    132
BRADY, J E 119 209
BRAGONIER, Rev 81 87 D 15
    Rev D G 69 81 90*96 117 169
    186 195 223 Daniel G 11 Rev
    Daniel G 188 Elizabeth Shin-
    dler 188 Jacob Jr 45 John
    Melville 188 Mrs M E 188

BRAGUNIER, Jacob 17 Rev M 52
BRAINARD, Rev Thomas 77
BRALL, Isaac 210
BRAND, Benj 163
BRANDENBERG, David 35
BRANDENBERGER, Daniel 24
   David 11 Isaac 24
BRANDENBURG, David 187
   Peter 41 S 219
BRANDENBURGER, H 11 Isaac
   11
BRANDERBERG, Sam'l 174
BRANDON, Col John 100
BRANE, Henry 198
BRANTNER, Jacob 17
BRAUCHER, Guelian 198
BREAKBILL, John 145
BRECHBILL, Fred 128 John 73
BRECKENRIDGE, Rev John 155
   Joseph Cabell 124 Margaret
   155 Rev Robert 148
BREDIN, John 99
BREECHBILL, Ann M 216
BREED, Rev W J 215
BREEKENRIDGE, Rev 223
BREIDENBERGER, Jacob 202
BREITENBACH, J 220
BRENDEL, Henry G 185 Melchoir 75 76
BRENDLE, Joseph 187
BRENGLE, Ann R 209 Jacob 83
   Mary C 86
BRENNEMAN, Rev John S 95
BRENNER, ___ 21 Esther 82
   Jacob S 132 180 Michael 132
BRENTLINGER, Susan 213
BRESSLER, Susan 131
BREWER, Mrs 1 Rev 113 Arthur
   214 Joseph 1* Susan A 93
BRICELAIN, Robert 147 Balty
   147
BRIDGER, Edw'd 188
BRIDGEMAN, Rev 112*

BRIDGMAN, Mr 18 Rev William
   45
BRIGGS, Joseph 201
BRIGHT, Margaret 137
BRINDLE, John 81 Veronica 81
BRINKER, Andrew 213 John 213
BRINKLE, Casper 200
BROADRIP, Catharine 169
BROADWELL, Mr 148
BROGUNIER, J 213
BROMBACK, Rachel 97
BROMBAUGH, James 204
BROMWELL, W 105
BRONK, Rev Robert 85
BRONSON, Rev E 145
BRONSTUTE, Basnil 176
BROST, Thoephilus 59
BROTHERTON, ___ 212
BROWER, ___ 164 216 Dr Daniel
   132
BROWN, ___ 116 220 Dr 107
   Judge 203 Rev 12 Catharine
   167 Catharine Ann 80 Chas
   202 Christian 14 David 3 86
   Ellen 203 Geo 148 Geo L 11
   15 Geo W 88 H I 95 H J 103
   106 Henry J 193 Rev Isaac B
   71 Rev J 216 Jacob 194 Rev
   Jno 33 115 John 117* 121
   219 Rev John 15 33 156 167
   198 John Sr 88 John W 165
   Jos 202 Joseph 202 Joseph
   Addison 203 Lydia 115 Mary
   151 163 Mary Ann 88 Mary W
   147 Rev Matthew 147 Samuel
   D 167 Thomas S 125 W A 136
   William 136 Wm 162*
BROWNBACH, John 152 Peter
   71 William 71
BROWNBACK, John 43 Wm 166
BROWNE, Peter A 98
BROWNELLER, Frederick 103
   Samuel 107

BROWNLEE, Nancy 186
BRUBAKER, Jacob 174 Jocob 135 Jos 198
BRUEN, ___ 1 Jane Augusta 71 John 71
BRUMBAUGH, Henry 167 Upton 167
BRUNER, Rev 63 82 108 140 Cath 17 Jno 75 John 127 166 216 Jonathan 17 Lewis 75 M 7 116 Rev Martin 73 132 155
BRUNNER, Rev 218 Catherine 13 Henry 166 Michael 166 Valentine J 123
BRYAN, Capt Benjamin 151 F 223 Fred'k 92 Susan M 151
BUCHANAN, Rev 96 125 Rev Edward Y 96 James 187 Dr
BUCHANAN, James A 208
BUCHECKER, Aaron 198
BUCHER, Judge 181 Rev 177 C 2 14 Daniel 191 Francis 194 G H 187 190 Geo 7 Geo H 186 George H 21 Rev J B 114 J C 115 210 Rev J C 21 35* 41* 45 50 58 62* 70* 76 79 86* 88 92* 94 103* 108 127 140 145 153 164 166 167 175 177* 179 181* 184 186 187 191* 198 201* 203 206 211 213 219* John C 90* 95 200 210 Maria 218 Sarah 124 Susan 18* 168 181
BUCHLER, S H 128
BUCHMAN, H 84
BUCHMANN, Henry 95
BUCHWALTER, David 95 George 166 Wm 166
BUCK, Jacob 50 99 John 179
BUCKEY, Ann Catharine 144 D 182 Daniel 201 Eveline Virginia 201 Mrs M 30 Mary 75 Susan 153

BUCKINGHAM, Mr 147
BUCKY, Charlotte 17
BUDD, S W 143
BUEHLER, Geo E 190 S H 218
BUFFINGTON, John 26 J 62
BULGER, D 116
BULL, James P 192
BULLARD, Bathsheba 132
BULOID, Robert 45
BUNDLE, Mr 199
BURG, Joseph 117
BURGESS, Rev Ebenezer 191
BURK, D 219 William 140 210
BURKHOLDER, Martha 66
BURKITT, H 11
BURNER, Jacob 115
BURNS, Mr 148 A 148*
BURNSIDE, Mary 196 Thos 196
BURNSIDES, James 83
BURROUGHS, Rev William 65
BURROWES, Thomas H 96 Thos H 154
BURROWS, Isaac B 96
BURTON, Hutchins G 53 R H 53
BURY, Joseph 184
BUSH, A 75 W 182 Wm 86
BUSHAR, G 69 213 D M 213 P M 69
BUSHONG, Jacob 160
BUTCHER, Eliza 64
BUTLER, Dr 3 Mr 107 E 3 Elizur 3 Dr H A 126
BUTT, John 185 190
BUTTERBAUGH, Henry 218
BUTTERWORTH, Pleasant 166
BUTTS, Mr 11
BUTZ, Daniel W 18 Polly 198
BUYER, William 124
BUZZARD, Ann Maria 92
BUZZEL, John R 109*
BYCK, Jonas 202
BYERLY, Andrew 138 Mary R 138

BYERS, Mary 222
BYRNE, Edmund 121
C_LLER, Daniel 97
CADOW, Mrs 134 William 134
CADWALLADER, Lydia 93
CADWELL, J 148
CAHOON, Samuel 134
CALDELEUGH, Anne Poyntell 56
  Robert A 56
CALDWELL, Prof 97 J 28 W 128
CALENDER, N 34 216
CALHOUN, Mrs 34 Andrew 189
  W B 101
CALLENDER, N 34 Norman 80
CAMP, David 124 Mary Ann 150
CAMPBEL, James 95 Margaret 38
CAMPBELL, John 159 Robt 121
CAMERON, James 223*
CANDY, Jacob 181 Matilda 113
CANNON, Rev F E 215
CANTANOS, Jose Maria 120
CAPE, John 156
CARES, Mr 102 Rev 92 210 Ann 181 J 42 Rev J 56 70 99 190 195 209 John 38 Rev John 15 26 38 133 163 195 199 201 214 P 195 209 Peter 195
CARIL, Joseph 144
CARKER, Daniel 103
CARL, Geo 170 221
CARLTON, Messrs 78 Eliza Janette 102 Thomas 102
CARMACK, John 186 Sarah 186
CARMAOTH, Hanson 190
CARNEY, Michael 121
CAROTHERS, Andrew 64 Ann 171 Elizabeth 103 Thos 171
CARPENTER, Alva 200* Col Henry 80 J 38 109 Jeremiah 213 Dr John S 96 Salome 96
CARR, Mrs 165 Otho 165
CARSON, J O 94 James O 42*

CASE, Chester 202
CASEY, H B 148 Henry 148 Thomas 92
CASHMAN, John 150 170
CASPER, ___ 148
CASSADY, Mary 121
CASSAT, Mrs 8
CASSEL, Elizabeth 124
CASSELBERY, William 166
CASTINI, ___ 219
CASTLE, Charles H 47 Elizabeth 219 Otho 219 Samuel N 79
CASTNER, Jesse 174 219 Jesse Jr 174
CATHCART, Rev Dr 11 Miss W 69
CELL, John 34
CELLY, Jonathan 138*
CEROEL, C A 53
CHAMBERLIN, Mr 3 Isaac 134
CHAMBERS, Mr 156 Arthur W 129 Capt Benjamin 109 Ellen De Witt 193 Geo 25 66 148 George 76 199 209 John 121 193 Mary 136 Sarah 15 109 Solomon 128 Thomas 209 Thos 209 Dr Wm 129
CHAMBERSBURG, H S 7
CHAMPLIN, Mrs Wm H 183
CHAMPNEYS, B 130 200
CHANDLER, Samuel 165
CHANEBAND, Mr 95
CHANEY, Elias 213
CHANNING, Dr W 107
CHAPIN, Rev Calvin 19
CHAPLINE, Jane 103
CHAPMAN, Mr 148 J 148
CHARITON, James 50 111
CHARLES, Capt 73
CHARTERS, Susannah 112
CHASE, Chester 202
CHAUNCEY, Dr 182
CHEANEY, Lewis 160

CHEEVER, Mr 107
CHENEY, Ezekial 54
CHENOWITH, Rexton 99
CHICKEM, ___ 156
CHILDERS, Hastur M 22 Matilda 22
CHORPENNING, Cyrus 204 Ellas 204 G 219 Geo 204 Henry 219 Peter 204
CHOYCE, Ann 174
CHRI_MAN, Henry 198
CHRISMAN, Henry 135 J 141 216
CHRISSMAN, John 192
CHRIST, John 159 Jonathan 31 Rebecca 31
CHRISTIAN, Daniel 24 Geo 38 J 99
CHRISTMAN, Ann 75 Chas 202 Joseph 80 Samuel 166
CHRONISTER, Mary 184
CHURCH, Mrs 53
CISNA, William 110
CLABAUGH, Harriet 190 John 190
CLAIR, Wm 121
CLAPP, Mrs 191 A 193 A Jr 193 Abraham 55 198 Barbara N 198 Col D 181 Col Daniel 132 Daniel F 181 Eliza 181 Elizabeth 174 Elizabeth A 132 George 174 Henry 198 J G 193 Capt J H 218 J Henry 198 John Sr 193 John 193 Joshua 193 Nathaniel B 170 Rebecca Louisa 218
CLARE, Mrs 223
CLARK, Capt 176 Rev 218 Caroline 72 Garret 198 Rev J A 131 J W 107 John 64 144 Josiah B 199 Mary 88 Rebecca Louisa 218 S S 148 Saml 176 Sarah Ann 82 Willis G 56

CLARKE, Adam 88 Ellen Marion 87 Mathew St Clair 87
CLARKSON, Rev Thomas B 60
CLARY, Rev J 134
CLAUSING, Lewis Henninger 62*
CLAYTON, ___ 99 W A 101
CLEARY, Rev John 70
CLEEN, Susan 187
CLEM, John 93 Snsan 93
CLEMENT, ___ 45 William A B 45
CLEN___ Michael 146
CLIFTON, C W 156
CLINCH, Gen 40
CLINE, Rev 59 Rev John P 94 Wm 65
CLINTON, Rev Mr 4
CLIPPINGER, Ant. 85 B Ann 85
CLODFELTER, Henry 28
CLOPER, John 58
CLOSE, Elijah 196
CLOTFELTY, J 185
CLOTH, Hen 205
CLUBB, Fred'k 121
CLUGSTON, Isaac 170 Capt John 147
COBE, B 177
COBLENTS, John Philip 219 Philip 219
COBLENTX, John Sr 164
COBLENTZ, Charles Washington 79 Dan'l 11 David 47 Eugenia Cleantha 198 Henry 45* 181 198 J 11 132 179 J P 132 184 219* Jno 11 John 11 35* 79 132* 179 219 John Sr 21 41* 201 John P 24 35 132 166 201 219 John Philip 79 Leonora 184 Maj P 180 Peter 11 Peter Jr 41*
COBLENTZSMITH, J 11
COBURN, Dr Charles 145
COCHRAN, Alfred Hamilton 187 Henry 41 132 187 John J 218

COCHRANE, Henry 166
COCKERILL, John 147
COE, Rev 215 Joseph D 219
COFFEE, J 121
COFFELT, Lydia 181
COFFROTH, Julian 152
COLBURN, Zera 195
COLDER, Mr 160 Mary Adaline 170
COLDSMITH, J D 187
COLE, Emily Ann 51 Sarah T 145
COLEMAN, C 102 Miss C 111 Catharine 102 213 Edward 113 Henry E 120 Nicholas 69 Thos Byrd 68 William 113
COLHOUN, Mrs 95 A 95 Alex. 112 121 M A 137 Mary 121
COLHOUSER, F 180 202
COLLIER, Dr 147
COLLIFLOWER, Rev 201 216 Elizabeth 94 G 30* Geo 94 George 95 99 Rev W 154 157 175 187 W F 198 Rev W F 167 181 198 William F 16 32 Rev Wm F 177
COLLIFLOWR, Rev W F 189
COLLINGS, Sarah Jane 210
COLLINS, Asahel 165 George 159 Rev John 56 Joshua 159 Richard 159
COMEGEYS, William 172
COMER, Wm 148
COMERFORD, ___ 116
COMINGO, Henry G 145
COMPTON, C 185 D 195
COMSTCOK, J L 101
CONDE, Rev Daniel T 79
CONLEY, John 176
CONRAD, Joseph 222 Logan 77 Susan 140 Rev W 79 199 213 William 16 Wm 213
CONVER, Samuel 166
CONWAY, Wm B 222
COOK, Mr 136 Adam 99 Eleanora R C 221 Geo 110 213 George 11 43 110 177 George Jr 74 154 Jacob 186 James 143 John 44 174 176 188 John B 221 John F 123 221 Martha Ann 123 Mary 18 Michael Sr 195 P 194 Peter 11 48* 173 Peter Sr 201 Wm 154
COOKE, ___ 116 Amos S 79 John B 194
COOKSTON, Jesse 197
COOKUS, John T 196 Sarah 196
COOLBAUGH, Margaret 15
COOLEY, Geo 163
COOLY, William 41
COONTZ, Charles 150 Jacob 150 191
COOPER, Maj 40 Miss 159 F 125 Jane 160 Rosanna 182 Samuel 160 Thomas 182 Thomas J 78 W 37
COOVER, John 214
COPES, Henry 121
COPPERSMITH, L F 221
CORBITT, Henry C 121
CORDMAN, Mathias 136
CORIGAN, ___ 116
CORN, Thos B 214
CORNISH, Capt Asa 220 Elam 220 Elisha 220* Lidia 220 Nathan 220 Newell 220 Norton 220
CORNMAN, Elenora 208
CORNWELL, Rev W 216
CORPENING, A 53 109 G 53
CORR, John 132
CORREE, David 28
CORREL, David 117 175
CORRELL, Catherine 102 D 53 69 David 69 180 John 102 180 P 53 Peter 202

CORT, Daniel 138 Daniel Jr 187
  Jacob 138
CORWELL, Henry 140
COSLEY, Eliza Jane 132 Mary 99
COSS, H 184
COST, Miss C 216 Cath. 78 G 11
  George 186 H 78 164 191 192
  Henry 11 32* 78 131 John 32
  125 180 Peter 110 Sam 206
  Sam'l 200 Samuel R 219
COUFFER, Rebecca 134
COULTER, Catharine M 116 D
  102* E P 117 Elkanah 98 J
  109 148 156* 188* John 86*
  116 188 W R 98
COUNTRYMAN, B 148
COUTER, Jacob 71 Mary 123
COVER, Mrs 87 Andrew 87
  Jacob 13 15 John 15 78
COVERLY, Dr Thomas Z 113
  Wells 170
COYNER, Mary 156
COWAN, J W 34 John W 34
  Mary 34 Thomas 34 Wm 126
COWEN, Rev 199
COWGAR, Jesse 126
COWLES, Rev George 121
COWPERWAITE, Jos 119
COX, Rev 82 J F 219
COXE, Wm S 109
COY, Jacob 132 180
COYLE, Eleanor 149
COYNER, Mary 156
CRABB, Louisa 59
CRAIG, Isabel W 145 Matthew
  150 Neville B 145
CRAIN, Joseph A 180
CRAMER, Mr 176 Christian 103
  204 David 17 32 Frederick 94
  H 94 Harriet 222 Henry 17 32
  34 73 Jacob 84 Col Jacob 47
  191 John 58 Joseph 64 L 186
  Lewis 17 32 Mary 17 Mary M

CRAMER (Continued)
  47 Philip H 17 Samuel 153
CRAMPTON, Eli 24 73 J 184 S
  184
CRANE, Dr F L 18
CRAUSE, Daniel 144 Jacob 219
  Peter 219
CRAWFORD, ___ 116 Mrs 198
  Rev 157 170 Edward 198
  Elizabeth R 141 Holmes 192
  Rev J 56 Rev J H 47 83 130
  181 214 218 Jacob 214 Rev
  John H 87 R 30 Robert 214 R
  Ross 121 Sarah B 38 T Hart-
  ley 25 38 Mrs T H 66
CREAGER, Solomon 19 66 84
CREE, James 175 Mary 142
CREIGH, Ann H 73 Dr John 73
  Rev R 184 Rev Tho 182 Rev
  Thos 209 Rev Thomas 35 73
  86 126 140 180 196 Rev Tho's
  86
CRESSLER, Ann C 131
CRESSMAN, Hannah 222
CRIDER, Jacob 198 John 69
CRILLEY, John B 134
CRINE, Maria 28 Decatur 28
  Peter G 27 28* Theodore 28
CRISWELL, Isabella 81 Jas 81
  John 126 Keziah 163 Marga-
  retta 126 Thomas G 134
CRITS, Job 180
CROCKER, Mr 128*
CRONE, Catharine 203 Conrad
  203
CRONISE, H 55 John 174
CROOKS, John 172 Rebecca 217
  Robert 217
CROOM, Mr H B 121
CROPPER, Thomas B 121
CROSS, Rev 223 Elizabeth 148
  Jacob 172 Susanna 213 Wil-
  liam 148

CROSSEL, John 195
CROSSLAN, Emanuel 53 136
    John 136
CROUSE, D 119 Daniel 69 105
    111 210 Samuel 164
CROUSER, Hannah 69
CROW, John 84
CROWELL, Col 55
CRULLE, Ann Maria 167
CRUM, Barbara 108 Henry 108
CRUMBERGER, D 214
CRUMMEL, Sarah 161
CULBERTSON, Mr 156 Mrs 78
    Anetta 151 Augustus 182
    Dorcas 138 Mrs Jos 32 Dr S
    D 182 Stephen 151 Dr William 95
CULP, Peter 197
CUMMING, Dr Robert 66
CUMMINGS, E 114 Eleanor P 114
CUMMINS, John B 83
CUNNINGHAM, Joseph 119
    Priscilla 138
CURFMAN, Catharine 192
CURREY, John 97 Susan 97
CURTIN, Andrew 184
CURTIS, G W P 79
CUSHING, David 128
CUSHWA, Capt 94 Benj 186 213
    D M 118 David 94 135 John C
    170 Jonathan 118 Sarah 186
    W A 184
CUSHWAS, D M 30
CUSTER, Phil 195
CUYLER, Rev 68 107
D___ETH, Cap 204
DAGGY, Jacob 207 M 207
DAILY, Henry 144
DALE, J M 121 M G 26
DALGARN, Mary Ellen 146
DALGREW, W S 121

DALLAM, Mr 219
DALLAS, T B 99
DANCHAUER, Mary 166
DANNER, Abraham 217 Ann M
    133 Charlotte 133 Daniel 166
    George 115 J R 214 Joel B
    150 183 Joseph 35 M 8 64
    119 190 Martin 146 147
DANY, Anna 116
DARBY, David 136 J 190 John 187
DARE, Susan 106
DARNER, J 190 John 24 213
    Lydia 88
DARST, Mary 147
DASHIELL, Mary E 83
DATROW, G 33 J 33
DAUBERMAN, George 146
DAUBERT, Charles 116
DAUGHERTY, ___ 119*
DAVENPORT, Catharine 151 213
DAVIDSON, Dr James 78
DAVIE, Rev J T Marshall 55
DAVIES, John W 162
DAVIS, Capt 157 C 181 Charles
    184 D L 176 David 166 Elias
    216 Hannah 97 Isaac 145 148
    Jane 95 132 Jesse 71 John
    199 Josiah 181 L 90 Levi 190
    Sam'l 174 Miss Sidney 165
    William S 99
DAVISON, John 95
DAY, Charles 87
DAYS, Catharine H 92
DEAL, Francis 56 Henry 95
DEAM, A 132 H 132
DEAN, Anna Mary 192 Margaret
    180 William 58 Wm 181
DEARDORF, Susannah 78
DEAVER, ___ 181
DEBERG, Mr 176
DeBOUCHERVILLE, Geo 125

DECHANT, Rev J W 12 16*
	Jacob William 11
DECHERT, E 213 Elijah 69
	Jonathan 57
DECK, Wm 202
DECKER, Daniel 16 G 182
	James 118 Michial 163
DEDECKER, Catharine 149
DEGENHARDT, Christian 13
DeHART, Capt 150
DEHOFF, ___ 213
DEHUFF, H 138 202
DEICHMAN, Dr 216
DEIFENBACHER, John 170
DEININGER, Mary 139
DEISCHER, Ellen J 116
DEITRICH, C 187
DeJAUNE, ___ 148
DELDVAN, E C 105
DELLENGER, Samuel 148
DELLERBACH, Dr 204
DELLINGER, Adam 38 David 98
	Fred'k 136 Jacob 53 Lewis 98
DEMME, Rev R C 95
DENIG, Catharine 176 Jane 222
	John 84 95 Lewis 35* 119
	173 193 195 201* Dr Robert
	H 165 Sarah 184
DENIUS, Rev S K 10 160 William
	Gellert 160
DENLER, Philip 174
DENNISTON, J 175
DENNY, Rev 109 110 148 Rev D
	38 59 60 126* 132 146 David
	180 Rev David 77 95 110 120
	121 133 134 180 197 Dr
	James 110 John F 209
	Margaret 133 134
DENTON, Rev Francis 38
DERING, Miss C 179 Cath 194
	Miss E 219
DERNER, John 11 41
DERR, David 145 Mary Ann 190

DERRINGER, Amanda Melvina
	155 Henry 155
DESCOMBES, Rev J 103 201
DeSELD_N, Mr 217
DeSELDING, Mr 217
DESHLER, Mrs 141
DESRIVIERES, Rodolphe 125
DETRICH, David 208 Margarret-
	ta R 208
DETWILER, ___ 206
DEVELBISS, David 17 George 17
DEVILBISS, Geo 32
DEVOR, June 58
DEWALT, Peter 99
DEWART, Lewis 14
DeWITT, Rev 77 Rev Wm R 107
DEYOUNG, Philip 202
DEYSERT, Catharine 221
DICK, A 151 213 N 151 213 S 13
DICKENSHIED, Anna Maria 173
	Dr C 216 Dr Charles 173
DICKEY, David 98 Elizabeth 77
DICKINSON, Rev 131 Rev Austin
	55
DIEFENBACHER, Henry 170
DIEFENDERFER, John 86
DIEFFENBACHER, Rev 70 Rev J
	70 Rev J F 2 10 55 76 126
	185 Rev J G 136 Rev Jacob G
	137 Jane C 10 Rev L E 102
DIEFFENDERFER, ___ 128 182
	Mrs Dr 148 216 C 181 J C
	184 Jacob 184 John 184
DIEFFENTHALER, Jacob 185
DIEHL, Adam 144 Elias 144
	Henry 141 John Jr 144 John
	Sr 144 Jonathan 144 Jonas
	144 Michael 144 Philip 144
	Samuel 122 Solomon 75 144
	Solomon Jr 144 Solomon Sr
	144
DIENER, Christian 219
DIETRICH, Christ'n 94

DIETUS, John T 128
DIETZ, Edward Lauman 210 J
    190 Jacob 210 217*
DIFFENBACHER, Rev J F 153
    Rev Jacob 15
DIFFENBAUCHER, Rev J F 214
DIFFENDERFER, __ 44 C 105
    Charles 167
DILLER, Dr David 170 Rev Jacob
    W 78
DILLON, Colly 148 Holly 148
    Sarah 107
DILWORTH, Taylor 131
DINGES, Philip 145
DISOWAY, G W 101
DITTO, John 94
DIVELBISS, Catharina Sophia
    219 Capt Geo 219
DIVELY, A 216 Abraham 74 144
    179 Margaret 144 Martin 144
DIXON, James 159
DOBLER, Christian 50 150
DODD, Mary Ann 160
DODGE, Rev Jonas 147 Rev N
    19 Nehemiah 15 19
DOERNBERG, Nicholas 144
DOHM, John 216
DOLBY, Capt 170
DOLL, Bernard 34 170 Cathrine
    50 Charles Edward 115 Christian W 16 D H 30 118 127*
    170 184 191* Daniel H 34 43
    170 Ezra 17 115 Jacob 180
    Jonas 139 Joseph F 149 Miss
    M 187 Rosanna 30 70 170
    Sarah 204
DOLLAND, Richard 121
DOLLINGER, Daniel 187
DOME, Sam'l 164
DONAGHUE, Peter 121
DONALDSON, Andrew 148
    Charles 198
DONAT, A 186 Abr 222

DONAVIN, Jeremiah 151
DONNELLEY, Mr 78 105 Catharine 105
DORNARICE, Elizabeth Ann 122
DORRANCE, James 90
DORWART, Samuel 73 107
DOSH, Elizabeth 52 W 187
DOUB, E 195
DOUBT, George 215
DOUGHERTY, __ 105 Mr 190
    James 125 Rody 184 Wm 151
DOUGHTY, John 202
DOUGLAS, Rev 179 Isaas 156
    James 148 R 15 38* 132 Rev
    R 70 153 181 192 203 219
    Robert 48 Rev Robert 69 74
    132 181
DOUGLASS, Isaac 83 Jas 148
    Rev M 30 Rev R 92 Rev Robert
    192
DOWNES, W H 132
DOWNEY, S J 117 174 Sam J
    180 Samuel J 38 W 184
DOWNING, Col 128* Thomas
    156
DOYLE, Mr 158 James 105 John
    99
DRAYER, John 191
DRECK, John 132
DREISBACH, Aron 215 Jacob
    215
DRENNER, Jeremiah 93
DREVITZ, Jacob 114
DREYER, Fredk 90 Susannah 90
DREYFUSS, Leopold 99
DRIESBACH, Jost 202 Margaretta 202 Michael 202
DRIESBAUCH, George 146
DRILL, Elizabeth Ann 204
DRINKER, Capt 121
DRUCKENMILLER, Daniel 95
DRUM, John 56 Simon 37 84
    148

DRUMBORE, Isaac 222
DRURY, Silas 176
DRYER, Frederick 148
DUBEC, J 125
DUBOIS, Mr 39
DUBOSE, Mr 41
DUBS, Rev J S 184
DUBBS, Brother 184 Rev 113 116 198 Cha's 87 J S 84 Rev J S 175 Moses 144
DUDEN, William 144
DUDLEY, Professor 97
DUDRAW, Jacob 188
DUDRO, Jacob 84 Rebecca 105
DUENGER, Rev R 43 156
DUER, Wm A 101
DUFF, __ 116
DUFFIELD, Rev G 75 James 36 154 200 Dr John 113 Josiah 175 177
DUFFY, Matthew 106
DULL, Frederick 174
DUNBAR, Matilda 81
DUNCAN, A E E 32 A S E 71 38 D 145 157 David 36 145 Elizabeth 164 James 145 Ja's 36 John B 126 Joseph 209 Margaret Ann 209 Wm 37
DUNHAM, Miss 148* Mr 128
DUNLAP, Eliza 90 Rev Robert W 150
DUNLOP, Deborah 73
DUNN, E 148 George H 189 James 121 Mrs Michael C 126
DUNWOODY, David 197
DUR, T 94 Thomas 94
DURBORAW, James S 96
DURYEE, Richard 25
DUSING, John 80
DUTCHER, William 26*
DUTERER, W 214
DUTRO, Philip 132
DUTROW, David 174

DUTTEROH, Samuel 11
DWIGHT, Mr 117 124 Frederick 148 Rev H G O 115* 117 196 Theodore Jr 101
DYCE, __ 152
DYER, Julia Ann 152
DYKES, Catharine 68 Mary Ann 70
DYOTT, Dr 190 R T W 183
E__ Solomon 62
E__H__LMAN, Jacob 184
E__PENSHIP, Henry 166
EAKLE, Mary 19 48 164 Wm 213
EARLS, John 32
EARLY, William 142
EARNEST, Sam 180
EARNST, Catharine 174 William 174
EASTON, Rev Jno S 103
EBAUGH, David 8 Rev J S 72 John 8
EBBERT, E 194 223 J 152 Jacob 199
EBERHART, Michael D 184
EBERLE, John 137
EBERLY, Daniel 207 John 82
EBERMAN, Ellen 116 John M 116
EBERT, Adam 146 Clarissa 146 D 221 Saml 166 Sarah 21
ECHELBERGER, Mary 97
ECHERT, Dr Geo N 198 Isaac 198 Peter 198
ECKART, Jacob 99
ECKER, Deborrah 166
ECKERMAN, Eleanor 49
ECKERT, Egbert 78 Frederick 106 Geo 204 George L 90 184 H 184* Henry 90 J K 184 John 111 William 184 Wm Jr 184
ECKMAN, John 56 115
ECKTON, Jetson 198

- 275 -

EDDY, Rev C 215
EDINGS, Mr 156
EDLEMAN, Margaret 204
EDWARDS, Gen 94 Mrs 223 J 53
   John 156 John W 170 Robert
   P 156 Samuel 223 Wm 156
EGGERS, Rev L 182 Rev L G 137
EHRHART, John W 166 Sarah
   116
EHRMAN, Sarah 99
EICHELBERGER, Barnitz 146
   147 Elizabeth Jane 113 Col
   Frederick 68 Henrietta 146
   147 Julia Ann 184 M 186
   Martin 113 148 Matthew 185
   Peter 214
EICHHOLTZ, John F 97
EIKER, S 223
EILENBERGER, D 184 H 184
EILER, Daniel 129
EISENBERG, E 184 John 166
   Lawrence 174 221
EISENBERGER, Samuel 105
EISENHARD, Mary 184
EISHELBERGER, Adam 56 Anna
   Mary 56
ELDER, Preston B 202
ELDRES, John 201
ELLIOTT, Mr 156 G 182 George
   M 96 J H 157
ELLIS, Mr 198 Elizabeth C 56
   Joseph 31
ELLISON, Stewart 121
ELLMAKER, Amos 98 Nath 98
ELLSWORTH, H L 138
ELMES, Thomas 32
ELY, Dr 96 Mrs R 70 91 95
   Rebecca 184
EMANNEL, ___ 41
EMBICH, Eliza Ann 110
EMERICH, Eliza 56 Peter 195
   215
EMERSON, Rev 222

EMLER, Joseph 144
EMORY, Mary 131
EMSCHWILLER, Ann Eliza 173
   Eliza 70 H 152 Henry 173
   Rebecca Adelaide 173
EMSEWILER, Ann E 201
ENGARD, Mrs C 156
ENGEL, William 215
ENGERD, Catharine 32
ENGLER, Chas 215 Joseph 215
ENSIGS, Elijah 176
ENTLER, Catharine 126 Elenora
   Amelia 209 P 216
EPPLY, Adam 124
ERDLE, Henry 146 Jacob 146
   John 146
ERMENTROUT, Miss C 213
   Catharine 107 H 107 111 121
   213 Rev H 213 Henry 69 213
   219 John 138 216
ERNSPERGER, ___ 99
ERNST, Rev 130 John M 126
   Margaret 192
ERWIN, Isaac 53 86
ESHBACH, Solomon 186
ESHBAUGH, David 222
ESPY, George R 195 J P 101
ESSIG, Sarah Jane 49
ESSOM, David 60 Maria 131
ETCHEBERGER, ___ 170 George
   182
ETIMIRE, David 175
ETTER, Mrs 159 Christian 159
EUDIG, John 148
EVANS, E L 202 H W 77 John
   126 202 Mary P 86 Philip 152
   Thomas 140
EVERETT, Edward 101
EVERHARD, J 11
EVERHART, Geo 179 George 179
   J 91 Maria Elizabeth 179
   Mich'l D 184
EVERSOLE, C 150

EVICK, Elizabeth Ann 132
EWALD, Hannah L 95
EWING, Nathaniel 99
EXLINE, Adam H 144 Daniel 144
   David 95 144 186 John 144
EYE, ___ 179 John 162
EYELENBERGER, David 15
   Henry 15
EYERMAN, Miss M 181
EYLER, Rachel 132 180
EYSTER, Eleanor 90 George 90
   Geo S 110 Michael 184
F___ Cynthia 191
FABER, C J 164 E 19 Edward
   203 Eve 28 194 F 19 J F 16
   Rev John Theobald 13*
FABLER, J 94
FAHNESTOCK, Benjamin 19
   Eliza 69 Mrs M 203 P 95 Dr P
   25 36 Samuel 19 69 80
FAILS, Sarah Ann 93
FALKENOR, William 144
FAMER, Isabella 141
FANSHAW, Daniel 63
FARNEY, J H 53
FARRELL, James 39
FARRINGTON, Mr 28*
FASSNACHT, Amos 129
FATZINGER, Thomas 202
FAUBLE, Jos D 186
FAUGHT, Julian 90
FAUHLE, Joseph 185
FAULKERSON, ___ 140
FAUSE, Frederick 144
FAUST, Rev Benjamin 12 Henry
   77 Peter 77
FAWBER, A 180
FAY, Rev Warren 19
FAYMAN, Geo 210
FEASER, Jacob 70
FEASTER, Elizabeth Eleanor 114
   H 116 Henry 114 J Sr 203
   John Sr 164

FECHEN, Barbara 81
FEDENIC, Rebecca 184
FEETE, Br 164 Brother 195 D
   175 Rev D 166 175 185 214
   Rev Dan'l 190 Daniel 16 32
   Rev Daniel 121 132 Henry 62
   Mary A 185
FEEZER, Jacob 196 Sarah 196
FEGLEY, Geo 202
FEGLY, David 132 Hannah 132
FEHL, Peter 118
FEID, Peter 139
FEIGHT, Henry 144
FELDEN, Christian 144
FELEKLEY, Jacob 53
FELGER, J 182
FELKER, Abr 213 John 213
FELLBAUM, Margaret 172
FELLTY, Philip 188
FELMLEE, Moses 91
FELTY, ___ 133
FENE_ Rev J 193
FENKE, Henry 191
FENNER, Henry 215
FENSTERMACHER, Ephraim
   184 Jona 202
FERGUSON, David 175 Jane 175
   Wm 168 213
FERRANT, William P 77
FERREN, Evelina 187
FERRIS, ___ 148
FETTER, Elvinia A 77 H 185
   Henry 51 185 Wm 139 197
FETTERER, Lewis 109
FETTERHOFF, Michael 14
FETTERMAN, Washington W 177
FETZER, Mary 136
FEUCHT, John 144
FICKES, Jacob 144 177 Josiah
   122
FIELD, Stephen 1
FIELDS, Ira 87 W R 132
FIERY, Joseph 171

FIESER, James 199 Rebecca 76
FILE, Elizabeth 108
FILSON, J R 99 Robert 152 208
FINDLAY, Mrs 207 Archibald I 74 217 E J 95 Eleanor 118 Col John 118 170 Mary 74 Sarah 25 95 William 217
FINDLEY, Catharine A 218
FINFROCK, Cath 142 Mary 184
FINFRUCK, Daniel 17
FINGER, __ 156 188 Daniel 109 Jos. 77 Mich 188 Michael 77 109 156 Peter 43 77 109 R 53
FINK, Emanl 216 John 32
FINLEY, Dr 102 Rev 187 Sarah 102
FINN, __ 116
FIPBER, J 53
FIROR, Daniel 84 133 Jacob 51 Sophia Barbara 137
FISCHER, Rev P S 219
FISHER, Mr 94 Ann 141 George 99 John 72 116 128 146* Joseph 180 214 Rev P S 11 45 70 80 139 179 197 208 Rev Peter S 99 Rev R 221 R A 95 156 Rev R A 179 Rev Richard A 95 106 S R 182 Rev S R 74* 107 116 148 153 168 182* 190 194 202 213* 220 223 Saml R 32* 70 Rev Saml R 78 83 93 95 196 William 77 146 199 214 William Sr 88 Wm 38
FISK, Dr 8 Julius 223
FISSLE, Lydia 124
FISTER, J 190 Jacob 11 14 John 11 24 35
FITZGERALD, John 166 174 Joseph T 174 Lehman 121
FLACK, George 95
FLANAGAN, Amelia 125 Jno 125* Lucretia B 125
FLANDERS, Christian W 16

FLEAGLE, D 132
FLEEK, Nicholas 200
FLEGEL, Samuel 192
FLEISHER, Christina 83
FLEMING, __ 210 Mr 100 Frances 206 J 148 James 200 John 210 Joseph 192* 200
FLEMMAN, Edward 148
FLETCHER, Richard 107
FLICKINGER, Daniel 195 John 120 195
FLIEGER, Andrew 137
FLINTON, Joseph 41
FLOHR, Elizabeth 77
FLOOK, Daniel 50 132 206 Elizabeth 186 Jacob 11 32 50 88 114 186 210 211 213 Jno 32 John 88 186 213 John H 32 Lewis Hamilton 114 Mary Jane 210 211 Matthias 208 Perry 186 Perry F 88 Phil 206 Philip 11 35 Susan 93
FLOYD, Gen John 113 Wm R 121
FLORY, Hannah 218
FLUBACHER, Charlotte 216
FLUCK, Abraham 199 H 133 Henry 144 152 J 11 Jacob 11 24 M 11
FOCKLER, George 123
FOERSCH, Rev 91 121 Rev J A 106
FOGEL, S W 152
FOGER, Jacob 88
FOGLE, Willoughby 120
FOIL, Moses 138 Sophia 72
FOLCK, Henry 216* J 168
FOLK, John Jr 144
FOLKNER, W 179
FOLLMER, Christian 215 D 198
FOLLY, Mrs 50
FOLMER, Philip 170
FONNEY, S S 150

FOOTE, Samuel 89 Rev W H 215
FORCE, Sophia 58
FORD, Dr 4 Eliza Ann 80
FORDNEY, William B 124
FORE, Eliza 45 Capt George 45
FOREMAN, Mr 71*
FORNEY, Adam 71 J H 77 Jacob 120 195 John 11 John W 218 Lewis J 11 Lewis S 213 Margaret 142 S S 214 Samuel S 100 Sarah 71 Sarah Amelia 100 Simon 131 Thomas 53
FORREST, Wm 101
FORREY, Dr 36 Catharine 36
FORSTER, John 145 John Jr 204
FORWARD, C 152 Chauncey 219
FORWOOD, Jac 133 Thoms 216
FOSTER, H F 77
FOTE, John Jr 122
FOTLER, Eliza 148 Filbin 148 Greke 148 J 148 Jacob 148 Joseph 148 Susan 148
FOUCK, Lewis 17
FOUK, George 26
FOULK, Ann 188
FOULKE, Barton 109
FOUSE, William 144
FOUST, Mrs 106 Christian 193 Daniel 181 193 George 106 Geo Sr 47 H 193 Henry 218 Levi 218 P 193 Rebecca 47 Sarah 181 W 193
FOUT, Greenberry 187
FOUTZ, Samuel 99
FOWLER, Ryan 132
FOX, Henry 121 John 213 Julian 166 Mary 166
FOXWELL, George 121
FRALEIGH, George 34 79
FRAMER, E 181
FRANCISCUS, Henry 155
FRANKLIN, ___ 148 Dr 151

FRANKLIN (Continued) Thomas E 124 Walter 43 Rev Walter E 92 Col Walter S 99
FRANKS, Catherine 77
FRANSOE, Chas 202
FRANTZ, Samuel 168
FRASE, Mich 202
FRASER, Capt 131*
FRASS, Jacob 190
FRAUNFELDER, Jac Jr 202 Jac Sr 202 Mich 202 Peter 202
FRAUTZ, Jesse 166
FRAVEL, Ann 137 B 180 Benj 149 Daniel H 177 Elizabeth M 149 Joseph 201 Samuel J 160
FRAZIER, ___ 212
FREANER, Henry 38
FREAS, John 141
FREDERICK, Philip 194 Samuel 11 208
FREEMAN, Elias 180 John G 148 Warren 156
FREESE, A P 166 Rev A P 186 201 222
FREEZE, Rev 153 Rev A P 116 129 133 137 143 148* 153 186 188 191 219 Andrew P 24 Ann M 135 Catharine 174 Franey 175 Geo 188 J P 197 John P 148 Samuel 175
FREEZLIN, John 98
FREIER, Bernhart 163 Henry 163 Peter 163
FREIMYER, W 198
FRENCH, A H 95 Francis B 80 Rev Ozro 191 Thomas 219 Tiberius 130
FRETZ, Jac 222
FREY, Anna Mary 94* Catharine 210 Elizabeth 184 Henry 94 Jacob 166 John 184 John B 139 Lydia 166 Michael 202 Moses 167

FREYDINGER, Catharine 97
   Christina 46
FREYMAN, Chas 184
FRICK, Anna 166 Fronica 166
   Henry 145 166* Jacob 184
   John 166
FRICKER, Jacob 213
FRIDGE, Alexander 182
FRIDINGER, John 116
FRIEDLANDER, Joseph R 190
FRIEND, Elijah 223 Freeman
   223 Harriet 223* John 223*
   Joseph 223 Mrs K T 203
   Reese 223
FRIES, Rev J H 88 150 156
FRIESE, Rev 201
FRITCHEY, Rev 43 J G 67 195
   Rev J G 98 102 156* 172 195
   219 Rev John G 117 175 188
FRITCHY, Rev J G 116 135
FROM, Jonas 156
FROMM, Jonas 201
FROST, Dr 130 Daniel Jr 14
FRUTCHEY, Mathias 215 William 166
FRUTCHY, Peter 215
FRUTTCHEY, Peter 215
FRY, Alonzo 95 Andrew 85
   Catherine 85 Jacob 146
   James 148 Mary 91
FRYSINGER, George Jr 203
FUHRMAN, Henry 166
FULLER, Rev William 115
FULLERTON, David 209 Ruth 34
   Thomas 147
FULTON, John 186
FULWILER, John 51 135 William B 129
FUNK, __ 38 Elizabeth 61 John
   17 Jos 216 Joseph 198 M 41
   Martin 51
FURLONG, Robert 177*
FURMAN, B 148

FURST, George 210 John 210
FUSS, J 187 Joseph 90
G__ Christian 28
G_TH, Jones 184
GABBY, Margaret C 120
GABEL, Elizabeth 91
GABLE, John 208
GAFFNEY, Barney 176
GALE, L H 101
GALWITH, Sarah Ann 198
GAMBER, Daniel 34
GAMBLE, Mr 101
GANT, Martin 32
GARDNER, Elizabeth 204 Ellenora 68 Ferdinand 120 Jacob 68
   M 190 Rebecca 204
GARLIU, Mary 30
GARNER, J 183 Wesley W 61 183
GARNETT, James M 101
GARRET, Mr 12
GARRETSON, Mr 39 Joseph 116
GARROT, Erasm. 79 Dr J D 186
GARROTT, Dr 219 Cordelia 153
   Dr J D 32 Dr John D 153
GARTHWAITE, J R 176
GARTMAN, Ab 15 Jacob 15
GARVER, Abr 192 Jacob 60 223
   Jacob Jr 181 John 52 Samuel
   32 Samuel Lewis 181
GASS, Jacob 95
GAST, C 148 200 Christian 73
GATES, __ 148 Rev C 61 79* 145
GAUGLER, William 146
GAUMP, Laura W 55
GAVER, David 41* Hannah M 41
   Lydia 167
GAY, Mrs 107 H 107*
GEAR, Rev Ezekiel T 213
GEATRELL, George 174
GEBHART, Rev J 26
GEDNEY, __ 40
GEIB, Christian 201

GEIGER, Rev 69 127 128 199 201 Ann Catharine 20 Rev J 138 179* Rev J J 32 Jacob 61 Rev Jacob 20 61 69 138 183
GEIMAN, Jacob 138
GEISER, John J 202
GEISSENHAINER, Rev F W Sr 152
GEISSINGER, Christian 184 Jacob 184
GEISTWEID, Rev George 9
GEISTWEIT, Rev Geo 112 Magdalena 112
GEISY, Mrs 197 J U 184
GELBERT, Dr Jesse 150
GEMBERLING, Philip 146
GENTIS, Isaac 180
GENTZEL, William 176
GEORGE, Mr 176 Abraham 102 John 13 Mrs R 187
GEPHART, Abs F 43 Rev J 103
GERET, Lydia 198
GERHARD, Abigail 166 Emanuel V 16 Rev H 124 216 Jonathan 166 Philip S 166 Rev W T 198 William F 1
GERHART, Rev 175 206 Abraham 174 George 95 Rev H 163 Rev I 99 128* 150 Isaac 26 Rev Isaac 62 83 84 86 97 98 103 114 131 137 139 152 195 John 174 Magdalena 174 Philip 174
GERHEART, Rev I 175 John 175
GERMAN, Rev 116 Jacob 137
GERMANTOWN, Frederick 215
GERTZENDANNER, Jonathan 95
GESEY, Charlotte 131
GETH, Lo_s_e 184
GETTIER, Julia 128 Peter K 128
GETZENDANNER, Abraham 33 Christian 160 Hannah Margaret 58 Jonathan 192

GETZENDANNER(Continued) Michael Jefferson 174
GEYER, J H 200
GIBBONS, Mathew 74
GIBSON, Chief Justice 83 Annie 83 James 148 Robt 148 Sarah 104 Sarah Ann 128
GIEB, Elizabeth 100
GIESSNER, Rev G 33
GIESY, J U 184
GILBERT, D 201 Rev E W 54 J 201 Jacob 80 114 Dr Jesse 164 John 19 111 Martha 136 Samuel 38
GILL, Catharine 199 Dr John 88 Richard 78 Thomas Jr 196
GILLAN, Thomas 214
GILLAND, Thomas 140
GILLELAND, James C 77
GILLESPIE, Eliza 141 Wm 141
GILLIA, Wm P 120
GILMORE, Rebecca 64
GILPEN, S 180
GIRVAN, Hannah 148
GISINER, J S 216 T S 200
GITT, John 199
GITTINGER, Geo 17 195 Wm 209
GLACE, Jacob 175
GLANTZ, J 145
GLASS, George 146
GLASSER, George 148
GLATZ, J 223
GLENN, John 81
GLESNER, Rev G 19 Rev Geo 14
GLESSNER, Rev 50 97 130 Rev G 33* 111 152 Rev G M 17 Rev G W 153 213 223 Rev Geo 171 201 J 190 Wm 127
GLODFELTER, G 132 John 132
GLODFELTY, Joseph 213
GLONINGER, Dr 138 John 13 41
GLOTFELTER, Geo 180 John 180

GO___ George 215
GOBRECHT, Esther 69 Rev J 69 Rev John 138 Rachel 138 W D 119
GODDARD, Charles 101
GOETSCHIUS, Rev Samuel 85
GOLD, Thomas 215
GOLDEN, T 11
GOLDMAN, Miss A 181 Annette 18 Thomas 145
GOOD, Rev 26 47 132 Jos 26 Mrs Jos 164 Joseph 69 104 Mrs Joseph 177 Mary Ann 179 R 104 Rev W A 28 58 69 134 201 Rev Wm A 41 51 59 132 179
GOODMAN, Mrs 37 Harriet 51 John H 51 Rev J R 83
GOODMANSON, Peter 107 Wilhelmina 107
GOOLEY, ___ 116
GORDON, Martin Jr 50 Matthew 81 Rebecca Ann 114
GORNER, Jacob 152
GORSHON, Sophia 129
GOSHEN, R 116 132
GOSHER, Richard 172 Solomon 172
GOSNAL, L W 38
GOSSLER, P 95
GOSSMAN, George 17
GOTSCHALL, John 166
GOTTINGER, Geo 32
GOTTWALD, Rev Daniel 151
GOTTWALT, Jacob 214
GOULBOURN, Joseph 223
GOULD, Samuel 214
GOWAN, Jonathan 118
GR_DER, John Jr 215
GRACEY, Rev 165 Rev R 134 175
GRAEB, Henry 182
GRAEBER, Rev 108
GRAFF, Hilary 214 John 37

GRAHAM, Ann J 100 David 106 David P 148 George C 121 J 53 Maj Jno 100 N 45 William 188 Wm 223
GRANGER, Rev Arthur 54
GRANT, John 70
GRATER, ___ 164 216
GRAVER, Mary 103
GRAVES, Rev Dietrich 14 Ellen 200 William J 138*
GRAY, Anna 132 180 Harrison 107 J 195 Ryan 132 180 Wm H 121
GREEN, ___ 55 Elizabeth 28 Dr 107 Dr N J 219 R C 73
GREENAWALT, C 202 David 138 E 200 Eliza 57 Godfrey 126 Jacob 181 John 59 Mary 174 Mary Anna 36 Sophia 126
GREENE, Rev David 19
GREENFIELD, Hugh 170
GREENLEAF, Rev 125
GREENWOOD, Mr 156
GREER, J H 145
GREGER, Abraham 174
GREGG, Mrs 48 Mrs A 60 Rev 62 Rev Jarvis 63 Margery 145
GREGORY, Ellen Mary 92 O 156 Robert 92
GRICE, John 99 76
GRIER, Rev 124 Jane 124 Martha 43 Rev R S 114 139
GRIFFIN, Wm 219*
GRIFFITH, Jacob 172
GRIFFITHS, James 93
GRIGGS, Eliza 41 Thomas 21
GRIM, Benjamin 79 Catharine 79 Danl 79 Joseph S 82 P 191
GRIMES, Amelia 38 George 164 Geo W 107 James 181 John 80 90 Mary 114
GRINDER, Amelia 188 Michael 103

GRING, D 62 Rev D 62 156 170 179 186 198 Rev Daniel 71
GRINNEL, Mr 79
GRISCOM, John 101
GROFF, Jacob 95 John 175 Joseph 17
GROSS, Abraham 49 168 Elizabeth 202 H Sr 221 Henry 41* J I 105 Maria 168 Mary 145 Peter 184 Rachel 49
GROSSMAN, ___ 84 Dr 36 David 116 M 199 Michael 28 Samuel 84
GROVE, Aaron 187 Ann Elizabeth Post 187 Daniel 186 Elizabeth Sarah 127 F 177 Francis 133 Geo 24 216 Henry 151 J 50 Jacob 50 56 195 John 182 187 219 Joseph 163 M 199 Philip 19 21 33 99 Philip Sr 11 Rebecca 99 Samuel 127 Susan 34 74 150 191 Susan Catharine 151
GROVER, N M 175 William 214
GRUBB, David Jr 66 Edward B 125 H 206 Henry 163 Henry Jr 163 Jane M 126 John 163 Joseph 126 Capt Joseph 182 Samuel 94 163 Sarah Ann 49 David Jr 66
GRUBER, Jacob 17
GUELICH, J 138 179 Jacob 192
GULDIN, Henr'ta Catherine 168 Henrietta Frederica Theresa 168 Rev J 43 Rev J C 50 66 71 86 166 Rev John C 168
GULDING, Rev J G 105
GULICK, Ira Condict 25 Peter J 25
GULLUHER, Hugh L 99
GUMP, Elias 75
GUNDAKER, Clementine M 55 Michael 55

GUNN, ___ 1
GURGIS, Joseph 195
GURLEY, Rev 79
GUSS, Susanna 49
GUTELIUS, Mr 199 Rev 56 71 73 74 76 89 H 133 190 214 Rev S 19 33* 145 150 199 216 221 Rev Samuel 50 138 199
GUTH, ___ 184 Charles 116 Daniel A 184 Elias 184 G__ine 184 Gideon 184 Henry 184 Joseph 184
GUTZLAFF, ___ 57 Mrs 112 Rev 112 Charles 18
GUYER, W 84
GWYNN, ___ 73
HA___ Daniel 198
H__TZ, Peter 184
HAAF, George 113
HAAK, Jacob 69
HABER, Peter 184
HABLISTON, H 182 Rev H 79 Brother Henry 102* Rev Henry 73
HACKE, Rev 73 77 141 Juliana 141 Rev N P 77 81 87 95 172
HACKMAN, Michael 166
HADE, J 157 Jacob 84 90 99 210 Jacob Jr 182 Mrs M 187
HAFER, Everhard 184
HAGAN, Mrs 191 Michael 100
HAGENBUCH, Stephen 180
HAGERMAN, J 215 Joshua 215
HAGUS, William 141
HAHN, Conrad 215 Elias 93 Elizabeth 190 George 215 George Jr 215 Henry 210 Philip 215 Samuel 72 Dr W B 84 163
HAIGIS, Philipina 67
HAINES, Elizabeth Browne 54 Reuben 54
HAINS, Julia 138

HAINTZ, Jona 202
HALDEMAN, H 34 Mrs M A 186
HALE, R I 210
HALEMAN, John 204
HALL, Constable 92 Mrs 147 Mr
   128 A M 149 James 121 John
   184 John L N 103 Rev Levi
   147 Mich 180 Mira 149 Rev W
   M 215 William 107 Wm M 91
HALLER, Charles 74 Jacob 46
   139 181
HALLETT, Wm P 198*
HALLEY, William 180
HALLIET, Paul 184 Stephen 184
HALLOCK, Homan 218
HALSEY, Rev Luther 19 Richard
   D 44
HAMBLIN, Mr 138
HAMBRIGHT, ___ 164
HAMER, Jasper 148 Solomon
   115
HAMILTON, Mrs 216 A 156
   Benjamin 180 Jane 104 P
   216* T 216 Rev W T 216
HAMLINE, Jonas 144
HAMLUN, John 73
HAMM, Rev J W 121
HAMMAN, M 180
HAMMEL, Mary Ann 93
HAMMER, G 199 John 144 Mary
   215
HAMMET, David 192
HAMMON, J 2 Joseph H 2
HAMMOND, B 115 Elizabeth 73
   181 Lavina 54 Jacob 181
   M, 131 Martin 17 45 Michael 73
HAMOT, Miss 168
HAND, Rev 215
HANDESHELL, John 76
HANDWERK, Sarah 198
HANDY, Benjamin 176
HANE, Catharine Mary 121
   Christiana C 59 John 121

HANE_ Barbara 180
HANENKAMPF, Dr 151 Mary
   Elizabeth 151
HANES, Barbara 132 William
   175
HANNA, Martha 190
HAPE, Mrs 166 Jacob 166
HARBAUGH, Jacob 192 John
   192
HARBERT, Margaretta 75
HARBISSON, Mr 14
HARE, John 110
HARGATE, Ann Maria 97 David
   105
HARGET, John 32
HARGETT, Juliann 51 Sam'l 95
HARIMAN, Joseph 184
HARKEY, Rev 102 125
HARLEY, O F 86
HARMAN, Peter 117 R 53
HARMON, W 132
HARMONY, J 190 John 139 143
   Nancy 143 P 190
HARN, George 150
HARNER, Ann 174 Anothony 144
   Fred'k 220 G 220 Rosana 174
HARNEY, Col 219
HARNISH, Christian 179 John
   116 S 184 Sam'l Jr 184
   Samuel 14 179* 220 Samuel
   Jr 94 Samuel Sr 74 179
   Tobias 14
HARP, David 66
HARPEL, Rev 67
HARPER, Messrs 37 Ellen 184 G
   K 110 Geo K 77 95 George K
   95 Georgiana 77 Henrietta
   150 James 184 John 37 220
   Mary 110 Thomas 150
HARRIS, A 33 Charles B 130
   Dicey 22 George 147 George
   W 17 H 219 Huston 22 Rev
   Isaiah 87 James 139

HARRIS (Continued)
　Dr John 100 Mary Ann 107
　Richard 77 Susan 148 Thos J
　149 Wm 148
HARRISON, ___ 148 Mary 172
　Thos 169
HARRY, J K 103 Jane K 165
　Silas 165
HART, Mr 183 C 60 Dr G W 109
　John 185 Mary 60
HARTELL, John 33
HARTER, Andrew 145 Thos 184
HARTMAN, Mr 37 Granville 16 J
　190 Jno 119 Mary Ann 221
　Philip 70 R 205
HARTRANFT, John 166
HARTSHORNE, William M 200
HARTZEL, Capt Elias 222 J G
　127
HARVEY, ___ 106
HASSON, J 135
HASTINGS, E M 56
HATCH, ___ 220
HATHFIELD, Eliza 118
HAUER, Priscilla 111
HAUGH, Paul 15 70 198* Wm 70
　107
HAUS, John 77
HAUSER, Cath 202 John 210
HAUSMAN, Henry 145 Judith
　198 Polly 198
HAUTZ, Christian 146 Rev John
　12
HAVEN, John 93
HAVERSTICK, B 195 W E 37
HAWK, Abraham 29 Catharine
　90 L 205 Tho 220
HAWKER, Abr 180 Abraham 132
HAWKINS, William 135
HAWN, D 70
HAWPE, John 74 John Sr 198
HAY, Benjamin Franklin 190
　Charles A 16 John 190

HAYDEN, James 214
HAYES, Dr R P 98
HAYS, Mr 37 Andrew 89 Dr J C
　103 James 48 75
HAYWARD, Dr George 147
HAZELIUS, Rev E 53
HEAFNER, John 19 179
HEAGY, Henry 143 James 150
　John 214 Margaret Elizabeth
　143 Rob 195
HEART, Charles W 199 Jacob
　176 Sarah Ann 176
HEATH, Maj 156* Nancy 119
HEBBARD, Capt 40
HEBERLIG, B 202 John 179
　Sam'l 202 Samuel 150
HECBROTH, Emma 77
HECK, Catharine 99 Daniel
　Smith 213 Dan'l 213 Geo 32
　George 105 Jacob 50 90 Maj
　Jacob 213 Ludwig 99 Madison
　72
HECKART, Peter 190
HECKERMAN, Henry 164
HECKERT, Ann 84 Geo A 16
　John 114 Peter 84
HECKMAN, Adam 158 Archi-
　medes 167 J 216
HEDGES, Eliza 128 J 101 Josiah
　128 Julia Ann 23 July Ann 8
HEDRICK, A 204 G 204 John 38
　48 138 S 204
HEEBNER, Abraham 166 Antho-
　ney 166 Rev Balser 166 David
　S 166 Henry 166
HEFFEDITZ, T L 70
HEFFELK, Leon 208
HEIDRICH, Baltzer 166 175
HEIGELROTH, Jonathan 128
HEIGERT, Rudo'ph 192
HEIGHT, Adam 95
HEILMAN, J 202 Jacob 200 John
　138

HEIM, Catharine 125 Rev J W 125
HEINDEL, Christiana 188
HEINEG, Cha's 202
HEINER, Rev 93 123 200 216 E 153 Rev E 18 19 30 33 36 38* 44 49 63 68 70 79 114 128 139 148 153 167 181 182 184 186 208* 220 Elias 13 44 79 Rev Elias 221 John 70* 103 John Jr 44 117 164 Martha Virginia 63 Mary 103
HEINLY, Maria 198
HEINZERLING, Tobias 144
HEISER, Mr 38
HEISLER, Cath 124 Jacob 166
HEIST, J G 77
HEISTAND, Ab'm 202 Dav 202
HEISTER, Dr Isaac 70 John 50
HEITSHU, Cath 156 Catharine 32 Harriet 73 Israel 70 110 P 200 Philip 73 W 200 Wm 24 74
HELFENSTEIN, Rev 99 123 211 Rev A 171* Rev A Jr 97 Rev Albert Jr 145 Rev J 106 169 170 173 175 Rev J Jr 216 Rev S 150* Rev S Jr 70* 104
HELFENSTINE, Rev 151 Charlotte A 132 Rev Jonathan 132
HELFERICH, Daniel 15 Daniel Jr 15
HELFFENSTEIN, A 180 Rev A 180 Albert Jr 181 Rev J 176 184 190 197 208 218 Rev Jac 115 Rev S Jr 190 204* 223
HELLER, Chas 207 David 202 George 213 Rev J 126 129 132 152* 162 179 199 215 221 Jacob 202 Jacob S 215 Jeremiah 16 34 Solomon 215 William 76
HELLMAN, D 152 Mich 213

HELM, D 56 Daniel 199
HELMS, Andrew 223
HELMSTETLER, P 138 201
HELSINGER, Jacob 51
HEMPHILL, Rev Andrew 116 Thomas 64
HENDEL, Rev 164 184 Bernard 103 Rev 37 Rebecca 103 Dr W 121 Wm 13 Wm B 47
HENDERSON, ___ 148 Rev Hugh 72 L F 53 Logan 115* Stephen 144 William 22
HENKEL, Lucinda 179
HENNEBERGER, John J 152
HENNIGH, Henry K 170
HENNINGER, Lewis C 62*
HENNY, Polly 145
HENRICH, John 202
HENRY, Mr 34 Alex 19 Alexander 223 Charles 121 G G 218 Rev Robt 138
HENSEL, Rev 201 Rev J 74 156* J C 198 Rev J C 132 143 153 Jeptha 70 John C 16 24 Michael 38 181
HENSELL, Rev J C 198 223* Mary A 146 Michael 19 146
HENSHAW, Rev 83 Washington 146
HENWIEX, John 145
HEPBURN, Dr William 103
HERBAUGH, E 38 H 38 Henry 160 J 38
HERGESHEIMER, G 145 J 192
HERMAN, Dr A J 164 198 Rev A L 86 102 116 164 Rev Augustus L 120 Rev C G 111* 198 Charles Frederick 111 Rev Charles G 120* 126 Daniel 143 Rev F L Jr 56 John 24 44 199 Joseph 218 Rev L C 200 Rev Lewis C B 81 156 Maria F 120 Dr W 179

HERON, A 105 J 105
HERR, Mr 205 C 210 Catharine
 153 Charlotte 203 Conrad 99
 153 157 D 164 J 219 William
 M 153
HERRING, Henry 94 145 Jacob
 132 180
HERSHBERGER, Elizabeth 144
 John 119 Rebecca E 182
HERSHEY, Catharine 127
HERSPERGER, Henry 24
HERSTER, Daniel 198
HERTZ, Rev 205 220 D 116 174
 181* Rev D 132 137 174* 181
 195* 217 Rev Daniel 11 167
 186
HERTZEL, Andrew 215 George
 215 Philip 69
HERZ, Rev D 217
HESS, Abraham 131 Jacob 99
 Jeremiah 215 Lactitia 207
 Letitia 150 Rev Samuel 139
 Simon 210 Stephen 215
HESSON, Joseph 30
HESSONG, Elizabeth Ann
 Rebecca 79 Sarah Ann 198
HETICH, Dr Andrew 125
HETTINGER, Henry 145
HEWES, S J 206 W 156 200
HEWITT, Thos 121 Geo W 107
HEWLETT, Narcissa J 22
HEY, Christian 175
HEYSER, Ann 69 Catharine 21
 Jacob 21 69 195 201 W 91
 173 174 William 28 181 187
 195 201 Capt William 69
 William Sr 67 Wm 25 95 131
HICKEL, C 12 Chr 15 Christopher 18*
HICKLE, Christian 115 Christopher 157
HICKOCK, Wm P 95

HICKS, ___ 55 Charity E 134
 Capt David 134 J 190 James
 G 22 James H 22 John 111
HIESTER, J B 138 202 Mrs J B
 187 John 74 T M K 145 W
 187 Wm 76
HIGBEE, D 148*
HIGGINBOTHAM, Jno 40
HIGGINS, Rev 145
HIGH, Esther 69 107 Hester 213
 Mary 86
HIGHBARGER, Joseph 72
HIGHBEE, Rev 56
HILBESH, Henry 146
HILBISH, John 146
HILDEBRAND, D 111 Daniel 84
 Elizab 172 John 33 Wm 100
HILEMAN, Jacob 98
HILGERT, Frantz 215 Isaac 215
 John 215
HILL, Mrs 15 Rev 79 Capt Alfred
 121* Benjamin 174 Henry 19
 129 Josephine Rachel Elenora
 15 Mary 15 Oliver 95
HILLEGAS, Charles 200* Frederick 144 Jacob 144 Josiah 99
HILLEGASS, Adam 163 Charles
 166 Rebecca 166 Samuel 166
HILLGERD, Isaac 18 Peter 18
 Philip 18
HILTON, Henry K 186
HIMBURY, Elizab 115 John 139
HIMES, Samuel 56
HINDES, Michael 172* Sanes
 172
HINDS, M 188 Michael 17
HINE, John 66
HINEA, Wm 214
HINKLE, John 180 Susanna 218
HINTSH, Father 156
HIPPLE, Jesse 195
HIRSH, Eliza 99 Philip 99

HISER, Jacob 166
HISS, Jacob Sr 205
HISSONG, Fred'k 168 Joseph 204
HITZLER, __ 40
HITCHEL, C 38
HIVELY, Michael 215
HIVLING, Abr 180
HOAK, Jacob 57
HOCKE, George 182
HODGES, Nelson 128
HOEGH, Jacob 113
HOFFEDITZ, Brother 215 Rev 190 195 203 204 216 Juliann 190 T L 184 Rev T L 184 Rev Th L 37 Rev Theod L 143 Theo C W 173 Theod C W 178 Theodore C W 16
HOFFER, Mrs 111 Christian 145 George 111
HOFFERT, C 197 Daniel 222
HOFFHEIN, Rev Emanuel 216
HOFFIUS, Dr 185 187 190 J H 13 144
HOFF, MAN, Rev JOHN, 152
HOFFMAN, __ 140* Ann 19 Catharine 131 Catherine 153 Christian 18 46 150 D Jr 220 Daniel 143 Daniel Jr 50 David 195 216 Eliza 192 F 38 Frederick 115 153 George 103 220 H 220 Hannah 98 Henrietta 135 Dr J 14 Rev J N 93 125 176 182 Jacob 131 James 19* John 17 24 164 181 184 Rev John N 57 Joshua 28 117 213 Josiah Qgden 85 M 216 Michael 128 153 Rebecca 57 Samuel 174 Susan 153 Susannah H 56 W 188 William 74 Wm 204

HOFFMEIER, Rev 216 Ann Elizabeth Cocky 113 C F 37 41 74 103 160 199 Rev C F 107 115 200 Charles F 56 Gertrude 105 Rev J H 105 J W 111 Rev J W 58 103 111 113 118 153 206 John Calvin 169 Rev John H 142 Rev John W 84 126 127 169 John Wm 11 Rev John Wm 47 66 142
HOFFMEIR, C F 73 Rev J W 18 93 Rev John W 17
HOFFMEYER, C F 28 Rev J H 19
HOFFMIER, Rev 208 George Henry 184 Rev J 184 J W 184 Rev J W 51 184* Rev John H 187 Rev John W 191
HOFIUS, Dr 105 174 179 221 J H 179 Dr J H 119 207 Peter Dechert 207
HOGAN, __ 128 Angeline 71 Lawrence 71
HOGE, Jesse 109
HOKE, Adam 192 Daniel 53 F A 53 Franklin W 135 Col J 53 John 156 188 Col John 86 117 M 15 Marcus C 115 Michael 117
HOLBEN, Peter 174
HOLCOMB, Michael 99
HOLLAND, James 198 John W 167 Joseph 121 Zacharia 130
HOLLIDAY, __ 195 Adam 105 Sarah 105
HOLLINGER, John 56
HOLLINGSHEAD, Isaac 109
HOLLOWBUSH, Mary 87
HOLMAN, Mr 160
HOLSEY, A P 101
HOLSHAUSER, Caspar 103
HOLSHOUSER, C 199

HOLSTEIN, Mr 28*
HOLTER, W 221
HOLTZ, Nicholas 17
HOLTZMAN, Peter 26
HOMMAN, J 84 Sarah 84
HOOD, John 210
HOOPER, Miss Julian 139
HOOT, G 174 P 174 Peter 166
  Philip 166
HOOVER, Christian 56 F W 99
  195 216 Fr W 9 Margaret 190
  Martin 145 205 Philip 174
  195
HOPKINS, Mr 221
HOPLER, Joseph 214
HOPPIN, Esther 121
HORINE, Jno 61 Susan 61
HORN, Abr 156 John 150
HORNBAKER, Mrs 160
HORTON, Susan Ophelia 115
HOSACK, Dr David 39
HOSKINS, George 67
HOSKYNS, Rev John H 83
HOSLER, Daniel 132 218 John
  107 W J 107
HOSSINGER, Jacob 180
HOSSLER, D 210 Jacob 48 119
  John 142
HOSTERMAN, John 145
HOTTEL, D 152 201 Daniel 55
  216 Geo 152 198 George 189
  Henry 109 Isaac 70 137 154
  201 Maria Cath 189 Wm 76
HOTTENSTEIN, Isaac 146
HOUCK, George 215 Henry 86 J
  94 John 170* 197 Michael 17
  Savillah 166
HOULSHAUSER, C 53
HOUSE, Milly 206*
HOUSER, A 53 Abraham D M
  194 Elias 181 Eliz 76 Eliza 99
  J E 32 Jacob 214 Maria 33 76
  99 Samuel 172

HOUSTON, Esquire 118 Mr 124
  Joseph 92 Miss Marion 193
  Rev William F 138
HOUTZ, Dr 14 159 Dr Daniel 21
HOUZELOT, Daniel H 213
HOW, Messrs 214
HOWELL, Aaron 28 Jesse M 83
HOWER, D 169 Geo 202 J E M
  169
HOWERTER, Elizabeth 129
HOWITTS, Dr Godfrey 200
  Richard 200 William 200
HOWLAND, G 45*
HOWPE, John 132
HOYER, Miss 37 George 208
  Miss S 181 Sarah 18
HUBBARD, Edward 176 S 190
  Samuel 19 Samuel James 212
  Sarah Ann 212 T S 148
  Thomas S 212 W J 19
HUBER, Frederick 70 Maria 99
  152 207 Philip 70
HUBLER, George 145 Henry 50
  159 201
HUDSON, Jonathan 55
HUEY, Robert M 18 Dr W 148
HUFFEET, Mary 213
HUFFER, Henry 90 Sarah A 213
HUFFERD, Sarah 82
HUFFERT, Daniel 192
HUFFMAN, S 53
HUGHES, Manasseh 50 Rev
  Thomas Edgar 151 Wm 60
  106
HUGUS, Christiana 86 Wm 203
HUIL, R 53
HULL, Gabriel 144 Rev L 45 P 30
  Peter 133
HUME, ___ 54 Rev David W 191
HUMES, Hamilton 84 Rachel 84
  Samuel 84
HUMMELSTINE, Catharine 141
HUMPHREY, M 121

HUMPHREYS, Dr Charles 198
  Henry 219 Dr William R 140
HUMRICKHOUSE, Frederick 17
  Mary 216 Peter 88 216
HUNT, Mrs 150 Elizabeth 108
  Rev T P 91
HUNTER, Dr 147 J 134 John
  105 N V R 198 William 106
  Wm 51 95
HUNTSBERGER, Elias 81
HUPPEL, Thomas 215
HURSH, Jacob 56
HURST, Mrs 148 Jacob 201 S
  Decatur 121
HURTZ, Sarah 81
HUSSEY, Rev Geo St C 150 Rev
  Geo St Clair 96 Peter Cook 96
HUSTON, Anna Mary 118 Wm
  148
HUTCHINS, Rev Benjamin 43
HUTCHINSON, Mr 156 Robert
  156*
HUTCHISON, Mr 156 Adeline
  146 John 146
HUTTER, E W 149
HUTZELL, John 184*
HUYETT, Catharine E 148
  Charles 219 D 192* Daniel
  219 Jacob 50 192 219 John
  159 P L 148 Samuel 219
HYATT, Wm 62
HYDE, Francis 105 Samuel 105
HYLE, John 179
IBBEKEN, Rev H 203 Rev H G
  203
IBEKEN, Rev H B 19
ICKES, Sarah 185
ICOFF, Adolph 62 Mary 62
IDE, Rev 199
IKERD, George 117
INGERSOLL, Charles 219
  Charles J 219 Joseph 219
INGLES, Martha 26

INGOLD, Ambrose 47 J 148 Joel
  83
INGRAM, ___ 128
INNES, Susan 181
INSKEP, Wm H 148
IRVIN, John 137 John Jr 122
  Mary 137
IRVINE, Elizabeth 103 John 103
IRWIN, Col 50 Jacob 174 John
  50 121 Susan 50
ISENBERG, B 50 Enoch 50
ISENBERGER, Rebecca 218
ITNIRE, Ann Eliza 211 Henry
  211
JACK, Maj Joseph 78 Sarah 78
JACKSON, George 129* Henry
  121 Lydia 72 Thomas 75
JACOB, Henry 184 S 105
JACOBS, Rev 209 Rev Cyrus H
  68 Cyrus S 176
JACOBY, Daniel 128 John 202
JACQUES, Dr Lancelot 92 Sarah
  92
JAEGER, Jona 216
JAMES, David 148 Rev John W
  65 Robert E 215 Thomas 160
JAMIESON, A 203 Alexander 164
  J 181
JANES, Thomas 53 86 99 109
JANEWAY, Dr 107
JANNEY, H 148 J 148
JANTZ, Ruben 202
JARDINE, Mr 112
JARRETT, Harrietta 170
JAUDON, Samuel 119
JEFFERS, Mr 37
JEFFERSON, Thomas 73
JEHL, Elizabeth 184
JENKINS, Ellen 124 Frances 91
  Phebe 70 Robert 70 Wm 124
JENKS, Dr Wm D 100
JENNINGS, Mr 160 Rev George
  67 Timothy 73

JERG, John 184
JESUP, Gen 88
JETURS, Benedict 53
JETTUN, B 98
JEWETT, Capt 191 Ellen 177*
   Joseph 128
JOB, Eliza 87
JOHNS, Eli 176 Elizabeth 186
JOHNSON, __ 212 Dr 152 110
   David 28 Elizabeth 132 Jacob
   77 James 217 Maria 181
   Martha Maria 148 Richard 86
   132 Robert 176 Silas 148
   Simeon S 106 Rev Stephen
   181 Col Thomas 209 Gov
   Thos 100 William 64 William
   Cost 209
JOHNSTON, Dr Benjamin 176
   Edward 79 James 191 Jane A
   180 Rev John 193 Thomas
   129* W 190 William 115
JONES, Abner 97 Agnes 223
   David A 16 Elias 174 Eliza-
   beth 87 Hannah 81 Jacob 198
   James W 101 Job 148 Joel
   87* John 174 Raph 186
   Raphael 222 Sidna 219 Wm S
   78
JONEY, J C 202
JORDAN, Cath 180 Charles 15
   76 Jacob 38 115 Jonah 198 L
   180 Lewis 180 Sarah 115
JOSEPH, E 156
JUCAS, __ 181
JUDSON, Rev Albert 193
JUNKIN, John 49 87
K_SLER, Rebecca Ann 219
KAEMERER, Rev David 19
KAGG, John 144
KAHL, Catharine 176 Jacob 176
KAIGN, Andrew 121
KAMP, David 145

KANE, Mr 99 Mrs 4
KANN, Geo 78
KAPP, Magd 56
KARCH, J 202
KARN, Rev 95 Geo 32 William 21
KARPER, Frederick 181
KAUFFMAN, N 166
KAUFMAN, Henry 50 H W 73
KAUTZ, Christian 146
KAVANAUGH, Rev 199
KAY, G B 133 177 Rev James
   149
KAYLER, F 199*
KEAFAUVER, Geo 219 George
   219 Capt J 213 John 219
   Jonathan 180 Mary Ann 219
KEAFAUVRE, Jacob 184
KEAGY, Jacob 206
KEAL, Daniel 37 Geo 58
KEALHOFER, Maj George 151
KEALHOFFER, A C 82 John 82
KEAN, J 148
KEANEDY, Jas 121
KEARNEY, Elizabeth 192 Francis
   154
KEATING, Rev Thomas J 139
KEDDLE, Sam'l 190
KEEDY, J 50 200 John D 17 24
   107 150 John J 219 Samuel
   200 206
KEEFER, Abraham 80 Catharine
   182 Dewalt 80 Rev E 184 Rev
   Ephraim 91 Geo 135* Hannah
   125 Jeremiah 125 Josiah 129
   M 121 Mary 72 Moses 44
   Nicholas 69 Samuel 184 Ste
   phen 119
KEEK, Sam'l L 184
KEELY, Henry 43
KEEN, Elijah 56 Henry 56 Henry
   Jr 198 Jacob 56 Joshua 56
   Samuel 121

KEENER, Christian 107 Geo 188
KEFAUVER, Daniel 79 G 201 J
  11 John 32 181 Mary Catha-
  rine 79 Sarah 79
KEFFEY, Jacob 184
KEHNEL, Hilary 198
KEILER, Elizabeth 59 Susan 170
KEIM, Benneville 151 George D
  B 167 Matilda H 151 Susan D
  B 167 Wm H 78
KEIN, Capt Daniel D B 95
KEIPER, David 201
KEISER, J 182 Joseph 110
KEISTER, Mary Ann D 126
KELCHNER, Julia 198
KELKER, Miss 210 Fred'k 168
  210 R F 206 Rosanna 168
  Sabina 90
KELLER, Mr 11 200 Rev 78 124
  125 141 Abraham 16 Adam
  181 187 215 Anthony 184
  Catharine 50 D 11 David 136
  145 203 219 Rev E 221 Eliz
  190 Elizabeth 136 138 Rev
  Emanuel 97 Ezra 26 Fred 198
  Frederick 90 Geo 180 195*
  George 56 79 Henry 138 143
  J H 221 Jacob 133 145 186
  214 215 220 Jno 94 John 14
  32 70 94 145 159* 175 186
  191 202 219 Rev John 138
  John Jr 70 132 203 John Sr
  179 201 219 John H 215
  Jonathan 50* Josephus 50
  Lawrence 55 177 Miss M 70
  Maria 164 Mary 11 164 Philip
  215 Samuel 64 Sarah 88 95
  William 45
KELLEY, James 105 Margaret
  184
KELLY, John Sr 106 200 Thos
  217
KELSEY, G H 148

KELSO, Joanna 72 Wm 72
KELTNER, Elizabeth 186 Jacob
  186
KEMMERER, Jacob 87 Jesse
  202 John 124 202
KEMP, Abraham 17 174 C 30
  Catharine 122 Christian 75
  Christian F 173 Christian
  Franklin 170 Daniel 170
  David 17 Col Henry 13 Jos
  156 Walter 122
KEMPER, James 107 P H 107
KENEDY, J A 53
KENNARD, Mr 198
KENNEDY, Mr 121 Rev 94 113
  James M 78 Lazarus 93
  Michael 148* Rev R 134 138
  Rev Robert 78 129 Rosamond
  H 95 Susan S 219 Thomas 95
KENNEL, George 184 Jacob 184
KENNODE, John 223
KENZER, N E 95
KEPHART, Peter 164 Susanna
  164
KEPLINGER, Eliz 15 Elizabeth
  38 70
KEPPEL, Jacob 73 Veronika 73
KERBLE, Miss Francisco 195
KERCHER, Danial 72
KERFOOT, Rev 92
KERLINGER, John 127 Sarah
  Ann 127
KERN, Adam 166 Charles 184
  Edw 181 215 Edward 184 Geo
  185 Henry 184 Jacob 14
  James 184 John 184 198
  Joseph 184 Lenhart 215 Mary
  215 Thomas 184 Peter J 214
KERNEY, Nancy 95
KERR, John S 56 Rev Leander
  95 Margaretta Chambers 56
  Maria 199
KERSCHNER, Sarah 116

KERSHNER, A 180 Andrew 38
  117 Ann Maria 79 Catharine
  87 Elenora 52 Gustavus 213
  Jacob 76 81 Jonathan 87
KESLER, George 83
KESSELRING, Christiana 106
  George 91
KETRON, Marg 198 Margaret
  182
KETTEMAN, ___ 180
KETTERMAN, ___ 132
KEYSER, George 187 Jacob 188
  Samuel 186
KIBBE, Lt 216
KICHLE, James 184
KICHLINE, Aaron 202
KIDD, B 184
KIEFER, Dewalt 15 E 30 Rev E
  179 E C 30 Geo 132 180 M 48
KIEFFER, Rev 176 188* Abraham 24 E 186 Rev E 139 181
  190 210* Ephraim 16 71
  Ephram 28 F 181 Rev F 181
  Hannah 168 Jonathan 210
  Jos 199 Joseph 215 M 145
  M___ 28 N 199 Rebecca 222
  Stephen 210 222
KIEGGER, E 194
KIEHL, Mr 138 Geo 8 38 George
  17
KIFFER, George 213
KILGORE, Jesse 127
KILGOUR, Charles J 114
KILKER, Sabina 90
KILLIAN, Jesse 129 Lucy 129
KILLINGER, John 141 145 195
KILMER, Mary 127 Miss P 179
KILPATRICK, Samuel 162
KIMES, Jno 71 Sarah Ann 146
KINDLEBERGER, Dr T 193
KINER, Abby 198

KING, Miss 128 Mr 1 Mrs 166
  Alexander 220 Ann Maria 199
  Catharine 176 G 190 Geo 219
  George 26 28 119 Henry 195
  Jacob 195 John 188 214
  Martin 180 Robert 76
KINGSBURY, Rev 157
KINGSLEY, Mr 208
KINKLE, W H 106 Wm 95
KINNEARD, James 176
KINSEY, John 82
KIP, Isaac L 85
KIPP, Samuel 159*
KIRCHOFF, Mary 68
KIRKER, James 114
KIRKNERS, Stephen D 141
KIRKPATRICK, Benjamin 86
  Jane 86
KIRSH, ___ 156
KIRTLAND, Rev O L 148 222
  Sarah Ann 222
KISLER, Paul 98
KITCHELL, Rev A W 60
KITE, Adeline 38
KITTOE, Dr Edward 32
KLAUSER, Wm 184
KLECKNER, Philip 214
KLEIS, Margaretta 217
KLINE, Mrs 92 Rev 217 Henry 99
  John 87 146 John 156 Rev
  John P 123
KLINGENSMITH, John 195
KLINGLER, Jacob 184 Mary 78
KLOPP, P Jr 190 P Sr 190
KLUTS, Geo 117
KLUTTS, Paul 103
KLUTZ, Geo 180 Paul 180
KNAAB, Elizabeth 188
KNABB, H 220 Jacob 93 Peter Jr
  93
KNAPP, Horton O 79

KNAUFF, Mr 107
KNAUS, Jonas 202 Paul 184
KNAUSE, Rev Charles 34
KNAUSS, __ 146
KNECHT, Abraham 202 Christian 202 John 202 Solomon 202
KNEPPER, Adam 115 Jona 219
KNERE, John 172
KNERR, Jonas 184
KNIPE, Rev 72 216 Rev J B 36 91* 131 184 Sarah 124
KNODE, Elizabeth 86 Geo 86 George 86 132 H 14 184 Henry 74 179 184 J 184 John 11 45 John F 191 John M 206 213 L H 184 Lewis 50 94 174 Maria 86 Nancy 164 213
KNODLE, George 171
KNOUFF, Margaret 186
KNOUSE, Rev C 216 Rev Charles 45
KNOWER, Eli 166
KNOWLES, Mrs 223 Frederick 223* Rev J D 150
KNOX, Rev 149 Benj 210 Joseph 115 Margaretta 115
KOBLENTZ, Philip 11
KOCH, Adam 202 Jacob 138 Wm 77
KOEHLER, Cath 202
KOH, John 202
KOHLER, J 200
KOHRT, Jacob 84
KOLB, John Michael 59
KOLBY, Cath 196 George 196
KOLLE, Charlotte 181
KOLLER, J 11
KOLP, Geo 166
KONIGMACHER, Hannah 186
KOOGLE, A 70

KOOGLER, __ 132 180
KOOKEN, J 204 J Jr 95 J Sr 204 John 48 69 110 John Jr 75 John Sr 179
KOONS, __ 164 216 Mrs 8 A 206 Abr'm 166 Adam 144 Benj 74 Danl 144 Fred'k 105 Henry 144 190 James 166 John 163 Nicholas 144 P 202
KOONTZ, Conrad 214 George W 114 Jacob 70 Joseph 70 Michael 175
KOPPENSHAFER, Jonathan 139
KORCK, Dr 1
KORUB, Lewis 190
KOTZEBUE, __ 62
KRAMER, Geo 148* George 210 Michael 56
KRANTZ, J 179 John 61 138
KRATZ, P N 81
KRATZER, Peter 202 Valentine 166
KRAUSER, Hannah 121
KRAUTH, Rev C P 55 124 Louisa C 124
KREB, William 145
KREBS, G 85 Rev John M 89 193 Sarah H 89
KREIDER, Philip 145
KREIS, Jonathan 188
KREMER, A H 75 Amos E 72 Amos H 75 103 Rev Amos H 222 Franklin W 145 John 145 W 145
KREPS, __ 33* 133 Isaac 150
KRIBBEL, Melcher 166
KRIDER, John 13
KRIEBEL, Abraham 163 166 175 Andrew 163 Benj 163 Rev David 163 Joseph 163 166 Melchion 175

KRISCHNER, Abraham 198
KRISE, Abraham 60 Abraham Sr 107 Daniel 214 Jacob 156 192 Jonathan 210
KRISELER, Sophia 219
KROFT, Frederick 127
KROH, Rev 13 D 210 Rev H 188 204 J 94* Jacob 94* 143 168 Sarah 168
KROM, Anna 190 Wm 223
KRONMILLER, Thomas 145
KROTZER, Susannah 189
KROUSER, Hannah 102
KRUG, J V 19
KRUM, George 175
KRUMBHAUR, Lewis 42
KRUPP, Isaac 163
KRYDER, Jacob 201
KUCHNER, Daniel 202
KUGLER, Elizabeth 184
KUHN, Rev A 133
KUHNS, David 187 200 Rev E 191 Henry 185 Henry Jr 187
KUKIN, Jacob 184 John 214
KULP, J 154 Jacob 195
KUNKEL, John 17 50
KUNKLE, G Z 200
KUNKLEMAN, P 210
KUNTZ, Dan'l 202 John 202 Joseph 202 S C 202
KURTS, John C 219
KURTZ, Abraham 174 Adam 215 Andrew 215 Rev B 57 Rev Benjamin 121 Joseph 215 Mary Catharine 57
KYLE, Geo 219 Jno 94
LA_A, Capt Moses 65
LABAUGH, Jos 216 Joseph 70
LAIRD, David 121 Mary Ann 101 William 101
LAKIN, Abr 41 Eleanora 41 Harriet Ann Elizabeth 108 Martha A M 221 Susan 78

LAKIN (Continued) W 221* Capt Wm 41 78
LAMAR, ___ 158* Charles 156* G B 156 John 211 Robert Johnson 211 Rebecca 156*
LAMB, Mr 107 David 91
LAMBERT, Jacob 8 203 Jane M 144 Mary 97
LAMM, J 190
LANCASTER, Sabina 90
LANDER, Rebecca 111
LANDERS, Wm C 139
LANDIS, Henry 163 John 139 220
LANDON, James 128
LANE, Elliott T 187 Jane B 187 Joseph E 132 Mary 196 Mary G 104 Dr N B 104
LANG, David John 98
LANGE, D P 202 Daniel P 15
LANGEKER, Isaac 166
LANGHAM, J 185 James 164
LANNEAU, J F 33*
LANTZ, Daniel 62 156 Daniel Jr 120 J 53 Rev J 180 Jacob 53 Rev John 180* 199 204 S 53 188 Sam'l 86 Samuel 156
LAPPON, A H 192 Allexander H 219
LARETZ, A H 98 Daniel 98
LAROUQUE, J M 105
LASHELLS, E 146
LATHAM, Elizabeth 172
LATHROP, Hannah Joanna 162
LATIMER, J B 8
LAUB, Christ 202
LAUBACH, Adam Jr 215 Joseph 18 48 166 Peter 190
LAUBAUGH, Jos 216*
LAUBOTH, Cassandra 199
LAUCKS, G W 190
LAUFFER, Henry 95 Mary Ann 95

LAUMAN, George 59
LAURENCE, Susannah 197
   William 197
LAURIE, Rev 79
LAUTON, Jane 167
LAW, Charles Jr 71 George 182
LAWALL, W H 141
LAWMAN, Margaret 198
LAWRENCE, J C 106 Luther
   194* Mills 128
LAWRIE, Rev 87
LAWVER, Henry 119
LAY, Mr 131
LAYBOLD, John 174
LAYMAN, A 184
LEACOCK, Abner 98
LEADER, Eve Ann 152 Henry
   144 187 Maj Henry 152 John
   216
LEAKIN, Capt W 192
LEAMAN, C 184 Clarissa 90
LEAS, F 71 Francis 121 H 148
   Nancy Amanda 121
LEASER, Daniel 103
LEASURE, Elizabeth 77 John 77
LEAZER, Daniel 36 Lydia 36
LEBER, Henry 37
LEBLANC, __ 125
LEBO, Joseph 98
LECHLEITNER, Dr M 219
LECKRON, Jacob 17 John 19
LECRONE, John 121
LEE, Elisha 105 Nathan 153* Z
   C 79
LEEPS, Solomon 223
LEESER, D 11
LEET, Horace 166
LEFEVER, Abr 187 E 33 Enoch
   33 Geo 200 Jacob 183
LEFEVRE, E 133
LEHMAN, Abraham 123 B 133
   Peter 92
LEHR, Enos 215

LEIB, Joseph 168
LEIBY, James 160 S 194* Sam'l
   87 Samuel 170 180 195
LEIDIG, Eliza 82
LEIDY, Mr 11 Rev 106 C 128 Rev
   G 128 221 Rev Geo 95 162 186
   George 33 174 223 Rev
   George 11 Henry 34 174 J 94
   Jacob 166 John 94 166 190*
   Levi 174 Mary 169 Samuel
   166 174 William 174 Zachari-
   ah 166
LEIGHDER, Henry 24
LEIGHTER, Catharine Ann 175
   Henry 177 179 187 Jacob 175
LEINAWEAVER, Dr 138
LEINBACH, C H 143 151 220*
   Charles H 71 198 T H 116 175
LEIS, Adam 151 Rev J A 201
LEISENRING, C 198 Conrad 196
LEITER, __ 199 Ann C 199 D
   120 David 185 Rev George 93
   Jos 205 Joseph 58* 214 Rev S
   129 S B 164 185 Rev S B 120
   164 185 199 Samuel B 16
LEIZENRING, John 202
LEMMON, Margaret 46
LENHERR, John 200
LENGS, G 99
LENHART, Christiana 150 David
   90
LENHERR, John 73
LENKER, Elizabeth 97
LENTZ, Jonathan 198 Miss L
   180
LEOMAN, Geo 38
LEONARD, Daniel 117 Elizabeth
   216 H 184 Jacob 78 181 Peter
   38 78 Sol 201
LEOPOLD, G A 115 Rev G A 115
   156 Rev Geo 38 Rev Geo A
   115
LEPPO, __ 199 Mr 120

LERCH, Mr 176 Adam 202
   Amelia G 130 Christian 202
   Dan'l B 202 Rev D B 130 Geo
   141 Jacob 164* John 202
   Jonas 202 Samuel 186
   Thomas 202
LESHER, Benneville 198 Samuel
   172
LESHY, J 206 Jacob 15
LEVAN, David 198 Julia 159
LEVER, Samuel 33
LEVERS, Joseph 198
LEVERGOOD, Peter 84
LEVY, Charles 168 Joshua 95*
   Mrs Joshua 95
LEWARS, James 15 170 222
LEWIS, Capt 37 Arthur 121
   Benjamin 148 Emanuel N 215
   Robert 121 Stephen 133 T D
   176
LEYBURN, Mr 124
LEYMASTER, Rev Jacob 16
LIBBEY, Elisha 176
LIBHART, J J 51
LICHTENWALDER, P 14
LIDDLE, John A 53
LIDY, ___ 140
LIGHDER, Henry 11 P 11
LIGHDERT, Joseph 17
LIGHT, Adam 152 Catharine 15
   Maria 152
LIGHTER, Jacob 219 Peter 179
LIGHTNER, Abraham 94 J L 195
   James H 16 John 137 142
LIMMERICK, Rev D 39
LINAFELDER, Jacob 144
LIND, Abraham 138
LINDAMOOD, Elizabeth 157
LINDERMAN, Isaac 163
LINDSAY, Thomas 163
LINDSLEY, Silas C 130
LINE, Jacob 213
LINEBACH, F 145 R E 148 S 145

LINEFELDER, Rachel 144
LINEHAN, Henry 105
LINEWEAVER, Dr 202
LINGENFELTER, I 168
LINGLE, Jacob 180 Joseph 16
   94
LINHEART, George 126
LINN, Rev 34 196 Ann H 122
   Jacob 51 Rev James 73 84
   122
LINSLEY, Mary J 199
LINTNER, Rev Geo A 26
LINTON, Samuel 174
LINTZ, Wm 184
LIPPARD, John F 76
LIPPY, George 213
LIPSCOMB, Rev 125
LITAKEDS, J 53
LITTLE, Catharine 130 Elizabeth
   184 James 117 Joseph 130
   Mary Ann 131 P 95 Dr P 35 P
   W 101* Dr P W 69 184 198
   Peter 131 Sarah Elizabeth 117
   Susanna 35
LIVERS, D M 143 209 David M
   48
LIVES, Rev Mark 79
LIVINGSTON, George 80
LLOYD, Samuel H 99
LOB, Henry 184
LOCHBAUM, Samuel 90
LOCHER, Chas 213
LOCHMAN, Rev A H 94
LOCK, George W 114
LOCKART, Dr 211
LOCKE, Mr 117 Edwin 79
LODER, Rob S 166 Robert 202
LOGAN, Elizabeth 50
LOHR, Wm 186
LONG, Dr 131 A 166* Abraham
   215 Maj Abraham 205
   Andrew 121 Elizabeth 95
   George 38 Hannah 131 Isaac

LONG (Continued)
 136 Isaac H 83 J C 176 J K
 176 J L 166 Jacob 69 87
 Jesse 205 John 8 148 John A
 215 Joseph 70 92 Michael
 180 Rebecca 114
LONGACKER, Peter 166
LONGENECKER, Daniel 166
LONGNECKER, David 107
LOOSE, Elizabeth 69 Peter 213*
LORENTZ, F 203
LORETZ, A H 53
LOTZ, W 164 Wm 69
LOUCKS, Henry 166
LOUDERBACK, Rev Alfred 115
LOUGERBEAM, Harrison 91
LOUGH, A 199 Abr 152 W 179
LOUGHRIDGE, George 61
LOUNT, Samuel 147
LOVE, Rev Robert 167 Wm 64
LOVEJOY, Mr 156 A 156
LOWMAN, Louisa 111
LOY, J F 177* Rev J F 133 John R 144 Martin 144
LUCAS, Virginia 131 William 131
LUCKEN, Wm 24
LUCKENBAUGH, Elizabeth 128
LUCKETT, Lloyd 114 Lloyd W L 114
LUDWIG, Benjamin 184 George E 151 Matilda 81 Peter 184
LUDY, Nicholas 50
LUPFER, David 51 221 Mich'l 56
LUTZ, Mr 11
LYNCH, D 194 Mary Jane 125
LYNE, James 148
LYNN, James 121
LYON, John 14
LYSINGER, John 184
LYTLE, John 148
M'CAULY, Charles F 16
M'CALL, ___ 94
M'CALMONT, Alex'r 202

M'CARTY, ___ 220
M'CLEARY, Andrew 13
M'CLEERY, William 89
M'CLELLAN, Mrs 58 (Mc LELLAND)
M'CLINTIC, Professor 137
M'CLURE, Mrs 11
M'COMMON, Alexander 17
M'CORD, Eliza 84
M'COY, Mary 61
M'CREERY, Wm 192
M'DONALD, Charles 79
M'DONELLS, Gen 55
M'DOWELL, Dr John 197 Mary M 140 Thomas 140
M'ELROY, Jnae 61 Samuel 61
M'ENALLY, Rev Peter 152
M'FALL, Jas 121
M'FARLANE, James 145
M'FERREN, Henry 143
M'GILLAN, Elizabeth 121
M'GINTY, R J 214
M'GUIRE, Isaac 40 James 71*
M'ILVAIN, Mary 95 Robert 95
M'ILVAINE, James Monroe 192 Robert 192
M'KEAN, J 86
M'KEE, James 86
M'KIM, James 204
M'KINNEY, Rev David 122
M'KINSTRY, William D 65
M'KNIGHT, Rev J 25 38
M'LAUGHLIN, Henry 110
M'LEAN, Judge 88 Rev C G 170 Fergus 88
M'LEOD, Alexander 165
M'MILLAN, Mr 77
M'NAUGHTON, Peter 61
M'PHELLAMY, John 121
M'PHERSON, Nancy 197
McABOY, Rev P L 214*
McAFFEE, Jane 126
McCASSEL, Jeremiah 176

McCAULEY, Charles 21 Isaac 19 Isaac H 81 Joseph 71 Thomas 209
McCAYAND, Robert 180
McCLAIN, John 32
McCLEAN, Rev D V 71 Sam'l 170
McCLEARY, Andrew 33 C 37 Mrs N 191
McCLEERY, Mrs 94 Nancy 164
McCLELLAN, Dr H 64 190 Mrs Wm C 121 (Mc LELLAND)
McCLELLAND, Mrs 30 76 (Mc LELLAND)
McCLINTIC, Jane 95 Capt John 59 Mary 59
McCLURE, James 174 Mary 221
McCORMICK, Jane 200
McCOY, A 156 200 Alexander 106 Denton J 169 Jamas Jr 62 James 102
McCRAE, Hamilton 176
McCRONE, Wm B 121
McCULLOCH, Mr 193 Ellen A 103
McCULLOH, Nancy 95 Th G 95
McCULLOUGH, Joseph 182
McDADE, Catharine 140
McDOWALL, Dr John 159 Margaret 159
McDOWEL, Mrs M 193
McDOWULL, Rev John R 79
McDUFFIE, John 159
McELROY, G W 37 Rev J 78 149 Marianne F 78
McFARLAND, D 175 Jas B 148*
McFEREN, Jacob 52
McFINLEY, Henry 176
McGARVEY, Caroline 196 Edward 196
McGEE, Ann Eliza 130
McGIGHEN, Mary 190
McGILL, Rev Alexander 103

McGINNIS, Jonathan W 132
McGLINCHY, James 132*
McGOWAN, Findlay 91
McGUINLEY, Rev A A 175
McILROY, Mary Jane 190 Samuel 190
McILVAIN, J M 185 James M 185
McILVAINE, J P 184 James P 90
McKANE, Hugh 184
McKESSON, Judge 134 Martha G 134 Wm 77
McKIBBIN, Col Wm 85
McKIM, (see MeKIM)
McKINNEY, Rev David 137 Joseph 58 Thos F 196
McKINSTRY, William 182 Wm 101 162
McKNIGHT, Rev J 179
McLANAHAN, Sarah 149
McLANE, John 187
McLAUGHLIN, Henry 191 223
McLEAN, Rev W 196
Mc LELLAND, Wm 214 (M'CLEL-LAN, McCLELLAN, McCLEL-LAND)
McMAHAN, Jas 191
McMICHAEL, Morton 99
McMILLEN, Robert 138
McMURTRIE, David 75
McNAIR, Ann 201
McNULTY, J 220
McPHERSON, E B 103 Elizabeth 115 Horatio 57 John B 115 (see also MePHERSON)
McROBERTS, Janetta A 111
McVICKERS, James 144
McWILLIAMS, Ann Thomas 142 William 145
MACE, George 61
MACK, Paul 144
MACKEY, Rebecca Ann 129
MACNAMARA, Col 206 Mary 206

MADDEN, J 148* Jas 148
MADEIRA, George A 46 209
　Martha 46
MADISON, James 60
MAGUIRE, James L 223
MAHN, A 14 Adam 24 Christopher 11 D 11 David 24 G 190 Geo 11 Geo A 92 George 11 J A 179 191 J Adam 11 John 11 17
MAHON, Martha B 150
MAIN, J Adam 92 Leanna 93
MAISH, Jacob 222
MALLORY, Alpheus 138 Norman 163
MALONY, Sarah Jane 114
MANAHAN, H 148
MANN, A M 148 Abraham 215 David 144 Ferdenand 215 J M 148 Jacob 33 Job 144 John 144 John G 215 Peter 105 106 144 220 Phil 220 Philip 105 177 179 Rethiel 79 Solomon 190
MANNING, Richard J 53
MANSON, Hannah 79
MANTZ, Caspar 95 Casper 219 Charles 187 John 198 Matilda 190
MAPPS, Sarah 121
MARCH, Samuel 184
MARIS, Eliza A 177 Dr George W 103
MARK, D N 214 J 33 214 Jacob 124 N 33
MARKEL, Hannah 222
MARKLEY, Daniel 77 H 200 Harriet 77 Henry 217
MARKLY, D 195 Henry 41
MARQUART, Geo 147
MARSHALL, Mrs 95 Dorcas 94 George Sr 94 Peter 197 William 121

MARTHER, John 144
MARTIN, Dr 60 Abiah 70 223 Rev Charles 102 Elizabeth 60 George 32 Geo H 110 Henry 121 J G 185 J S 188 John 17 24 John G 75 John S 61 Joseph 196 202 Mary 166 Sam'l 213 Sarah 166 Stephen 24 W 135
MARTINS, Miss 162 Sarah 216
MARTSON, John M 120
MASON, Eveline 181 Capt James 181 John M 1 Rev Thomas 79
MASSY, Jacob 192 Wm 121
MATDORF, Mary 144
MATEER, William M 180
MATIS, Marianna 175
MATTER, Elizabeth 152
MATHIAS, Eliza Ann 170 Jacob 170 Joseph 150
MATTHEW, Dr 107
MATTHIAS, Mrs 143 Rev J J 143
MATZ, G 116
MATZER, Margaret 142
MAUCK, Ann 124
MAUL, Edward 121
MAULSBY, Mr 133
MAURER, John 144
MAURY, Rachel 132
MAUS, Elizabeth 138 Jacob 138 John 191
MAWRER, Jacob 153
MAXFIELD, L 179 Levi 61 138
MAXWELL, Samuel 187 W J 68
MAY, Rev 131 Daniel 95 180 Ellen C 95 Jane 188
MAYBURRY, W 187 Wm 173 178
MAYER, Professor 4 Rev 95* Abraham 214 Ann 114 Anna Barbara 95 Elizabeth 86 Frederick 145 Col G 107 Col Geo 13 124 George Louis 95 Rev J 166 174 179 181 185

MAYER (Continued)
  187 201 204 216 Jacob 179
  193 201 215 Rev Jacob 30 95
  163 166 174 200 202 John
  103 192 Rev L 91 Margaretta
  181 Serena Angelica 124
MAYHUGH, James P 217
MAYERS, A 86 Polly 134 Susan 86
MAYOR, Jesse 196
MEARS, Saml 128
MECANDLESS, William 92
MECHTLY, Fred 115
MEDHART, Rev 77
MEHAFFEY, Andrew 115
MEHRCOM, Conrad 202 Jacob 202
MEIXSEL, Mr 11 Philip 11
MEIXSELL, P 207
MeKIM, John Jr 105
MENGOUS, Anna Aspasia 1
MENNICKEN, J 148
MENSER, Jos 193
MENTZER, Sarah 223
MePHERSON, W Y 180
MERCER, Maria 202
MERCHANT, Samuel 58
MEREDITH, Mr 219
MERKEL, D G 180
MERRIL, Caroline 68
MERRILAT, Dr J C M 223
MERTZ, John 202 Peter 146 Philip 146 Solomon 86
MESSENGER, __ 184
MESSER, Rev Asa 73
MESSINGER, Aaron 195 Charles J 215 Geo Jr 202 Geo Sr 202 Geo G 202 Isaac 216 Jac 215 Jac P 202 Jos 202 Mich 202
METCALF, John 204
METCALFE, W 210 Wm 69 162
METTICK, John S 219

METZ, Conrad 215 Henry 215 J 53 Thomas 215
METZGAR, Gerhart 73
METZGER, Frederick Elder 110 George 198 215 Gerhart 56 107 John 202 P 160 Peter 215
MEYER, Emanuel 218 F C 146 Isaac 184 John 146 John Sr 71 Reuben 198 Valentine 45 103 181
MEYERS, Barbara Ann 93 Rev Jacob 56
MICHAEL, A 99 Alexander 3878 Christoper 1124 Henry 24 92 Henry D 16 John 11 24 35 121* 166 Sophia 192 W H 53
MICHALS, Christ 190
MICHLER, Thomas 215
MICHTLY, Frederick 210*
MICKE, Lewis 215
MICKEY, Francis 103
MICKLY, Henry 46
MIDDLECAUFF, Sam'l 97
MIDDLEKAUF, David Jr 76 David Sr 76
MIDDLEKAUFF, Amelia 205 Charles 218 D 11 D M 213 Daniel 219 223 Dan'l Sr 174 191 Danlel M 180 218 David 67 93 160 Hannah 209 Henry 24 92 Hezekiah 67 J C 213 Jacob 17 Jacob Sr 11 Mary Ann 209 S S 205 Samuel 174
MIDDLETON, Daniel Wesley 56 R W 223* Robert F 89 Sarah Patton 89
MIESS, F 190 Martin 210
MILES, Rev Geo I 84 John 167
MILEY, Col Curtis 95
MILHOUSE, Susan 184
MILLEISEN, Ann Elizabeth 136 G 136

MILLER, ___ 148 Mr 140 Rev 218
  Ann E 195 Aquila B 8 Caleb
  98 Casia 181 Cath 206
  Catharine 33 222 D 87 D P
  217 D V 166 Daniel 94 Daniel
  P 131 David 148 Eleanor 208
  Elizabeth R 74 G 209 George
  76 130 170 Geo Jr 156 H 217
  Rev H 19 77 91 Henry 95 111
  Rev Henry 111* 145 J 62 187
  J G 185 195 203* J P 209 Jac
  33 Jacob 28 110 148* 180
  181 194 202 206 Jacob C 51
  Jacob H 69 Jacob P 10 12 34*
  Jno 33 John 17 24 38 72 76
  90* 103 109 156 181 184*
  221 222 Col John 208 John
  Jr 200 Joseph 26 206 Linius
  Wilson 163 Malvina 15
  Margaretta 60 Maria 116
  Mary 33 72 74 127 182 216
  Michael 223 Mich'l 191 Polly
  184 Mrs S 187 Samuel 93 162
  Capt Samuel 195 Rev Samuel
  155 Samul 213 Sarah 136
  Seb 220 Sebastian Jr 181
  Sebastian Sr 181 Solomon
  110 Susan 103 152 169 Gen
  Thomas C 99 Rev W 77 W A
  176 William 95 Wm Clinton
  131
MILLS, Rev George 141 N J 176
  Richard 204 W J 40
MILNOR, Rev 115
MINER, Charles 223 Law L 148
MINES, F S 55
MINGEL, Isaac 144
MINICH, C F 18 Elizabeth 182
  Geo 179 Mary 28 Mary A 134
MINNICK, Joseph 95
MISH, G 34 200 Mrs Geo 188
  John B 13

MITCHELL, ___ 121 B 148*
  George 192 Mary 124 Samuel
  150 218 Susan B 32
MITTAG, Catharine Louisa 211
MIX, Capt 101
MIXSELL, Ann Eliza 76 C 76
MOFFATT, Rev J N 33
MOHLER, Mary 167
MOHR, Dan 195
MOLER, Samuel 24
MONTGOMERY, ___ 147 Daniel
  S 198 David M 51 Mary 121
  Dr Robert 184
MOODY, Capt 175 Rev 180 Rev
  John 127
MOON, Dan'l 195
MOORE, Mr 4 109 Cornelia S 77
  Eli 202 Jacob 164 216 John
  76 John C 77 Peter P 34
  Philip H 34 Rev Richard
  Channing 78 Sarah Ann 92 W
  138 202 Wm 13
MOOSE, Elizabeth 118 Hen 193
  Henry 103 John 199 Levi 99
MOREA, Catharine 191
MORGAN, Margaret 123 Mary 61
  W Duane 46
MORITZ, Jacob 103 Joseph 33
  83 Joshua 142 Margaretta
  103 Peter 28 Saml S 203
  Samuel S 150 198
MORRIN, Margaret 136
MORRIS, Mr 15 Mrs 15 Barbara
  126 Charles 198 Evan 78 H D
  210 Rev J G 73 116 John 93
  Dr John 126 Sibilla Stone 78
  William E 196
MORRISON, Mr 112 Mrs 210 Rev
  112 Catharine 71 E 50 Ellen
  44 Sam'l Jr 186
MORRITZ, Joseph 70
MORROW, James 95 162

MORSE, Gardner 110 S F B 62
MORTIMORE, John 144
MORTON, Catharine 47 William 87
MOSAS, Adam 144
MOSE, George 61
MOSER, Mrs C 166 Charlotte 32 John 181 Margaret 166
MOSHER, Daniel 48 Hugh 48 John 48
MOSIER, ___ 94
MOSLEY, Frank 223
MOSS, Charles 79 Jonathan 79
MOSSER, Fanny 142
MOSTELLER, A 200
MOSTENER, A 99
MOTT, Samuel C 219*
MOTTER, Eliz A 32 Elizabeth Ann 103 George 103 Mrs H 70 Harriet 33 179 Isaac 79 J 179 Joshua 15 60 Lewis 79 Lewis Sr 90
MOTZ, Andrew 53 George M 117 John 117 145 John Jr 156 188
MOURY, Anthony 132
MOWEN, George 99
MOWER, G 190 Peter 167
MOYER, Abraham 190 Absalon 185 Henry 201 Henry Jr 201 Jacob Jr 201 John 145 184 Jonathan 184 Leonard 184 Magdalena 166 P 116
MUELHAEUSER, John 126
MUELLER, Ernst Wilhelm 113
MUENCH, C 160 Danl E 216 J 62
MUENICH, Daniel A 26 Jacob 26
MUETTER, Dr 206
MUHLENBERG, Henry A 139 Rev Wm A 78
MULL, Aaron 57 84 163 174
MULLEDOR, Mrs 191

MUMMA, F 199
MUMMERT, John 114
MUNDAY, Capt 177
MURDOCH, Thomas 83
MURPHY, Mr 136 J 47 Wm W 132
MURRAY, ___ 210 Hariet 183 James 121 John 39* 183 Sarah 39 William 141 Rev Wm M 26
MURTAUGH, ___ 158 John 132*
MUSS, Frederick 174
MUSSELMAN, Ann 82 D 200
MUSSER, ___ 184
MUTERSBAUGH, John 118
MYER, Burkhardt 198 J J 181
MYERS, ___ 150 Abraham 218 Ann Sophia 97 Catharine 99 196 Dorcas E 218 Elizabeth 93 George 176 H 200 Henry 77 185 191 Maj Henry 79 J 156 J F 132 J H 200 J J 128 Jacob 33 117 150 Col Jacob 19 115 Jacob F 180 John 215 John Jr 136 Joseph 108 Nancy 183 Rachel 215 Rose Anna 222 Samuel 47 Sarah 215 Singleton 145 180
MYRIC, Theodore C 121
MYTINGER, Ann 125
NAGEL, John 103 Wm F 202
NAGLE, Mrs 37 E 19 Geo 193
NASH, Mr 40
NASON, Joseph D 121
NAUGLE, J 77
NEAL, Mr 148 Minerva 114
NEEDY, William 172
NEFF, A 76 164 Maj John 139 Malinda Ann 167
NEGLY, Leonard 111
NEIDIG, ___ 213 David 83 197
NEIDIGH, Adam 145
NEIGHBOURS, John 70

NEIHART, Daniel 88
NEIL, Elizabeth 85 John Jr 103
NEIMAN, Peter 163
NEINSTEDT, Henry C 120
NELSON, Rev A Kirkpatrick 149
NETZ, Henry 166
NEVIN, Andrew 174
NEVINS, Mrs 25 Rev William 25
NEWCOMER, Christian 92 Eliza 111 142 John 148 Joseph 38 Joshua 87 Maria 171 Martin 111 Mary 213 Sarah 92
NEWHARD, Geo 202 Jonas Jr 202 Jos 202 Rev P 181 Peter 184 Susan 202
NEWKIRK, George 93 Margaret 93 Matthew 91
NEWLAND, E 164
NEWMAN, Geo 156 Jacob 75 76 Martin 148 194 Samuel 45
NEWROTH, Conrad 202
NEYSWANGER, Christian 153
NICE, Wm 15
NICHODEMUS, Frederick 144 Henry 144 Jacob 117 144 201 John 32 117 144 Margaret 144
NICHOLS, Rev E N 215 John Randolph 196
NICHOLSON, Sarah 131
NICHOME, Lenhart 144
NICKEY, Barbara 59
NICKOME, Jonathan 144
NICODEMUS, Capt Abraham 76
NIEZ, Rev 126
NILES, Professor 107
NILL, Charles Wright 213 James 93 213
NIMERICK, Lydia 132
NIMMO, Wm 121
NISEWANDER, Sarah 172
NISSLEY, Herman 220
NITTERHOUSE, Philip 195 201

NIXON, William 138
NOBLE, Rev Mason 68 Wm 90
NOE, Mr 128
NOECKER, C 186 Maria 99
NOEL, Catharine 101 John 101 184
NOFSKERT, Emanuel 145
NOLAND, Elizabeth 219 St George Callender 121
NOLL, John 150
NOLLAU, Rev Lewis 126
NORTH, Elijah 148
NORTON, Sarah E 177
NOTTINGHAM, Glorvinn Elizabeth 53 Dr John 53
NOVINGER, Joseph 175 Leah 175
NOYES, Daniel 19 Capt John 76
NUBECK, Jacob 71*
NULL, George 181 John 99
NUSBAUM, Samuel 144
NUSS, Lawrence 124
NUSSEAR, James 16
NUTZ, Leonard 181
NYCE, John 215 Jonathan 207 Levi 43 175
NYCUM, Eve 185 John 75 133 144 Simon 144 W 221 Wm 186
NYMAN, H 216 Henry 141 168 Henry Sr 57 61 Susannah 61
OAKS, Susan 198
OAT, Mrs 166 191
OBERLY, Anthony 202 Miss J 164 Jesee 202 Julian 207
OBERTEUFFER, Charles A 49
OBLINGER, Daniel 198
O'BRIEN, Nancy D 218
O'CALLAGHAN, Dr 125
OCKLEY, Jacob 105
ODENHEIMER, Mr 19
ODENWELDER, B 207 Bernard 194

OERTEL, Rev Maximilian 126
OGDEN, Col Aaron 196
OGLE, C 134 John 17 Peter 117
OHL, George 210 John 186 Mary 184
OLEWINE, John 202
OLIVE_ Thomas 168
OLMSTEAD, Denison 101 Rev James Munson 55
OLYPHANT, Mr 131
OMWAKE, Jacob 193 Susan 145
O'NEAL, D 148
OPPENHEIMER, Samuel 144
ORAM, William 132
ORBISON, Eleanor 100 William 100
ORNDORF, Geo 179
ORR, Robert 43
ORT, Jacob 194
OSBORN, C 148 Rev Joel 175 S 148 Truman 181
OSBORNE, Rev T 164
OSGOOD, Elhira Brown 147 Samuel M 147
OSTAINGER, Isaac 49
OSTER, F 185 Frederick 144 Jacob 219
OSTLER, J 160
OSWALD, Rev J 55 Dr John 111 Rev Jonathan 122 Rev Solomon 122
OTT, Barney 219 Mary 15 Michael 144 Peter Jr 215 Samuel 163 W 185
OTTER, William Jr 172
OTTO, H 128 Harbet 144
OUIMET, Andre 125
OUTERBRIDGE, Capt 30
OVENBAGH, W 10
OVER, John 150 Mary A 222
OVERHOLSER, Jacob C 163
OVERKERSH, Rebecca Ann 211
OWENS, Mr 128

OYER, John 91 Louisa 91
OYERLY, Rudolph 87
OYLER, Andrew 130
OYSTER, David Wm 140 Eve 82
PACKARD, F A 101
PAGUE, Samuel 68 135
PAINE, Capt 101
PAINTER, Frances 90 Rev Joseph 43
PAISLEY, Rev W D 132
PALISGROVE, Joseph 34
PALLOCK, __ 222
PALMER, Col 170 Rev 92 Emily 170 Frederick 183
PALSGROVE, Joseph 118
PANEBECKER, N 166
PANNEBAKER, Daniel 166
PAPINEAU, Mr 125
PARISH, __ 148
PARKER, Dr 112 Euphemia B 125 Isaac B 125 John G 147 Mary 148 Stafford H 192 W 148* W B 148 Wm 148
PARKMAN, Mr 156
PARKS, Joseph 184 Margaret 61
PARLEY, John 44
PARSON, Ruben 202
PARTENHEIMER, Jacob 134
PATTERSON, Elizabeth 188 Rev James 125 John 70 S D 99
PATTINGALL, Benjamin 219
PATTNAN, John 148
PATTON, Mr 148 Ann 75 Cath 184 J 204 James 38 John 48 181 204 M 185 Matthew 138 William 78
PAUL, Hannah 166 John 106 186
PAULDING, Rachel 192
PAULI, Rev Augustus 116 Rev W 102* 164 William 68 Rev William 219 Rev Wm 47 69
PAULING, James M 99

PAULUS, Adam 33
PAXTON, J D 84
PAYNE, Mr 200 Barbara Ann 99
   Samuel 94 Wm B 89
PEACOCK, James 73 200
PEAK, Ephraim 40 Rebecca 40
PEAL, Miss 128 Mrs 128
PEARSON, Capt 156* G 95 Geo
   223 George 99 Jacob 215
   Mary Ann 99 Philip Sr 215
PECKMAN, Samuel 110
PEDRICK, John R 49
PEEBLES, Rev J 75 Rev John
   100 Rev R K 108
PEERS, B C 101
PEFFER, Sarah Ann 179
PENCE, Geo 154 Rev J 56 133
   John 103 Rev John 103 201
PENNINGTON, Isaac 88 Mary L
   49 Mrs Robert 106 S H 101
PENNYPACKER, Daniel 95
PENNYWITT, J 187 John 38 115
   Susan 167
PENSIL, Charles 75 Peter 190
PENTZ, George 33
PENTZER, V 58 181 Valentine 95
PENTZINGER, Rosanna 127
PEPLE, Catharine 197
PEPPER, John 103
PERKINS, Rev 191 Col Ephriam
   172 Martha S 172
PERRAULT, J B 50 Ovide 125
PERIN, Capt 148*
PERLMER, Thomas 202
PERRIN, Capt 147
PERRINE, Matthew La Rue 44
PERRY, Mr 162 Mrs 162* Ann L
   127 Rev G B 97 Rev J 151
   James 196
PETER, __ 11 Casper 184 Daniel
   184* Henry 184 John 184
   Nathan 184 William 198
PETERMAN, Jacob 132 166

PETERS, A 37 41 Abr 1999 C
   200 G S 128 Isaac
   146 P 150 194 Philip 174
PETERSON, __ 132 180 J 132
PETRIKIN, James M 145
PFEIFFER, Benjamin 175
PHEASANT, Ann Maria 118
   Rachel 97
PHEBUS, John 56
PHELIM, J 148
PHELPS, Dr 73 Rev A A 198
   Zerua Amelia 73
PHENICA Joseph 115 Mary 115
PHENICO, Joseph 117 Mary 117
PHILIPPE, John 103
PHILIPPI, George 148
PHILLIPS, Mrs 157 Geo M 91
PHIPHER, Geo 209
PHYSIC, Dr Philip Syng 128
PICKING, Sarah 56 Susannah 80
PIERCE, Rev 107 Joseph H 144
PIERPONT, Rev 107
PIGGFORD, Robt 121
PILE, Geo 219
PINNEO, Misses 25 95
PIPER, Ann 86 Daniel 131 Elias
   208
PLASTERER, Conrad 138
PLEASANT, Edward 121
PLEASANTS, Mr 148 Ann Catharine 68 B F 68 Charles 149
   William 219
PLITT, Mr 26
PLOTZ, Philip 111 Rebecca 111
POAG, Martha 55
POE, __ 206 Susannah M 86
POFFENBERGER, George 130
   Rachel 130
POINDEXTER, Carter B 121
POLK, Duval 41 G Duval 41 J R
   W 43 R J W 154* Robert 41
POLLARD, D 107
POMICH, Peter Jr 184

POMP, Eleanora 43 Peter 141
   Rev Thos 11 13 43 69 Thomas
   H R 16 W H 198 Wm H 43
PONTIUS, F 217 Frederick 179
   Joseph 146
POOL, Ann C 186 Ann R 206
   John 148 Ruth 34* Saml 34*
POOR, Charles S 16
POORMAN, John 187
PORKELT, Elizabeth 172
PORTER, Charles W 116 Frederick W 223 Rev G D 198 Rev George 35 Margaret 73 Susannah L 198
POST, Ann Elizabeth 187 S 148
POTTER, Mr 188 J 156 200* James 60 106* 156 179 200 201 James Jr 81 William 108 William W 219
POWELL, T C 148
POWERS, Elizabeth 167
POWLES, Jacob 123 Joseph 95 Louisa Ann 123
PRENTICE, Rev Joseph 40
PRENTISS, Horace 22* Narcissa 45
PRESTON, Col 128*
PRETZ, Mrs A 181 Christian 184
PRETZMAN, _ 38 Sam 180 Samuel 17
PRICE, Dr 176 Armisted 30 Emily 83 Polly 47 Dr William B 83
PRIGG, Edward 133
PRINCE, P 38 Peter 115
PRINTZ, P 175 Solomon 175 William 181
PRITTS, J 30 Joseph 95
PROCTOR, Mr 3
PROPTS, Amelia 132 John 179
PROTZMAN, S 8
PROUDFIT, Dr 79 Rev 198
PRUGH, John 180

PRY, Samuel 69 200
PUMPHREY, George S 70
PURSEL, James 92
PUTMAN, Peter 103 214
PYLE, Henrietta A 138 Mary D 133
QUANTRILL, Thomas 72
QUARLE, Joseph 206
QUAY, Ellen 184 Sarah 72
QUIG, Abr 86
QUIGLY, Joseph 127 Mary 127
RADCLIFF, P W 101
RADEBAUGH, Mr 128 John 129 Rebecca M 129
RADER, Adam 132 180
RAESLEY, Jacob 215 Jacob Jr 215 Jacob Sr 215 Samuel 215*
RAFFELSBERGER, W 216
RAFINESQUE, C S 203
RAHAUSER, A C 187 Amelia 56 Elizabeth 4 Rev E 168 Rev F 35 49 52 70 Rev Frederick 4 168 Gideon 180 H J 15
RAHM, Martin 19
RAHOUSER, D W 203
RAIGUEL, A 195 Abraham 111 John H 111
RAMP, Benjamin 121 Jacob 164 210
RAMSBURG, Elizabeth 17* Henry 131 Mary Ann 144 Rebecca 17
RAMSDALE, Daniel 34
RAMSEY, Margaretta 160
RAMSOUR, A 53 98 Dr A 86 117 156 Ald 53 Andrew 188 D 53 86 188* D F 77 Daniel 156 David 77 86 98 117 156 David J 86 Eli 86 Henry F 156 J 53 77 86 156 188 J Jr 77 Jacob 53 77 86 98 117 156 188 Jacob Jr 109 Jacob A 98

RAMSOUR (Continued)
   John 86 117 156 188 Sol 188*
   Solomon 53 77 86 109 156
RANDALL, S W 99
RANDOLPH, Dr 65 Lucy Jane 78
   Martha 73 Gen Thomas 78
   Thomas Jefferson 73 Thomas
   Mann 73
RANK, Isaac 168
RANKIN, A 86 Catharine 62
   Elizabeth B 62 John 100
   Robert G 101* Rev W C 75 86
   98 99 109 180 Rev Wm 38
   Wm C 38 53 62 72 Rev Wm C
   62 72
RANSBERG, C 94
RANSBERK, Christian 94
RANSON, Benjamin 83
RASHIG, Francis M 16
RASSMAN, Rev Henry 12
RATHBURN, Benjamin 150
RATHFON, Jacob 103
RATHFONG, Leonard 37
RAUCH, Rev 143 193 201 222 D
   156 Dr F A 195 H J 187
RAUM, John 119
RAUSH, Miss Julian 190
RAUTZAHN, Benjamin 88 D 11
   Delenah 88
RAVERTZ, Jacob 121
RAWLE, Ann 121 Mary W 121
   William 50
RAWLINGS, James 168
RAWN, William 211
RAY, Jessey 64
RAYMOND, E 148
REA, Andrew 114
READ, Almon H 202 Harriet 190
   James 140* John M 80 Miss
   Julian 82 Sarah Ann C 80
REAL, Otho 121
REAM, Dr John 197 Sapara 190

REBAUGH, Eliz 181 Rev J 119
   131 136 140 145* 160 172
   182 187* 192 195 201 222
   Rev John 118 174
REBER, Dan'l 184 George 184
   John 174 179 Samuel 194
REBERT, Jonas 221
REBO, J B 50 Rev John 48 Rev
   John B 50
REBOUGH, Rev 26 Rev J 13 33
   54* 61 72 74 76 93 107 109
   167 204 213 Rev J B 21 John
   69 Rev John 11 54* 213* Sev E
   24
REBUCK, C 193 J 193
RECHTER, Peter 146
RECK, Cath 190
RECKENBAUGH, Martin 117
RECKER, Frederick 60
RECKS, George 150
REDGRAVE, Mr 123
REED, Abraham 166 And 192
   Andrew 84 163 D 191 J 107
   Jacob 166 John 97 M 220
   Martha 175 Michael 192
   Philip 80 166 Th D 53 William
   172
REEL, D 118 Daniel 43
REEN, Nathan 202
REESE, Dr 79 Catharine 144
   Jacob 174 Rev John S 76
REEVE, Samuel 167 Susan D B
   167
REEVES, Mary 81 William 91
REFFLEY, Frederick 96
REICH, Abraham 202
REICHENBAUCH, Samuel 116
REIFF, B 58* Benj 163 209
   Benjamin 179 Mary 181
   Michael 163 W 166 William
   166 Wm 94 216
REIFSNYDER, John 216

REIGART, Amos E 16 Henry M 16
REIGEL, Jacob K 202
REIGHLEY, Chas 17 George A 55
REIKA, Rev 77
REILAND, S 194
REILLY, Anna 121 James 146 Mary Ann 121 Wilson 95 188
REILY, ___ 19 Mr 12 56 J R 143
REIMENSNYDER, John J 151
REIMUND, H 216 Henry 105 Michael 144
REINBOLD, Elizabeth 116
REINECKE, Rev 105 John 126
REINECKER, George 131
REINEMANN, Augustus 170
REINER, Geo 50 George 50 Peter 30
REINHAARDT, John 117
REINHARDT, F 195 F D 172 F W P 156 Col J 53 L 195 Lawson 156 P 195
REINHART, Eliza 184 Margaret 179 Margaretta 184 Susan 77
REISENGER, Catharine E 199
REITER, ___ 43 203 Andrew 203
REITZEL, Elizabeth 155 209 Elizabeth Matilda 218 John 155 200 Philip 166* 200* 218
REITZELL, Elizab 140 Philip 179
RELYEA Margaret 118
REMAILY, Charles 184 George 184 Isiah 184 John 184
REMICK, Jonas 148
REMSBERG, Henry 24 Jacob 221 John 35 John Jr 35 132 S 221 Sebastion Jr 78
REMSBURG, Eliza 13 Elizabeth 33 Frederick 32 J 11 John 201 Sebastian 17
REMSHART, Mrs N 188
RENCH, Angelica 126 Daniel 126
RENDER, Jacob 166

RENINGER, Joseph 99
RENN, Philip 179
RENNER, Jacob 17 Rebecca 167 Solomon 88
RENNOLL, Julia 199
RENSCH, John 60
RENTCH, Andrew 50 Joseph 93 209
REPH, Sam'l 202
RETTICH, Richard P 131
RETTUE, Adeline 181
REWALT, Anna 198 W 181 Wm 76 198
REX, John 174
REXROAD, Emanuel 132
REXROAT, F 179
REYER, Conrad 202 Wm 202
REYNOLDS, George 146 J 156 James 209 John 169 Margaret 185 Mary 1 Susan 209 Thomas 110 W 65 William 105 Wm 163 Rev Wm M 154
RHEA, Elizabeth 182
RHOADE, Rev John 88
RHOADES, Charles 146
RHOADS, Daniel 123
RHODE, Frances 56 Paul 144
RHODES, Henry 174 Rev J 81 Susan 174
RICE, Mrs 95 Gertrude V D 47 Grafton J 50 Rev H L 28* 34 35* 80 90 Rev Henry L 25 36 46 50 72* 75 82 95* 101 John 180* Rev John H 7
RICHARD, H 181 Maria 181
RICHARDS, Rev 106 Benjamin W 19 Guy 47 John S 218 Luther 155
RICHARDSON, Isabella 121 J C 148
RICHEY, William 49
RICHLINE, Jacob 202
RICHMOND, Henry 184

RICHNER, John 166
RICHSTEIN, G 181 Geo 128
RICKENBACH, M 131
RICKENBAUGH, __ 11 D 213
   Henry 11 Jac 64 M 38 41 45
   48 58* 76* 131 174 180* 191
   197 213 223* Martin 28 95
RICKSTINE, Samuel 91
RIDDLE, Ariana 184 Rev D H
   117 Rev David H 145 H R 94
   J Stewart 216 James 60 John
   Stewart 188 Joseph 144
   Margaret R 138 191 Mary 188
   Rebecca 60
RIDENOUER, John 179
RIDENOUR, John 14
RIDGELY, Commodore 121 E
   213 G W 101
RIEDY, Barnard 96
RIEGEL, Rev D 216 Daniel 177
   215 Jacob 215 Philip 215
   William 215
RIEKENBACH, M 8
RIFE, Abraham 135 Eliza 148
RIGGBY, Mrs 41
RIGGS, Mr 218 Elias 218
RIGHTER, Helen 61
RIKE, Christian 180 Jacob 132
   John 180
RIKER, Jacob 180
RILE, C C 32 64 H 166 Henry
   104 Henry H 174 John 70
   104 166 174 Margaret 174 W
   32 William 64
RILLEMORE, Mary 30
RIMER, Rev Geo 82
RINEHART, Isaac 189 Mrs M 38
RINGEL, Mrs 202 Ann 138
RINGWALT, J 205
RINKER, Absolom 15 70* Elizab
   70* Capt Jacob 177 John 102
   Mary 177 S 177 Samuel 154

RIPLEY, __ 148 Gen Eleasar W
   189
RIPPLE, __ 132 Lewis 174
   Matilda 174
RIPPON, Rev 88*
RISINGER, Mr 165
RITCHEY, Atcheson 182
RITNER, Gov 98 Margaret 98
RITTER, Jacob 219 John 128
   221 Samuel 71
RITZ, Rev Solomon 93
RIVINUS, Edward F 120
RIXSTINE, Saml 216
ROACH, Margaret 121
ROAN, Jacob 201
ROBAUGH, Rev 12 Rev J B 12
ROBB, Jacob 121
ROBERT, William 74
ROBERTS, Mr 57 160 Rev 211
   Amelia 97 John 43 121 W
   Milnor 83
ROBERTSON, Dr F M 209 John
   69 Mary 69 William 82
ROBINSON, __ 177* Martha 78
ROC, Jane 54
ROCHELLE, Col 128 Mrs 128*
ROCHESTER, Judge 156
ROCK, George 144 John 186
ROCKEFELLER, P F 34* Peter F
   12
ROCKFELLER, P F 10
RODEMAN, Thomas 56
RODENMAYER, J 182 John 44
RODENMEYER, George C 123
RODERICK, Lewis 32 Louis 78
RODGERS, Com John 162
RODNEY, H F 121
RODRICK, L 192 221 Lewis 24
ROEMER, Mrs 184 Adam 187
   Christian 50 Elizabeth 162 F
   187 222 Frederick 162 R 115
ROESDLEY, John 215

ROESLE, John 202 Jos 202
ROFFELSBERGER, W 220
ROFFENSBERGER, P 41
ROGERS, Erastus 40* J S 101 J T 215 Margaret P 73
ROHR, Jacob 33
ROHRBACK, H B 200 Wm 24
ROHRER, Davod 176 John H 50
ROLLER, J 156
ROLLIN, David 175
ROMAN, Sarah Alcorn 54 W 54
ROMICH, Peter Sr 184
ROMIG, Dr 182 John 184 Mrs M 182
ROMSOUR, A 98
RONDEBUSH, M 174 Salome 166
ROOP, Mrs C 164
ROOPERT, John 184
ROPP, Solomon 74
ROSAMON, H 8
ROSEBERRY, Jeremiah MD, 68
ROSENBERGER, A 180 181 Anthony 21 David 168 Jacob 154
ROSS, A 105 Capt Isaac 144 J 105 James 204 John 213
ROSSEN, T 202
ROTER, Rev M 155
ROTH, J 94
ROTHROCK, Rev 60 61 65 Mary 65 Rev Samuel 124
ROUCH, Martha 186 Martin 38
ROUDEBUSH, Samuel 166
ROUDENBUSH, S 222
ROUNSAVILLE, Miss 203 M 46 78 99 138 181 201
ROUSER, Daniel 19 133
ROUSH, George 67 Maria 67 Mary Ann 95
ROUZER, D 139 Sarah A 139
ROWE, Anthony 142 Mary Ann 93

ROWLAND, Isaac B 177 Rev William 145
ROYER, Daniel 143 David 220 Jonathan 175
RRIZER, Rev P 73
RROTHERTON, Rev Robert 212
RUBLE, Henry 184
RUBY, Henry 37 199 John 199
RUCH, Christ 202
RUDD, F 45 Frederick 76
RUDISEL, Sol 98
RUDISILL, Adam 100 Mary 218
RUDY, Elizabeth 45 Fred'k 11 32 Rev J 56 Rev Jehn 34 John 1045 Rev John 12 34*
RUMBAUGH, Samuel 114 William 114
RUMER, Adam 150 174 John F 174
RUMPFF, Eliza 179 Vincent 179
RUNK, Cath 175 Michael 175
RUNKEL, Rev William Sr 12
RUP, Amanda 168
RUPLEY, F 143 F A 150 Simon 44
RUPP, D 190 Geo 115 John G 136 Jonathan 131 Melvina 133
RUSH, Richard 8 Samuel 213
RUSS, John A 83
RUSSEL, Alexander 121 David 206 John 121 Wm 198
RUSSELL, Alexander 50
RUTER, ___ 212
RUTH, Catharine 168 Rev F J 133 Jacob 215 John 199 Veronica 124
RUTHERFORD, Abel 53
RUTHRAUFF, Rev 56 149 Charles 16 J Sr 129 W R 26
RYAN, W 220
RYNDELS, John 144
RYON, Washington 198

S_EFF, Abraham 184
SA_LEY, R 53
SADLER, Samuel 121
SAEGER, C 184 Jonathan 184 214 Joseph 184 Rebecca 164
SAGER, Mary 215 Mrs R 181
SAHM, Mary 210 Rev P 124 161
SAILER, John 8 Peter 11 24
SAILOR, Mr 105 Henry 66 Susan 51
SALLADA, Jacob 195
SALSBURY, Stephen 217
SALT, John 202
SAMPSON, Wm C 12
SAMSEL, Rebecca 50
SANCHEZ, Joseph F 120
SAND, __ 62
SANDER, Peter 24
SANDERS, Mr 157 Rev J L 94 135
SANDS, __ 62 Thomas 147
SANDT, Adam 202 Charles 202 Jonas 202 Leonard 202 Mary M, 202 Philip 202
SANFORD, John W 92
SANGREE, A 179
SANTZ, George 15
SARGENT, Delight 108 L M 107 N 101
SASSEMAN, John 166
SAUL, James 121
SAUNDERS, Dr 149 Isaac 175 James 175
SAUTMAN, Sarah 174
SAVAGE, Susan A 204 Rev Thomas 204*
SAVERBIER, Anna 73
SAVOY, William 153
SAYLOR, Charles 215 Sarah 190
SCANLON, Hugh 153
SCHAEFFER, Baltzer 107 Rev C F 79 Rev Charles 126 Rev D G 99 Rev F D 42 Robert 166

SCHAFFER, George 24 Peter 24 206
SCHAFFNER, H B 116 Jacob 26
SCHARFF, John 187
SCHAUFFLER, Mr 124
SCHAUMAN, Stephen 15
SCHEIB, Barbara 166 Geo 166 George 179 John 166
SCHEIBLY, Elizabeth 221 John 221
SCHELL, Judge 204 Ab 192 Abraham 144 Elizabeth 144 E D 144 Henry 144 Maria 144 Peter 75 144 179
SCHELLENBERGER, Mich'l 166
SCHENK, Capt 78 Peter 198
SCHEPLIN, __ 162
SCHERMERHORN, J F 11
SCHERTZER, Jacob 144
SCHLA_CH, N 166
SCHLATER, Henry 174 John 174 John Jr 174 Ulrich 174 William 174
SCHLATTER, Miss A 204 Ann 216 John 166 Rev Michael 46 Rachael 46
SCHLEIFER, Samuel 166
SCHLEIGH, Henry 8 John 174 211 223
SCHLEY, John 24 32 95 Mary 174 Michael 199
SCHLI_HTER, Jacob 163
SCHLOSSER, Rev G 204
SCHMECK, Jacob 138
SCHMUCKER, Dr 8 Catharine 73 Rev J G 73
SCHNEBLY, Messrs 200 Col D 11 24 184 D H 181 Dan 180 Daniel 24 65 80 Dan'l 117 Daniel H 120 Col David 11 56 Mrs David 184 Elizabeth 93 John 213 John Sr 135 Margaret 65 80

SCHNECK, Mrs 14 Adeline 120 B
  S 193 201 Rev B S 11* 14* 18
  32* 35 51 53 60 66 89 90 96
  110 123 127 134 135 143 144
  145 150 155 160 168 181 183
  186 202 211 220 222 Benja-
  min 183 Rev Benjamin S 141
  218 Dr H 14 116 142 Mrs R R
  181
SCHNEIDER, Alfred 215 221
  Anth 204 Rev Benj 200 Elias
  198 Fred'k 181 Hen 156 W 62
SCHNIDER, Maria 168
SCHOCH, Abraham 146
SCHOENEBRUCH, Julia Ann 76
SCHOLL, Dan'l 184 David 184
  Elias 32 Rev J 87 Jacob 174
  Rev Jacob 49 Michael 174
  Samuel 174
SCHOSSER, Stephen 184
SCHRACK, ELIZABETH, 166
SCHREINER, Henry J 138
SCHREIVER, David 30* Jacob 30
SCHRIVER, David 214 Henry
  214
SCHUCK, Peter 215
SCHUG, Henry 202 Sam'l 202
  Sandt 202 Wm 202
SCHULTZ, Amos 163 C K 163
  Caspar 166 Rev Charles W
  203 Geo 166 Salome 166
SCHULTZE, H F W 55
SCHUMACHER, Lewis 198
SCHWALM, Philip 195
SCHWANCK, George 174
SCHWARTZ, H 45 Henry 45
  Jacob 202
SCHWARZ, Benj 217
SCHWENK, George 163
SCOTT, Gen 140 141 Mr 105
  Hugh 214 Rev James 71 Jas
  D 210 Rev John W 70 Thomas
  157
SCOVIL, Mary 106
SCRIBA, Victor 132
SCULL, Rev William 78
SCULLY, Jacob 204
SEABOLD, Lucinda 56
SEABROOK, Robert 156
SEABROOLS, Wm J 120
SECHLER, Rev 120 Ann 184
  Cynthia 72 Henry 69 199 Rev
  J 110 118 120 127 139 170
  183 185 195* 199 201 218
  Rev Jacob 138 143
SEELY, Eliza 63
SEESNOP, Ann 184
SEIBEGBUTH, Jonas 202
SEIBERT, Catharine 213 Henry
  193 195 Henry J 184 Jacob
  202 John 143 Justina Eliza-
  beth 143 M 213 Michael 15
  38* 127 170 Mich'l 125 Maj
  Peter 180 Rev Samuel 179
  Samuel R 143 W H 209 Wil-
  liam 195 Wm 141
SEICHRIST, Christian 172 Eliza-
  beth 172 John Breneman 172
SEIDENSTRICKER, J B 139
SEIM, John 148
SEIME, John 148
SEIP, Savina 198
SEIPEL, David 202 Martin 202
SEIPT, George 166
SEITS, Jacob 59
SEITZ, Mr 11
SELDEN, William 192
SELLERS, Martha 22 Mary 182
SEMER, J W 152
SENSENY, Dr A 192 Dr A H 132
  Christian H 175
SENT, Col John 198
SENTMAN, Solomon 79
SENTZ, Jesse 128 Joel 186
SERVER, Jacob 163
SEUDER, Jacob 111

SEWARD, Jonas H 39
SEWELL, Rev E W 147 John 121
SEXTON, Edward 148*
SEYFFERLY, C Wilhelmina 121
SEYMOUR, William 121
SHADE, Henry 166
SHAEFFER, Rev 85 Rev Charles
  F 93 Elizabeth 85 Henry 11
  26 (SHEFFER)
SHAFER, ___ 179 A 171 Ann
  Rosina Virginia 171 Caroline
  B 74 Catharine 19 Daniel 42
  55 101 George 11 164 H J
  171 Hen 216 Henry 117 Jacob
  184 216 Jesse 138 179 John
  11 69 John Jr 21 38 180
  Leonard 74 Lydia 137 Mrs M
  E 41 Peter 11 32 Susanna
  218 Wm 167
SHAFF, Henry 214
SHAFFER, Dr 95 D 210 Daniel
  110 162 Geo 219 George 24
  199 Henry 180 Jacob 130 150
  John 24 John Jr 132 180
  Michael 219 Peter 8 24 163 R
  41* Rebecca
SHAFFNER, H B 51 Rev H B 56
SHANE, Joseph 37
SHANK, H 132
SHANNON, Edward 82 John 132
  160 180 Margaretta 190
SHANTZ, Jacob 184
SHARER, Henry 213 Jno 192
SHARK, Ann 174
SHARP, Agnes Margaret 164 Rev
  Alexander 58 Henry A 218
  Jacob 37 Nathan 42 Robert
  164 William 164
SHARPE, Rachel 121
SHARRETS, Rev N 83
SHARRETZ, Jacob 127
SHARSWOOD, Mr 219

SHAW, Mr 181 Hugh 117 P 204
  Peter 215 Rachel 203 Thomas
  55 145
SHAWEN, Grafton 198
SHEA, Mrs S B 203 Susan 19
  Susan B 46
SHEARER, F 152 Frederick 103
  Jacob 221 Rebecca 138
SHECKELS, Merrit 121
SHEELY, Joseph 222
SHEETS, John 19
SHEETZ, Daniel 93 George 148
  John 223
SHEFFER, Dr 79 D 138 Daniel
  192 John 202 Joseph 202
  Mary 79 Peter 202
SHEFLER, W F 28
SHEIB, John 192
SHEIBLY, B 185
SHEIDER, Christian 152
SHEIMER, Joseph 159
SHELL, John N 38 181 192 Peter
  13
SHELLER, Mary 192
SHELTON, John 217
SHENEBERGER, G 135 G Sr 135
  Ma___et 145
SHEPHERD, Amelia 70 Henrietta
  21 James 21 Serena 21
SHEPLEY, Sarah 98
SHERBURN, H 216
SHERP, George 202
SHERTZ, Elizabeth 82
SHERTZER, David 145
SHERWOOD, ___ 148
SHETRON, John 159
SHICK, Mary 76 77
SHIDY, Peter 184
SHIEMER, Joseph 194
SHILICH, Mary 95
SHIMER, Jacob 138 Jesse 202
  John 50 166

SHINDLE, Elizabeth E 149 John
    93
SHIREY, Adam 187
SHIRK, D 202 Elizabeth 164
    Henry 76 132 191 J 13 Matthias 46 W 132
SHITZ, Andrew 175 Jacob 186
SHIVE, Jacob 174
SHIVELY, Mrs 11 John 191 Dr
    John D 191 Miss Julian 80
SHMEIER, Sam'l 202
SHOAF, D 201 203 David 203
SHOBER, Jacob 138
SHOCH, Samuel 202
SHOEMAKER, Elizab 186 George
    144 H P 95 Henry 144 Jac 24
    Philip J 95 144 179 Wm 202
SHOFF, David 56 Michael 193 V
    79*
SHOLL, Mr 102 Rev F A 15 78
    George 219 Rev J 112 221
    Rev Jacob 87 142 Mary 156
SHOLLENBERGER, Elijah 199
    Jacob 180
SHOOK, Rev Geo 12 Rev George
    A 101 Sarah 140
SHOOP, Mary 123
SHOOTS, D 192
SHORA, John 103 Mary 103
SHOTVILLE, Mr 202
SHOVER, Jacob 19 36 182
SHOWERS, Jacob 34 127
SHOWMAN, Dr 79 John S 54
SHRADER, George 222 John 127
SHREADER, Priscilla 150
SHRINER, Jacob 36
SHRIVER, Abraham 95 Andre K
    89 Ann 69 Ann E 184 Charles
    95 D 133* David 11 33* 78
    150 Henry 33 120 141 150
    Isaac 76 190 Jacob 69 132
    John 81 Julianne 190 Louisa
    184 Margaret 76 Sarah 184

SHROCK, John 197
SHROM, Barbara 92 Joseph 79
    Joseph Sr 92
SHROYER, John 180
SHUCK, Bro 211 Mrs 211
SHUFORD, A H 109 Abel 53 Abel
    A 156 Andrew 117 E S 53
    Elkanah 195 Elvira 98 G R 53
    George 98 J J 84 156* J S 53
    Jacob 98 109 Philip 156
    Sarah E 156 Susan 98
    Thomas 53 Thomas R 98
SHULL, A 53 David 116 Jacob
    124
SHULTZ, D 164 David 74 132
    198 223 I 164 P 190 Peter 38
    R 190 Samuel E 145
SHULTZE, H F W 103
SHULZE, Rev Christopher 166
SHUMAKER, Jacob 21
SHUMAN, A B 26 Jacob 144
    Simon 193
SHUPING, A 53
SHUTZ, John 156
SHYBLER, Jacob 73
SHYER, Phebe Ann 110
SICELOFF, E 53
SIDES, Jacob 72
SIECFRIED, John 81
SIEGEL, Simon 215
SILBER, M 145
SILBERT, C 182
SILICK, Elizabeth 118
SILL, Iaseah 144
SIMARD, Dr 125
SIMMON, Dan'l 179
SIMMONS, Miss 128* Mr 160
    Nicholas 61
SIMMS, Mary 126
SIMPSON, Mrs 98 Michael T 65
SIMPSONS, Dr S 53
SINCLAIR, A 34* Mary 34
SINE, George 192

SINSNEY, Hiram 99
SKELLY, William 37
SKILLY, William 84
SKINNER, Archilbald 209 Porcia 38
SKYLES, John 144
SLAER, Ann 51
SLAMAKER, Peter 179
SLATE, Israel P 202
SLAUGHTER, Rev 80
SLAYBAUGH, Maria 32
SLAYMAKER, N E 95
SLEMMER, Jacob 148
SLICK, Mr 195 James 30
SLIFER, Henry 175
SLINGLUFF, Levi 45
SLOAN, Dr 36 Mrs 36 Jonathan H 146 Mrs S 24 Susan 111 209 Samuel 78 Dr William J 91
SLOOP, Jacob 102
SLOYER, George 86
SLYDER, William 176
SMALL, D 130 Daniel 26 37 46 G 190 Geo 18 64 George 10 11 70 164 Hen 195 John 221 Joseph 8 195 Lawrence 8 Maria 83 P A 64 Robert M 169 Capt Wm 83
SMALTZ, Cath 184 Catharine 187 Rev J H 11 13 32* 70 91 166 179 181 188 Rev John H 107
SMELSER, Mary Ann H 95
SMELTZER, Hannah 152
SMITH, ___ 206 Dr 195 Mr 28 101 115 Parson 89 Rev 121 Ameilia C 219 B 185 Mrs B M 10 24 181 Barbara 15 Barbara M 213 Catharine R 121 Catherine 99 Charles D 166 Conrad 207 Constatine 40 Cornelius J Jr 206 D 30 99

SMITH (Continued)
Daniel 24 33 David 115 Eli 17 78 182 Rev Eli 79 Eliz 216 Elizabeth 48 77 140 Fred 162 Fred'd 25 Fred'k 95 144 Frederick 181 196 G W 202 Geo 19 Rev Geo A 131 George 54 H 106 186 Gerrit 202 Harriet 94 Henry 17 22 24 95 99 102* 128 148 Capt Henry 94 Hiram R 199 Isaac 160 Isabella 196 J C 68 J G 32 J Logan 195 201 Jacob 17 21 87 90 146 181 186 James M 53 John 28 42 56 57 80 95 121 128 132 144* 162* 173 174 181* 187 193 201 John Cotton 19 John G 32 John J 11 43 132 177 213 Capt John L 184 Joseph 11 24 99 Levi 71 Rev Lewis Jr 96 Lucia G 79 Lydia 196 Marcia M 79 Margaret 54 Margaret Ann E 121 Martin 218 Mary 33 78 119 192 Mary Elizabeth 128 Mary Loutzenheiser 57 Mary M 83 Matthew 118 Michael 121 157 Nancy 96 129 Noah 156 Mrs Noah 156 Patrick 156 Peter 95 Richard Somers 87 Samuel 86* 150 192 215 Rev Samuel 154 Sarah Ann 184 Sarah L 79 Sophia 188 Susan 201 T N 105 Valent 195 Volney 182 William 121 William H 59 61 Wm 148 150
SMOOT, Geo H 99
SMURR, John 70 192
SMYSER, Daniel M 106 George Matthew 106 Henry 122 Susan 122
SNAPP, Jacob B 180 Jos 180 Joseph 201 202*

SNAVELY, J 202 Joseph 166
SNECK, Rev B S 10 Magdalena 179
SNIDER, ___ 214 Mr 134 Mrs Christian 184 George 75 Henry L 80 J 190 Jacob 150 Jacob Sr 196 Jeremiah 156 Jeremiah Jr 195 201 John 28 Col John 89 Mary 89 P 204 Peter 37 121
SNIVELY, Andrew 30 32 191* Capt Casper 218 Catharine 50 Henry 30 61 Maj Henry 94 145 Jacob 50 92 121 John C 191 Joseph 79 181 Mary A 79 Melchior 111
SNOOK, Daniel 111 Dan'l 66
SNOWDEN, Thomas 128
SNYDER, ___ 33* 133 Mr 11 Benjamin 210 Charles 202 Christianna 220 Daniel 76 David 112 Ezra J 124 127 Geo 194 George 195 Hen 170 216 Henry 51 103 Jacob 202 John 103 John L 134 Jonas 202 Jonathan 132 180 Mary 166 190 202 Mary Ann 166 N 171 Peter 92 164 202 216 Peter Sr 220 Mrs S 164 Samuel 164 Simon 28 149 202 Sophia 216 SO___ Rev B S 32
SODER, Jacob 205
SOHN, Henry 24
SOLANO, ___ 40
SOLES, Mr 147
SOMERVILLE, Sarah J 154
SONDER, P 221
SONNENDECKER, Rev H 213 Rev Henry 213
SORIN, Rev Mathew 101
SOUDER, Jacob 69 Michael 21 P 164 Peter 35

SOUTH, Joseph 126 Susan 145
SOUTHARD, Samuel L 101
SOWERS, ___ 182
SPANG, Martha 137
SPANGLER, Mrs Dr 187 Alex K 16 Barbara 150 D 190 195 201 Eleanor 91 Elizabeth 214 Elizabeth S 94 Emanuel 43 Ferdinand L 73 Geo 183 George 141 J 190 Jacob 119 Jane 43 John 33 Lydia 30 72 Margaret 8 Mary H 43 Col Michael 94 Peter 163 Sarah Ellen 163 Z 64
SPARE, F 143
SPATZ, Jacob 175
SPEAR, B 216
SPECH, Sarah 49
SPECHT, Mary 195
SPEECE, Rev Dr Conrad 44 Lewis 175
SPEER, Dr A 194 Lydia W 194 Mrs O 216
SPEESE, Harriet 137
SPEICHER, J 219
SPEILMAN, Jonas 136
SPERA, Henry 97
SPICER, Richard 144
SPICKLER, Elizabeth 119
SPIESE, Mrs 176
SPIEGLER, Susan 81
SPIELMAN, Daniel 17 John 54 John M 180 Margaret 171 Sam 180
SPIESE, Charles A 166 H 159 Lewis 105
SPINNER, Abraham 184 John 184
SPOHR, Sam'l 184
SPOTTSWOOD, James 175 Jane 175
SPRECHER, Rev S 98 Rev Sam'l 170 Rev Samuel 73

SPRIHLMAN, Miss A 213
SPRINGER, Joseph 164
SPROBT, James 95
SPROLE, Rev 81 W T 19 56 115
   William T 171
SPROUT, James 144
ST_I__ Elizabeth 174
STAFFERT, Anna 113
STAHL, Geo 198 J 190 W 185
   William 144
STAKE, ___ 195 Edward G W 195
STALEY, John 11 Joseph 11 195
   Rev S 21 Stephen Jr 70 William 144
STALL, Daniel 107
STALLINGS, John P 121
STALLSMITH, Susan 122
STALSMITH, ___ 214
STALY, John 24 Joseph 195 204
   Stephen 24*
STAMBAUGH, John 187 Martin 99 Sam'l 152
STAMM, H 219
STANDENOUR, Jacob 144
STANFORD, Elizabeth 44
STANGER, Dr J 109
STANTON, Eliza 198
STARK, Daniel 168
STARNER, Jacob 133
STATLER, Emanuel 144 John S 144 S 143 Samuel 128
STAUB, H 38 179 Henry 70 J 190 Jacob 188
STAUBS, Sarah Ann 124 127
STAUFFER, Eliza 103 William K 163 Wm D 186
STEARLY, Daniel 163
STEBBINS, N G 223
STECH, George 134
STECKEL, Daniel 200 Sarah 184
STEDMAN, Rev James O 75
STEEL, Jacob 132
STEELE, Jacob 180 John 109

STEES, Miss 210
STEFFEY, Martin 78
STEFFY, M 133
STEHLEY, Mrs J A 188 Jacob 64
   John A 16
STEHLY, John 62 Joseph 215
STEIN, A G 198 220 Elias 79 F 148 Peter 99
STEINER, Abraham 94 Christian 13 David C 144 E 13 Jacob 13 Jesse 16 131 John 166 John A 75 97 John H 166
STEINMENTZ, Marion Edwardinia 67
STELTZ, Solomon 87
STEM, Margaret 116 Mary 152 194 Peter 181 Reuben 198 Samuel 215
STEMBLE, J 132 Jacob 180
STEMM, Ab'm 202 Sam'l 202
STEMPLE, Fred 11
STENDLER, David 86
STEPHEN, Sanford 184
STEPHENS, Lydia 30 127 184 Nancy 119
STERER, __ 44
STERLING, A W 111 114*
STERNER, Jacob 33
STETLER, Joseph 184
STEUART, George 81
STEUDEN_OWER, Jacob 168
STEVENS, Rev 131* Rev Edwin 105 Thaddeus 99
STEVENSON, A R 26 Henrietta 196
STEVER, David 44 Jacob 44 John 222
STEWARD, ___ 170 Dr 122 Andrew 167 Catharine W 167
STEWART, ___ 184 Mrs 128 Ann Maria 101 Rev J 81 Lucetta 175 Margaret 184 Thomas 202 W 198 Wm 202

STICKEL, __ 84 Edman 184
  Henry 174 208 Michael 213
STILT, John 222
STIMMEL, Henry 214
STINE, Michael 210
STINER, Rev Conrad 119 Jacob
  119
STITZEL, Henry 31
STIVES, Tunis J 198
STO__R, Wm 32
STOCKER, Bernard 202 Rev
  John 73
STOCKMAN, D 30 221 George
  Nelson 219 H 30 192 221
STOCKTON, Mr 105
STODDARD, Charles 19
STOEHR, Philip 95 193
STOEVER, C F 26 Rev C F 130
STOFLIT, John 202
STOHRM, Catharine 159
STOKES, Mr 105 Henry 148
  Montfort 92
STOLTZ, Catharine 109
STONE, Calvin R 148* David 174
  Wheelock S 121 Rev Wm 139
STONEBRAKER, Geo 148 Harvey
  126 Henry 181 Joseph 33
  Samuel 33 W 191 William 76
  Wm 32 117
STONEBREAKER, Hester Ann
  191 Joseph 191 Maria 191
STONER, M M 166 S P 223
  Samuel 171
STONESIFER, Eve 124
STONG, Barbara 166 Frederick
  166 Henry 166 John 166
  Philip 166 Richard 166
STORK, Jonathan 184
STORKE, Theophilus 26 Rev
  Thoephilus J 125
STORY, John 215
STOUCH, Barbara 185 Peter 131
STOUFER, George 50

STOUFFER, Henry 145 John 139
  Marks 107 S 185
STOUT, Jacob 216
STOVER, Adam 145 Jacob 145
  Jacob E 145 John 145
STRACK, Jonathan 192
STRADER, Capt 176
STRASBACH, Adam 76
STRASBERGER, Rev J 162 Rev J
  A 174 179 John 184
STRASBURGER, Rev J 222
STRASSBURGER, Rev J A 222*
  Louisanna 222
STREALY, John 185
STREBIG, William 182 Wm 72
STREHER, Catharine 175
STRICKLAND, __ 212 Geo Jr 99
  Samuel 116
STROB, Rev 131
STROBEL, Rev P 193 Rev Philip
  A 124
STROCK, Mary A 172
STROH, Rev N J 85
STROHL, Nich 202
STROUP, W J 216
STROUSE, Maria 150
STRUCK, John 45
STRUNK, John 36 207 Joseph
  174
STUCK, Chas 210
STUCKEY, J 184
STUDY, J 214 Ludwig 33
STULL, Adam 17
STUMP, Jonathan 77
STURGES, John W 77
STURTEVANDT, J M 101
SUBER, Daniel 38 David 38 E 53
  Micheal 38 Sitchel 38
SUDDARDS, Rev 131 Rev Wm
  138
SUESSEROTT, Christian L 92
  Eleanor 182
SUFFICOOL, Isaac 115 117

SUGERT, S T 73
SUGS, __ 40
SULLIVAN, M 203
SULTNER, Christian 81
SULTZBACH, H 156
SULTZER, Thomas D 221
SUMMER, A 179
SUMMERS, A 38 70 Abraham 11 Chris 11 J 11 J S E 77 Jacob 117 John 11 P A 77
SUMMEY, Widow 53 G 38 77 James J 53 Peter 38 98
SUMNER, Jacob 41
SUMPTION, Isaac 202
SUTER, C 216
SUTHERLAND, Gen 147 Sarah 39 Wm B 39*
SUTTER, Ann Maria 126
SWAIN, Dr 205 Theophilus H 121
SWAN, Ann M 154 Robt 121
SWARTZ, B 205
SWENEY, Jos 216
SWIFEL, Josephine 208
SWIFT, Rev E P 50 Joseph 148
SWIGART, Elizabeth 80 John 196 Peter 214
SWIGERT, Peter 28
SWING, Joel 181
SWINGLEY, Benjamin 127
SWISHER, Sarah 208
SWITZER, Henry 170
SWOPE, Adam 216 Jacob 116 John 14 Julia Ann 216 Mary Ann 93 P 14 Peter 14 97 Dr W 159 Dr Wm 14
SWOOP, John 179*
SWOOPE, John 179* Mary 184 Peter Sr 205 Dr W 219
SYLVIES, Isaac 73
TABB, Jacob 97
TABER, Henry F 69 William 69
TAGGART, Ja's 87

TALBOTT, __ 94
TALHELM, Ann Maria 109
TALMADGE, Rev Mr 4
TANNER, Barbara 104
TAPPAN, A 13 Arthur 32 John 19
TATE, Dr A C 206* David 50
TATUM, Willia 121
TAUGHINBAUGH, Elizabeth 127 Nicholas 127
TAYLOR, __ 184 Rev 107 Rev B C 166 L 123 Rebecca 53 Richard 110 Thomas 217
TEED, __ 148
TEEL, Adam 215
TEMPLE, Daniel 218
TENNENT, Rev Gilbert 107
TENPLIN, Sam'l P 202
TEWE, Thomas 176
THEIBER, Mary 76
THELIER, __ 147
THOMAS, __ 147 Mr 148 Abraham 146 Ann Cath 115 Ann Eliza 95 C 30 C K 201 Conrad 80 Daniel 184 Dan'l 11 E 106 195 Emanuel 115 217 Francis Ephraim 114 Geo 11 George 51 205 George Jr 187 Hen 11 Henry 51 99 127 Jacob 11 24 32 186 187 Jno 24 John 11 32 150 204 Mrs M 148 Maria 104 Michael 17 32 P 30 Peter 114 Prissilla 131 Samuel 95 Susan 170 205
THOMPSON, __ 128 148 Gen 40 Andrew 162 Benaiah 174 Eliza Ann 140 James 83 Jas 148 John 99 Moses 137 Sarah 91 167 Wm E 167
THOMSON, Judge 182 A 95 Alex'r 25 Barbara 208
THORNBURG, George 195
THORPE, __ 31
THRONE, Rebecca 76

- 320 -

TICE, Cath 199 Daniel H 213
   John 174 John Jr 17 38 John
   Sr 17 Peter 15 91 199 203
TIERNAN, Luke 220
TITUS, ___ 71
TITZEL, Henry 142
TOBIN, F M 148
TODD, William 144 Wm H 155
TOMPKINS, Able 174
TOMS, Jacob S 186
TOOL, Miss E 106
TOWNE, Capt 12
TRACY, Mr 132
TRAINER, Albert 71*
TRAUP, John 24
TRAUTMAN, Peter 148*
TRAVELLI, Mr 57 Mrs 57 Rev
   Joseph S 50*
TRAVENIER, Frans 125
TRAXEL, Jacob 184 John 184*
   Peter 184* Stephen 184
TRAXELL, Salley Ann 184
TRAXELT, Phebe 184
TRENKLE, Geo 182
TRIMBLE, James 41
TRITT, George 99 Peter 150
TROUB, Adam 95 David 95 John 197
TROUBTMAN, Ann 195
TROUP, Mr 197 A 213 Adam 213
   David 197 John 68 Joseph 186
TROUTMAN, G 187 G Sr 191
   Geo Sr 128 L M 148 187
   Lavinia 99 M 182 Michael 110
TROXEL, Cath 182 Catharine 33
   Charles 166 Frederick 137
   Jacob 15 33 Jno 15 John 19
   Peter 15 19 36 148 179
TRUAX, Stephens 147
TRUMAN, Matthew 197
TRUMBAUER, Henry 95

TRUMBLE, A 216 Adam 21 186
TSIHOPP, Margaret 114
TUCKER, Rev 101 Rev Charles
   145 Rev Robert 107
TURBUT, Edward 94
TURNBULL, Benjamin L 214
TURNER, Mr 216 F 98 J 175
   Mary Ann 55
TUSSEY, Daniel 115
TUTTLE, Wm P 106*
TUTWILER, John 145
TWIGGS, Major 156
TYLER, Rev Joseph D 223
TYNG, Rev 131 Rev Stephen H 56
TYRELL, Thomas 195
TYSON, James 40 Jonas 166
UHLER, Andrew 202 Isaac 98
   Mary 139 Valentine 202
UHRICH, Valentine 74
UHRIG, Valentine 79
ULERY, Daniel 17
ULRICH, Charles 97 G 190 Rev
   John 151 Mich'l 204 Valentine 26
UMSTEAD, Robert 50
UNANGEST, Henry 202 Philip 215
UNANGST, Joseph 14
UNCLES, F 16
UNCLESBY, Belinda 191
UNDERWOOD, Felix 176
UNGER, Lydia 183
UNITY, Pleasant 37
UNMSTEAD, Robert 166
UPDEGRAFF, Susan 177
UPPERMAN, Conrad 19
URBAN, Joseph 72
URIE, Col John 85
VAN BIBBER, Abraham 16
   Washington C 16
VAN DERVOOT, Rev John C 53

VAN DUZEE, Wm S 79
VAN DYKE, Ellen 70 Rev Hamilton 52 Henrietta 56 Lydia 107 190 Wm 70
VAN HOFF, Louisa 130
VAN HOOK, Isaac 148
VAN LEAR, Dr William 100
VAN NOSTRAND, Angelina 78 Lozee 78
VAN PATTON, P S 207
VAN PELT, R 179
VAN RANSSALAER, Stephen 19
VAN READ, Charles 202
VAN RENSELLAER, J 101
VAN RENSSELAER, Stephen 183
VAN TREIS, Samuel 86
VALLENDER, N 223
VANDERANDER, Isaac 179
VANDERAU, Adam 174 Catharine 28
VANDERAW, Consentine 174
VANDEROW, Jacob 204
VANDERSLICE, T 220
VANDERSLOOT, Rev Fred W 8
VANDYKE, Dr C 18 Rev H 18 Mary 135
VANFOSEN, Michael 166
VANNEMAN, Richard 81
VAUGHN, Dr 148
VETHAKE, Henry 63
VIRL, Robert 95
VISTTMAN, D W 148
VOGELSONG, ___ 19 128 William G 16
VOIGHT, Rev 95 Rev H E F 86
VONDERAU, Adam 62 William 142 Wm 76
VONDERAW, Adam 197 William 164
VONEADA, Philip 166
VONFASSEN, Michael 214
VONNEADA, Philip 181
VOUST, John 184 Thomas 184

VROOM, John P 53
WACHTER, Jacob 93 John 93 167 Michael 213
WACK, Barbara 166 Elizabeth A 166 Emeline B 174 Rev G 99 174 Garret C 174 Rev Geo 124 George 214 Rev George 166 179 214 Gerret C 174 Philip 166
WADDEL, Sophia 100
WADDLE, Sophia 53 56
WADE, Ebenezer 170
WAGENSELLER, Jacob 146 William P 146
WAGER, Mr 40
WAGNER, Mrs 187 Rev 202 Anna Maria 112 Augustus 148 Cath 185 Christian 131 D 4 Rev D 112 Daniel 217 Daniel S 16 Geo 202 Rev H 11 138 202 Rev Henry 15 Jacob 26 M M 159 S 185 190 Samuel 64 139 140 Valentine 67 W 24 119 190 200 William 10 Wm 200
WAGONER, A M 156 Elias 152
WAITE, Benjamin 165 James 147
WAKER, Hannah 88
WALDORF, Jane Eliza 101
WALDSCHMIDT, William 146
WALDSON, William 129
WALK, Fred'k 206 Joseph B 206
WALKER, Judge 78 Elizabeth 170 175 J O 76 John 94 John Sr 166 Joseph 170 Margaretta 151
WALL, Arthur 208
WALLACE, Rev 95 Rev B J 199 H O 199 J A 53 J B 145 Jno 95 Rev John 70 Lydia Martha 95 Mary 36 Wm 150 Wm H 90
WALTER, Jacob 144

WALTERS, Dr Albert G 219 Mary 201 Philip 179
WALTHAUR, Christopher 81 Dorothy 81
WALTON, Wm 53
WALTZ, John G 145
WAMNER, Rev 33
WAMPLER, Mrs 50 79 188 Clarissa 33* Elizabeth 145 Hannah 167 Julia Ann 190 J Lewis 167 Lewis 80 145 210
WAMPOLE, Rev Jacob 133
WANNER, Aaron 166 Dewalt 166 John 166 Peter 166
WARACK, Catharine 43
WARD, Capt 191 A 98 C 156 Nancy 99 Thomas 99 Sheriff Wm 92
WARDNER, John A 54
WARFIELD, Henry R 189
WARG, Daniel 215
WARLACK, M 53 P 38
WARLICH, Peter 77 109 Solomon 77
WARLICK, ___ 156 188 Maxwell 116 Solomon 188
WARMPOLE, Fred 163
WARNER, ___ 153 Erastus 165 Francis 202 John S 176
WARREN, Col 40
WARTON, Eliza 97 Samuel 97
WASHABAUGH, D 179 Dan'l 144
WASHINGTON, R 95 Col W R 31
WASSER, Elias K 145
WATERS, Elanor 95 John 71 William 121
WATKIN'S, 2Mr 148
WATSON, Rev 115 Elizabeth 103 Rev James 197 John W 55 Dr W 65
WATT, Robert 148 Thos 148
WATTS, Mr 148 Joseph 99 Robert 148

WAUGHEMANN, Peter 95
WAY, Frederick 80 Susannah 80
WAYNE, Thomas 121
WE_K, Elias 191
WEAGLY, Mary Ann 145 Samuel C 222
WEAST, Jos 168 Joseph 54
WEATHERHOLD, Wm 202
WEATHERHOLTZ, J 132 Joel 180
WEAVER, ___ 220 Adam 148 Ann Rebecca 198 D 190 Daniel 18 38 66 Elizabeth 213 Geo 145 202 Hannah 181 Helena 184 Jacob 35 76 164 203 206 215 John 145 166 187 198 213 Julia Ann 137 Ohn 191 S 191 Samuel 95 213 W 181
WEBB, Rev 12 Arthur B 59 Eliza 130 James B 217 James Watson 138* Wm Charlton 13
WEBBER, Mrs 148 Benj 162
WEBER, Benj 162 Benjamin 166 Elizabeth 148 Emaline M 166 G 107 Geo 55 107 190 Col George 201 John 166 174 195 Maria M 166 Mrs W 201
WEBSTER, Abner 148 Dan'l 62 Daniel 63 Edward 115 Rev Richard 148
WEEBER, G F 77
WEED, Mrs 77 Henry 77
WEICKEL, Henry 166 179 Jacob 166
WEIDE, Charles 116
WEIDMAN, Rev P 43 Rev Paul 43
WEIDNER, D 120 128 148 156 191 David 90 104 128 132 J 116 Jacob 32
WEIERBACH, Benjamin 174
WEIKEL, Jacob 174
WEIKERT, John Jr 33

WEIL, Benj 163
WEILER, G 37
WEINBRENNER, Christian 144
WEIR, A K 197 Abraham K 197
WEIS, Brother 17 Rev George 79*
WEISE, Wendel 174
WEISEL, George 166 J 185
   James 105 199 Philip 186
WEISER, Rev 166 Mrs C 156
   Cassandra 55 D 87 95 Rev D
   16 87 95 173 219 D J 219
   Daniel 73 Rev Dan'l 179 G
   111 Samuel Sr 55
WEISS, Joseph 181
WEIST, M John 138
WEITZEL, E 219 W 219
WEITZELL, Henry 202
WELCH, Rev Johnson 99
WELKER, Chr 213 Christian 111
   G C 219 G W 95 Geo C 194
   George 179
WELLER, Ludwig 103
WELLS, David 46 Wm P 138
WELSCH, V W 76
WELSH, Mrs 68 Benjamin 68 J
   175 J R 111 Jacob 74 Jacob
   R 121 James 142 John Sr 99
   Lewis 80 Margaret 219
   Michael 219* Rachel 55 V W
   62
WELSHANS, Henry 179 191
WELTY, D 15 George B 141 H 15
   Henry 24 J B 26 117 168*
   John B 13 72 117 219 Sam'l
   191 Samuel 41 William 90
WELTZ, J B 201
WENDEL, Leonard 128
WENNER, J 110 Jon 110 Jona
   188 Jonathan 21 Sarah 184
   W 188
WENNIG, Francis 152
WENRICH, Miss 106
WENTZ, Mrs 8 J B 64 Jacob 202
   John 202
WERNER, Daniel 82 George 215
   Henry 213
WERT, Sarah 210
WERTSNER, George 174
WERTZ, Geo 28 H 36 Henry 24
   182 Martha L 28 Rachel 182
WESCOTT, Capt 198
WESSEBHEFT, Dr Wm 11
WEST, James M 121
WESTHEAVER, M 37*
WESTON, Wm 190
WETZEL, Jacob 179
WETZELL, Henry 146* Jacob
   146 Joseph 146
WEVER, John 195
WEYANT, John 77
WH TE, Charles W 83
WH_TMAN, Philip 215
WHALEY, T 156 W 156
WHARTON, Martha M 218
WHEELAND, Michael 176
WHEELER, Henry 171
WHETSTONE, Jacob 144 John
   144 Samuel 144 174
WHISLER, Andrew 162
WHITE, __ 148 Mr 148 Rev 78
   Dyer 110 Isaac 138 JM 34
   Rev N G 126 Rev N W 86
   Thomas 53 Rev Wm 62
WHITEHEAD, Mary 95 Peter 95
   148
WHITEMAN, Henry 34
WHITENER, Daniel 109
WHITFIELD, Rev George 107
WHITMAN, Dr Marcus 45*
WHITMOR, Nicholas 17
WHITMORE, Daniel 117 Eliza-
   beth 46* Fredd'k 203 John 46
   John W 141 Joseph B 144
   Luke 106 Michael 35

WHITNEY, D 70 Stephen 45
WICKHAM, John 95 Matilda 137
WIEDRICH, C 30
WIESELL, James 144 John 144
    Philip 144
WIEST, Christopher 105 Elizabeth 144 Hiram 61 John 105
WIESTLING, B 111 Dr Benj 111 Mrs H 200 Harriet 18 95 Mary 54 Dr Sam'l 54
WIKERT, __ 56
WILCOX, Abner 79 Amos 28 Nathan 28
WILEY, Rev 130 John 92
WILFANG, John 55 117 Mrs L 117 Lavina 53
WILHIDE, Margaret Ann 103 Samuel 103
WILL, Mr 11 Elizabeth 187 George 33* 133 150 214 H 199 Margaret E 120
WILLARD, Rev H 184 Henry 32 John 32
WILLERS, Rev D 24 150* 156 174 194 Rev Dietrich 11 110
WILLEY, __ 148
WILLIAMS, __ 200 Francis 121 Halsey 148* Jacob 28 Jas 121 John 121 Joseph 99 Rev Joshua 165 166 Laura Sophia 130 Gen O H 130 R 159 Robert L 81 Solomon 144 W T J 148
WILLIAMSON, Rev James 103 Warren R 126
WILLIARD, Catharine 168 Dewalt 186 G W 21 Geo W 32 George 64* 133 George W 138 Rev H 150 184 197 Henry 16 21 32 Rev Henry 118 138 184 John 11 24 118 186 216 Mary 11 Sarah 21
WILLIER, Joseph 152

WILLIS, Adeline 216
WILSON, __ 119* Dr 36 Mr 160 Alvira 156 Alvirah 188 Charles 129 David 76 179 Fleming 121 Geo M 127 Rev H R 126 151 Rev Henry R 117 Rev Henry R Sr 150 James 58 75 94 Rev James 150 John 105 John R 128 Mary Ann 59 Maxwell 67 Richard 91 Sally M 83 Stephen 175 Thomas H 184 W 180 191 William 138 144 Wm 102
WILT, Margaret 222 P 214 W A 187 214 Wm A 214*
WINCHESTER, Rev S G 102
WINEBRENNER, Rev C 179 Chas 120 Christian 152 Henry 50 71 P 71 Sarah Ann 56
WINGARD, Lydia 188
WINGERT, Isaac 152
WINN, Capt Joseph 222
WINNEBRENNER, Rev John 124
WINROTH, Henry 11
WINROTT, Samuel 56 W 192
WINSLOW, Rev 71 72
WINSTON, James 202
WINT, Solomon 181 W 190
WINTER, Christian 173*
WINTERS, Rev 78 Rev D 38* 147 180 184 David 17 Rev David 132 Elizabeth 219 John 219 Valentine 180
WIRE, David 21 William 110
WIRT, Mr 102 Rev 156* Catharine 89 Christian 118 Daniel 139 Elizab 139 Emeline Margaretta 74 Henry 33 50* 74 89 110 195 Jacob 120 175 Louisa 110 Wm E 16
WIRTH, Fidel 210
WISE, __ 156 199 Mr 120 A 187 A Jr 187 Alpheus 198

WISE (Continued)
  Christiana 74 D 156 John
  Fred'k 209 Jos 206 Joseph 76
  86 198 Richard 17 24 W 188
WISEMAN, James 115
WISENAIL, H 38
WISNER, Rev B B 19
WITHERELL, ___ 106
WITHERSPOON, Rev 77
WITMER, Henry 145
WITMIRE, Sam 192
WITT, Jacob 147
WITTY, W 220
WITZEL, Jacob 83
WOLBERT, ___ 184 Frederick 59
WOLF, ___ 150 A 37 Adam 155
  Anthony 200 Augustus 141
  Barnard 25 C 185 Edward L
  16 F 191 John 145 John Jr
  180 Joseph 144 Paul 200
  Sarah 188
WOLFE, Adam 127
WOLFELSPERGER, John 223
WOLFERSBERGER, John 38 174
  Joseph 192
WOLFERSPERGER, Geo 95 John
  17 166
WOLFF, Brother 195 Rev 43 131
  141 Mrs B 184 Rev B 164 216
  Rev B C 18 28 76* 77 121
  159* 181* 194 207 Barnard
  95 173 193 195 201* Rev
  Barnard C 152 Bernard C 131
  C 222 C D 118 Christian 46
  78 182 Christian D 115 Eliza-
  beth 46 46 Fred 135 Frederick
  141 Geo 15 19 26 74 118 135
  164 Rev J 164 J G 216 Rev J
  G 141 145 152 162 181 190
  216 J W 132 Jacob 145 182
  John 150 John G 16 Rev
  John G 95 152 164 Joseph
  126 Ninetta 141 Sophia 54

WOLFFARD, John 166
WOLFINGER, Daniel 41
WOLFKILL, Leah 221
WOLFORD, J 179
WOLFORT, Jno 200
WOLFSBERGER, John 13
WOLLISON, ___ 176
WOMELSDORF, Mr 176
WONDERLY, Wm S 114
WOOD, Alva 101 Rev George W
  148 Hannah 129
WOODBRIDGE, Wm 106 Wm C
  101
WOODFORD, Lyman 98
WOODRING, Capt 181 Henry
  184 Michael 184* Wm N 202
WOODS, Rev J S 81 Professor
  Leonard Jr 198
WOODWARD, Robert C 163 Wm
  W 84
WOOLAM, Dan'L, 184
WOOLVERTON, John 101
WORCESTER, ___ 45 Mr 3*
WORLEY, Barbara 75 John 32
WORMAN, Leidy 166
WORNER, Gottleib 195
WORTZ, Cathatharine 198 Henry
  74 202 Lewis 198
WRIGHT, James 187 R K 117
  Thomas J 95
WROE, John 207
WUNDER, Dr H S 21
WYNANT, H 216 Henry 115
WYNCOOP, Rev 65 82
WYNKOOP, Jefferson 11 Rev
  Richard 93 148
YAKEY, Barbara 50 John 21 188
  Simon 21 50
YANOVER, ___ 40
YASTE, Samuel 11
YATES, John O 196
YEAST, Elizabeth 130
YEATZ, Patrick 160 P 129

YELT, Jacob 44
YINGLING, Benjamin 179 David 179 Joshua 76
YINGST, Isaac 175
YOCKEY, Hannah 220
YODER, B 198 Capt John 43
YOHE, Mrs 216 Maria 159
YOHN, Jacob 170
YONSON, Jacob 215
YONTZ, J 203 John 201 203 Samuel 11 69 141 Wm 11 146
YORKE, ___ 217
YOST, A 104 Abr 216 Abraham 150 174 Benj B 163 Daniel 221 David G 209 John 163 Martin 192 Mary 174 Sarah 174
YOUMANS, John 40
YOUNG, ___ 133 Capt 148 Dr 164 Mrs 4 Adam 46 145 Andrew S 16 Ben 211 Daniel 4 David 190 Frances B 124 Jacob 14 127 204 211 James 53 Jno 202 John 19 144 197 John C 124 Mary A 59 Mary Ann 43 Mich 202 P 43 Peter 77 192 Dr Robert T 151 Sam'l 179 Samuel 138 Dr Samuel 160 163 173 Samuel P 120 Sarah A 172 Sophia P 18 145 William 47 Dr William 192
YOUNGHEN, George 69
YOUNGMAN, George 99
YOURTEE, Aaron 140
ZACHARIAS, Rev 33 91 121 130 Mrs C Z 181 Catharine Z 18 Christian 56 D 2 18* 30 32 Rev D 33 50* 55 59 75 86 94 95* 97 105 114 115 131 143 156 174 185 186 192 195 198 Rev Daniel 8 51 56 139 154 196 Jane 8 Rev K 144 M 38 70 S 200 202 Sam 94

ZEARFASS, Samuel 174
ZECK, Dietrick 93
ZEIGLER, Rev 184 199 David 208 Rev J 152 Jacob 210 Rev Jacob 166
ZELLER, Rev D 181 Daniel 41 174 219 David 95 219 Rev J 159 194 John 168 194 Rev Jon 94 Jonathan 64 Rev Jonathan 14 50 Oliver 213 Samuel 219
ZELLERS, Rev Mr 45 D 213 Daniel 58 97 David 76 Mrs H H 42 J 13 Rev J 42 74* 174 Jno 76 Rev Jona 174 Rev Jon'a 143 Rev Jonathan 74 Oliver 96
ZERBE, David 103
ZIEGENFUSZ, Geo 202
ZIEGER, Samuel 133
ZIEGLER, ___ 11 Rev 100 Rev D 33 190 Daniel 13 45 Rev Daniel 177 Emanuel K 55 Rev J 175 179 Jacob 78 107 Rev Jac 133 177 179 198 John 78 105 177* 178 Susanna 125
ZILFING, Michael 166
ZIMMERMAN, B 33 Catharin 188 David 33 E 221 Elizabeth 17 118 G 30 Geo 17 223 Geo T 201 George 18 118 H 213 Henry 11 32 198 J 30 213 J S R 188 Jacob 17 Jno 137 John 11 17 36 105 198* Col John 135 John P 133 214 Lilly Ann 18 M 195 Mary 135 Mich 186 Michael 58 75 84 129 214 P 56 Peter 203 Rebecca 202 Sarah 90
ZIMMERS, Frederick 130
ZINN, Geo 37 George 87 194 John 18
ZIPPAR, ___ 177

ZIRKLE, Benjamin 167
ZOCCHI, Rev 170
ZODY, Conrad 150
ZOLLICKOFFER, Rev Daniel 147
ZUCK, Susan 94
ZUILCH, Rev J 55 152 200
ZURCHER, James 223
ZWISLER, C 182 Rev C 110* 182
    J Jr 223 James Jr 17

www.ingramcontent.com/pod-product-compliance
Lightning Source LLC
Chambersburg PA
CBHW070935230426
43666CB00011B/2441